The Thousand Best Poems in the World. First series-containing five hundred poems. Selected and arranged by E. W. Cole. (The Thousand Best Poems in the World. Second series-containing five hundred poems. Selected and arranged by Ernest Hope.).

Edward William. Cole, Ernest Hope

The Thousand Best Poems in the World. First series-containing five hundred poems. Selected and arranged by E. W. Cole. Fiftieth thousand. (The Thousand Best Poems in the World. Second series-containing five hundred poems. Selected and arranged by Ernest Hope.).

THE THOUSAND BEST POEMS IN THE WORLD.

FIRST SERIES—CONTAINING FIVE HUNDRED POEMS.

SELECTED AND ARRANGED

BY

E. W. COLE.

FIFTIETH THOUSAND

LONDON:
HUTCHINSON & CO.
25, PATERNOSTER SQUARE.

MELBOURNE: COLE'S BOOK ARCADE.

BRITISH MUSEUM

THE LIBRARY OF THE FUTURE.

TO BE COMPOSED ENTIRELY OF THE CREAM OF HUMAN THOUGHT AND KNOWLEDGE.

Friendly Reader,—I propose to start a cheap, comprehensive, and concise library, to be called the "Federation of the World Library." It is to consist of the hundred best books in the world, one book the best of its kind on each subject of human knowledge, such as astronomy, geology, geography, history, biography, poetry, botany, chemistry, electricity, architecture, mechanics, navigation, mathematics, natural history, grammar, medicine, agriculture, cookery, religion, law, politics, fun, and so on, up to 100 volumes, which will comprise all the important branches of human knowledge and thought. Each of these books must be carefully prepared for the purpose, and can each be made to contain the best of human knowledge on the subject treated of. It is astonishing how easily and perfectly this can be done within a small compass. A moderate-sized song book will hold all the best songs in the world; a moderate-sized poetry book will hold all the best poems in the world; a moderate sized wisdom book will hold all the wisest sayings in the world; a moderate-sized book, carefully prepared, of astronomy, geology, geography, chemistry, botany, or any of the sciences, will give a clear knowledge of the principles of each of those sciences. Such a library of 100 volumes of, say, 600 pages each can be produced to sell at £10, thus bringing all the most important knowledge, and all the most beautiful thoughts, within the reach of every human being. Books are multiplying so fast now, that no man can know even the titles of them all, much less read their contents, therefore, a desirable thing, and an absolute necessity of the future, will be to pick the grain out of so much chaff, and preserve it in condensed libraries for the ready instruction, elevation and gratification of universal humanity. I have called it the "Federation of the World Library," because I believe that the cream of human thought, collected into a convenient form, and brought within the reach of everyone, will do much to spread the principles of right and truth and friendship—to make men think rightly and consequently alike, and so bring about the federation of the human race. Mankind, as a whole, have infinitely greater regard for right and truth than they have for wrong and falsehood, and it is the high destiny of the Press to develop and nurture this good tendency in man, by spreading and re-spreading abroad those great principles of right and truth, until everyone shall become a right thinker; and no small part of the duty of the Press is to collect the best knowledge, and the best thoughts existing in the world, and bring them before every reading being, in the form of convenient libraries, as above indicated. As one unit amongst the many, I am trying to do my share in carrying out this object; I have little leisure time, but I hope to be able to publish a few of these "Best Books in the World." I have already published two—one entitled "Cole's Funny Picture Book," of which I have sold 50,000; it is the best child's book in the world; and the "Fun Doctor," of which I have also sold 50,000, is the best fun book in the world. And I am just about to publish three others—namely, "The Thousand Best Songs in the World," "The Thousand Best Poems in the World," and "The Five Thousand Wisest Sayings in the World." Of course, I shall not make these selections with the completeness that they will be done later, but I shall have the satisfaction of having done something towards initiating the greatest and most valuable necessity of the future, namely: *A cheap and universal library for all mankind.*

E. W. COLE, Book Arcade, Melbourne.

LEDICATION.

This series of books is hopefully and lovingly dedicated to the Unity of Man.

PREFACE.

This little book of poetry contains fully half of the favourite poetic gems of the world collected together for the first time. Campbell defines poetry as the "Eloquence of Truth." Shelley defines it as "Men's best Thoughts, expressed in their best language, in their happiest moments," and certainly poetry contains the noblest of human thought expressed in the most telling, the most pleasing, and the most easily remembered form. All the best poetic gems in the world can be put into a convenient volume, and sold for two or three shillings. Has it not, then, up to the present been a great loss to humanity that this has not been done? If poems containing great and noble truths beautifully expressed exist in the world, surely it is better that every thinking being should have the opportunity of reading them, and anyone collecting them into a convenient form, or even spreading them abroad in any part of the world, when so collected, is really promoting the mental and moral progress, and happiness, of mankind. There is not one person in a thousand that ever read half the poems collected into this small book, and I have no hesitation in saying that if any thoughtful person reads this volume through, small as it is, they will be the happier for it. No thinking person can read these gems from that dozen grand and noble poets of humanity: Burns, Hood, Wordsworth, Mackay, Swain, Sims, Longfellow, Whittier, Lowell, Carleton, Felicia Hemans, and Letitia E. Landon, without being better, wiser, and happier for having done so. And I would here express my deep obligation and thanks to the following, who have granted very kind permission for the insertion of poems: to Charles Mackay, for poems on pp. 86, 112, 153, 180, 205, 215, 216, 247; to George Bell & Sons, for Adelaide A. Proctor's poems, pp. 149, 213; to Kegan Paul, Trench & Co., for Archbishop Trench's poems, pp. 219, 277; to Clement Scott, for 'Story of a Stowaway," p. 188, from his "Lays and Lyrics;" to George R. Sims, for "Billy's Rose," p. 60, and "The Road to Heaven," p. 69; to Gerald Massey, for poems on pp. 51, 147, 163, 177, 223, and to Wells Gardner, Darton and Co. for the Bishop of Bedford's poem, "Was Lost and is Found."

The pieces in this collection may not all be what a severe critic would call good poetry. I have selected them for their soul-stirring ideas rather than for their mere poetic embellishment. A grand idea which produces noble resolves, or a humane recital which brings tears of sympathy into the eyes, although given in simple, or even in ungrammatical language, is of far greater value to mankind than volumes, or dozens of volumes, of exquisite obscurities or "sublime nonsense." It is largely of these simple-touching poems dear to the heart of humanity rather than to the head that this book is composed. It is said by some, and I think rightly, that poetry acts upon human beings with a soothing effect like music. Fuller calls it "music in words." Certainly the reading of beautiful poems has an intellectually pleasing and soothing effect upon troubled minds. This beneficial effect has been appreciated by millions in the past, and I believe that hundreds of millions in the future will more frequently take up their favourite book of poetry to read themselves, or say to some dear friend in the spirit, if not in the words of one of the best poets of humanity:—

"Come, read to me some poem,
  Some simple and heartfelt lay,
That shall soothe this restless feeling,
  And banish the thoughts of day.

Come, read from the treasured volume
  The poem of thy choice,
And lend to the rhyme of the poet
  The beauty of thy voice.

And the night shall be filled with music,
  And the cares that infest the day
Shall fold their tents, like the Arabs,
  And as silently steal away."

Appeal to the Intelligent Reader for Advice and Assistance.

Friendly Reader,—I wish to make this collection of the Thousand Best Poems as perfect as possible, and therefore ask your advice and assistance. The pieces here collected, most of them, I think, are the best in the world, but of course there are many good ones with which I am unacquainted, and some, most probably, I might say most certainly, that I have adopted will have in later editions to be left out as inferior, and I would respectfully ask the opinion of thinking persons into whose hands this book may come to point out any in it that in their opinion should be left out, and also to send any poem or the name of a poem which they consider should be included. Perhaps there are a million printed poems in the world, and to pick out the thousand best is no small difficulty, but mankind is equal to it, and it will be done. The thousand best are worth more than the remaining 999,000 all put together. Of course poems differ greatly in value; probably in the thousand best there are approximately 100 first-class, 300 second-class, and 600 third-class.

By almost universal consent Gray's "Elegy," Goldsmith's "Deserted Village," Longfellow's "Psalm of Life," and others are held to belong to the first-class; the second-class is also moderately easy to decide upon, but the third-class is the most difficult to deal with. It requires great knowledge, great judgment, and an entire absence of prejudice to properly decide the relative position of each poem. Of course, there is great difference of opinion in many cases which are the best poems. Some people say that Longfellow's "Psalm of Life" is not one of the hundred best, and yet, speaking as a bookseller of great experience, I can assert that it is read more, verse for verse, than the whole of Milton's and Homer's poems put together, and, short as it is, is held by some to be doing more good to mankind.

I would ask anyone favouring me with contributions *not* to send original poems, as I am sure in most cases disappointment only could follow by their non-insertion, for of all the poems written in the world not one in ten thousand is good enough for this selection. This may seem a startling statement, but it is quite true. There are probably a million poems written in the world every year, and yet not a ten-thousandth part, that is, one hundred poems, are equal to the best poems of the best poets, such as Byron, Burns, Longfellow, Mrs. Hemans, &c. Of course the natural egotism of mankind makes each particular writer think that his or her production is exceptionally good, as every mother thinks that her own baby is the best; nevertheless, the fact remains that of all the millions of poems produced the number is very small indeed that will bear the criticism of the world, and live for ages by virtue of their intrinsic worth, and it is only such that can go into the Thousand Best Poems.

One more remark:—It will be said that a collection of the thousand best poems in the English language is not a collection of the thousand best poems in the world. I know it is not, but it is nearly so. At the present moment half the literature of the world is in the English language, and by far the best half. All the world cannot show such an array of famous poets as English-speaking countries can. And besides, nearly all the best thoughts of other nations, ancient and modern, are either translated into English, or have been infused into English literature. It is largely this unparalleled comprehensiveness of English literature, spontaneous and acquired, that will cause the English language to become the universal one.

CONTENTS.

INDEX TO SUBJECTS

CONTENTS.

Poems about Home.

HOME, SWEET HOME.

Payne.

'Mid pleasures and palaces, though we may roam,
Be it ever so humble, there's no place like home;
A charm from the skies seems to hallow us there,
Which, seek through the world, is ne'er met with elsewhere.

Home, home, sweet, sweet home,
There's no place like home.

I gaze on the moon as I trace the drear wild,
And feel that my parent now thinks of her child;
She looks on that moon from her own cottage door,
Through woodbines whose fragrance shall cheer me no more.

Home, home, sweet, sweet home, &c.

An exile from home, splendour dazzles in vain,
O, give me my lowly thatched cottage again;
The birds singing gaily that came at my call,
Give me them with the peace of mind, dearer than all.

Home, home, sweet, sweet home, &c.

MAKE HOME BEAUTIFUL.

Make your home beautiful; bring to it flow'rs,
Plant them around you in bud and in bloom;
Let them give life to your loneliest hours,
Let them bring life to enliven your gloom.
Make your own world one that never has sorrowed,
Of music, and sunshine, and gold summer air:
A home world whose forehead care never has furrowed,
And whose cheek of bright beauty will ever be fair.

Make your home beautiful; weave round its portal
Wreaths of the jasmine, and delicate sprays
Of red fruited woodbine, with gay immortelle,
That blesses and brightens wherever it strays;
Gather the blossoms, too, one little flower,
Varied verbena or sweet mignonette,
Still may bring bloom to your desolate bower,
Still may be something to love and to pet.

Make your home beautiful; gather the roses;
Hoard in the sunshine with exquisite art;
Perchance they may pour, as your darkness closes,
That summer sunshine down into your heart!
If you can do so, oh! make it an Eden
Of beauty and gladness! remember 'tis wise,
'Twill teach you to long for that home you are needing,
That heaven of beauty beyond the blue skies.

HOME.

Goldsmith.

But where to find that happiest spot below,
Who can direct, when all pretend to know?
The shuddering tenant of the frigid zone
Boldly proclaims that happiest spot his own;
Extols the treasures of his stormy seas,
And his long nights of revelry and ease:
The naked negro, panting at the Line,
Boasts of his golden sands and palmy wine,
Basks in the glare, or stems the tepid wave,
And thanks his gods for all the good they gave.
Such is the patriot's boast, where'er we roam,
His first, best country ever is at home.

HOME.

Montgomery.

There is a land, of every land the pride,
Belov'd by heaven o'er all the world beside;
Where brighter suns dispense serener light,
And milder moons emparadise the night;
A land of beauty, virtue, valour, truth,
Time-tutor'd age, and love-exalted youth;
The wandering mariner, whose eye explores
The wealthiest isles, the most enchanting shores,
Views not a realm so bountiful and fair,
Nor breathes the spirit of a purer air.
In every clime the magnet of his soul,
Touch'd by remembrance, trembles to that pole;
For in this land of heaven's peculiar grace,
The heritage of nature's noblest race,
There is a spot of earth, supremely blest,
A dearer, sweeter spot than all the rest,
Where man, creation's tyrant, casts aside
His sword and sceptre, pageantry and pride;
While in his soften'd looks benignly blend,
The sire, the son, the husband, brother, friend.
Here woman reigns; the mother, daughter, wife,
Strews with fresh flowers the narrow path of life:
In the clear heaven of her delightful eye
An angel-guard of loves and graces lie.
Around her knees domestic duties meet,
And fireside pleasures gambol at her feet.
Where shall that land, that spot of earth, be found?
Art thou a man?—a patriot?—look around;
Oh, thou shalt find, howe'er thy footsteps roam,
That land thy country, and that spot thy home.

MAKE HOME BEAUTIFUL.

More than building showy mansions,
More than dress or fine array,
More than dome of lofty steeples,
More than station, power, sway;
Make your home both neat and tasteful,
Bright and pleasant, always fair,
Where each heart shall rest contented,
Grateful for each beauty there.

More than lofty, swelling titles,
More than fashion's luring glare,
More than Mammon's gilded honours,
More than thought can well compare;
See that home is made attractive,
By surroundings pure and bright,
Trees arranged with taste and order,
Flowers with all their sweet delight.

Seek to make your home most lovely,
Let it be a smiling spot,
Where, in sweet contentment resting,
Care and sorrow are forgot!
Where the flowers and trees are waving,
Birds will sing their sweetest song,
Where the purest thoughts will linger,
Confidence and love belong.

There each heart will rest contented,
Seldom wishing e'er to roam,
Or, if roaming, still will cherish
Mem'ries of that pleasant home;
Such a home makes man the better,
Sweet and lasting its control;
Home, with pure and bright surroundings,
Leaves an impress on the soul.

MY OWN FIRESIDE.

Alaric A. Watts.

My own fireside! Those simple words
Can bid the sweetest dreams arise;
Awaken feeling's tenderest chords,
And fill with tears of joy mine eyes.
What is there my wild heart can prize
That doth not in thy sphere abide,—
Haunt of my home-bred sympathies,
My own—my own fireside!

A gentle form is near me now;
A small white hand is clasped in mine:
I gaze upon her placid brow,
And ask, What joys can equal thine?
A babe, whose beauty's half divine
In sleep his mother's eyes doth hide;
Where may love seek a fitter shrine,
Than thou—my own fireside!

What care I for the sullen war
Of winds without, that ravage earth?
It doth but bid me prize the more
The shelter of thy hallowed hearth:—
To thoughts of quiet bliss give birth:
Then let the churlish tempest chide,
It cannot check the blameless mirth
That glads my own fireside!

My refuge ever from the storm
Of this world's passion, strife, and care;
Though thunder-clouds the skies deform,
Their fury cannot reach me there;
There all is cheerful, calm, and fair;
Wrath, envy, malice, strife, or pride
Hath never made its hated lair
By thee—my own fireside!

Thy precincts are a charmèd ring,
Where no harsh feeling dares intrude,
Where life's vexations lose their sting,
Where even grief is half subdued,
And peace, the halcyon, loves to brood.
Then let the world's proud fool deride:
I'll pay my debt of gratitude
To thee—my own fireside.

Shrine of my household deities,
Bright scene of home's unsullied joys!
To thee my burthened spirit flies,
When Fortune frowns or Care annoys!
Thine is the bliss that never cloys,
The smile whose truth hath oft been tried;
What, then, are this world's tinsel toys
To thee—my own fireside!

Oh, may the yearnings, fond and sweet,
That bid my thoughts be all of thee,
Thus ever guide my wandering feet
To thy heart-soothing sanctuary!
Whate'er my future years may be,
Let joy or grief my fate betide,
Be still an Eden bright to me,
My own—my own fireside!

Poems about Wives.

MY WIFE.

Come, Posy, help me with your lays,
And give your choicest meed of praise,
To her with whom I spend my days.
My Wife!

I courted her with honest pride,
Preferred her to all girls beside;
She afterwards became my bride,
My Wife!

Who is it that governs home so well,
That it is pleasant there to dwell,
Wherein she reigns by magic spell?
My Wife!

Who is it that I call "my dear,"
And think of when both far and near,
Whose presence helps my heart to cheer?
My Wife!

Who is my best and truest friend,
Whose love all other's does transcend,
Whose faithfulness ne'er knows an end?
My Wife!

Who is it, when all friends forsake,
Most steadfast stands my part to take,
Whose constancy will *ne'er* forsake?
My Wife!

Who is it in misfortune's hour,
When adverse clouds begin to lour,
Strives hard to check their dark'ning power?
My Wife!

Who is it meets me with sweet smiles,
Which oft my weary heart beguiles—
My stubborn spirit reconciles?
My Wife!

Who cares for me with anxious brow,
And best attention does bestow
When illness lays my body low?
My Wife!

Do thou attend my dying bed,
And wipe death's sweat from off my head,
Let then thy soothing power be shed,
My Wife!

CHARACTER OF A HAPPY WIFE.

Wordsworth.

She was a phantom of delight
When first she gleamed upon my sight,
A lovely apparition, sent
To be a moment's ornament:
Her eyes as stars of twilight fair:
Like twilight's too, her dusky hair;
But all things else about her drawn
From May-time and the cheerful dawn;
A dancing shape, an image gay,
To haunt, to startle, and waylay.

I saw her upon nearer view,
A spirit, yet a woman too!
Her household motions light and free,
And steps of virgin liberty;
A countenance in which did meet
Sweet records, promises as sweet;
A creature not too bright or good
For human nature's daily food;
For transient sorrows, simple wiles,
Praise, blame, love, kisses, tears, and smiles.

And now I see with eye serene
The very pulse of the machine;
A being breathing thoughtful breath,
A traveller betwixt life and death;
The reason firm, the temperate will,
Endurance, foresight, strength and skill,
A perfect woman, nobly planned;
To warn, to comfort, and command:
And yet a spirit still, and bright
With something of an angel light.

A GOOD WIFE.

Samuel Rogers.

His house she enters—there to be a light
Shining within, when all without is night;
A guardian angel o'er his life presiding,
Doubling his pleasures, and his cares dividing;
Winning him back when mingling in the throng,
From a vain world we love, alas, too long,
To fireside happiness, and hours of ease,
Blest with that charm, the certainty to please.
How oft her eye read his; her gentle mind
To all his wishes, all his thoughts inclined:
Still subject—ever on the watch to borrow
Mirth of his mirth, and sorrow of his sorrow.

A KISS AT THE DOOR.

WE were standing in the doorway,
My little wife and I:
The golden sun upon her hair
Fell down so silently;
A small white hand upon my arm,—
What could I ask for more ·
Than the kindly glance of loving eyes,
As she kissed me at the door?

I know she loves with all her heart
The one who stands beside,
And the years have been so joyous,
Since first I called her bride;
We've had so much of happiness
Since we met in years before,
But the happiest time of all was when
She kissed me at the door.

Who cares for wealth of land or gold,
For fame or matchless power?
It does not give the happiness
Of just one little hour.
With one who loves me as her life—
She says she loves me more—
As I thought she did this morning,
When she kissed me at the door.

At times it seems that all the world,
With all its wealth of gold,
Is very small and poor indeed,
Compared with what I hold;
And when the clouds hang grim and dark,
I only think the more
Of one who waits the coming step
To kiss me at the door.

If she lives till age shall scatter
Its frost upon her head,
I kn w she'll love me just the same
As the morning we were wed.
But if the angels call her,
And she goes to heaven before,
I shall know her when I meet her,—
For she'll kiss me at the door.

UNFINISHED STILL.

A baby's boot, and a skein of wool,
Faded and soiled and soft;
Odd things, you say, and no doubt you're right,
Round a seaman's neck this stormy night,
Up in the yards aloft.
Most like it's folly, but mate, look here:
When first I went to sea
A woman stood on the far-off strand,
With a wedding-ring on the small soft hand,
Which clung so close to me.
My wife, God bless her! The day before,
She sat beside my foot,
And the sunlight kissed her yellow hair,
And the dainty fingers, deft and fair,
Knitted a baby's boot.
The voyage was over; I came ashore;
What, think you, found I there?
A grave the daisies had sprinkled white;
A cottage empty, and dark as night,
And this beside the chair.
The little boot, 'twas unfinished still—
The tangled skein lay near,
But the knitter had gone away to rest,
With the babe asleep on her quiet breast,
Down in the churchyard drear.

TO A WIFE DURING SICKNESS.

Cornelius Neale.

I said I would love thee in want or in wealth,
Through cloud and through sunshine, in sickness, in health,
And fear not, my love, when thy spirits are weak,
The troth I have plighted I never may break.

Ay, sickness; but sickness it touches the heart
With a feeling, where how many feelings have part;
There's a magic in soothing the wearisome hour,
Pity rears up the stem, and hope looks for the flower.

The rose smells as sweetly in sunshine and air,
But the greenhouse has all our affection and care;
The lark sings as nobly while soaring above,
But the bird that we nurse is the bird that we love.

I have loved thee in sickness, I'll love thee in health;
And if want be our portion, why love be our wealth;
Thy comfort in sorrow, thy stay when most weak,
The troth I have plighted I never will break.

THE FARMER'S WIFE.

Up with the birds in the morning—
  The dew-drops glow like a precious gem;
Beautiful tints in the skies are dawning,
  But she's never a moment to look at them.
The men are wanting their breakfast early;
  She must not linger, she must not wait;
For words that are sharp and looks that are surly
  Are what men give when meals are late.

To glorious colour the clouds are turning,
  If she would but look over hills and trees;
But here are the dishes and here is the churning—
  Those things must always yield to these.
The world is filled with the wine of beauty,
  If she could but pause and drink it in;
But pleasure, she says, must wait for duty—
  Neglected work is committed sin.

The day grows hot and her hands grow weary;
  Oh for an hour to cool her head,
Out with the birds and the winds so cheery!
  But she must get dinner and bake the bread.
The busy men in the hayfield working,
  If they saw her sitting with idle hand,
Would think her lazy and call it shirking,
  And she could never make them understand.

They do not know that the heart within her
  Hungers for beauty and things sublime;
They only know that they want their dinner—
  Plenty of it—and "just in time."
And after the sweeping and churning and baking,
  And dinner dishes are all put by,
She sits and sews, though her head is aching,
  Till time for supper and "chores" draws nigh.

Her boys at school must look like others,
  She says as she patches their frocks and hose;
For the world is quick to censure mothers
  For the least neglect of children's clothes.
Her husband comes from the field of labour;
  He gives no praise to the weary wife;
She's done no more that has her neighbour;
  'Tis the lot of all in country life.

But after the strife and weary tussle
  With life is done, and she lies at rest,
The nation's brain and heart and muscle—
  Her sons and daughters—shall call her blest.
And I think the sweetest joy of heaven,
  The rarest bliss of eternal life,
And the fairest crown of all will be given
  Unto the wayworn farmer's wife.

THE INVENTOR'S WIFE.

E. T. Corbett.

It's easy to talk of the patience of Job. Humph! Job had nothin' to try him:
If he'd been married to 'Bijah Brown, folks wouldn't have dared come nigh him.
Trials indeed! Now, I'll tell you what—if you want to be sick of your life
Jest come and change places with me a spell— for I'm an inventor's wife.
And sech inventions! I'm never sure, when I take up my coffee pot
That 'Bijah hain't been "improvin'" it, and it mayn't go off like a shot.
Why, didn't he make me a cradle once that would keep itself a-rockin'?
And didn't it pitch the baby out, and wasn't his head bruised shockin'?
And there was his patent "peeler," too—a wonderful thing I'll say;
But it had one fault—it never stopped till the apple was peeled away.
As for locks, and clocks, and mowin' machines, and reapers, and all such trash,
Why 'Bijah's invented heaps o' them, but they don't bring in no cash.
Law! that don't worry him—not at all; he's the aggravatinest man—
He'll sit in his little workshop there, and whistle, and think, and plan,
Inventin' a Jew's harp to go by steam, or a new-fangled powder-horn,
While the children's goin' barefoot to school, and the weeds is choking our corn.
When 'Bijah and me kep' company he warn't like this, you know,
Our folks all thought he was dreadful smart—but that was years ago.
He was handsome as any pictur' then, and he had such a glib, bright way—
I never thought that a time would come when I'd rue my wedding day;
But when I've been forced to chop the wood, and tend to the farm beside,
And look at 'Bijah a-settin' there, I've jest dropped down and cried.
We lost the hull of our turnip crop while he was inventin' a gun,
But I counted it one of my marcies when it bu'st before it was done;
So he turned it into a "burglar alarm." It ought to give the thieves a fright—
'Twould scare an honest man out of his wits ef he sot it off at night.
Sometimes I wonder ef 'Bijah's crazy, he does sech cur'ous things;
Hev I told you about his bedstead yet? 'Twas full of wheels and springs;
It hed a key to wind it up, and a clock face at the head;
All you did was to turn them hands, and at any hour you said,
That bed got up and shook itself, and bounced you on the floor,
And then shet up, jest like a box, so you couldn't sleep any more.
Wa'al, 'Bijah he fixed it all complete, and he sot it at half-past five,
But he hadn't more'n got into it, when—dear me! sakes alive!
Them wheels began to whizz and whirr! I heerd a fearful snap,
And there was that bedstead, with 'Bijah inside, shet up, just like a trap!
I screamed, of course; but 't wa'n't no use. Then I worked the hull long night
A-tryin' to open the pesky thing. At last I got in a fright;
I couldn't hear his voice inside, and thought he might be dyin',
So I took a crowbar and smashed it in. There was 'Bijah peacefully lyin',
Inventin' a way to git out ag'in. That was all very well to say,
But I don't believe he'd have found it out if I'd left him in all day.
Now, sence I've told you my story, do you wonder I'm tired of my life?
Or think it strange I often wish I warn't an inventor's wife?

THE GAMBLER'S WIFE.

Coates.

Dark is the night! how dark!—no light! no fire!
Cold, on the hearth, the last faint sparks expire!
Shivering she watches by the cradle-side,
For him who pledged her love—last year a bride!

"Hark! 'tis his footstep! No—'tis past! 'tis gone;
Tick!—tick!—How wearily the time crawls on!
Why should he leave me thus? He once was kind!
And I believed 'twould last:—how mad!—how blind!

"Rest thee, my babe!—rest on!—'Tis hunger's cry!
Sleep! —for there is no food! the font is dry!
Famine and cold their wearing work have done;
My heart must break!—And thou!"——The clock strikes one.

"Hush! 'tis the dice-box! Yes, he's there, he's there!
For this, for this, he leaves me to despair!
Leaves love! leaves truth! his wife! his child!—for what?
The wanton's smile—the villain—and the sot!

"Yet I'll not curse him! No! 'tis all in vain!
'Tis long to wait, but sure he'll come again!
And I could starve and bless him, but for you,
My child!—*his* child!—Oh fiend!"——The clock strikes two.

"Hark! how the sign-board creaks! The blast howls by!
Moan!—Moan!—A dirge swells through the cloudy sky!
Ha! 'tis his knock! he comes! he comes once more—
'Tis but the lattice flaps! Thy hope is o'er!

"Can he desert me thus? He knows I stay
Night after night in loneliness to pray
For his return—and yet he sees no tear!
No! no! it cannot be. He will be here.

"Nestle more closely, dear one, to my heart!
Thou'rt cold! thou'rt freezing! But we will not part.
Husband!—I die!—Father!—It is not he!
Oh Heaven! protect my child!"——The clock strikes three.

They're gone! they're gone! The glimmering spark hath fled,
The wife and child are numbered with the dead!
On the cold hearth, out-stretched in solemn rest
The child lies frozen on its mother's breast!
—The gambler came at last—but all was o'er—
Dead silence reigned around—he groaned—he spoke no more!

Poems about Husband and Wife.

THE WIFE TO HER HUSBAND.

"You took me, William, when a girl, unto your home and heart,
To bear in all your after fate a fond and faithful part;
And, tell me, have I ever tried that duty to forego,
Or pined there was not joy for me when you had sunk in woe?
No; I would rather share your tear than any other's glee;
For though you're nothing to the world, you're all the world to me.
You make a palace of my shed, this rough hewn bench a throne;
There's sunlight for me in your smiles, and music in your tone.
I look upon you when asleep—my eyes with tears grow dim;
I cry, 'O Parent of the poor, look down from heaven on him;
Behold him toil from day to day, exhausting strength and soul;
Oh, look with mercy on him, Lord, for thou canst make him whole!'
And when at last relieving sleep has on my eyelids smiled,
How oft are they forbade to close in slumber by our child?
I take the little murmurer that spoils my span of rest,
And feel it as a part of thee I lull upon my breast.
There's only one return I crave, I may not need it long,
And it may soothe thee when I'm where the wretched feel no wrong;
I ask not for a tender tone, for thou wert ever kind;
I ask not for less frugal fare, my fare I do not mind;
I ask not for attire more gay—if such as I have got
Suffice to make me fair to thee, for more I murmur not.
But I would ask some share of hours that you on clubs bestow—
Of knowledge which you pride so much, might I not something know?
Subtract from meetings amongst men each eve an hour for me;
Make me companion of your soul, as I may safely be.
If you will read, I'll sit and work, then think when you're away;
Less tedious I shall find the time, dear William, of your stay.
A meet companion soon I'll be for e'en your studious hours,
And teachers of those little ones you call your cottage flowers;
And if we be not rich and great, we may be wise and kind;
And as my heart can warm your heart, so may my mind your mind."

LOVE LIGHTENS LABOUR.

[The moral, or lesson, of this poem is well expressed by its title. The hardest work becomes easy when it is done for those whom we love, and who love us. Here the wife was utterly disheartened by the amount of hard work before her; but a few kindly words from her husband cheered her so, that she got through her day's work without feeling it the least irksome.]

A good wife rose from her bed one morn,
And thought with a nervous dread
Of the piles of clothes to be washed, and more
Than a dozen mouths to be fed.
There's the meals to get for the men in the field,
And the children to send away
To school, and the milk to be skimmed and churned;
And all to be done this day.

It had rained in the night, and all the wood
Was wet as it could be;
There were puddings and pies to bake, besides
A loaf of cake for tea.
And the day was hot, and her aching head
Throbbed wearily as she said:
"If maidens but knew what good wives know,
They would be in no haste to wed."

"Jennie, what do you think I told Ben Brown?"
Called the farmer from the well;
And a flush crept up to his bronzëd brow.
And his eyes half bashfully fell.
"It was this," he said, and, coming near,
He smiled, and, stooping down,
Kissed her cheek, "'Twas this: that you were the best
And the dearest wife in town!"

The farmer went back to the field, and the wife,
In a smiling and absent way,
Sang snatches of tender little songs
She'd not sung for many a day.
And the pain in her head was gone, and the clothes
Were white as the foam of the sea;
Her bread was light, and her butter was sweet,
And as golden as it could be.

"Just think," the children all called in a breath,—
"Tom Wood has run off to sea;
He wouldn't, I know, if he'd only had
As happy a home as we."
The night came down, and the good wife smiled
To herself, as she softly said,
"'Tis so sweet to labour for those we love,
It's not strange the maids will wed!"

BETSEY AND I ARE OUT.

Will Carleton.

DRAW up the papers, lawyer, and make 'em good and stout:
For things at home are crossways, and Betsey and I are out—
We, who have worked together so long as man and wife,
Must pull in single harness for the rest of our nat'ral life.

"What is the matter?" says you. I swan its hard to tell!
Most of the years behind us have passed by very well!
I have no other woman, she has no other man—
Only we've lived together as long as we ever can.

So I have talked with Betsey, and Betsey has talked with me,
And we have agreed together that we can't never agree:
Not that we've catched each other in any terrible crime:
We've been a-gathering this for years, a little at a time.

There was a stock of temper we both had for a start,
Although we never suspected 'twould take us two apart;
I had my various feelings, bred in the flesh and bone:
And Betsy, like all good women, had a temper of her own.

The first thing I remember whereon we disagreed
Was something concerning heaven—a difference in our creed;
We argued the thing at breakfast, we arg'ed the thing at tea:
And the more we arg'ed the question the more we didn't agree.

And the next that I remember was when we lost a cow,
She had kicked the bucket for certain, the question was only—how?
I held my own opinion, and Betsey another had;
And when we were done a-talkin', we both of us was mad.

And the next that I remember, it started in a joke;
But full for a week it lasted, and neither of us spoke.
And the next was when I scolded because she broke a bowl.
And she said I was mean and stingy, and hadn't any soul.

And so that bowl kept pourin' dissensions in our cup;
And so that blamed cow-creature was always a-cumin' up;
And so that heaven we arg'ed no nearer to us got,
But it gave us a taste of something a thousand times as hot.

And so the thing kept workin', and all the self-same way;
And always somethin' to arg'e, and somethin' sharp to say;
And down on us came the neighbours, a couple dozen strong,
And lent their kindest services to help the thing along.

And there has been days together—and many a weary week—
We was both of us cross and spunky, and both too proud to speak;
And I have been thinkin' and thinkin', the whole of the winter and fall,
If I can't live kind with a woman, why, then, I won't at all.

And so I have talked with Betsey, and Betsey has talked with me,
And we have agreed together that we can't never agree;
And what is hers shall be hers, and what is mine shall be mine;
And I'll put it in the agreement, and take it to her to sign.

Write on the paper, lawyer—the very first paragraph—
Of all the farm and live-stock that she shall have her half;
For she has helped to earn it, through many a weary day,
And it's nothing more than justice that Betsey has her pay.

Give her the house and homestead—a man can thrive and roam,
But women are skeery critters, unless they have a home;
And I have always determined, and never failed to say,
That Betsey should never want a home if I was taken away.

There is a little hard money that's drawing tol'rable pay,
A couple of hundred dollars laid by for a rainy day;
Safe in the hands of good men, and easy to get at;
Put in another clause there, and give her half of that.

Yes, I see you smile, sir, at my givin' her so much;
Yes, divorce is cheap, sir, but I take no stock in such!
True and fair I married her, when she was blithe and young;
And Betsey was al'ays good to me excepting with her tongue.

Once, when I was young as you, and not so smart, perhaps,
For me she mittened a lawyer, and several other chaps;
And all of them was flustered, and fairly taken down,
And I for a time was counted the luckiest man in the town.

Once when I had a fever—I won't forget it soon—
I was hot as a basted turkey and crazy as a loon;
Never an hour went by me when she was out of sight—
She nursed me true and tender, and stuck to me day and night.

And if ever a house was tidy, and ever a kitchen clean,
Her house and kitchen were as tidy as any I ever seen;
And I don't complain of Betsey, or any of her acts,
Excepting when we've quarrelled, and told each other facts.

So draw up the paper, lawyer, and I'll go home to-night,
And read the agreement to her, and see if it's all right;
And then, in the mornin', I'll sell to a tradin' man I know,
And kiss the child that was left to us, and out in the world I'll go.

And one thing put in the paper, that first to me didn't occur,
That when I am dead at last she'll bring me back to her;
And lay me under the maples I planted years ago,
When she and I was happy before we quarrelled so.

And when she dies I wish that she would be laid by me,
And, lying together in silence, perhaps we will agree;
And, if ever we meet in heaven, I wouldn't think it queer
If we loved each other the better because we quarrelled here.

HOW BETSEY AND I MADE UP.

Will Carleton.

GIVE us your hand, Mr. Lawyer: how do you do to-day?
You drew up that paper—I s'pose you want your pay.
Don't cut down your figures: make it an X or a V;
For that 'ere written agreement was just the makin' of me.

Goin' home that evenin' I tell you I was blue,
Thinkin' of all my troubles, and what I was goin' to do;
And if my horses hadn't been the steadiest team alive,
They'd've tipped me over for certain, for I couldn't see where to drive.

No—for I was labourin' under a heavy load;
No—for I was travellin' an entirely different road;
For I was a-tracing over the path of our lives ag'in,
And seein' where we missed the way, and where we might have been.

And many a corner we'd turned that just to a quarrel led,
When I ought to've held my temper, and driven straight ahead;
And the more I thought it over the more these memories came,
And the more I struck the opinion that I was the most to blame.

And things I had long forgotten kept risin' in my mind,
Of little matters betwixt us, where Betsey was good and kind;
And these things flashed all through me, as you know things sometimes will
When a feller's alone in the darkness, and everything is still.

"But," says I, "we're too far along to take another track,
And when I put my hand to the plough, I do not oft turn back,
And 'tain't an uncommon thing now for couples to smash in two;"
And so I set my teeth together, and vowed I'd see it through.

When I come in sight o' the house, 'twas some'at in the night,
And just as I turned a hill-top I see the kitchen light;
Which often a han'some pictur' to a hungry person makes,
But it don't interest a feller much that's going to pull up stakes.

And when I went in the house, the table was set for me—
As good a supper's I ever saw, or ever want to see;
And I crammed the agreement down my pocket as well as I could,
And fell to eatin' my victuals, which somehow didn't taste good.

And Betsey, she pretended to look about the house,
But she watched my side coat-pocket like a cat would watch a mouse;
And then she went to foolin' a little with her cup,
And intently readin' a newspaper, a-holding it wrong side up.

And when I'd done my supper, I drawed the agreement out,
And gave it to her without a word, for she know'd what 'twas about;
And then I hummed a little tune, but now and then a note
Was busted by some animal that hopped up in my throat.

Then Betsey she got her specs from off the mantel shelf,
And read the article over quite softly to herself;
Read by little and little, for her eyes is gettin' old,
And lawyers' writin' ain't no print, especially when it's cold.

And after she'd read a little she gave my arm a touch,
And kindly said she was afraid I was 'lowin' her too much:
But when she was through, she went for me, her face a-streamin' with tears,
And kissed me for the first time in over twenty years!

I don't know what you'll think, sir—I didn't come to inquire—
But I picked up that agreement, and stuffed it in the fire;
And I told her we'd bury the hatchet alongside of the cow;
And we struck an agreement never to have another row.

And I told her in the future I wouldn't speak cross or rash
If half the crockery in the house was broken all to smash;
And she said, in regards to heaven, we'd try and learn its worth,
By startin' a branch establishment and runnin' it here on earth.

And so we sat a-talkin' three-quarters of the night,
And opened our hearts to each other until they both grew light;
And the days when I was winnin' her away from so many men
Was nothing to that evening I courted her over again.

Next mornin' an ancient virgin took pains to call on us,
Her lamp all trimmed and a-burnin' to kindle another fuss;
But when she went a pryin' and openin' of old sores,
My Betsey rose politely, and showed her out of doors.

Since then I don't deny but there's been a word or two;
But we've got our eyes wide open, and know just what to do;
When one speaks cross the other just meets it with a laugh,
And the first one's ready to give up considerable more than half.

Maybe you'll think me soft, sir, a-talking in this style,
But somehow it does me lots of good to tell it once in a while;
And I do it for a compliment—'tis so that you can see
That that there written agreement of yours was just the makin' of me.

So make out your bill, Mr. Lawyer; don't stop short of an X;
Make it more if you want to, for I have got the cheques.
I'm richer than a National Bank, with all its treasures told,
For I've got a wife at home now that's worth her weight in gold.

THE BLACKSMITH'S STORY.

Frank Olive.

WELL, no! my wife ain't dead, sir, but I've lost her all the same;
She left me voluntarily, and neither was to blame.
It's rather a queer story, and I think you will agree—
When you hear the circumstances—'twas rather rough on me.

She was a soldier's widow. He was killed at Malvern Hill;
And when I married her she seemed to sorrow for him still;
But I brought her here to Kansas, and I never want to see
A better wife than Mary was for five bright years to me.

The change of scene brought cheerfulness, and soon a rosy glow.
Of happiness warmed Mary's cheeks and melted all their snow.
I think she loved me some—I'm bound to think that of her, sir,
And as for me—I can't begin to tell how I loved her!

Three years ago the baby came, our humble home to bless:
And then I reckon I was nigh to perfect happiness;
'Twas hers—'twas mine—; but I've no language to explain to you,
How that little girl's weak fingers our hearts together drew!

Once we watched it through a fever, and with each gasping breath,
Dumb, with an awful, wordless woe, we waited for its death;
And, though I'm not a pious man, our souls together there,
For Heaven to spare our darling, went up in voiceless prayer.

And when the doctor said 'twould live, our joy what words could tell?
Clasped in each other's arms, our grateful tears together fell.
Sometimes, you see, the shadow fell across our little nest,
But it only made the sunshine seem a doubly welcome guest.

Work came to me a plenty, and I kept the anvil ringing;
Early and late you'd find me there a hammering and singing;
Love nerved my arm to labour, and moved my tongue to song,
And though my singing wasn't sweet it was tremendous strong!

One day a one-armed stranger stopped to have me nail a shoe,
And while I was at work, we passed a compliment or two;
I asked him how he lost his arm. He said 'twas shot away
At Malvern Hill. "At Malvern Hill! Did you know Robert May?"

"That's me," said he. "You, You!" I gasped, choking with horrid doubt;
"If you're the man, just follow me; we'll try this mystery out!"
With dizzy steps, I led him to Mary. God! 'Twas true!
Then the bitterest pangs of misery, unspeakable, I knew.

Frozen with deadly horror, she stared with eyes of stone,
And from her quivering lips there broke one wild despairing moan.
'Twas he! the husband of her youth, now risen from the dead.
But all too late—and with bitter cry, her senses fled.

What could be done? He was reported dead. On his return.
He strove in vain some tidings of his absent wife to learn.
'Twas well that he was innocent! Else I'd 've killed him, too
So dead he never would have riz till Gabriel's trumpet blew!

It was agreed that Mary then between us should decide,
And each by her decision would sacredly abide;
No sinner, at the judgment-seat, waiting eternal doom,
Could suffer what I did, while waiting sentence in that room.

Rigid and breathless, there we stood, with nerves as tense as steel,
While Mary's eyes sought each white face, in piteous appeal.
God! could not woman's duty be less hardly reconciled
Between her lawful husband and the father of her child?

Ah, how my heart was chilled to ice, when she knelt down and said:
"Forgive me, John! Here is my husband! Here! Alive! Not dead."
I raised her tenderly, and tried to tell her she was right,
But somehow, in my aching breast, the poisoned words stuck tight!

"But, John, I can't leave baby"—"What! wife and child!" cried I;
"Must I yield all! Ah, cruel fate! Better that I should die.
Think of the long, sad, lonely hours, waiting in gloom for me—
No wife to cheer me with her love—no babe to climb my knee!

"And yet—you are her mother, and the sacred mother love
Is still the purest, tenderest tie that Heaven ever wove.
Take her, but promise, Mary— for that will bring no shame—
My little girl shall bear, and learn to lisp her father's name!"

It may be in the life to come, I'll meet my child and wife;
But yonder by my cottage gate, we parted for this life;
One long hand-clasp from Mary, and my dream of love was done!
One long embrace from baby, and my happiness was gone!

AULD ROBIN GRAY.

Lady Anna Barnard.

WHEN the sheep are in the fauld, when the cows come hame
When a' the weary warld to quiet rest are gane;
The woes of my heart fa' in showers frae my ee,
Unken'd by my gudeman, who soundly sleeps by me.

Young Jamie loo'd weel, and sought me for his bride;
But saving ae crown piece, he'd naething else beside.
To make the crown a pound, my Jamie gaed to sea;
And the crown and the pound, O they were baith for me!

Before he had been gane a twelvemonth and a day,
My father brak his arm, our cow was stown away!
My mother she fell sick—my Jamie was at sea—
And Auld Robin Gray, oh—he came a courting me.

My father cou'dna work, my mother cou'dna spin;
I toil'd day and night, but their bread I cou'dna win;
Auld Rob maintain'd them baith, and, wi' tears in his ee,
Said, 'Jenny, oh! for their sakes, will ye marry me?'

My heart it said na, and I looked for Jamie back;
But hard blew the winds, and his ship was a wrack:
His ship it was a wrack! Why didna Jamie dee?
Or, wherefore am I spar'd to cry out, Woe is me!

My father argued sair—my mother didna speak,
But she look'd in my face till my heart was like to break;
They gaed him my hand, but my heart was in the sea;
And so Auld Robin Gray, he was gudeman to me.

I hadna been his wife, a week but only four,
When mournfu' as I sat on the stane at my door,
I saw my Jamie's ghaist—I cou'dna think it he,
Till he said, 'I'm come hame, my love, to marry thee!'

O sair, sair did we greet, and mickle say of a';
Ae kiss we took, nae mair—I bade him gang away.
I wish that I were dead, but I'm no like to dee;
For O, I am but young to cry out, Woe is me;

I gang like a ghaist, and I carena much to spin,
I darena think o' Jamie, for that wad be a sin.
But I will do my best a gude wife aye to be,
For Auld Robin Gray, oh! he is sae kind to me.

THE CONTINUATION.

The wintry days grew lang, my tears they were a' spent:
Maybe it was despair I fancied was content.
They said my cheek was wan; I cou'dna look to see—
For, oh! the wee bit glass, my Jamie gaed it me.

My father he was sad, my mother dull and wae;
But that which griev'd me maist, it was Auld Robin Grey;
Though ne'er a word he said, his cheek said mair than a',
It wasted like a brae o'er which the torrents fa'.

He gaed into his bed, nae physic wad he take;
And oft he moaned and said, 'It's better for her sake,'
At length he looked upon me, and called me "his ain dear,'
And beckoned round the neighbours as if his hour drew near.

'I've wronged her sair,' he said, 'but ken't the truth o'er late;
It's grief for that alone that hastens now my fate;
But a' is for the best, since death will shortly free
A young and faithful heart that was ill-matched wi' me.

'I loo'd and sought to win her for many a lang day;
I had her parents' favour, but still she said me nay;
I knew na' Jamie's luve: and oh! it's sair to tell—
To force her to be mine, I steal'd her cow mysel!

'O what cared I for Crummie! I thought of naught but thee,
I thought it was the cow stood twixt my luve and me.
While she maintained ye a', was you not heard to say,
That you would never marry wi' Auld Robin Gray?

'But sickness in the house, and hunger at the door,
My bairn gied me her hand, although her heart was sore
I saw her heart was sore—why did I take her hand?
That was a sinfu' deed! to blast a bonnie land.

'It was na very lang ere a' did come to light;
For Jamie he came back, and Jenny's cheek grew white.
My spouse's cheek grew white, but true she was to me;
Jenny! I saw it a'—and oh, I'm glad to dee!

'Is Jamie come!' he said; and Jamie by us stood—
'Ye loo each other weel—oh, let me do some good—
I gie you a', young man—my houses, cattle, and kine,
And the dear wife hersel, that ne'er should hae been mine.'

We kissed the clay-cold hands—a smile came o'er his face;
'He's pardon'd,' Jamie said, 'before the throne of grace,
Oh, Jenny! see that smile—Forgi'en I'm sure is he,
Wha could withstand temptation when hoping to win thee?'

The days at first were dowie; but what was sad and sair,
While tears were in my ee, I kent mysel nae mair;
For, oh! my heart was light as any bird that flew,
And, wae as a' thing was, it had a kindly hue.

But sweeter shines the sun than e'er he shone before,
For now I'm Jamie's wife, and what need I say more?
We hae a wee bit bairn—the auld folks by the fire—
And Jamie, oh! he loo's me up to my heart's desire.

LAND POOR.

J. W. Donovan.

I'VE had another offer, wife, a twenty acres more,
Of high and dry prairie land, as level as a floor.
I thought I'd wait and see you first, as Lawyer Brady said,
To tell how things will turn out best, a *woman* is ahead.

And when this plot is paid for, and we have got the deed,
I'll say that I am satisfied—it's all the land we need;
And next we'll see about the yard, and fix the house up some,
And manage in the course of time to have a better home.

WIFE.

There's no use of talking, Charles—you buy that twenty more,
And we'll go scrimping all our lives, and always be *land poor*.
For thirty years we've tugged and saved, denying half our needs,
While all we have to show for it is *tax receipts and deeds!*

I'd *sell* the land if it were mine, and have a better home,
With broad, light rooms to front the street, and take life as it come.
If we could live as others live, and have what others do,
We'd live enough sight pleasanter, and have a plenty too.

While others have amusements and luxury and books,
Just think how stingy we have lived, and how this old place looks.
That other farm you bought of Wells, that took so many years
Of clearing up and fencing in, has cost me many tears.

Yes, Charles, I've thought of it a hundred times or more,
And wondered if it really *paid* to be always land poor,—
That had we built a cosy house, took pleasure as it come,
Our children, once so dear to us, had never left our home.

I grieve to think of wasted weeks and years and months and days,
While for it all we never yet have had one word of praise.
Men call us rich, but we are poor—would we not freely give
The land with all its fixtures *for a better way to live?*

Don't think I'm blaming you, Charles—you're not a whit to blame.
I've pitied you these many years, to see you tired and lame.
It's just the way we started out, our plans too far ahead;
We've worn the cream of life away, *to leave too much when dead.*

'Tis putting off enjoyment long after we enjoy,—
And after all too much of wealth seems useless as a toy,—
Although we've learned, alas, too late! what all must learn at last,
Our brightest earthly happiness is buried in the past.

That life is short and full of care, the end is always nigh,
We seldom half begin to live before we're doomed to die.
Were I to start my life again, I'd mark each separate day,
And never let a single one pass unenjoyed away.

If there were things to envy, I'd have them now and then,
And have a home that was a home, and not a cage or pen.
I'd sell some land if it were mine, and fit up well the rest,
I've always thought and think so yet—small farms well worked are best.

FIVE-AND-TWENTY YEARS AGO.

Ah, good wife, have you forgotten,
  Days when you were young and fair?
Time of rosy cheeks and dimples,
  Time of sunny golden hair?
Not a thought of toil could vex us,
  Grief and care we did not know;
You and I were young together
  Five-and-twenty years ago.

In the strength of hopeful manhood,
  Lithe and straight and tall I stood;
And you waited close beside me,
  Crowned with blooming womanhood:
Now life's twilight shades are falling,
  While the years crowd on apace,
And on heart and form and feature,
  Care and grief have left their trace.

We have heard the church-bell tolling,
  We have filled pale hands with flowers,
We have robed our precious darlings
  For the grave's dark, lonely hours;
We have seen the wee chairs vacant,
  Aged friends we've bid "Good-bye;"
O'er green graves we've wept together—
  Ah! how often! you and I.

But the summer's bloom is followed
  By the "sere and yellow leaf,"
And the golden harvest comes not,
  Till we break the burdened sheaf.
Hearts may love in sunny weather,
  When youth's freshest roses glow,
That can ill betide the waiting
  For the ripening years of snow.

But the rapture of love's morning
  Brightens still our noon-tide ray,
And hope paints a glorious sunset
  For our last declining day:
And or long or short the journey,
  That our lagging feet may know,
Love is ours, the love we plighted,
  Five-and-twenty years ago.

ARE THE CHILDREN AT HOME?

EACH day when the glow of sunset
  Fades in the western sky,
And the wee ones, tired of playing,
  Go lightly tripping by,
I steal away from my husband—
  Asleep in the easy chair,
And watch from the open doorway
  Their faces fresh and fair.

* * * * *

Alone in the dear old homestead,
  That once was full of life,
Ringing with girlish laughter,
  Echoing with boyish strife,
We two are waiting together,
  And, oft as the shadows come,
With tremulous voice he calls me,—
  "It is night, are the children home?"

"Yes, love," I answer him gently,
  "They're all home long ago;"
And I sing in my quivering treble,
  A song so soft and low,
That the old man drops to slumber,
  With his head upon his hand,
And I tell to myself the number—
  Home in the better land,—

Home, where never a sorrow
  Shall dim their eyes with tears!
Where the smile of God is on them,
  Through all the summer years!
I know!—yet my arms are empty,
  That have fondly folded seven,
And the mother's heart within me
  Is almost starved for heaven.

* * * * *

Sometimes in the dusk of evening,
  I do but shut my eyes,
And the children are all about me—
  A vision from the skies;
The babes whose dimpled fingers
  Did lose the way to my breast,
And the beautiful ones, the angels,
  Passed to the world of the blest.

With never a cloud above them
  I see their radiant brows,
My boys that I gave to freedom,
  The red sword sealed their vows!
In a war for holy freedom,
  Twin brothers bold and brave,
They fell! and the flag they died for
  Thank God! floats over their grave.

A breath, and the vision is lifted
  Away on the wings of light,
And again we two are together,
  Alone, alone, in the night.
They tell me his mind is failing,
  But I smile at idle fears;
He is only back with the children
  In the dear and peaceful years.

* * * * *

And still as the summer sunset
  Fadeth away in the west,
And the wee ones, tired of playing,
  Go trooping home to rest,
My husband calls from his corner,
  "Say, love, have the children come?"
And I answer with eyes uplifted,
  "Yes, dear, they are all at home."

THE DIAMOND WEDDING.

Come sit close by my side, my darling,
  Sit up very close to-night;
Let me clasp your tremulous fingers
  In mine, as tremulous quite.
Lay your silvery head on my bosom,
  As you did when 'twas shining gold;
Somehow I know no difference,
  Though they say we are very old.

'Tis seventy-five years to-day, wife,
  Since we knelt at the altar low,
And the fair young minister of God
  (He died long years ago)
Pronounced us one, that Christmas eve—
  How short they've seemed to me,
The years—and yet I'm ninety-seven,
  And you are ninety-three.

That morn I placed on your finger
  A band of purest gold;
And to-night I see it shining
  On the withered hand I hold.
How it lightens up the memories
  That o'er my vision come!
First of all is the merry children
  That once made glad our home.

There was Benny, our darling Benny,
  Our first-born pledge of bliss,
As beautiful a boy as ever
  Felt a mother's loving kiss.
'Twas hard—as we watched him fading
  Like a floweret day by day—
To feel that He who had lent him
  Was calling him away.

My heart it grew very bitter
  As I bowed beneath the stroke;
And yours, though you said so little,
  I knew was almost broke.
We made him a grave 'neath the daisies
  (There are five now, instead of one),
And we've learned, when our Father chastens,
  To say, "Thy will be done."

Then came Lillie and Allie—twin cherubs,
  Just spared from the courts of heaven—
To comfort our hearts for a moment:
  God took as soon as He'd given.

Then Katie, our gentle Katie;
  We thought her very fair,
With her blue eyes soft and tender,
  And her curls of auburn hair.

Like a queen she looked at her bridal
  (I thought it were you instead);
But her ashen lips kissed her first-born,
  And mother and child were dead.
We said that of all our number
  We had two, our pride and stay—
Two noble boys, Fred and Harry;
  But God thought the other way.

Far away, on the plains of Shiloh,
  Fred sleeps in an unknown grave:
With his ship and noble sailors
  Harry sank beneath the wave.
So sit closer, darling, closer—
  Let me clasp your hand in mine:
Alone we commenced life's journey,
  Alone we are left behind.

Your hair, once gold, to silver
  They say by age has grown;
But I know it has caught its whiteness
  From the halo around His throne.
They give us a diamond wedding
  This Christmas eve, dear wife;
But I know your orange-blossoms
  Will be a crown of life.

'Tis dark; the lamps should be lighted;
  And your hand has grown so cold.
Has the fire gone out? how I shiver!
  But, then, we are very old.
Hush! I hear sweet strains of music:
  Perhaps the guests have come.
No—'tis the children's voices—
  I know them, every one.

On that Christmas eve they found them,
  Their hands together clasped;
But they never knew their children
  Had been their wedding guests.
With her head upon her bosom,
  That had never ceased its love,
They held their diamond wedding
  In the mansion house above.

Poems about Mother.

A MOTHER'S LOVE.

A MOTHER'S love—how sweet the name!
What is a mother's love?
A noble, pure and tender flame,
Enkindled from above,
To bless a heart of earthly mould,
The warmest love that can't grow cold—
This is a mother's love.

To bring a helpless babe to light.
Then, while it lies forlorn,
To gaze upon that dearest sight,
And feel herself new-born;
In its existence lose her own,
And live and breathe in it alone—
This is a mother's love.

Its weakness in her arms to bear,
To cherish on her breast;
Feed it from love's own fountain there,
And lull it there to rest;
Then, while it slumbers watch its breath,
As if to guard from instant death—
This is a mother's love.

To mark its growth from day to day,
Its opening charms admire,
Catch from its eye the earliest ray
Of intellectual fire;
To smile and listen when it talks,
And lend a finger when it walks—
This is a mother's love.

THE MOTHER IN THE SNOW-STORM.

Seba Smith.

THE cold winds swept the mountain's height,
And pathless was the dreary wild,
And 'mid the cheerless hours of night,
A mother wandered with her child;
As through the drifting snows she pressed
The babe was sleeping on her breast.

And colder still the winds did blow,
And darker hours of night came on,
And deeper grew the drifting snow;
Her limbs were chilled, her strength was gone:
"O God!" she cried, in accents wild,
"If I must perish, save my child!"

She stripped her mantle from her breast,
And bared her bosom to the storm,
And round the child she wrapped the vest,
And smiled to think her babe was warm.
With one cold kiss one tear she shed,
And sunk upon her snowy bed.

At dawn a traveller passed by,
And saw her 'neath a snowy veil;
The frost of death was in her eye,
Her cheek was cold, and hard, and pale.
He moved the robe from off the child—
The babe looked up and sweetly smiled!

MY MOTHER'S VOICE.

John Harris, a Cornish Miner.

I HEAR it in the busy throng;
I hear it when alone;
I hear it in the rock-ribb'd earth,
The same melodious tone.
I hear it when my heart is sad;
I hear it when I'm gay.
It floats around me everywhere,
The sweetest voice for aye!

It leads me back when life was new;
Tells of those happy hours
I passed in childhood's sunny vale,
Among the opening flowers.
Talks to me of my mountain home,
That home of homes to me,
Engraven on my heart of hearts,
For ever there to be.

The music of this voice I hear
Above the world's rough roar,
Like whispers from another sphere,
Some calm Elysian shore;
Sweet harp-notes from the lyre of Time,
Around me and within,
They gush with conquering ecstacy,
To lure my soul from sin.

THE MOTHER AND CHILD.

Roger.

Her by her smile how soon the stranger knows;
How soon by this the glad discovery shows!
As to her lips she lifts the lovely boy.
What answering looks of sympathy and joy!
He walks, he speaks. In many a broken word
His wants, his wishes, and his griefs are heard,
And ever, ever, to her lap he flies,
When rosy sleep comes on with sweet surprise.
Lock'd in her arms, his arms across her flung,
(That name most dear for ever on his tongue),
As with soft accents round her neck he clings,
And, cheek to cheek, her lulling song she sings,
How blest to feel the beatings of his heart,
Breathe his sweet breath, and kiss for kiss impart,
Watch o'er his slumbers like the brooding dove,
And, if she can, exhaust a mother's love.

A MOTHER'S LOVE.

Emily Taylor.

Hast thou sounded the depth of yonder sea,
And counted the sands that under it be?
Hast thou measured the height of Heaven above?
Then mayest thou mete out a mother's love.

Hast thou talked with the blessed, of leading on
To the throne of God some wandering son?
Hast thou witnessed the angel's bright employ?
Then mayest thou speak of a mother's joy.

Evening and morn hast thou watched the bee
Go forth on her errands of industry?
The bee for herself hath gathered and toil'd,
But the mother's cares are all for her child.

Hast thou gone with the traveller Thought afar,
From pole to pole, and from star to star?
Thou hast—but on ocean, earth or sea,
The heart of a mother has gone with thee.

There is not a grand, inspiring thought,
There is not a truth by wisdom taught,
There is not a feeling pure and high,
That may not be read in a mother's eye.

And ever since earth began, that look
Has been to the wise an open book,
To win them back from the love they prize
To the holier love that edifies.

There are teachings on earth, and sky, and air,
The heavens the glory of God declare,
But more loud than the voice beneath, above,
He is heard to speak through a mother's love.

A MOTHER'S GRIEF.

T. Dale.

To mark the suff'rings of the babe
  That cannot speak its woe,
To see the infant's tears gush forth,
  Yet know not why they flow:
To meet the meek, uplifted eye,
  That fain would ask relief,
Yet cannot tell of agony—
  This is a mother's grief.

Through dreary days and darker nights
  To trace the mark of death,
To hear the faint and frequent sigh,
  The quick and shorten'd breath;
To watch the last dread strife draw near,
  And pray that struggle brief,
Though all is ended with its close—
  This is a mother's grief.

To see in one short day decay'd
  The hope of future years;
To feel how vain a father's prayers,
  How vain a mother's tears;
To think the cold grave now must close
  O'er what was once the chief
Of all the treasured joys on earth—
  This is a mother's grief.

Yet, when the first wild throb is past
  Of anguish and despair,
To lift the eye of faith to heaven,
  And think, "My child is there!"
This best can dry the gushing tears—
  This yield the heart relief;
Until the Christian's pious hope
  O'ercomes a mother's grief.

THE MOTHER'S FIRST GRIEF.

From "Knickerbocker."

She sits beside the cradle,
  And her tears are streaming fast,
For she sees the present only,
  While she thinks of all the past:
Of the days so full of gladness,
  When her first-born's answering kiss
Thrilled her soul with such a rapture
  That it knew no other bliss.
O, those happy, happy moments!
  They but deepen her despair,
For she bends above the cradle,
  And her baby is not there!

There are words of comfort spoken,
  And the leaden clouds of grief
Wear the smiling bow of promise,
  And she feels a sad relief:
But her wavering thoughts will wander,
  Till they settle on the scene
Of the dark and silent chamber,
  And of all that might have been!
For a little vacant garment,
  Or a shining tress of hair
Tells her heart in tones of anguish,
  That her baby is not there!

She sits beside the cradle,
  But her tears no longer flow,
For she sees a blessed vision,
  And forgets all earthly woe;
Saintly eyes look down upon her,
  And the Voice that hushed the sea
Stills her spirit with the whisper,
  "Suffer them to come to Me."
And while her soul is lifted
  On the soaring wings of prayer,
Heaven's crystal gates swing inward,
  And she sees her baby there!

TIRED MOTHERS.

A LITTLE elbow leans upon your knee,
Your tired knee, that has so much to bear;
A child's dear eyes are looking lovingly
From underneath a thatch of tangled hair.
Perhaps you do not heed the velvet touch
Of warm, moist fingers, folding yours so tight;
You *do not* prize this blessing overmuch,
You almost are too tired to play to-night.

But it is blessedness! A year ago
I did not see it as I do to-day—
We are so dull and thankless, and too slow
To catch the sunshine till it slips away.
And now it seems surpassing strange to me
That, while I bore the badge of motherhood,
I did not kiss more oft and tenderly
The little child that brought me only good.

And if some night when you sit down to rest
You miss this elbow from your tired knee,
This restless, curling head from off your breast,
This lisping tongue that chatters constantly;
If from your own the dimpled hands had slipped,
And ne'er would nestle in your palms again;
If the white feet into their grave had tripped,
I could not blame you for your heartache then.

I wonder so that mothers ever fret
At little children clinging to their gown;
Or that the footprints when the days are wet
Are ever black enough to make them frown.
If I could find a little muddy boot,
Or cap, or jacket on my chamber floor;
If I could kiss a rosy restless foot,
And hear its patter in my home once more;

If I could mend a broken cart to-day,
To-morrow make a kite to reach the sky—
There is no woman in God's world could say
She was more blissfully content than I.
But, ha! the dainty pillow next my own
Is never rumpled by a shining head;
My singing birdling from its nest is flown—
The little boy I used to kiss is dead.

PREPARING FOR SUNDAY.

PLACING the little hats all in a row,
Ready for church on the morrow, you know;
Washing each wee face and little black fist,
Getting them ready and fit to be kissed;
Putting them into clean garments and white—
That is what mothers are doing to-night.

Spying out holes in the little worn hose,
Laying by shoes that are worn through the toes,
Looking o'er garments so faded and thin—
Who but a mother knows how to begin?
Changing a button to make it look right—
That is what mothers are doing to-night.

Calling the little ones all round her chair,
Hearing them lisp forth their soft evening prayer,
Telling them stories of Jesus of old,
Who loves to gather the lambs to his fold;
Watching they listen with childish delight—
That is what mothers are doing to-night.

Creeping so softly to take a last peep,
After the little ones all are asleep;
Anxious to know if the children are warm,
Tucking the blanket round each little form;
Kissing each little face rosy and bright—
That is what mothers are doing to-night.

Kneeling down gently beside the white bed,
Lowly and meekly she bows down her head,
Praying as only a mother can pray,
"God guide and keep them from going astray."

THE HAND THAT ROCKS THE WORLD.

INFANCY, the tender fountain,
  Ever may with beauty flow;
Mother's first to guide the streamlets;
  From them souls unresting grow—
Grow on for the good or evil,
  Sunshine streamed or darkness hurled;
For the hand that rocks the cradle
  Is the hand that rocks the world.

Mother, how divine your mission
  Here upon our natal sod!
Keep, oh, keep the young heart open
  Always to the breath of God!
All true trophies of the ages
  Are from mother-love impearled,
For the hand that rocks the cradle
  Is the hand that rocks the world.

Blessings on the hand of mother!
  Fathers, sons, and daughters cry,
And the sacred song is mingled
  With the worship in the sky—
Mingles where no tempest darkens,
  Rainbows ever gently curled;
For the hand that rocks the cradle
  Is the hand that rocks the world.

SMITING THE ROCK.

The stern old judge, in relentless mood,
Glanced at the two who before him stood;
She was bowed and haggard and old,
He was young and defiant and bold,—
Mother and son; and to gaze at the pair,
Their different attitudes, look and air,
One would believe, ere the truth were known,
The mother convicted and not the son.

There was the mother; the boy stood nigh
With a shameless look, and his head held high.
Age had come over her, sorrow and care;
These mattered but little so he was there,
A prop to her years and a light to her eyes,
And prized as only a mother can prize;
But what for him could a mother say,
Waiting his doom on a sentence day.

Her husband had died in his shame and sin;
And she a widow, her living to win,
Had toiled and struggled from morn till night,
Making with want a wearisome fight,
Bent over her work with resolute zeal,
Till she felt her old frame totter and reel,
Her weak limbs tremble, her eyes grow dim;
But she had her boy, and she toiled for him.

And he,—he stood in the criminal dock,
With a heart as hard as a flinty rock,
An impudent glance and a reckless air,
Braving the scorn of the gazers there,
Dipped in crime, and encompassed round
With proof of his guilt by captors found,
Ready to stand, as he phrased it "game,"
Holding not crime, but penitence, shame
Poured in a flood o'er the mother's cheek
The moistening prayers where the tongue was weak,
And she saw through the mist of those bitter tears
Only the child in his innocent years;
She remembered him pure as a child might be,
The guilt of the present she could not see;
And for mercy her wistful looks made prayer
To the stern old judge in his cushioned chair.

"Woman," the old judge crabbedly said—
"Your boy is the neighbourhood's plague and dread;
Of a gang of reprobates chosen chief;
An idler, and rioter, ruffian and thief,
The jury did right, for the facts were plain;
Denial is idle, excuses are vain.
The sentence the court imposes is one—"
"Your honour," she cried, "he's my only son."

The constables grinned at the words she spoke,
And a ripple of fun through the court-room broke;
But over the face of the culprit came
An angry look and a shadow of shame.
"Don't laugh at my mother!" loud cries he;
"You've got me fast, and can deal with me;
But she's too good for your coward jeers,
And I'll—" then his utterance choked with tears.

The judge for a moment bent his head,
And looked at him keenly, and then he said:
"We suspend the sentence,—the boy can go;"
And the words were tremulous, forced and low.
"But say!" and he raised his finger then—
"Don't let them bring you hither again.
There is something good in you yet, I know;
I'll give you a chance—make the most of it—Go!"

The twain went forth, and the old judge said;
"I meant to have given him a year instead.
And perhaps 'tis a difficult thing to tell
If clemency here be ill or well.
But a rock was struck in that callous heart,
From which a fountain of good may start;
For one on the ocean of crime long tossed,
Who loves his mother is not quite lost."

NAPOLEON AND THE SAILOR.

A TRUE STORY.

Campbell.

Napoleon's banners at Boulogne
Armed in our island every freeman,
His navy chanced to capture one
Poor British seaman.

They suffered him—I know not how—
Unprisoned on the shore to roam;
And aye was bent his longing brow
On England's home.

His eye, methinks, pursued the flight
Of birds to Britain half-way over,
With envy, they could reach the white,
Dear cliffs of Dover.

A stormy midnight watch he thought,
Than this sojourn would have been dearer,
If but the storm his vessel brought
To England nearer.

At last, when care had banished sleep,
He saw one morning—dreaming—doating,
An empty hogshead from the deep
Come shoreward floating.

He hid it in a cave, and wrought
The livelong day laborious; lurking
Until he launched a tiny boat
By mighty working.

Heaven help us! 'twas a thing beyond
Description, wretched: such a wherry
Perhaps ne'er ventured on a pond,
Or crossed a ferry.

For ploughing in the salt sea-field,
It would have made the boldest shudder,
Untarred, uncompassed, and unkeeled,
No sail—no rudder.

From neighbouring woods he interlaced
His sorry skiff with wattled willows;
And thus equipped he would have passed
The foaming billows—

But Frenchmen caught him on the beach,
His little Argo sorely jeering;
Till tidings of him chanced to reach
Napoleon's hearing.

With folded arms Napoleon stood,
Serene alike in peace and danger;
And in his wonted attitude,
Addressed the stranger:—

"Rash man that would'st yon channel pass
On twigs and staves so rudely fashioned;
Thy heart with some sweet British lass
Must be impassioned."

"I have no sweetheart," said the lad;
"But—absent long from one another—
Great was the longing that I had
To see my mother."

"And so thou shalt," Napoleon said,
"You've both my favour fairly won;
A noble mother must have bred
So brave a son."

He gave the tar a piece of gold,
And with a flag of truce commanded
He should be shipped to England Old,
And safely landed.

Our sailor oft could scantily shift
To find a dinner plain and hearty;
But never changed the coin and gift
Of Bonaparte.

THE SENTINEL; OR, "WHO'S THERE?"

Vogl.

See that poor soldier, who ne'er speaks
  Nor laughs nor weeps, I'm told;
His heart would seem of iron formed,
  His face of marble cold.

As sentinel in duty bound,
  He once stood at his post.
And gazed with sorrow down the vale,
  In night and darkness lost.

For then the plague was raging wild,
  That spares not old or young;
His aged mother lived down there—
  That thought his heart had wrung.

He knows not if she lives or if
  Her head is now laid low;
For no one dares to mount on high,
  And none descend below.

And there in darkness night alone
  He stood on that steep height,
And still along that silent vale
  He gazed with longing sight.

But greater longing still has seized
  His aged mother's breast;
Alone in that poor cabin, she
  No more in peace can rest;

She only thinks upon her son,
  No longer can she stay;
To find him out—to hear his fate—
  She hastens now away.

And through the dark and stormy night,
  She wanders forth alone;
"O God! but let me hear two words
  From that dear child's own tongue!

She climbed the hill with weary steps,
  The wind was raging high;
Her brow was moist with fear and dread,
  Her breast heaved many a sigh.

Soon had she reached the height when, lo!
  A rude voice cries: "Who's there?"
Her knees bend low, she trembles all,
  To speak she does not dare!

And once again: "Who's there?" but, oh
  She finds no word or sound!
For in that rude harsh sentinel,
  Her own loved son she found.

Once more resounds that call—"Who's there?"
  The third time and the last.
She tries to speak—a loud report
  Is heard and all is past!

"I have thee!" cries the sentinel,
  And loads his gun again;
But, sudden, through his mind there runs
  A thought of grief and pain.

It seemed as if that shot had pierced
  Right through his own warm heart;
And yet he knew, what he had done
  Was duty on his part.

Just then through dark and heavy clouds
  Broke out the moon's pale light;
"Who was it, then, who climbed up here
  Alone, this dreary night?"

He found the corpse, and gazed, and stood,
  As sudden turned to stone;
For there before him bleeding lay
  His mother dear—his own.

ROCK ME TO SLEEP.

Mrs. Akers.

BACKWARD, turn backward, O Time, in your flight;
Make me a child again, just for to-night!
Mother, come back from that echoless shore;
Take me again to your heart as of yore,—
Kiss from my forehead the furrows of care,
Smooth the few silver threads out of my hair,
Over my slumbers your loving watch keep,—
Rock me to sleep, mother,—rock me to sleep!

Backward, flow backward, O tide of the years!
I am so weary of toil and of tears,—
Toil without recompense, tears all in vain,—
Take them and give me my childhood again!
I have grown weary of dust and decay,—
Weary of flinging my soul-wealth away,—
Weary of sowing for others to reap,—
Rock me to sleep, mother,—rock me to sleep!

Tired of the hollow, the base, the untrue,
Mother, O mother, my heart calls for you!
Many a summer the grass has grown green,
Blossomed and faded—our faces between—
Yet with strong yearning and passionate pain,
Long I to-night for your presence again:
Come from the silence so long and so deep,—
Rock me to sleep, mother,—rock me to sleep!

Over my heart in the days that are flown,
No love like mother-love ever has shone,—
No other devotion abides and endures,
Faithful, unselfish, and patient like yours,—
None like a mother can charm away pain
From the sick soul and world-weary brain:
Slumbers soft, calm, o'er my heavy lids creep,—
Rock me to sleep, mother,—rock me to sleep!

Come, let your brown hair, just lighted with gold,
Fall on your shoulders again as of old,—
Let it drop over my forehead to-night,
Shading my faint eyes away from the light!
For, with its sunny-edged shadows once more,
Haply will throng all the visions of yore;
Lovingly, softly, its bright billows sweep,—
Rock me to sleep, mother,—rock me to sleep!

Mother, dear mother! the years have been long
Since last I listened your lullaby song:
Sing, then, and unto my soul it shall seem
Womanhood's years have been only a dream;
Clasped to your heart in a loving embrace,
With your light lashes just sweeping my face,
Never hereafter to wake or to weep,—
Rock me to sleep, mother,—rock me to sleep!

BEAUTIFUL HANDS.

The following poem was written by Mrs. Ellen H. Gates, the author of "Your Mission" and other gems, upon seeing her aged mother's wrinkled and worn hands lying in her lap, as she sat by her side:—

SUCH beautiful, beautiful hands!
They are neither white nor small,
And you, I know, would scarcely think
That they were white at all.
I've looked on hands of form and hue—
A sculptor's dream might be,
Yet are these aged wrinkled hands
Most beautiful to me.

Such beautiful, beautiful hands!
When her heart was weary and sad
These patient hands kept toiling on
That the children might be glad.
I often weep when looking back
To childhood's distant day;
I think how these hands rested not
When mine were at their play.

Such beautiful, beautiful hands!
They are growing feeble now,
And time and toil have left their mark
On hand, and heart, and brow.
Alas! Alas! the nearing time—
The sad, sad day to me,
When 'neath the daisies, out of sight,
These hands must folded be.

But, oh! beyond these shadowy lands,
Where all is bright and fair,
I know full well these dear old hands
Will palms of victory bear;
Where crystal streams, through endless years,
Flow over golden sands,
And where the old grow young again,
I'll clasp my mother's hands!

SOMEBODY'S MOTHER.

From "Our Boys and Girls."

THE woman was old, and ragged, and grey,
And bent with the chill of the winter's day;
The street was wet with a recent snow,
And the woman's feet were aged and slow.
She stood at the crossing and waited long
Alone, uncared for, amid the throng
Of human beings who passed her by,
Nor heeded the glance of her anxious eye.
Down the street, with laughter and shout,
Glad in the freedom of school let out,
Came the boys, like a flock of sheep,
Hailing the snow piled white and deep,
Past the woman so old and grey,
Hastened the children on their way,
Nor offered a helping hand to her,
So meek, so timid, afraid to stir,
Lest the carriage wheels or the horses' feet
Should crowd her down in the slippery street.
At last came one of the merry troop,
The gayest laddie of all the group;
He paused beside her, and whispered low,
"I'll help you across if you wish to go."
Her aged hand on his strong young arm
She placed, and so, without hurt or harm,
He guided her trembling feet along,
Proud that his own were firm and strong.
Then back again to his friends he went,
His young heart happy and well content.
"She's somebody's mother, boys, you know,
For all she's old, and poor, and slow;
And I hope some fellow will lend a hand
To help my mother, you understand.
If ever so poor, and old, and grey,
When her own dear boy is far away."
And "somebody's mother" bowed low her head
In her home that night, and the prayer she said
Was—"God be kind to the noble boy,
Who is somebody's son, and pride, and joy!"

MADE HOME HAPPY.

IN an old churchyard stood a stone,
  All weather-marked and stained,
The hand of time had crumbled it,
  And only part remained,
Upon one side I could just trace
  " In memory of our mother ; "
An epitaph which spoke of " home "
  Was chiselled on the other.

I'd gazed on monuments of fame
  High towering to the skies ;
I'd seen the sculptured marble tower
  Where a great hero lies ;
But by this epitaph I paused
  And read it o'er and o'er
For I had never seen inscribed
  Such words as these before.

" She always made home happy,"
  What noble record this,
A legacy of memory sweet,
  To those she loved and left.
And what a testimony given,
  By those who knew her best,
Engraven on this plain rude stone
  That marked their mother's rest.

A noble life but written not
  In any book of fame ;
Among the list of noted ones
  None ever saw her name ;
For only her own household knew
  The victories she had won,
And none but they could testify,
  How well her work was done.

A MOTHER.

Mary Wright.

THERE came one day, to join the angel throng,
  A woman, bowed through serving oft in pain ;
And as she meekly stood her form grew strong,
  And long-lost youthful beauty dawned again.
Yet more was giv'n—for all, with wonder fraught,
  Bent low before the sweetness of her face ;
Crying—what marvel hath this woman wrought,
  To be thus clothed with such sweet mighty grace !
The one of seraph tongue made answer low—
  One talent only hers, a faithful heart ;
And she abroad but little could bestow,
  So much was needed for her mother part.
And *this* with love she almost made so fair,
  That there, she was an angel unaware.

ON THE RECEIPT OF MY MOTHER'S PICTURE.

Cowper.

OH that those lips had language! Life has passed
With me but roughly since I heard thee last.
Those lips are thine—thy own sweet smile I see,
The same that oft in childhood solaced me;
Voice only fails, else how distinct they say,
"Grieve not, my child, chase all thy fears away!"
The meek intelligence of those dear eyes
(Blest be the art that can immortalize,
The art that baffles Time's tyrannic claim
To quench it!) here shines on me still the same.
Faithful remembrancer of one so dear,
O welcome guest, though unexpected here!
Who bid'st me honour with an artless song,
Affectionate, a mother lost so long,
I will obey, not willingly alone,
But gladly, as the precept were her own;
And, while that face renews my filial grief,
Fancy shall weave a charm for my relief.
Shall steep me in Elysian reverie,
A momentary dream, that thou art she.
My mother! when I learned that thou was't dead.
Say, was't thou conscious of the tears I shed?
Hovered thy spirit o'er thy sorrowing son,
Wretch even then, life's journey just begun?
Perhaps thou gav'st me, though unfelt, a kiss;
Perhaps a tear, if souls can weep in bliss—
Ah, that maternal smile!—it answers—Yes.
I heard the bell tolled on thy burial day,
I saw the hearse that bore thee slow away,
And, turning from my nursery window, drew
A long, long sigh, and wept a last adieu!
But was it such?—It was.—Where thou art gone
Adieus and farewells are a sound unknown.
May I but meet thee on that peaceful shore,
The parting word shall pass my lips no more!
Thy maidens, grieved themselves at my concern,
Oft gave me promise of thy quick return.
What ardently I wished, I long believed,
And disappointed still, was still deceived;
By expectation every day beguiled,
Dupe of to-morrow, even from a child.
Thus many a sad to-morrow came and went,
Till, all my stock of infant sorrows spent,
I learned at last submission to my lot,
But, though I less deplored, thee ne'er forgot.
Where once we dwelt our name is heard no more,
Children not thine have trod my nursery floor;

And where the gardener Robin, day by day
Drew me to school along the public way,
Delighted with my bauble coach, and wrapt
In scarlet mantle warm, and velvet-capt,
'Tis now become a history little known,
That once we called the pastoral house our own.
Short lived possession! But the record fair.
That memory keeps of all thy kindness there,
Still outlives many a storm, that has effaced
A thousand other themes less deeply traced.
Thy nightly visits to my chamber made
That thou might'st know me safe and warmly laid;
Thy morning bounties ere I left my home,
The biscuit, or confectionery plum;
The fragrant waters on my cheeks bestowed
By thine own hand, till fresh they shone and glowed;
All this, and more endearing still than all,
Thy constant flow of love, that knew no fall,
Ne'er roughened by those cataracts and breaks,
That humour interposed too often makes:
All this still legible in memory's page,
And still to be so to my latest age,
Adds joy to duty, makes me glad to pay
Such honours to thee as my numbers may;
Perhaps a frail memorial, but sincere,
Not scorned in Heaven, though little noticed here.
Could Time, his flight reversed, restore the hours,
When, playing with my vesture's tissued flowers,
The violet, the pink and jessamine,
I pricked them into paper with a pin,
(And thou was't happier than myself the while,
Would'st softly speak, and stroke my head, and smile)
Could those few pleasant days again appear,
Might one wish bring them, would I wish them here?
I would not trust my heart—the dear delight
Seems so to be desired, perhaps I might.—
But no—what here we call our life is such,
So little to be loved, and thou so much,
That I should ill requite thee to constrain
Thy unbound spirit into bonds again.
My boast is not, that I deduce my birth
From lines enthroned, and rulers of the earth,
But higher far my proud pretensions rise—
The son of parents passed into the skies.
And now, farewell—Time unrevoked has run
His wonted course, yet what I wish is done,
By contemplation's help, not sought in vain,
I seem to have lived my childhood o'er again;
To have renewed the joys that once were mine,
Without the sin of violating thine;
And, while the wings of fancy still are free,
And I can view this mimic show of thee,
Time has but half succeeded in his theft—
Thyself removed, thy power to soothe me left.

XV.—THE MOTHER AND HER DEAD CHILD.

David Moir (Delta).

WITH ceaseless sorrow, uncontrolled,
The mother mourned her lot;
She wept, and would not be consoled,
Because her child was not.

She gazed upon its nursery floor—
But there it did not play;
The toys it loved, the clothes it wore,
All void and vacant lay.

Her house, her heart, were dark and drear,
Without their wonted light;
The little star had left its sphere,
That there had shone so bright.

Her tears, at each returning thought,
Fell like the frequent rain;
Time on its wings no healing brought,
And Wisdom spoke in vain.

Even in the middle hour of night
She sought no soft relief;
But, by the taper's misty light,
Sat nourishing her grief.

'Twas then a sight of solemn awe
Rose near her like a cloud:—
The image of her child she saw,
Wrapped in its little shroud!

It sat within its favourite chair;
It sat, and seemed to sigh;
And turned upon its mother there
A meek, imploring eye.

"O child! what brings that breathless form
Back from its place of rest?
For, well I know, no life can warm
Again that livid breast.

The grave is now your bed, my child;
Go, slumber there in peace!"
"I cannot go," it answered mild,
"Until your sorrow cease.

I've tried to rest in that dark bed,
But rest I cannot get;
For always, with the tears you shed,
My winding-sheet is wet.

The drops, dear mother! trickle still
Into my coffin deep:
It feels so comfortless, so chill,
I cannot go to sleep!"

"O child! those words—that touching look,
My fortitude restore:
I feel and own the blest rebuke,
And weep thy loss no more."

She spoke, and dried her tears the while;
And, as her passion fell,
The vision wore an angel smile,
And looked a fond farewell!

Poems about Parents.

OVER THE HILL TO THE POOR HOUSE.

Will Carleton.

OVER the hill to the poor-house I'm trudgin' my weary way—
I, a woman of seventy, and only a trifle grey—
I, who am smart an' chipper, for all the years I've told,
As many another woman that's only half as old.

Over the hill to the poor-house—I can't quite make it clear!
Over the hill to the poor-house—it seems so horrid queer!
Many a step I've taken, a toilin' to and fro,
But this is a sort of a journey I never thought to go.

What is the use of heapin' on me a pauper's shame?
Am I lazy or crazy? am I blind or lame?
True, I am not so supple, nor yet so awful stout;
But charity ain't no favour, if one can live without.

I am willin' an' anxious and ready any day
To work for a decent livin', and pay my honest way;
For I can earn my victuals, an' more too, I'll be bound,
If anybody only is willin' to have me round.

Once I was young an' han'some—I was, upon my soul—
Once my cheeks were roses, my eyes as black as coal;
And I can't remember, in them days, of hearin' people say,
For any kind of a reason, that I was in their way.

'Tain't no use of boastin', or talkin' over free,
But many a house an' home was open then to me;
Many a han'some offer I had from likely men,
And nobody ever hinted that I was a burden then.

And when to John I was married, sure he was good and smart,
But he and all the neighbours would own I done my part;
For life was all before me, an' I was young and strong,
And I worked the best that I could in tryin' to get along.

And so we worked together; and life was hard but gay,
With now and then a baby for to cheer us on our way;
Till we had half a dozen, an' all growed clean an' neat,
An' went to school like others, an' had enough to eat.

So we worked for the childr'n, and raised 'em every one;
Worked for 'em summer and winter, just as we ought to've done;
Only perhaps we humoured 'em, which some good folks condemn,
But every couple's childr'n's a heap the best of them.

Strange how much we think of our blessed little ones!—
I'd have died for my daughters, I'd have died for my sons;
And God He made that rule of love; but when we're old and grey
I've noticed it sometimes somehow fails to work the other way.

Strange, another thing; when our boys an' girls were grown,
And when, exceptin' Charley, they'd left us there alone;
When John, he nearer an' nearer come, an' dearer seemed to be,
The Lord of Hosts, He come one day, an' took him away from me.

Still I was bound to struggle, an' never to cringe or fall—
Still I worked for Charley, for Charley was now my all;
And Charley was pretty good to me, with scarce a word or frown,
Till at last he went a-courtin', and brought a wife from town.

She was somewhat dressy, an' hadn't a pleasant smile—
She was quite conceity, and carried a heap o' style;
But if ever I tried to be friends, I did with her, I know,
But she was hard and proud, an' I couldn't make it go.

She had an edication, an' that was good for her;
But when she twitted me on mine, 'twas carryin' things too fur;
An' I told her once 'fore company (an' it almost made her sick),
That I never swallowed a grammar, or e't a 'rithmetic.

So 'twas only a few days before the thing was done—
They was a family of themselves, and I another one;
And a very little cottage one family will do,
But I never have seen a house that was big enough for two.

An' I never could speak to suit her, never could please her eye,
An' it made me independent, an' then I didn't try;
But I was terribly staggered, an' felt it like a blow,
When Charley turned ag'in me, an' told me I could go.

I went to live with Susan, but Susan's house was small,
And she was always a hintin' how snug it was for us all;
And what with her husband's sisters, and what with childr'n three,
'Twas easy to discover that there wasn't room for me.

An' then I went to Thomas, the oldest son I've got,
For Thomas's buildings 'd cover the half of an acre lot;
But all the childr'n was on me—I could'nt stand their sauce—
And Thomas said I needn't think I was comin' there to boss.

An' then I wrote to Rebecca, my girl who lives out west,
And to Isaac, not far from her—some twenty miles at best;
And one of 'em said 'twas too warm there for any one so old,
And t'other had an opinion the climate was too cold.

So they have shirked and slighted me, and shifted me about—
So they have well-nigh soured me, an' wore my old heart out;
But still I've borne up pretty well, an' wasn't much put down,
Till Charley went to the poor-master, an' put me on the town.

Over the hill to the poor-house—my childr'n dear, good-by!
Many a night I've watched you when only God was nigh;
And God'll judge between us; but I will always pray
That you shall never suffer the half I do to-day.

OVER THE HILL FROM THE POOR HOUSE.

Will Carleton.

I, WHO was always counted, they say,
Rather a bad stick any way,
Splintered all over with dodges and tricks,
Known as "the worst of the Deacon's six;"
I, the truant, saucy and bold,
The one black sheep in my father's fold,
"Once on a time" as the stories say,
Went over the hill on a winter's day—
Over the hill to the poor-house.

Tom could save what twenty could earn;
But *givin'* was somethin' he ne'er would learn;
Isaac could half of the Scripture's speak—
Committed a hundred verses a week;
Never forgot and never slipped;
But "Honour thy father and mother" he skipped.
So *over the hill to the poor-house.*

An' Charley an' 'Becca meant well, no doubt,
But any one could pull 'em about.
An' all o' our folks ranked well, you see,
Save one poor fellow, and that was me;
An' when one dark an' rainy night,
A neighbour's horse went out o' sight,
They hitched on me, as the guilty chap
That carried one end o' the halter-strap.
An' I think, myself, that view of the case
Wasn't altogether out o' place;
My mother denied it as mothers do,
But I am inclined to believe 'twas true.
Though for me one thing might be said—
That I, as well as the horse, was led;
And the worst of whisky spurred me on,
Or else the deed would have never been done.
But the keenest grief I ever felt
Was when my mother beside me knelt,
An' cried an' prayed, till I melted down,
As I wouldn't for half the horses in town.
I kissed her fondly, then an' there,
An' sworn henceforth to be honest and square.
I served my sentence—a bitter pill
Some fellows should take who never will;
And then I decided to go "out West,"
Concludin' 'twould suit my health the best;
Where, how I prospered, I never could tell,
But fortune seemed to like me well,
An' somehow every vein I struck
Was always bubbling over with luck.
And better than that, I was steady an' true,
An' put my good resolutions through.
But I wrote to a trusty old neighbour an' said,
"You tell 'em, old fellow, that I am dead,
And died a Christian; 'twill please 'em more,
Than if I had lived the same as before."
But when this neighbour he wrote to me,
"Your mother's in the poor-house," says he,

I had a resurrection straightway,
An' started for her that very day.
And when I arrived where I was grown,
I took good care that I shouldn't be known;
But I bought the old cottage through and through,
Of some one Charley had sold it to;
And held back neither work nor gold,
To fix it up as it was of old.
The same big fire-place wide an' high,
Flung up its cinders toward the sky;
The old clock ticked on the corner-shelf—
I wound it and set it agoin' myself;
An' if everything wasn't the same,
Neither I nor money was to blame;
Then—*over the hill to the poor-house.*

One blowin' blusterin' winter's day,
With a team an' cutter I started away;
My fiercy nags was as black as coal;
(They some'at resembled the horse I stole);
I hitched an' entered the poor-house door—
A poor old woman was scrubbin' the floor;
She rose to her feet in great surprise,
And looked, quite startled, into my eyes;
I saw the whole of her troubles' trace
In the lines that marred her dear old face;
"Mother!" I shouted, "your sorrows is done!
You're adopted along o' your horse-thief son,
Come *over the hill from the poor-house!"*

She didn't faint; she knelt by my side,
An' thanked the Lord, till I fairly cried.
An' maybe our ride wasn't pleasant an' gay,
An' maybe she wasn't wrapped up that day;
An' maybe our cottage wa'n't warm and bright,
An' maybe it wasn't a pleasant sight,
To see her a-gettin' the evenin's tea,
An' frequently stoppin' and kissin' me;
An' maybe we didn't live happy for years,
In spite of my brothers' and sisters' sneers,
Who often said, as I have heard,
That they wouldn't own a prison bird;
(Though they're gettin' over that, I guess,
For all of 'em owe me more or less);
But I've learned one thing; an' it cheers a man
In always a-doin' the best he can;
That whether, on the big book, a blot
Gets over a fellow's name or not,
Whenever he does a deed that's white,
It's credited to him fair and right.
An' when you hear the great bugle's notes,
An' the Lord divides his sheep an' goats;
However they may settle my case,
Wherever they may fix my place,
My good old Christian mother, you'll see,
Will be sure to stand right up for me,
With *over the hill from the poor-house.*

THE OLD MAN GOES TO TOWN.

J. G. Swinerton.

WELL, wife, I've been to 'Frisco, an' I called to see the boys,—
I'm tired, an' more'n half deafened with the travel and the noise;
So I'll sit down by the chimbly, and rest my weary bones,
And tell how I was treated by our 'ristocratic sons.

As soon's I reached the city, I hunted up our Dan—
Ye know he's now a celebrated wholesale business man.
I walked down from the depo'—but Dan keeps a country seat—
An' I thought to go home with him, an' rest my weary feet.

All the way I kep' a-thinkin' how famous it 'ud be
To go a'round the town together—my grown-up boy an' me—
An' remember the old times, when my little "curly head"
Used to cry out "Good-night, papa!" from his little trundle-bed.

I never thought a minit that he wouldn't want to see
His gray an' worn old father, or would be ashamed of me;
So when I seen his office, with a sign writ out in gold,
I walked in without knockin'—but the old man was too bold.

Dan was sittin' by a table, an' a-writin' in a book;
He knowed me in a second, but he gave me such a look;
He never said a word o' you, but axed about the grain,
An' ef I thought the valley didn't need a little rain.

I didn't stay a great while, but inquired after Rob;
Dan said he lived upon the hill—I think they call it Nob;
An' when I left, Dan, in a tone that almost broke me down,
Said, "Call an' see me, won't ye, whenever you're in town?"

It was rather late that evenin' when I found out Robert's house;
There was music, lights and dancin' and a mighty big carouse.
At the door a nigger met me, an' he grinned from ear to ear,
Sayin', "Keerds ob invitation, or you nebber git in here."

I said I was Rob's father; an' with another grin,
The nigger left me standin', and disappeared within.
Rob came out on the porch—he didn't order me away;
But said he hoped to see me at his office the next day.

Then I started fur a tavern, fur I knowed there, anyway,
They wouldn't turn me out so long's I'd money fur to pay.
An' Rob an' Dan had left me about the streets to roam,
An' neither of them axed me if I'd money to git home.

It may be the way o' rich folks—I don't say 'at it is not—
But we remember some things Dan and Rob have quite forgot.
We didn't quite expect this, wife, when twenty years ago,
We mortgaged the old homestead to give Rob and Dan a show.

I didn't look fur Charley, but I happened just to meet
Him with a lot o' friends o' his'n, a-comin' down the street.
I thought I'd pass on by him, for fear our youngest son
Would show he was ashamed o' me, as Rob and Dan had done.

But as soon as Charley seen me, he, right afore em all,
Said: "God bless me, there's my father!" as loud as he could bawl.
Then he introduced me to his frien's, an' sent 'em all away
Tellin' 'em he'd see 'em later, but was busy for that day.

Then he took me out to dinner, an' he axed about the house,
About you an' Sally's baby, an' the chickens, pigs, and cows;
He axed about his brothers, addin' that 'twas ruther queer,
But he hadn't seen one uv 'em fur mighty nigh a year.

Then he took me to his lodgin', in an attic four stairs high—
He said he liked it better, cause 'twas nearer to the sky.
An' he said: "I've only one room, but my bed is pretty wide,"
An' so we slept together, me and Charley, side by side.

Next day we went together to the great Mechanics' Fair,
An' some o' Charley's picters was on exhibition there.
He said if he could sell 'em which he hoped to pretty soon,
He'd make us all a visit, an' "be richer than Muldoon."

An' so two days an' nights we passed, an', when I come away,
Poor Charley said the time was short, an' begged me fur to stay.
Then he took me in a buggy an' druv me to the train,
An' said in just a little while he'd see us all again.

You know we thought our Charley would never come to much;
He was always readin' novels an' poetry an' such.
There was nothing on the farm he ever seemed to want to do,
An' when he took to paintin' he disgusted me clear through!

So we gave to Rob and Dan all we had to call our own,
An' left poor Charley penniless to make his way alone;
He's only a poor painter; Rob and Dan are rich as sin;
But Charley's worth the pair of 'em with all their gold thrown in.

Those two grand men, dear wife, were once our prattling babes—an' yet
It seems as if a mighty gulf 'twixt them an' us is set;
An' they'll never know the old folks till life's troubled journey's past,
An' rich an' poor are equal underneath the sod at last.

An' maybe when we all meet on the resurrection morn,
With our earthly glories fallen, like the husks from the ripe corn,
When the righteous Son of Man the awful sentence shall have said,
The brightest crown that's shining there may be on Charley's head.

THERE'S BUT ONE PAIR OF STOCKINGS TO MEND TO-NIGHT.

An old wife sat by her bright fireside,
  Swaying thoughtfully to and fro.
In an ancient chair whose creaky frame
  Told a tale of long ago;
While down by her side on the kitchen floor,
Stood a basket of worsted balls—a score.

The old man dozed o'er the latest news,
  Till the light of his pipe went out,
And, unheeded, the kitten, with cunning paws,
  Rolled and tangled the balls about;
Yet still sat the wife in the ancient chair,
Swaying to and fro in the firelight glare.

But anon a misty tear-drop came
  In her eye of faded blue,
Then trickled down a furrow deep,
  Like a single drop of dew;
So deep was the channel—so silent the stream—
The good man saw naught but the dimmed eye-beam.

Yet he marvelled much that the cheerful light
  Of her eye had weary grown,
And marvelled he more at the tangled balls;
  So he said in a gentle tone,
"I have shared thy joys since our marriage vow,
Conceal not from me thy sorrows now."

Then she spoke of the time when the basket there
  Was filled to the very brim,
And how there remained of the goodly pile
  But a single pair—for him.
"Then wonder not at the dimmed eye-light,
There's but one pair of stockings to mend to-night.

"I cannot but think of the busy feet,
  Whose wrappings were wont to lie
In the basket, awaiting the needle's time,
  Now wandered so far away;
How the sprightly steps to a mother dear,
  Unheeded fell on the careless ear.

"For each empty nook in the basket old,
  By the hearth there's a vacant seat;
And I miss the shadows from off the wall,
  And the patter of many feet;
'Tis for this that a tear gathered over my sight
At the one pair of stockings to mend to-night.

"'Twas said that far through the forest wild
  And over the mountains bold,
Was a land whose rivers and darkening caves
  Were gemmed with the rarest gold;
Then my first-born turned from the oaken door,
And I knew the shadows were only four.

"Another went forth on the foaming waves
  And diminished the basket's store—
But his feet grew cold—so weary and cold—
  They'll never be warm any more—
And this nook in its emptiness, seemeth to me
  To give forth no voice but the moan of the sea.

"Two others have gone towards the setting sun,
  And made them a home in its light,
And fairy fingers have taken their share
  To mend by the fireside bright;
Some other garments their baskets fill—
  But mine! Oh, mine is emptier still.

"Another—the dearest—the fairest—the best—
  Was ta'en by the angels away,
And clad in a garment that waxeth not old,
  In a land of continual day.
Oh! wonder no more at the dimmed eye-light,
While I mend the one pair of stockings to-night."

WHERE IS YOUR BOY TO-NIGHT?

Life is teeming with evil snares,
The gates of sin are wide,
The rosy fingers of pleasure wave,
And beckon the young inside.
Man of the world with open purse,
Seeking your own delight,
Pause ere reason is wholly gone—
Where is your boy to-night?

Sirens are singing on every hand,
Luring the ear of youth,
Gilded falsehood with silver notes
Drowneth the voice of truth.
Dainty ladies in costly robes,
Your parlours gleam with light,
Fate and beauty your senses steep—
Where is your boy to-night?

Tempting whispers of royal spoil
Flatter the youthful soul
Eagerly entering into life,
Restive of all control.
Needs are many, and duties stern
Crowd on the weary sight;
Father, buried in business cares,—
Where is your boy to-night?

Pitfalls lurk in the flowery way,
Vice has a golden gate:
Who shall guide the unwary feet
Into the highway straight?
Patient worker with willing hand,
Keep the home hearth bright;
Tired mother, with tender eyes—
Where is your boy to-night?

Turn his feet from the evil paths
Ere they have entered in;
Keep him unspotted while yet he may;
Earth is so stained with sin;
Ere he has learned to follow wrong,
Teach him to love the right;
Watch ere watching is wholly vain—
Where is your boy to-night?

Poems about Children.

ONLY A BABY SMALL.

ONLY a baby small,
Dropped from the skies;
Only a laughing face,
Two sunny eyes.

Only two cherry lips,
One chubby nose;
Only two little hands,
Ten little toes.

Only a golden head,
Curly and soft;
Only a tongue that wags
Loudly and oft.

Only a little brain,
Empty of thought;
Only a little heart,
Troubled with naught.

Only a tender flower
Sent us to rear;
Only a life to love
While we are here.

Only a baby small,
Never at rest;
Small, but how dear to us,
God knoweth best.

PAYING HER WAY.

WHAT has my darling been doing to-day,
To pay for her washing and mending?
How can she manage to keep out of debt
For so much caressing and tending?
How can I wait till the years shall have flown,
And the hands have grown larger and stronger?
Who will be able the interest to pay,
If the debt runs many years longer?

Dear little feet! How they fly to my side
White arms my neck are caressing;
Sweetest of kisses are laid on my cheek;
Fair head my shoulder is pressing.
Nothing at all from my darling is due—
From evil may angels defend her—
The debt is discharged as fast as 'tis made,
For love is a legal tender.

THE LITTLE MISCHIEF.

ONLY a wee little mortal,
Asleep on the nursery floor,
'Mid a pile of neglected playthings,
Which litter the whole room o'er.
Two little fat arms lying
Over a curly head,
And smiles which awaken the dimples,
Parting the lips so red.

Here's dolly with arms and legs broken,
And a terrible crack on her head,
And her cheeks washed white as a lily,
That once were so rosy and red.
Poor Fido, the puppy, is whining;
Poor fellow, no wonder you wail!
I wonder what mischievous fingers
Fastened that cup to your tail!

It was only that wee little mortal,
Asleep on the nursery floor;
And nurse stands aghast at the litter
Which covers the whole room o'er.
Well pick them up patiently, nurse,
Over and over again,
E'en though that bundle of mischief
Will make all your labor but vain.

Better a home with a baby,
And a floor all littered with toys,
Than one that is empty for ever
Of childish prattle and noise.
So here's a kiss for the darling!
On forehead, mouth, and chin,
And wherever I find a dimple
I'll smuggle the kisses in.

BEAUTIFUL CHILD.

W. A. H. Sigourney.

Beautiful child by thy mother's knee,
In the mystic future what wilt thou be?
A demon of sin, or an angel sublime—
A poison Upas, or innocent thyme—
A spirit of evil flashing *down*
With the lurid light of a fiery crown—
Or gliding *up* with a shining track,
Like the morning star that ne'er looks back.
Daintiest dreamer that ever smiled,
Which wilt thou be, my beautiful child?

Beautiful child in my garden bowers,
Friend of the butterflies, birds and flowers,
Pure as the sparkling crystalline stream,
Jewels of truth in thy fairy eyes beam.
Was there ever a whiter soul than thine
Worshipped by love in a mortal shrine?
My heart thou hast gladdened for two sweet years
With rainbows of hope through mists of tears—
Mists beyond which thy sunny smile,
With its halo of glory, beams all the while.

Beautiful child, to thy look is given
A gleam serene—not of earth, but of heaven;
With thy tell-tale eyes and prattling tongue,
Would thou could'st ever thus be young,
Like the liquid strain of the mocking bird,
From stair to hall thy voice is heard;
How oft in the garden nooks thou'rt found,
With flowers thy curly head around,
And kneeling beside me with figure so quaint,
Oh! who would not dote on my infant saint!

Beautiful child, what thy fate shall be,
Perchance is wisely hidden from me;
A fallen star thou may'st leave my side,
And of sorrow and shame become the bride—
Shivering, quivering, through the cold street,
With a curse behind and before thy feet,
Ashamed to live, and afraid to die;
No home, no friend, and a pitiless sky.
Merciful Father—my brain grows wild—
Oh! keep from evil my beautiful child!

Beautiful child, may'st thou soar above,
A warbling cherub of joy and love;
A drop on eternity's mighty sea,
A blossom on life's immortal tree—
Floating, flowering evermore,
In the blessed light of the golden shore.
And as I gaze on thy sinless bloom
And thy radiant face, they dispel my gloom;
I feel He will keep thee undefiled,
And His love protect my beautiful child.

CHILDREN.

A DREARY place would be this earth
Were no little people in it;
The song of life would lose its mirth
Were there no children to begin it.

No little forms, like buds, to grow,
And make the admiring heart surrender;
No little hands on breast and brow,
To keep the thrilling love-chords tender.

No rosy boys, at wintry morn,
With satchels to the school-house hasting;
No merry shouts as home they rush,
No precious morsel for their tasting.

Tall, grave, grown people at the door,
Tall, grave, grown people at the table;
The men on business all intent,
The dames lugubrious as they're able;

The sterner souls would get more stern,
Unfeeling natures more inhuman,
And man to stoic coldness turn,
And woman would be less than woman.

Life's song, indeed, would lose its charm,
Were there no babies to begin it;
A doleful place this world would be,
Were there no little people in it.

MY NEIGHBOR'S BABY.

ACROSS in my neighbor's window,
With its drapings of satin and lace,
I see, 'neath his flowing ringlets,
A baby's innocent face.
His feet in crimson slippers,
Are tapping the polished glass,
And the crowd in the street look upward,
And nod and smile as they pass.

Just here in my cottage window,
Catching flies in the sun,
With a patched and faded apron,
Stands my own little one.
His face is as pure and handsome
As the baby's over the way,
And he keeps my heart from breaking
At my toiling every day.

Sometimes when the day is ended,
And I sit in the dusk to rest,
With the face of my sleeping darling
Hugged close to my lonely breast,
I pray that my neighbor's baby
May not catch Heaven's roses all,
But that some may crown the forehead
Of my loved one as they fall.

And when I draw the stockings
From his little weary feet,
And kiss the rosy dimples
In his limbs, so round and sweet,
I think of the dainty garments
Some little children wear,
And that my God withholds them
From mine so pure and fair.

May God forgive my envy—
I know not what I said;
My heart is crushed and troubled—
My neighbor's boy is dead!
I saw the little coffin
As they carried it out to-day;—
A mother's heart is breaking
In the mansion over the way.

The light is fair in my window;
The flowers bloom at my door;
My boy is chasing the sunbeams
That dance on the cottage floor;
The roses of health are blooming
On my darling's cheek to-day,
But the baby has gone from the window
Of the mansion over the way.

THE UNFINISHED PRAYER.

"Now I lay," repeat it, darling;
"Lay me," lisped the tiny lips
Of my daughter, kneeling, bending
O'er her folded finger-tips.
"Down to sleep." "To sleep," she murmured,
And the curly head dropped low;
"I pray the Lord," I gently added,
'You can say it all, you know."

"Pray the Lord," the word came faintly,
Fainter still, "My soul to keep;"
Then the tired head fairly nodded,
And the child fell fast asleep.
But the dewy eyes half opened
When I clasped her to my breast,
And the dear voice softly whispered,
"Mamma, God knows all the rest."

GRANDPAPA'S SPECTACLES.

Mrs. M. L. Rayne.

Oh, mother, what will Grandpa do?
He's gone away to Heaven,
Without the silver spectacles
That uncle John had given;
How can he read the papers there,
Or find his hickory staff?
He'll put his coat on wrong side out,
And make the people laugh.

And when he takes the Bible down
And wipes the dusty lid,
He'll never find his spectacles
Within its cover hid;
There won't be any little girl
He likes as well as me,
To run and hunt them up for him
And put them on his knee.

Oh dear! he'll never find the place
About "the wicked flee,"
And how the bears ate children up;
(That used to frighten me);
So, mother, if you'll dress me up
Just like an angel bright,
I'll fix our ladder 'gainst the sky,
And take them up to-night.

LITTLE TOMMY, OR THE BLOW.

"O NEIGHBOUR, I'm so frighten'd,
Poor little Tommy's hurt;
He came in where the clean clothes lay,
All over mess and dirt.

"He would not mind me when I spoke,
And toss'd the things about,
Iron'd and folded as they were,
And sorted to send out.

"And he was saucy when I spoke,
And said what he ought not;
Unluckily a stick was near—
You know my temper's hot.

"I struck at him a sharp quick blow
It chanc'd upon his head:
I can't believe it while I speak,
He fell down—like one dead.

"He's better now, but do come in,
I'm very sad at heart;
It seems to me there's something wrong,
More than the pain and smart."

The child lay with a dreary look,
And an unmeaning gaze;
The doctor came and did his best,
But there he lay for days.

The blow has hurt the tender brain—
Poor little naughty child!
It was a punishment too sharp;
Try, mothers to be mild.

Not word and blow with thoughtless haste,
And then this bitter grief—
A malady that none can reach,
No doctors give relief.

And never strike a young child's head,
That tender part the brain
Is slightly cover'd, and if hurt,
May never heal again.

Poor little Tommy! now he lies
A little idiot boy;
And no one knows what he may feel
Of suffering or of joy.

He meets his mother's anxious gaze
With calm unmeaning smile;
And little knows the agony
That wrings her heart the while.

Poor mother, in your patient love
You're never hasty now,
And tears and kisses shower down
Upon his fair young brow.

OUR IDOL.

Close the door lightly,
  Bridle the breath,
Our little earth Angel
  Is talking with death;
Gently he woos her,
  She wishes to stay,
His arms are about her,
  He bears her away!
Music comes floating
  Down from the dome;
Angels are chanting
  The sweet welcome home.

Come, stricken weeper!
  Come to the bed,
Gaze on the sleeper;
  Our idol is dead!
Smooth out the ringlets,
  Close the blue eyes;
No wonder such beauty
  Was claim'd in the skies;
Cross the hands gently
  O'er the white breast;
So like a wild spirit
  Stray'd from the blest.

THE LITTLE WINTER GRAVE.

Sheldon Chadwick.

Our baby lies under the snow, sweet wife,
  Our baby lies under the snow,
Out in the dark with the night,
  While the winds so loudly blow.
As a dead saint thou art pale, sweet wife,
  And the cross is on thy breast;
Oh, the snow no more can chill
  That little dove in its nest.

Shall we shut the baby out, sweet wife,
  While the chilling winds do blow?
Oh, the grave is now its bed,
  And its coverlid is snow.
Oh, our merry bird is snared, sweet wife,
  That a rain of music gave,
And the snow falls on our hearts,
  And our hearts are each a grave.

Oh, it was the lamp of our life, sweet wife,
  Blown out in a night of gloom;
A leaf from our flower of love,
  Nipped in its fresh spring bloom.
But the lamp will shine above, sweet wife,
  And the leaf again shall grow,
Where there are no bitter winds,
  And no dreary, dreary snow.

SLEEP, LITTLE BABY, SLEEP.

Sleep, little baby, sleep!
  Not in thy cradle bed,
Not on thy mother's breast
  Henceforth shall be thy rest,
But with the quiet dead.

Yes, with the quiet dead,
  Baby, thy rest shall be!
Oh! many a weary one,
  Under life's fitful sun,
Would fain lie down with thee.

Flee, little tender child!
  Flee to thy grassy nest;
There the first flowers shall blow;
  The first pure flake of snow
Shall fall upon thy breast.

And when the hour arrives
  From earth that sets me free,
Thy spirit will await
  The first at heaven's gate,
To meet and welcome me.

THE GOLDEN STAIR.

Put away the little dresses,
  That the darling used to wear,
She will need them on earth never,
  She has climb'd the golden stair.
She is with the happy angels,
  And I long for her sweet kiss,
Where her little feet are waiting,
  In the realm of perfect bliss.

Lay aside her little playthings,
  Wet with mother's pearly tears,
How we shall miss our little darling
  All the coming weary years!
Fold the dainty little dresses,
  That she never more will wear,
For her little feet are waiting,
  Up above the golden stair.

Kiss the little curly tresses,
  Cut from her bright golden hair,
Do the angels kiss our darling,
  In that realm so bright and fair?
Oh! we pray to meet our darling
  For a long, long sweet embrace,
Where the little feet are waiting,
  And we meet her face to face.

Angels whisper that our darling
  Is in lands of love so fair,
That her little feet are lightly
  Climbing up the golden stair.

MY BUD IN HEAVEN.

One bud the Gardener gave me,
A fair and only child,
He gave it to my keeping,
To cherish undefiled;
It lay upon my bosom,
It was my hope, my pride;
Perhaps it was an idol
Which I must be denied.

For just as it was opening
In glory to the day,
Came down the heavenly Gardener
And took the bud away.
Yet not in wrath He took it,
A smile was on His face;
And tenderly and kindly
He bore it from its place.

Fear not, methought he whispered,
Thy bud shall be restored,
I take it but to plant it
In the garden of my Lord.
Then bid me not to sorrow,
As those who hopeless weep,
For He who gave hath taken,
And He who took can keep.

And night and morn together,
By the open gate of prayer,
I'll go unto my darling,
And sit beside him there.
I know 'twill open for me,
Poor sinner tho' I be,
For His dear sake who keeps it
And keeps my bud for me.

THE LITTLE DARLING'S SHOE.

There is a sacred, secret place,
Baptised by tears and sighs,
Where little half-worn shoes are kept
From cold unfeeling eyes.

They have no meaning, save to her
Whose darling's feet have strayed
Far from the sacred folds of love,
Where late in joy they played.

The impress of a little foot,
How can it be so dear!
How can a little half-worn shoe
Call forth a sigh or tear!

'Tis more than dear, 'tis eloquent
Of grace and beauty fled;
It wakes the sound of little feet—
Sweet sound for ever fled!

It whispers to the mother's ear
A tale of fondest love;
It tells her that the little feet—
Now tread the fields above.

Oft has she bathed it with her tears,
Oft kiss'd it o'er and o'er:
If it were filled with costliest gems,
She could not love it more.

MEASURING THE BABY.

R. A. Browne.

We measured the riotous baby
Against the cottage wall—
A lily grew at the threshold,
And the boy was just as tall!
A royal tiger lily,
With spots of purple and gold,
And a heart like a jewelled chalice,
The fragrant dew to hold.

Without, the blackbirds whistled
High up in the old root trees,
And to and fro at the window
The red rose rocked her bees;
And the wee pink fists of the baby
Were never a moment still,
Snatching at the shine and shadow,
That danced on the lattice-sill!

His eyes were wide as blue-bells—
His mouth like a flower unblown—
Two little bare feet, like funny white mice,
Peeped out from his snowy gown;
And we thought with a thrill of rapture
That yet had a touch of pain,
When June rolls around with her roses,
We'll measure the boy again.

Ah me! In a darkened chamber,
With the sunshine shut away,
Through tears that fell like bitter rain,
We measured the boy to-day;
And the little bare feet that were dimpled,
And sweet as a budding rose,
Lay side by side together,
In the hush of a long repose;

Up from the dainty pillow,
White as the risen dawn,
The fair little face lay smiling,
With heaven's light o'er it drawn.
And the dear little hands, like rose-leaves
Dropped from a rose, lay still.
Never to snatch at the sunshine
That crept to the shrouded sill!

We measured the sleeping baby
With ribbons white as snow,
For the shining rosewood casket
That waited for him below;
And out of the darkened chamber
We went with a childish moan—
To the height of the sinless angels
Our little one had grown!

LITTLE WILLIE.

Gerald Massey.

POOR little Willie,
  With his many pretty wiles ;
Worlds of wisdom in his look,
  And quaint, quiet smiles ;
Hair of amber, touch'd with
  Gold of Heaven so brave ;
All lying darkly hid
  In a workhouse grave.

You remember little Willie,
  Fair and funny fellow ! he
Sprang like a lily
  From the dirt of poverty.
Poor little Willie !
  Not a friend was nigh,
When from the cold world
  He crouch'd down to die.

In the day we wander'd foodless,
  Little Willie cried for "bread ;"
In the night we wander'd homeless,
  Little Willie cried for "bed."
Parted at the workhouse door,
  Not a word we said ;
Ah ! so tired was poor Willie !
  And so sweetly sleep the dead.

'Twas in the dead of winter
  We laid him in the earth ;
The world brought in the new year
  On a tide of mirth.
But for the lost little Willie
  Not a tear we crave ;
Cold and hunger cannot wake him
  In his workhouse grave.

We thought him beautiful,
  Felt it hard to part ;
We loved him dutiful :
  Down, down, poor heart !
The storms they may beat,
  The winter winds may rave ;
Little Willie feels not
  In his workhouse grave.

No room for little Willie ;
  In the world he had no part ;
On him stared the Gorgon-eye
  Through which looks no heart.
"Come to me," said Heaven ;
  And if Heaven will save,
Little matters though the door
  Be a workhouse grave.

OUR LITTLE BOY THAT DIED.

Robinson.

I AM all alone in my chamber now,
  And the midnight hour is near,
And the fagot's crack and the clock's dull tick
  Are the only sounds I hear :
And over my soul, in its solitude,
  Sweet feelings of sadness glide ; [think
For my heart and my eyes are full, when I
  Of our little boy that died.

I went one night to my father's house—
  Went home to the dear ones all,—
And softly I opened the garden gate,
  And softly the door of the hall ;
My mother came out to meet her son ;
  She kissed me and then she sighed ;
And her head fell on my neck, and she wept
  For our little boy that died.

And when I gazed on his innocent face,
  As still and cold he lay,
And thought what a lovely child he had been
  And how soon he must decay,—
"O Death, thou lovest the beautiful !"
  In the woe of my spirit I cried ; [fair,
For sparkled the eyes, and the forehead was
  Of our little boy that died.

Again I will go to my father's house—
  Go home to the dear ones all,—
And sadly I'll open the garden gate,
  And sadly the door of the hall ;
I shall meet my mother, but never-more
  With her darling by her side ;
But she'll kiss me, and sigh and weep again
  For our little boy that died.

I shall miss him when the flowers come
  In the garden where he played ;
I shall miss him more by the fireside,
  When the flowers have all decayed ;
I shall see his toys and his empty chair,
  And the horse he used to ride ;
And they will speak, with a silent speech,
  Of our little boy that died.

I shall see his little sister again
  With her playmates about the door ;
And I'll watch the children in their sports
  As I never did before ;
And if in the group I see a child
  Like him, so laughing-eyed,
I'll love the face that speaks to me
  Of our little boy that died.

We shall all go home to our Father's house,—
  To our Father's house in the skies [blight
Where the hope of our souls shall have no
  And our love no broken ties ; [Peace,
We shall roam on the banks of the River of
  And bathe in its blissful tide ;
And one of the joys of our heaven shall be—
  Of our little boy that died.

PAPA'S LETTER.

I WAS sitting in my study,
  Writing letters, when I heard:
"Please, dear mama, Mary told me
  That you musn't be disturbed.

"But I'se tired of the kitty,
  Want some ozzer fing to do.
Writing letters is 'ou mama?
  Tan't I write a letter, too?"

"Not now, darling, mama's busy;
  Run and play with kitty, now,"
"No—no, mama; me wite letter,
  Ten you will show me how."

I would paint my darling's portrait,
  As his sweet eyes searched my face—
Hair of gold and eyes of azure,
  Form of childish witching grace.

But the eager face was clouded,
  As I slowly shook my head,
Till I said: "I'll make a letter
  Of you, darling boy, instead."

So I parted back the tresses
  From his forehead high and white,
And a stamp in sport I pasted,
  'Mid its waves of golden light.

Then I said: "Now, little letter,
  Go away and bear good news,"
And I smiled as down the staircase
  Clattered loud the little shoes.

Leaving me, the darling hurried
  Down to Mary in his glee:
"Mama's writing lots of letters;
  I'se a letter, Mary, see."

No one heard the little prattler,
  As once more he climbed the stair,
Reached his little cap and tippet,
  Standing on the table there.

No one heard the front door open,
  No one saw the golden hair,
As it floated o'er his shoulders
  On the crisp October air.

Down the street the baby hastened,
  Till he reached the office door,
"I'se a letter, Mr. Postman,
  Is there room for any more?

"'Cause this letter's going to papa;
  Papa lives with God, 'ou know;
Mama sent me for a letter;
  Does 'ou fink at I tan do?"

But the clerk in wonder answered,
  "Not to-day, my little man;"
"Den I'll find annozzer office,
  'Cause I must go if I tan."

Fain the clerk would have detained him
  But the pleading face was gone,
And the little feet were hast'ning,
  By the busy crowd swept on.

Suddenly the crowd was parted,
  People fled to left and right,
As a pair of maddened horses
  At that moment dashed in sight.

No one saw the baby figure.
  No one saw the golden hair,
Till a voice of frightened sweetness
  Rang out on the autumn air.

'Twas too late! a moment only
  Stood the beauteous vision there;
Then the little face lay lifeless
  Covered o'er with golden hair.

Rev'rently they raised my darling,
  Brushed away the curls of gold
Saw the stamp upon the forehead
  Growing now so icy cold.

Not a mark the face disfigured,
  Showing where a hoof had trod;
But the little life was ended—
  "Papa's letter" was with God.

LINES ON A STATUE OF HIS DEAD CHILD.

Richard Lane.

I SAW thee in thy beauty! Bright phantom of the past,
I saw thee for a moment—'twas the first time and the last;
And though years since have glided by of mingled bliss and care,
I never have forgotten thee, thou fairest of the fair!

I saw thee in thy beauty; thou wert graceful as the fawn,
When, in wantonness of glee, it sports along the lawn;
I saw thee seek the mirror—and when it met thy sight,
The very air was musical with thy burst of wild delight.

I saw thee in thy beauty! with thy sister at thy side—
She a lily of the valley, thou a rose in all its pride;
I look'd upon thy mother—there was triumph in her eyes;
And I trembled for her happiness, for grief had made me wise.

I saw thee in thy beauty! with one hand among her curls—
The other with no gentle grasp had seized a string of pearls;
She felt the pretty trespass; and she chid thee, though she smiled;
And I knew not which was loveliest—the mother or the child.

I saw thee in thy beauty! and a tear came to mine eye,
As I press'd thy rosy cheek to mine, and thought e'n thou could'st die.
My home was like a summer bower by thy joyous presence made,
But I only saw the sunshine, and felt alone the shade.

I *see* thee in thy beauty! for there thou seem'st to lie,
In slumber resting peacefully!—but, oh, the change of eye—
That still serenity of brow—those lips that breathe no more—
Proclaim thee but a mockery of what thou wert before.

I see thee in thy beauty! with thy waving hair at rest,
And thy *busy* little fingers folded lightly on thy breast
But thy merry *dance* is over, and thy little *race* is run,
And the mirror that reflected two, can now give back but one.

I see thee in thy beauty! with thy mother by thy side—
But her loveliness is faded, and quell'd her glance of pride;
The smile is absent from her lip, and absent are the pearls,
And a cap almost of widowhood conceals her envied curls.

I see thee in thy beauty! as I saw thee on that day—
But the mirth that gladden'd then my home, fled with thy life away;
I see thee lying motionless upon the accustom'd floor,
But my heart hath blinded both my eyes, and I can see no more.

LITTLE JIM.

E. Farmer.

The cottage was a thatch'd one,
The outside old and mean,
Yet everything within that cot
Was wondrous neat and clean.

The night was dark and stormy,
The wind was howling wild;
A patient mother knelt beside
The death bed of her child.

A little worn-out creature—
His once bright eyes grown dim;
It was a collier's only child—
They called him Little Jim.

And, oh! to see the briny tears
Fast hurrying down her cheeks,
As she offer'd up a prayer in thought—
She was afraid to speak,

Lest she might waken one she loved
Far better than her life;
For there was all a mother's love
In that poor collier's wife.

With hands uplifted, see, she kneels
Beside the sufferer's bed;
And prays that He will spare her boy,
And take herself instead.

She gets her answer from the child,
Soft fell these words from him,—
"Mother, the angels do so smile,
And beckon Little Jim.

"I have no pain, dear mother, now,
But oh! I am so dry;
Just moisten poor Jim's lips again,
And mother, don't you cry."

With gentle, trembling haste she held
The tea-cup to his lips;
He smiled to thank her, as he took
Three tiny little sips.

"Tell father when he comes from work,
I said 'good-night' to him;
And, mother, now I'll go to sleep,"—
Alas, poor Little Jim.

She saw that he was dying—
The child she loved so dear
Had uttered the last words that she
Might ever hope to hear.

The cottage door was opened
The collier's step is heard,—
The father and the mother meet,
Yet neither speak a word.

He knew that all was over,
He knew his child was dead;
He took the candle in his hand,
And walked towards the bed.

His quivering lips gave token
Of the grief he'd fain conceal,
And see his wife has joined him—
The stricken couple kneel.

With hearts bowed down with sadness
They humbly ask of Him,
In heaven, once more to meet again,
Their own poor Little Jim.

THE LOST LITTLE ONE.

We miss her footfall on the floor,
Amidst the nursery din,
Her tip-tap at our bedroom door,
Her bright face peeping in.

And when to Heaven's high courts above
Ascends our social prayer,
Though there are voices that we love,
One sweet voice is not there.

And dreary seems the hours, and lone,
That drag themselves along,
Now from our board her smile is gone,
And from our hearth her song.

We miss that farewell laugh of hers,
With its light joyous sound,
And the kiss between the balusters,
When good-night time comes round.

And empty is her little bed,
And on her pillow there
Must never rest that cherub head
With its soft silken hair.

But often as we wake and weep,
Our midnight thoughts will roam,
To visit her cold dreamless sleep,
In her last narrow home.

Then, then it is Faith's tear-dimm'd eyes
See through eternal space,
Amidst the angel-crowded skies,
That dear, that much-loved face.

With beckoning hand she seems to say,
"Though all her sufferings o'er,
Your little one is borne away
To this celestial shore.

"Doubt not she longs to welcome you
To her glad, bright abode,
There happy endless ages through
To live with her and God."

CHILDREN.

Longfellow.

COME to me, O ye children,
  For I hear you at your play,
And the questions that perplex me
  Have vanished quite away.

Ye open the eastern windows,
  That look towards the sun,
Where thoughts are singing swallows
  And the brooks of morning run.

In your hearts are the birds and the sunshine,
  In your thoughts the brooklets flow;
But in mine is the wind of Autumn,
  And the first fall of the snow.

Ah! what would the world be to us,
  If the children were no more.
We should dread the desert behind us
  Worse than the dark before.

What the leaves are to the forest,
  With light and air for food,
Ere their sweet and tender juices
  Have been hardened into wood,—

That to the world are children;
  Through them it feels the glow
Of a brighter and a sunnier climate
  Than reaches the trunks below.

Come to me, O ye children!
  And whisper in my ear
What the birds and the winds are singing
  In your sunny atmosphere.

For what are all our contrivings,
  And the wisdom of our books,
When compared with your caresses,
  And the gladness of your looks?

You are better than all the ballads
  That ever were sung or said;
For ye are living poems,
  And all the rest are dead.

THE LITTLE CHILDREN.

GOD bless the little children:
  We meet them everywhere;
We hear their voices round our hearth,
  Their footsteps on the stair;
Their kindly hearts are swelling o'er
  With mirthfulness and glee;
God bless the little children
  Wherever they may be.

We meet them 'neath each gipsy tent,
  With visage swarth and dun,
And eyes that sparkle as they glance
  With roguery and fun:
We find them fishing in the brook
  For minnows with a pin,
Or creeping through the hazel bush
  The linnet's nest to win.

We meet them in the lordly hall,
  Their stately father's pride;
We meet them in the poor man's cot—
  He has no wealth beside;
Along the city's crowded street,
  They hurl the hoop or ball.
We find them 'neath the drunkard's roof
  The saddest sight of all.

For there they win no father's love,
  No mother's tender care;
Their only friend the God above,
  Who hears the children's prayer.
But dressed in silks or draped in rags,
  In childish grief or glee,
God bless the little children
  Wherever they may be.

WATCHING FOR PAPA.

Up at the window are three little heads,
Lucy's and Willie's, and year-old Fred's;
What are they doing there all in a row,
Bobbing up, bobbing down, every way so?

Watching for papa to come home to tea,
Dear is their papa to all the little three,
Which pair of little eyes, sparkling and bright,
Think you will be first to see him to-night?

Hark! who is that now whose footsteps they hear?
Far out are heads stretched to see him draw near;
Somebody's papa, perhaps, but not theirs—
Up at three eager faces he stares.

Back from the window bobs each little head,
"Papa, make haste now," says dear baby Fred;
Now they all see him just coming in sight;
Hark, how they clap their hands, and scream with delight.

Happy at last, not a moment to wait,
Laughing and shouting they rush to the gate.
Joyfully papa the little troop meets,
Each rosy mouth with glad kisses he greets.

Up in his strong arms he takes little Fred,
Willie and Lucy go dancing ahead;
Into the house now all four of them come,
Mama stands smiling her bright welcome home.

Pulling and tugging they made him sit down,
One brings his slippers, another his gown,
Round him they hover and chatter with glee,
While they are waiting the summons to tea.

Little they know how their sweet loving ways
Comfort him after the wearisome days;
Arms full and lap full of dear little pets,
Now all his worries and cares he forgets.

MY BOYS.

Anson C. Chester.

The eldest has not finish'd yet
  The third of life's young years;
His eyes are blue as violets,
  And bright as evening's tears;
His hair is golden as the beams
  That usher in the dawn,
And softer than the tassels are
  That plume the growing corn:
His voice is sweeter to my ear
  Than lutes or woodland streams;
It rings amid my cares by day,
  And echoes in my dreams.

He has a hundred pretty ways,
  Which I delight to see!
I love him next to Heaven and her
  Who gave the child to me.
And when he nestles to my heart,
  And calls me by my name—
The only name he knows for me—
  I sigh no more for fame.
But think that having such a gem
  To wear upon my breast,
Contented should I be to leave
  The chaplets for the rest.

My other darling's little life
  In months is counted yet;
His eye is lustrous as a star,
  And black as burnish'd jet;
His hair is brown like forest leaves,
  When autumn's frost begin.
Four teeth have blossom'd in his mouth
  A dimple dents his chin;
His smile is like the smile that plays
  Upon a cherub's face—
He is a cherub, though he makes
  My home his dwelling-place.

No fear that we shall entertain
  "An angel unaware"—
That heavenly look upon his face,
  That glory on his hair,
Reminds us whence the darling came,
  And bids us not forget,
That He who lent the child to us
  Will come to claim him yet.

THE LITTLE "TORMENTS."

"O MOTHER! get my bonnet, do,
I want to go to play!"
"And hurry, mother, tie my shoe,
Or Jane will run away."
"O mother! do untie this string,
It's in a hateful knot,
And tell me where I put my sling,
I really have forgot."
"Mother, see here, my dress is loose,
I wish you'd hook it up;"
"Oh! dear, I want a drink so bad,
Ma, reach me down the cup."
"I've cut my finger, mother, oh!
Do tie a rag upon it:"
"And, mother here, do sew this string
Again upon my bonnet."
"O mother! pick these stitches up,
I've dropped some half-a-score;
And see! there's one all ravelled down
A dozen rounds or more."
"Mother, where is my skipping rope?"
"Mother, where is my hat?"
"Mother, help me to build my house."
"Mother, John plagues my cat."
Thus hour by hour, and day by day,
These little things intrude—
Till many a mother's anxious heart
Is wearied and subdued.
But let each mother calmly think
How much she has at stake;
How many thousand tiny drops
It takes to fill a lake:—
Remember that her noisy boy
A statesman true may be,
And strong in truth and right, may [teach
A nation to be free.
With glowing words of eloquence
Maintain Jehovah's plan,
Till vice shall hide its head with shame
And nations bless the man.
Or, when her head is growing grey,
The daughter, kind and true,
With feeling heart and ready hand,
The "little things" will do.
Let these reflections nerve and cheer
Each weary, fainting one,
With patient hope to do her work
Till all her work is done.
For not on earth can there be found
Through all life's varied plan,
A nobler, greater work than hers
Who rears an honest son.

CHILDREN.

Letitia Elizabeth Landon.

A WORD will fill the little heart
With pleasure and with pride;
It is a harsh, a cruel thing,
That such can be denied.

And yet how many weary hours
Those joyous creatures know;
How much of sorrow and restraint
They to their elders owe!

How much they suffered from our faults!
How much from our mistakes!
How often, too, mistaken zeal
An infant's misery makes!

We overrule and overteach,
We curb and we confine,
And put the heart to school too soon,
To learn our narrow line.

No: only taught by love to love,
Seems childhood's natural task;
Affection, gentleness, and hope,
Are all its brief years ask.

LET THE CHILD WORK.

HE who checks a child with terror,
Stops its play and stills its songs,
Not alone commits an error
But a great and moral wrong.

Give it play, and never fear it;
Active life is no defect,
Never, never break its spirit;
Curb it only to direct.

Would you stop the flowing river,
Thinking it would cease to flow?
Onward it must flow for ever;
Better teach it where to go.

LINES TO LITTLE MARY.

Caroline B. Southey.

I'M bidden, little Mary, to write verses unto thee:
I'd fain obey the bidding, if it rested but with me;
But the mistresses I'm bound to (nine ladies, hard to please)
Of all their stores poetic so closely keep the keys,
That 'tis only now and then—by good luck, as we may say—
A couplet or a rhyme or two falls fairly in my way.

Fruit forced is never half so sweet as that comes quite in season;
But some folks must be satisfied with rhyme, in spite of reason;
So, Muses, all befriend me,—albeit of help so chary,—
To string the pearls of poesy for loveliest little Mary.

And yet, ye pagan damsels, not over-fond am I
To invoke your haughty favours, your fount of Castaly:
I've sipped a purer fountain; I've decked a holier shrine;
I own a mightier mistress;—O Nature, *thou* art mine!

And only to that well-head, sweet Mary, I resort,
For just an artless verse or two,—a simple strain and short,—
Befitting well a pilgrim, way-worn with care and strife,
To offer thee, young traveller, in the morning track of life.

There's many a one will tell thee, 'tis all with roses gay;
There's many a one will tell thee, 'tis thorny all the way.
Deceivers are they every one, dear child, who thus pretend:
God's ways are not unequal; make Him thy trusted friend,
And many a path of pleasantness He'll clear away for thee,
However dark and intricate the labyrinth may be.

I need not wish thee beauty, I need not wish thee grace;
Already both are budding in that infant form and face.
I *will* not wish thee grandeur, I *will* not wish thee wealth;
But only a contented heart, peace, competence, and health;
Fond friends to love thee dearly, and honest friends to chide,
And faithful ones to cleave to thee, whatever may betide.

And now, my little Mary, if better things remain
Unheeded in my blindness, unnoticed in my strain,
I'll sum them up succinctly in "English undefiled,"—
My mother-tongue's best benison,—God bless thee, precious child!

ONLY A BOY.

Mrs. M. A. Kidder.

ONLY a boy, with his noise and his fun,
The veriest mystery under the sun,
As brimful of mischief and wit and glee,
As ever a human frame can be.
And as hard to manage as—what ! ah me!
'Tis hard to tell,
Yet we love him well,

Only a boy, with his fearful tread,
Who cannot be driven, but must be led;
Who troubles the neighbours' dogs and cats,
And tears more clothes, and spoils more hats,
Loses more tops and kites and bats,
Than would stock a store
For a year or more.

Only a boy, with his wild, strange ways,
With his idle hours and his busy days:
With his queer remarks, and his odd replies,
Sometimes foolish, and sometimes wise,
Often brilliant for one his size,
As a meteor hurled
From the planet world.

Only a boy, who will be a man,
If nature goes on with its first great plan;
If water or fire or some fatal snare,
Conspire not to rob us of this our heir.
Our blessing, our rest, our care,
Our torment, our joy!
"Only a boy."

THE SCHOOLBOY.

WE bought him a box for his books and things,
And a cricket-bag for his bat;
And he looked the brightest and best of kings
Under his new straw hat.

We handed him into the railway train
With a troop of his young compeers,
And we made as though it were dust and rain
Were filling our eyes with tears.

We looked in his innocent face to see
The sign of a sorrowful heart;
But he only shouldered his bat with glee,
And wondered when they would start.

'Twas not that he loved not as heretofore,
For the boy was tender and kind.
But his was a world that was all before,
And ours was a world behind.

'Twas not his fluttering heart was cold,
For the child was loyal and true;
And the parents love the love that is old,
And the children the love that is new.

And we came to know that love is a flower
Which only groweth down:
And we scarcely spoke for the space of an hour,
As we drove back through the town.

BILLY'S ROSE.

From Dagonet Ballads by G. R. Sims.

Billy's dead, and gone to glory—so is Billy's sister Nell:
There's a tale I know about them were I poet I would tell;
Soft it comes with perfume laden, like a breath of country air
Wafted down the filthy alley, bringing fragrant odours there.

In that vile and filthy alley, long ago, one winter's day,
Dying quick of want and fever, hapless, patient, Billy lay;
While beside him sat his sister, in the garret's dismal gloom,
Cheering, with her gentle presence, Billy's pathway to the tomb.

Many a tale of elf and fairy did she tell the dying child,
Till his eyes lost half their anguish, and his worn, wan features smiled:
Tales herself had heard hap-hazard, caught amid the Babel roar,
Lisped about by tiny gossips playing at their mother's door.

Then she felt his wasted fingers tighten feebly as she told
How beyond this dismal alley lay a land of shining gold,
Where, when all the pain was over—where when all the tears were shed—
He would be a white-frocked angel, with a gold thing on his head.

Then she told some garbled story of a kind-eyed Saviour's love,
How He'd built for little children great big playgrounds up above,
Where they sang and played at hop-scotch and at horses all the day,
And where beadles and policemen never frightened them away.

This was Nell's idea of heaven—just a bit of what she'd heard,
With a little bit invented and a little bit inferred.
But her brother lay and listened, and he seemed to understand,
For he closed his eyes and murmured he could see the Promised Land.

"Yes," he whispered, "I can see it—I can see it, sister Nell;
Oh, the children look so happy, and they're all so strong and well;
I can see them there with Jesus—He is playing with them, too!
Let us run away and join them, if there's room for me and you."

She was eight, this little maiden, and her life had all been spent
In the garret and the alley where they starved to pay the rent;
Where a drunken father's curses and a drunken mother's blows
Drove her forth into the gutter from the day's dawn to its close.

But she knew enough, this outcast, just to tell the sinking boy,
"You must die before you're able all these blessings to enjoy.
You must die," she whispered, "Billy, and I am not even ill;
But I'll come to you, dear brother,—yes, I promise that I will.

"You are dying, little brother,—you are dying, oh, so fast;
I heard father say to mother that he knew you couldn't last.
They will put you in a coffin, then you'll wake and be up there,
While I'm left alone to suffer in this garret bleak and bare."

"Yes, I know it," answered Billy. "Ah, but, sister, I don't mind,
Gentle Jesus will not beat me; He's not cruel or unkind.
But I can't help thinking, Nelly, I should like to take away
Something, sister, that you gave me, I might look at every day.

"In the summer you remember how the Mission took us out
To a great green lovely meadow, where we played and ran about,
And the van that took us halted by a sweet bright patch of land,
Where the fine red blossoms grew, dear, half as big as mother's hand.

"Nell, I asked the good, kind teacher what they called such flowers as those,
And he told me, I remember, that the pretty name was rose.
I have never seen them since, dear—how I wish that I had one!
Just to keep and think of you, Nell, when I'm up beyond the sun."

Not a word said little Nelly; but at night, when Billy slept,
On she flung her scanty garments, and then down the stairs she crept.
Through the silent streets of London she ran nimbly as a fawn,
Running on and running ever till the night had changed to dawn.

When the foggy sun had risen, and the mist had cleared away
All around her, wrapped in snowdrift, there the open country lay.
She was tired, her limbs were frozen, and the roads had cut her feet,
But there came no flowery gardens her poor tearful eyes to greet.

She had traced the road by asking—she had learnt the way to go;
She had found the famous meadow—it was wrapped in cruel snow;
Not a buttercup or daisy, not a single verdant blade
Showed its head above its prison. Then she knelt her down and prayed.

With her eyes upcast to heaven, down she sank upon the ground,
And she prayed to God to tell her where the roses might be found.
Then the cold blast numbed her senses, and her sight grew strangely dim;
And a sudden, awful tremor seemed to seize her every limb.

"Oh, a rose!" she moaned, "good Jesus—just a rose to take to Bill!"
And as she prayed a chariot came thundering down the hill;
And a lady sat there toying with a red rose, rare and sweet;
As she passed she flung it from her, and it fell at Nelly's feet.

Just a word her lord had spoken caused her ladyship to fret,
And the rose had been his present, so she flung it in a pet;
But the poor, half-blinded Nelly thought it fallen from the skies,
And she murmured "Thank you, Jesus!" as she clasped the dainty prize.

Lo! that night from out the alley did a child's soul pass away,
From dirt and sin and misery to where God's children play.
Lo! that night a wild, fierce snowstorm burst in fury o'er the land,
And that morn they found Nell frozen, with the red rose in her hand.

Billy's dead, and gone to glory—so is Billy's sister Nell,
Am I bold to say this happened in the land where angels dwell—
That the children met in heaven after all their earthly woes,
And that Nelly kissed her brother, and said "Billy, here's your rose?"

ONLY ME.

Caroline A. Mason.

A LITTLE figure glided through the hall ;
"Is that you, Pet ?" the words came tenderly ;
A sob—suppressed to let the answer fall—
"It isn't Pet, mamma, it's only me."

The quivering baby lips !—they had not meant
To utter any word could plant a sting,
But to that mother-heart a strange pang went ;
She heard and stood like a convicted thing.

One instant, and a happy little face
Thrilled 'neath unwonted kisses rained above ;
And from that moment Only Me had place
And part with Pet in tender mother-love.

SOME MOTHER'S CHILD.

Francis L. Keeler.

AT home or away, in the alley or street,
Wherever I chance in this wide world to meet
A girl that is thoughtless, or a boy that is wild,
My heart echoes softly, " 'Tis some mother's child."

And when I see those o'er whom long years have rolled
Whose hearts have grown hardened, whose spirits are cold—
Be it woman all fallen, or man all defiled,
A voice whispers sadly, "Ah ! some mother's child."

No matter how far from the right she has strayed ;
No matter what inroads dishonour has made ;
No matter what elements cankered the pearl—
Though tarnished and sullied, she is some mother's girl.

No matter how wayward his footsteps have been ;
No matter how deep he is sunken in sin ;
No matter how low is his standard of joy—
Though guilty and loathsome, he is some mother's boy.

That head hath been pillowed on some tender breast ;
That form hath been wept o'er, those lips have been pressed ;
That soul hath been prayed for, in tones sweet and mild ;
For *her* sake deal gently with—some mother's child.

PRAYING FOR SHOES.

A TRUE INCIDENT.

Paul Hamilton Hayne.

ON a dark November morning
  A lady walked slowly down
The thronged tumultuous thoroughfare
  Of an ancient seaport town.

Of a winning and gracious beauty,
  The peace of her pure young face
Was soft as the gleam of angels' dream
  In the calms of a heavenly place.

Her eyes were fountains of pity,
  And the sensitive mouth expressed
A longing to set the kind thoughts free
  In music that filled her breast.

She met, by a bright shop window,
  An urchin timid and thin,
Who with limbs that shook, and a yearning look,
  Was mistily glancing in

At the rows and varied clusters
  Of slippers and shoes outspread;
Some, shimmering keen, but of sombre sheen,
  Some purple and green and red.

His pale lips moved and murmured,
  But of what she could not hear,
And oft on his folded hands would fall
  The round of a bitter tear.

"What troubles you, child?" she asked him
  In a voice like the May-wind sweet,
He turned, and while pointing dolefully
  To his naked and bleeding feet—

"I was praying for shoes," he answered—
  "Just look at the splendid show!—
"I was praying to God for a single pair,
  The sharp stones hurt me so!"

She led him in museful silence
  At once through the open door,
And his hope grew bright like a fairy light
  That flickered and danced before.

And there he was washed and tended,
  And his small brown feet were shod,
And he pondered there on his childish prayer
  And the marvellous answer of God.

Above them his keen gaze wandered,
  How strangely—from shelf to shelf,
Till it almost seemed that he fondly dreamed
  Of looking on God himself.

The lady bent over and whispered,
  "Are you happier, now, my lad?"
He started; and all his soul flashed forth
  In a gratitude swift and glad.

"Happy?—Oh, yes!—I am happy!"
  Then-wonder with reverence rife—
His eyes aglow, and his voice sunk low,
  "Please tell me are you God's wife?"

"NOW THEY'LL HAVE ENOUGH OF FOOD."

Mrs. E. C. A. Allen.

A SAD WISH.—Said a poor little girl in the fourth ward of New York, as she was dying, "I am glad I am going to die, because now my brothers and sisters will have enough to eat!" Nothing could be written or thought more simply pathetic.—"AMERICAN JOURNAL."

WITHIN a hospital there lay
  A suffering child upon a bed;
The kindly doctor passed that way,
  He felt her pulse—he shook his head.

The silent sign—the pitying look—
  Did not escape her watching eye!
Her heart the mournful warning took,
  She felt—she knew that she must die.

The mother came to see her child,
  And heard the fiat of her doom;
Her wail was loud, her grief was wild,
  She could not yield her to the tomb.

"Dear mother! do not weep for me,"
  The gentle, patient sufferer cried:
"You've had hard work to feed us three,
  And clothe us, too, since father died.

"There's scarce been food enough for all
  When you have done your very best;
Oh! how I wanted to grow tall,
  That I could work to help the rest.

"But I am little, weak and thin,
  The least thing made my limbs to ache,
Mother! I hope 'tis not a sin,
  I'm glad I'm dying for your sake.

"Brother and sister will be good,
  They'll help and comfort you, you'll see;
And now they'll have enough of food,
  You'll have but two instead of three.

"And mother! I am going home,
  Plenty and happiness to share;
Mother! you'll all be sure to come?
  There's neither thirst nor hunger there.

"Father and I will watch for you—
  Willie—and you—and little Jane,
And when you get to heaven too,
  Dear mother, we shall meet again."

THE NEWSBOY'S DEBT.

ONLY last year, at Christmas-time, while pacing down the city street,
I saw a tiny, ill-clad boy—one of the many that we meet—
As ragged as a boy could be, with half a cap, with one good shoe,
Just patches to keep out the wind—I know the wind blew keenly too:

A newsboy, with a newsboy's lungs, a square Scotch face, an honest brow,
And eyes that liked to smile so well, they had not yet forgotten how:
A newsboy, hawking his last sheets with loud persistence. Now and then
Stopping to beat his stiffened hands, and trudging bravely on again.

Raised his torn cape with purple hands, said, "Papers, sir? *The Evening News!*"
He brushed away a freezing tear, and shivered, "Oh, sir, don't refuse!"
"How many have you? Never mind—don't stop to count—I'll take them all;
And when you pass my office here, with stock on hand, give me a call."

He thanked me with a broad Scotch smile, a look half wondering and half glad.
I fumbled for the proper "change," and said, "You seem a little lad
To rough it in the streets like this." "I'm ten years old on Christmas-day!"
"Your name?" "Jim Hanley." "Here's a crown, you'll get change there across the way."

"Or, were you hungry?" "Just a bit," he answered bravely as he might.
"I couldn't buy a breakfast, sir, and had no money left last night."
"And you are cold?" "Ay, just a bit; I don't mind cold." "Why, that is strange!"
He smiled and pulled his ragged cap, and darted off to get the "change."

"Why, where's the boy? and where's the 'change' he should have brought an hour ago?
Ah, well! ah, well! they're all alike! I was a fool to tempt him so.
Just two days later, as I sat, half dozing, in my office chair,
I heard a timid knock, and called in my brusque fashion, "Who is there?"

An urchin entered, barely seven—the same Scotch face, the same blue eyes—
And stood, half doubtful, at the door, abashed at my forbidding guise.
"Sir, if you please, my brother Jim—the one you give the crown, you know—
He couldn't bring the money, sir, because his back was hurted so.

"He didn't mean to keep the 'change.' He got runned over, up the street;
One wheel went right across his back, and t'other fore-wheel mashed his feet.
They stopped the horses just in time, and then they took him up for dead,
And all that day and yesterday he wasn't rightly in his head.

"They took him to the hospital—one of the newsboys knew 'twas Jim—
And I went too, because, you see, we two are brothers, I and him.
He had that money in his hand, and never saw it any more.
Indeed, he didn't mean to steal! He never stole a pin before.

"He was afraid that you might think he meant to keep it, anyway;
This morning when they brought him to, he cried because he couldn't pay.
He made me fetch his jacket here; it's torn and dirtied pretty bad;
It's only fit to sell for rags, but then, you know, it's all he had.

"When he gets well—it won't be long—if you will call the money lent,
He says he'll work his fingers off but what he'll pay you every cent."
And then he cast a rueful glance at the soiled jacket where it lay.
"No, no, my boy! take back the coat. Your brother's badly hurt, you say?

"Where did they take him? Just run out and hail a cab, then wait for me.
Why, I would give a thousand coats, and pounds, for such a boy as he!"
A half-hour after this we stood together in the crowded wards,
And the nurse checked the hasty steps that fell too loudly on the boards.

I thought him smiling in his sleep, and scarce believed her when she said,
Smoothing away the tangled hair from brow and cheek, "The boy is dead."
Dead? dead so soon? How fair he looked! One streak of sunshine on his hair,
Poor lad! Well, it is warm in heaven: no need of "change" and jackets there.

And something rising in my throat made it so hard for me to speak,
I turned away, and left a tear lying upon his sunburned cheek.

LUCY GRAY.

Wordsworth.

No mate, no comrade, Lucy knew;
She dwelt on a wide moor:
The sweetest thing that ever grew
Beside a cottage door!

You yet may spy the fawn at play,
The hare upon the green;
But the sweet face of Lucy Gray
Will never more be seen.

"To-night will be a stormy night,
You to town must go;
And take a lantern, child, to light
Your mother through the snow."

"That, father, I will gladly do;
'Tis scarcely afternoon—
The minster clock has just struck two,
And yonder is the moon."

At this the father raised his hook,
And snapped a faggot band;
He plied his work, and Lucy took
The lantern in her hand.

Not blither is the mountain roe;
With many a wanton stroke
Her feet disperse the powd'ry snow,
That rises up like smoke.

The storm came on before its time;
She wandered up and down.
And many a hill did Lucy climb,
But never reach'd the town.

The wretched parents all that night
Went shouting far and wide;
But there was neither sound nor sight
To serve them for a guide.

At daybreak on a hill they stood,
That overlooked the moor;
And thence they saw the bridge of wood,
A furlong from the door.

They wept, and turning homeward, cried,
"In heaven we all shall meet,"
When in the snow the mother spied
The print of Lucy's feet!

Half breathless from the steep hill's edge,
They tracked the footmarks small;
And through the broken hawthorn hedge,
And by the long stone wall;

And then an open field they cross'd—
The marks were still the same;
They tracked them on, nor ever lost,
And to the bridge they came.

They follow'd from the snowy bank
Those footmarks, one by one,
Into the middle of the plank—
And further there were none!

You yet may spy the fawn at play,
The hare upon the green;
But the sweet face of Lucy Gray
Will never more be seen.

CASABIANCA.

Felicia Hemans.

The boy stood on the burning deck,
Whence all but he had fled;
The flame that lit the battle's wreck,
Shone round him o'er the dead.

Yet beautiful and bright he stood
As born to rule the storm;
A creature of heroic blood,
A proud, though childlike form.

The flames roll'd on—he would not go
Without his father's word;
That father, faint in death below,
His voice no longer heard.

He call'd aloud—"Say, father, say
If yet my task be done!"
He knew not that the chieftain lay
Unconscious of his son.

"Speak, father!" once again he cried,
"If I may yet be gone!"
And but the booming shots replied,
And fast the flames roll'd on.

Upon his brow he felt their breath,
And in his waving hair;
And looked from that lone post of death,
In still yet brave despair;

And shouted but once more aloud,
"My father, must I stay?"
While o'er him fast, through sail and shroud
The wreathing fires made way.

They wrapt the ship in splendour wild,
They caught the flag on high,
And stream'd above the gallant child,
Like banners in the sky.

There came a burst of thunder sound—
The boy—oh! where was he?
Ask of the winds that far around
With fragments strewed the sea,

With mast, and helm, and pennon fair
That well had borne their part;
But the noblest thing that perished there
Was that young faithful heart.

THE THREE SONS.

Rev. J. Moultrie.

I HAVE a son, a little son, a boy just five years old,
With eyes of thoughtful earnestness, and mind of gentle mould;
They tell me that unusual grace in all his ways appears,
That my child is grave and wise of heart beyond his childish years.
I cannot say how this may be; I know his face is fair,
And yet his chiefest comeliness is his sweet and serious air;
I know his heart is kind and fond, I know he loveth me,
But loveth yet his mother more, with grateful fervency.
But that which others most admire is the thought which fills his mind,
The food for grave inquiring speech he everywhere doth find.

Strange questions doth he ask of me when we together walk;
He scarcely thinks as children think, or talks as children talk.
Nor cares he much for childish sports, dotes not on bat or ball,
But looks on manhood's ways and works, and aptly mimics all.
His little heart is busy still, and oftentimes perplext,
With thoughts about this world of ours, and thoughts about the next.
He kneels at his dear mother's knee—she teacheth him to pray,
And strange, and sweet, and solemn then are the words which he will say.
Oh, should my gentle child be spared to manhood's years like me,
A holier and a wiser man I trust that he will be;
And when I look into his eyes, and stroke his thoughtful brow,
I dare not think what I should feel were I to lose him now.

I have a son, a second son, a simple child of three;
I'll not declare how bright and fair his little features be,
How silver sweet those tones of his when he prattles on my knee;
I do not think his light blue eye is like his brother's, keen,
Nor his brow so full of childish thought, as his hath ever been;
But his little heart's a fountain pure of kind and tender feeling,
And his every look's a gleam of light, rich depths of love revealing.
When he walks with me, the countryfolk who pass us in the street

Will speak their joy and bless my boy, he looks so mild and sweet.
A playfellow is he to all, and yet, with cheerful tone,
Will sing his little song of love when left to sport alone.
His presence is like sunshine, sent to gladden home and hearth,
To comfort us in all our griefs, and sweeten all our mirth.
Should *he* grow up to riper years, God grant his heart may prove
As sweet a home for heavenly grace as now for earthly love;
And if, beside his grave, the tears our aching eyes must dim,
God comfort us for all the love which we shall lose in him.

I have a son, a third sweet son; his age I cannot tell,
For they reckon not by years and months where he is gone to dwell.
To us for fourteen anxious months his infant smiles were given,
And then he bade farewell to earth, and went to live in heaven.
I cannot tell what form his is, what looks he weareth now,
Nor guess how bright a glory crowns his shining seraph brow.
The thoughts that fill his sinless soul, the bliss which he doth feel,
Are numbered with the secret things which God will not reveal;
But I know (for God hath told me this) that he is now at rest,
Where other blessed infants be, on their Saviour's loving breast.
I know his spirit feels no more this weary load of flesh,
But his sleep is bless'd with endless dreams of joy for ever fresh.

I know the angels fold him close beneath their glittering wings,
And soothe him with a song that breathes of heaven's divinest things,
I know that we shall meet our babe (his mother dear and I)
Where God for aye shall wipe away all tears from every eye.
Whate'er befalls his brethren twain, *his* bliss can never cease;
Their lot may here be grief and fear, but *his* is certain peace.
It may be that the tempter's wiles their souls from bliss may sever,
But, if our own poor faith fail not, *he* must be ours for ever.
When we think of what our darling is, and what we still must be;
When we muse on *that* world's perfect bliss, and *this* world's misery;
When we groan beneath this load of sin, and feel this grief and pain,
Oh! we'd rather lose our other two than have him here again.

NOT ONE TO SPARE.

Mrs. E. L. Beers.

This beautiful poem tells how a poor man and wife refused the offer of a rich friend's comfortable provision, if they would give him one of their children.—*I believe it is the most pathetic poem in the world.*

WHICH shall it be? Which shall it be?
I looked at John—John looked at me;
Dear, patient John, who loves me yet
As well as though my locks were jet.
And when I found that I must speak,
My voice seemed strangely low and weak:
"Tell me again what Robert said!"
And then I, listening, bent my head.

"This is his letter;
"'I will give
A house and land while you shall live,
If, in return, from out your seven,
One child to me for aye is given.'"
I looked at John's old garments worn,
I thought of all that John had borne
Of poverty, and work, and care,
Which I, though willing, could not share;
I thought of seven mouths to feed,
Of seven little children's need,
And then of this.
"Come, John," said I,
'We'll choose among them as they lie
Asleep;" so, walking hand in hand,
Dear John and I surveyed our band.
First to the cradle light we stepped,
Where Lilian the baby slept,
A glory 'gainst the pillow white.
Softly the father stooped to lay
His rough hand down in loving way,
When dream or whisper made her stir,
And huskily he said: "Not her!"

We stooped beside the trundle-bed,
And one long ray of lamp-light shed
Athwart the boyish faces there,
In sleep so pitiful and fair;
I saw on Jamie's rough, red cheek,
A tear undried. Ere John could speak,
"He's but a baby, too," said I,
And kissed him as we hurried by.

Pale, patient Robbie's angel face
Still in his sleep bore suffering's trace;
"No! not for gold untold, not him,"
He whispered while our eyes were dim.

Poor Dick! bad Dick! our wayward son,
Turbulent, reckless, idle one—
Could he be spared? "Nay, He who gave,
Bade us befriend him to the grave;
Only a mother's heart can be
Patient enough for such as he;
And so," said John, "I would not dare
To send him from her bedside prayer."

Then stole we softly up above
And knelt by Mary, child of love.
"Perhaps for her 'twould better be,"
I said to John. Quite silently
He lifted up a curl that lay
Across her cheek in a wilful way.
And shook his head: "Nay, love, not thee,"
The while my heart beat audibly.

Only one more, our eldest lad,
Trusty and truthful, good and glad,
So like his father. "No, John, no!
I cannot, will not, let him go."
And so we wrote in courteous way,
We could not give one child away;
And afterwards toil lighter seemed,
Thinking of that of which we dreamed,
Happy in truth that not one face
Was missed from its accustomed place;
Thankful to work for all the seven,
Trusting the rest to One in heaven.

THE ROAD TO HEAVEN.

A STORY OF WATERLOO BRIDGE.

Geo. R. Sims, from "Lifeboat" and other poems.

How is the boy this morning?
  Why do you shake your head?
Ah! I can see what's happened—
  There's a screen drawn round the bed
So poor little Mike is sleeping
  The last long sleep of all,
I'm sorry, but who can wonder
  After that dreadful fall?

Let me look at him, Doctor,
  Poor little London waif!
His frail barque's out of the tempest,
  And lies in God's harbour safe.
It's better he died in the ward here,
  Better a thousand times,
Than have wandered back to the alley
  With its squalor and nameless crimes.

Too young for the slum to sully,
  He's gone to the wonder land,
To look on the thousand marvels
  That he scarce could understand.
Poor little baby outcast,
  Poor little waif of sin,
He has gone, and the pitying angels
  Have carried the cripple in.

Didn't you know his story?
  Ah! you weren't here, I believe,
When they brought the poor little fellow
  To the hospital, Christmas eve.
It was I who came here with him,
  It was I who saw him go
Over the bridge that evening
  Into the Thames below.

'Twas a raw, cold air, that evening,
  A biting Christmas frost
I was looking about for a collie—
  A favourite dog I'd lost.
Some ragged boys, so they told me,
  Had been seen with one that night,
In one of the bridge recesses,
  So I hunted left and right.

You know the stone recesses,
  With the long broad bench of stone,
To many a weary outcast
  As welcome as monarch's throne.

On the fiercest night you may see them,
  As crouched in the dark they lie
Like the hunted vermin striving
  To hide from the hounds in cry.

The seats that night were empty,
  For the morrow was Christmas Day,
And even the outcast loafers
  Seemed to have slunk away.
They had found a warmer shelter—
  Some casual ward, maybe—
They'd do one morning's labour
  For the sake of the meat and tea.

I fancied the seats were empty,
  But, as I passed along,
Out of the darkness floated
  The words of a Christmas song
Sung in a childish treble—
  'Twas a boy's voice, harsh with cold,
Quavering out the anthem
  Of angels and harps of gold.

I stood where the shadows hid me,
  And peered about until
I could see two ragged urchins,
  Blue with the icy chill,
Cuddling close together,
  Crouched on a big stone seat—
Two little homeless Arabs,
  Waifs of the London street.

One was singing the carol,
  When the other with big round eyes—
It was Mike—looked up in wonder
  And said: "Jack, when we dies
Is that the place as we goes to—
  That place where yer dressed in white,
And has golding harps to play on,
  And it's warm, and jolly, and bright?

"Is that what they means by 'eaven
  As the misshun coves talk about,
Where the children's always happy,
  And nobody kicks 'em out?"
Jack nodded his head assenting,
  And then I listened and heard
The talk of the little Arabs—
  Listened to every word.

Jack was a Sunday scholar—
  So I gathered from what he said—
But he sang in the road for a living;
  His father and mother were dead.
And he had a drunken granny,
  Who turned him into the street:
She drank what he earned, and often
  He hadn't a crust to eat.

He told little Mike of heaven—
  In his rough untutored way,
He made it a land of glory
  Where the children play all day.
And Mike, he shivered and lis'ened,
  And told *his* tale to his friend.
How he was starved and beaten—
  'Twas a tale one's heart to rend.

He'd a drunken father and mother
  Who sent him out to beg
Though he'd just got over the fever,
  And was lame with a withered leg.
He told how he daren't crawl homeward,
  Because he had begged in vain,
And his parent's brutal fury
  Haunted his baby brain.

"I wish I could go to 'eaven,"
  He cried, as he shook with fright;
"If I thought as they'd only take me,
  Why I'd go this very night.
Which is the way to 'eaven?
  How d'ye get there, Jack?"
Jack climbed on the bridge's coping,
  And looked at the water black.

"That there's *one* road to 'eaven."
  He said, as he pointed down
To where the cold Thames water
  Surged muddy, and thick, and brown,
"If we was to fall in there, Mike,
  We'd be dead, and right through there
Is the place where it's always sunshine,
  And the angels has crowns to wear."

Mike rose and looked at the water:
  He peered in the big, broad stream.
Perhaps with a childish notion,
  He might catch the golden gleam
Of the far-off land of glory;
  He leaned right over and cried,
"If them are the gates of 'eaven,
  How I'd like to be inside!"

He'd stood but a moment looking—
  How it happened I cannot tell—
When he seemed to lose his balance,
  Gave a short, shrill cry, and fell;
Fell over the narrow coping,
  And I heard his poor head strike
With a thud on the stone work under,
  Then splash in the Thames went Mike.

We brought him here that evening—
  For help I had managed to shout,
A boat put off from the landing,
  And they dragged his body out.
His forehead was cut and bleeding,
  But a vestige of life we found.
When they brought him here he was senseless
  But slowly the child came round.

I came here Christmas morning,
  The ward was bright and gay
With mistletoe, green, and holly,
  In honor of Christmas Day.
And the patients had clean white garments,
  And a few in the room out there
Had joined in a Christmas service—
  They were singing a Christmas air.

They were singing a Christmas carol
  When Mike from his stupor awoke,
And dim on his wandering senses
  The strange surroundings broke.
Half dreamily he remembered
  The tale he had heard from Jack,
The song, and the white-robed angels
  The warm, bright heaven came back.

"I'm in 'eaven," he whispered faintly,
  "Yes, Jack must have told me true,"
And as he looked about him
  Came the kind old surgeon thro'.
Mike gazed at his face for a moment,
  Put his hand to his fevered head,
Then to the kind old doctor,
  "Please are you God?" he said.

Poor little Mike, 'twas heaven,
  This hospital ward to him.
A heaven of warmth and comfort;
  Till the flickering lamp grew dim.
And he lay like a tired baby
  In a dreamless gentle rest;
And now he is safe for ever,
  Where such as he are best.

This is the day of scoffers,
  But who shall say, that night
When Mike asked the road to heaven,
  That Jack didn't tell him right?
'Twas the children's Jesus pointed
  The way to the kingdom come,
For the poor little tired Arab,
  The waif of a London slum.

MY GIRL.

A LITTLE corner with its crib,
A little mug, a spoon, a bib,
A little tooth, so pearly white,
A little rubber ring to bite.

A little plate all lettered round,
A little rattle to resound,
A little creeping—see! she stands!
A little step 'twixt outstretched hands.

A little doll with flaxen hair,
A little willow rocking-chair,
A little dress of richest hue,
A little pair of gaiters blue.

A little school day after day,
A little "schoolma'am" to obey,
A little study—soon 'tis past—
A little graduate at last.

A little muff for wintry weather,
A little jockey-hat and feather,
A little sac with funny pockets,
A little chain, a ring, and lockets.

A little while to dance and bow,
A little escort homeward now,
A little party somewhat late,
A little lingering at the gate.

A little walk in leafy June,
A little talk while shines the moon,
A little reference to papa,
A little planning with mama.

A little ceremony grave,
A little struggle to be brave,
A little cottage on a lawn,
A little kiss—my girl was gone!

THE CHILDREN WE KEEP.

Mrs. E. V. Wilson.

THE children kept coming one by one,
Till the boys were five and the girls were three,
And the big brown house was alive with fun,
From the basement floor to the old roof tree.
Like garden flowers the little ones grew,
Nurtured and trained with tenderest care;
Warmed by love's sunshine, bathed in dew,
They blossomed into beauty rare.

But one of the boys grew weary one day,
And leaning his head on his mother's breast,
He said, "I am tired and cannot play:
Let me sit awhile on your knee and rest."
She cradled him close to her fond embrace,
She hushed him to sleep with her sweetest song,
And rapturous love still lightened his face
When his spirit had joined the heavenly throng.

Then the eldest girl, with her thoughtful eyes,
Who stood where the "brook and the river meet,"
Stole softly away into Paradise,
Ere "the river" had reached her slender feet,
While the father's eyes on the graves were bent,
The mother looked upward beyond the skies:
"Our treasures," she whispered, "were only lent;
Our darlings were angels in earth's disguise."

The years flew by, and the children began
With longings to think of the world outside;
And as each in turn became a man,
The boys proudly went from the father's side.
The girls were women so gentle and fair,
That lovers were speedy to woo and to win;
And with orange blooms in their braided hair,
Their old home they left, new homes to begin.

So, one by one the children have gone—
The boys were five and the girls were three;
And the big brown house is gloomy and lone,
With but two old folks for its company.
They talk to each other about the past,
As they sit together at eventide,
And say, "All the children we keep at last
Are the boy and girl who in childhood died."

THE GRAVES OF A HOUSEHOLD.

Mrs. Hemans.

They grew in beauty, side by side,
  They filled one home with glee ;—
Their graves are severed, far and wide,
  By mount, and stream, and sea.

The same fond mother bent at night
  O'er each fair sleeping brow ;
She had each folded flower in sight—
  Where are those dreamers now ?

One, 'midst the forest of the west,
  By a dark stream is laid—
The Indian knows his place of rest,
  Far in the cedar shade.

The sea, the blue lone sea hath one—
  He lies where pearls lie deep ;
He was the loved of all yet none
  O'er his low bed may weep.

One sleeps where southern vines are drest
  Above the noble slain ;
He wrapt his colors round his breast
  On a blood-red field of Spain.

And one—o'er her the myrtle showers
  Its leaves, by soft winds fanned ;
She faded 'midst Italian flowers—
  The last of that bright band.

And parted thus they rest, who played
  Beneath the same green tree ;
Whose voices mingled as they prayed
  Around one parent knee.

They that with smiles lit up the hall,
  And cheered with song the hearth—
Alas for love, if thou wert all,
  And naught beyond, O earth !

Poems about Sister.

A SISTER'S INGRATITUDE.

Geo. A. Merritt.

I ONCE was gay, as thou art now,
In fortune's festive hall;
With radiant gems I've decked my form
For banquet or for ball.
Yes—golden curls once clustered
Around my neck of snow;
And waving wreaths, bright coronals,
Have sported on my brow.

When asked to mingle with the throng
Or tread the giddy maze,
My fawn-like step was sure to win
The crowd's admiring gaze.
'Twas then I sought thy low-thatched roof,
Upon yon bleak hill's side;
Oh, how could I suppress my grief,
To see thy humbled pride!

I snatched thy feeble, fragile form
From poverty's cold brink;
The love of gold when duty bid,
Could never make me shrink.
But time soon turned the scale of wealth,
And fortune's glittering tide
Poured in thy lap its luxury,
And soon my fountain dried.

Amid the summer of my dreams,
By fate's cold, withering blast,
My hours of joy, and flowers of hope
Were blighted, crushed at last.
I turned to thee—I did not weep
The burden of my breast;
But humbly came beneath thy roof,
To seek a place of rest.

Recalling each endearing word,
In childhood's hour we knew;
The verdant lawn, the hills we loved,
The dear spot where we grew—
I hung my head upon my breast,
My woes still numbering o'er;
But, O, unfeeling sister, thou
Didst spurn me from the door.

But go—now triumph in thy pride,
'Mid revelry and song;
There, thou may'st find forgetfulness
Of this uncherished wrong.
But guard thy lips against my name—
The name they dare not speak;
Be sure the blush of honest shame
Will mantle on thy cheek.

THE NEGLECTED CHILD.

Ho ne Daney.

I NEVER was a favourite—
My mother never smiled
On me with half the tenderness
That blessed her fairer child;
I've seen her kiss my sister's cheek,
While fondled on her knee;
I've turned away to hide my tears—
There was no kiss for me!

And yet I strove to please, with all
My little store of sense;
I *strove* to please, and infancy
Can rarely give offence;
But when my artless efforts met
A cold, ungentle check,
I did not dare to throw myself
In tears upon her neck.

How blessed are the beautiful!
Love watches o'er their birth;
Oh beauty in my nursery
I learned to know thy worth;
For even *there* I often felt
Forsaken and forlorn,
And wished—for others wished it too—
I never had been born.

I'm sure I was affectionate—
But in my sister's face,
There was a look of love that claim'd
A smile or an embrace.
But when *I* raised my lip, to meet
The pressure children prize,
None knew the feelings of my heart—
They spoke not in my eyes.

But oh! that heart too keenly felt
The anguish of neglect;
I saw my sister's lovely form
With gems and roses deck'd;
I did not covet *them*, but oft
When wantonly reproved,
I envied her the privilege
Of being so beloved.

But soon a time of triumph came—
A time of sorrow too—
For sickness o'er my sister's form
Her venom'd mantle threw—
The features once so beautiful,
Now wore the hue of death;
And former friends shrank fearfully
From her infectious breath.

'Twas then, unwearied, day and night,
I watched beside her bed,
And fearlessly upon my breast
I pillowed her poor head.
She lived!—and loved me for my care,
My grief was at an end;
I was a lonely being once,
But now I *have* a friend.

Poems about Orphans.

THE ORPHAN BOY.

Mrs. Opie.

Stay, lady, stay for mercy sake,
And hear a helpless orphan's tale!
Ah, sure my looks must pity wake,
'Tis want that makes my cheek so pale.
Yet I was once a mother's pride.
And my brave father's hope and joy;
But in the Nile's proud fight he died,
And I am now an Orphan Boy.

Poor foolish child! how pleased was I,
When news of Nelson's victory came,
Along the crowded streets to fly,
And see the lighted windows flame!
To force me home my mother sought;
She could not bear to see my joy;
For with my father's life 'twas bought,
And made me a poor Orphan Boy.

The people's shouts were long and loud,—
My mother shuddering closed her ears:
"Rejoice! rejoice!" still cried the crowd,—
My mother answered with her tears.
"Oh, why do tears steal down your cheek,"
Cried I, "while others shout for joy?"
She kissed me and in accents weak,
She called me her poor Orphan Boy.

"What is an Orphan Boy?" I said,—
When suddenly she gasped for breath,
And her eyes closed. I shrieked for aid;
But ah, her eyes were closed in death!
My hardships since I will not tell;
But, now, no more a parent's joy,
Ah, lady! I have learned too well
What 'tis to be an Orphan Boy!

Oh, were I by your bounty fed!—
Nay, gentle lady! do not chide;
Trust me, I mean to earn my bread,—
The sailor's Orphan Boy has pride.
Lady, you weep! What is't you say?
You'll give me clothing, food, employ?—
Look down, dear parents, look and see
Your happy, happy Orphan Boy!

THE ORPHAN GIRL'S RECOLLECTIONS OF A MOTHER.

I have no mother! for she died
When I was very young;
But still her memory round my heart,
Like morning mists has hung

They tell me of an angel form,
That watch'd me while I slept,
And of a soft and gentle hand
That wip'd the tears I wept:

And that same hand that held my own
When I began to walk,
The joy that sparkled in her eyes
When first I tried to talk.

They say the mother's heart is pleas'd
When infant charms expand:
I wonder if she thinks of me
In that bright, happy land.

I know she is in heaven now,
That holy place of rest;
For she was always good to me—
The good alone are blest.

I remember, too, when I was ill,
She kissed my burning brow;
The tear that fell upon my cheek—
I think I feel it now.

And I have got some little books,
She taught me how to spell;
The chiding or the kiss she gave
I still remember well.

And then she used to kneel with me,
And teach me how to pray,
And raise my little hands to heaven,
And tell me what to say.

Oh, mother, mother! in my heart
Thy image still shall be,
And I will hope in heaven at last,
That I may meet with thee.

THE ORPHANS.

My chaise the village inn did gain,
  Just as the setting sun's last ray
Tipped with refulgent gold the vane
  Of the old church across the way.

Across the way I silent sped
  The time till supper to beguile
In moralising o'er the dead
  That mouldered round the ancient pile.

There many a humble green grave showed
  Where want, and pain, and toil did rest;
And many a flattering stone I viewed
  O'er those who once had wealth possest.

A faded beech its shadow brown
  Threw o'er a grave where sorrow slept
On which, though scarce with grass o'er-grown,
  Two ragged children sat and wept.

A piece of bread between them lay,
  Which neither seemed inclined to take;
And yet they looked so much a prey
  To want, it made my heart to ache.

"My little children, let me know
  Why you in such distress appear,
And why you wasteful from you throw
  That bread that many a one might cheer?"

The little boy, in accents sweet,
  Replied, while tears each other chased,
"Lady, we've not enough to eat—
  Ah! if we had we should not waste.

But sister Mary's naughty grown,
  And will not eat whate'er I say;
Though sure I am the bread's her own,
  For she has tasted none to-day."

"Indeed," the wan, starved Mary said,
  "Till Henry eat I'll eat no more;
For yesterday I got some bread,
  He's had none since the day before."

My heart did swell, my bosom heave,
  I felt as though deprived of speech;
Silent I sat upon the grave,
  And clasped the clay-cold hand of each.

With looks of woe too sadly true,
  With looks that spoke a grateful heart,
The shivering boy then nearer drew,
  And did his simple tale impart:

"Before my father went away,
  Enticed by bad men o'er the sea,
Sister and I did nought but play—
  We lived beside yon great ash tree.

But then poor mother did so cry,
  And looked so changed, I cannot tell;
She told us that she soon should die,
  And bade us love each other well.

She said that when the war was o'er
  Perhaps we might our father see;
But if we never saw him more,
  That God our father then would be.

She kissed us both and then she died,
  And we no more a mother have;
Here many a day we've sat and cried
  Together at poor mother's grave.

But when my father came not here,
  I thought if we could find the sea,
We should be sure to meet him there,
  And once again might happy be.

We hand in hand went many a mile,
  And asked our way of all we met;
And some did sigh, and some did smile,
  And we of some did victuals get.

But when we reached the sea, and found
  'Twas one great water round us spread,
We thought that father must be drowned,
  And cried, and wished we both were dead.

So we returned to mother's grave,
  And only long with her to be;
For Goody, when this bread she gave,
  Said father died beyond the sea.

Then since no parent we have here,
  We'll go and search for God around;
Lady, pray, can you tell us where
  That God, our Father, may be found?

He lives in heaven, mother said,
  And Goody says that mother's there;
So, if she knows we want his aid,
  I think perhaps she'll send him here."

I clasped the prattlers to my breast
  And cried, "Come both and live with me;
I'll clothe you, feed you, give you rest,
  And will a second mother be.

And God shall be your father still;
  'Twas he in mercy sent me here
To teach you to obey his will,
  Your steps to guide, your hearts to cheer!"

THE ORPHAN BOY.

Thelwall.

Alas! I am an orphan boy,
  With nought on earth to cheer my heart;
No father's love, no mother's joy,
  Nor kin nor kind to take my part.
My lodging is the cold, cold ground;
  I eat the bread of charity:
And, when the kiss of love goes round—
  There is no kiss, alas! for me.

Yet once I had a father dear,
  A mother, too, I wont to prize,
With ready hand to wipe the tear,
  If chanced a childish tear to rise:
But cause of tears was rarely found;
  For all my heart was youthful glee;
And, when the kiss of love went round,
  How sweet a kiss there was for me.

But, ah! there came a war, they say.
  What *is* a war? I cannot tell.
But drums and fifes did sweetly play,
  And loudly rang our village bell.
In truth it was a pretty sound,
  I thought; nor could I thence foresee
That when the kiss of love went round,
  There soon would be no kiss for me.

A scarlet coat my father took;
  And sword as bright as bright could be:
And feathers that so gaily look,
  All in a shining cap had he.
Then how my little heart did bound—
  Alas! I thought it fine to see,
Nor dreamt that, when the kiss went round,
  There soon would be no kiss for me.

My mother sigh'd, my mother wept—
  My father talked of wealth and fame;
But still she wept, and sigh'd and wept,
  Till I to see her did the same.
But soon the horsemen throng around,
  My father mounts with shout and glee;
Then gave a kiss to all around—
  And, ah! how sweet a kiss to me.

But when I found he rode so far,
  And came not back as heretofore,
I said it was a naughty war,
  And loved the fife and drum no more.
My mother oft in tears was drown'd,
  Nor merry tale nor song had she:
And when the hour of night came round
  Sad was the kiss she gave to me.

At length the bell again did ring—
  There was a victory, they said:
'Twas what my father said he'd bring,
  But, ah! it brought my father—dead!
My mother shriek'd—her heart was woe;
  She clasped me trembling to her knee:
And oh, that you may never know
  How wild a kiss she gave to me!

But once again—but once again
  These lips a mother's kisses felt;
That once again—that once again
  The tale a heart of stone would melt.
'Twas when upon her death-bed laid;
  (Oh, what a sight was that to see!)
"My child, my child," she feebly said,
  And gave a parting kiss to me.

So now I am an orphan boy,
  With nought below my heart to cheer:
No mother's love—no father's joy,
  Nor kin nor kind to wipe the tear.
My lodging is the cold, cold ground,
  I eat the bread of charity;
And when the kiss of love goes round,
  There is no kiss of love for me.

THE MITHERLESS BAIRN.

William Thom.

When a' ither bairnies are hushed to their hame,
By aunty, or cousin, or freaky grand-dame,
Wha stands last and lanely, an' naebody carin'?
'Tis the puir doited loonie,—the mitherless bairn.

The mitherless bairn gangs to his lane bed;
Nane covers his cauld back, or haps his bare head
His wee hackit heelies are hard as the airn,
And litheless the lair o' the mitherless bairn.

Aneath his cauld brow siccan dreams hover there,
O' hands that wont kindly to kame his dark hair;
But mornin' brings clutches, a' reckless an' stern,
That lo'e nae the locks o' the mitherless bairn.

Yon sister that sang o'er his saftly rocked bed
Now rests in the mools where her mammie is laid,
The father toils sair their wee bannock to earn,
An' kens na the wrangs o' his mitherless bairn.

Her spirit, that passed in yon hour o' his birth,
Still watches his wearisome wanderings on earth;
Recording in heaven the blessings they earn
Wha couthilie deal wi' the mitherless bairn.

O, speak him na harshly,—he trembles the while,
He bends to your bidding, he blesses your smile;
In their dark hour o' anguish the heartless shall learn,
That God deals the blow for the mitherless bairn.

LITTLE PHIL.

Mrs. Helen Rich.

"Make me a headboard, mister, smoothed and painted, you see;
Our ma she died last winter: and sister, and Jack, and me
Last Sunday could hardly find her, so many new graves about,
And Bud cried out: 'We've lost her,' when Jack gave a little shout.
We have worked and saved all winter—been hungry sometimes, I own—
But we hid this much from father under the old door stone.
He never goes there to see her; he hated her; scolded Jack
When he heard us talking about her and wishing she'd come back,
But up in the garret we whisper, and have a good time to cry,
Our beautiful mother who kissed us, and wasn't afraid to die.
Put on it 'that she was forty, in November she went away,
That she was the best of mothers, and we haven't forgot to pray;
And we mean to do as she taught us—be loving and true, and square,
To work and read, to love her, till we go to her up there.'
Let the board be white like mother" (the small chin quivered here)
And the lad coughed something under, and conquered a rebel tear.
"Here is all we could keep from father, a dollar and thirty cents,
The rest he has got for coal and flour, and partly to pay the rents."
Blushing the white lie over, and dropping the honest eyes,
"What is the price of headboards, with writing and handsome size?
Three dollars!" a young roe wounded just falls with a moan, and he,
With a face like the ghost of his mother, sat down on his tattered knee.
"Three dollars! and we shall lose her next winter, the grave and the snow!"
But the boss had his arms around him, and cuddled the head of tow
Close up to the great heart's shelter, and womanly tears fell fast—
"Dear boy, you shall never lose her, oh cling to your sacred past!
Come to-morrow, and bring your sister and Jack, and the board shall be
The best that the shop can furnish; then come here and live with me."

* * * * * * *

When the orphans loaded their treasure on the rugged old cart next day,
The surprise of a footboard varnish, with all that their love could say;
And "*Edith St. John, Our Mother!*" baby Jack gave his little shout,
And Bud, like a mountain daisy, went dancing her doll about.
But Phil grew white and trembled, and close to the boss he crept,
Kissing him like a woman, shivered, and laughed and wept:
"Do you think, my benefactor, in Heaven that *she'll* be glad?"
"Not as glad as *you* are, Philip, but finish this job, my lad."

GUILTY OR NOT GUILTY.

SHE stood at the bar of justice,
  A creature wan and wild,
In form too small for a woman,
  In features too old for a child;
For a look so worn and pathetic
  Was stamped on her pale young face,
It seemed long years of suffering
  Must have left that silent trace.

"Your name," said the judge, as he eyed her
  With kindly look yet keen,
"Is Mary McGuire, if you please sir,"
  "And your age?"—"I am turned fifteen."
"Well, Mary," and then from a paper
  He slowly and gravely read,
"You are charged here—I'm sorry to say it—
  With stealing three loaves of bread.

"You look not like an offender,
  And I hope that you can show
The charge to be false. Now tell me,
  Are you guilty of this, or no?"
A passionate burst of weeping
  Was at first her sole reply,
But she dried her eyes in a moment,
  And looked in the judge's eye.

"I will tell you just how it was, sir,
  My father and mother are dead,
And my little brother and sisters
  Were hungry, and asked me for bread.
At first I earned it for them
  By working hard all day,
But somehow times were bad, sir,
  And the work all fell away.

"I could get no more employment;
  The weather was bitter cold,
And the young ones cried and shivered—
  (Little Johnny's but four years old);—
So, what was I to do, sir?
  I am guilty, but do not condemn,
I *took*—oh, was it *stealing?*—
  The bread to give to them."

Every man in the court-room—
  Grey-beard and thoughtless youth—
Knew, as he looked upon her,
  That the prisoner spake the truth.
Out from their pockets came kerchiefs,
  Out from their eyes sprang tears,
And out from the old faded wallets
  Treasures hoarded for years.

The judge's face was a study—
  The strangest you ever saw,
As he cleared his throat and murmured
  Something about the *law*.
For one so learned in such matters,
  So wise in dealing with men,
He seemed on a simple question,
  Sorely puzzled just then.

But no one blamed him or wondered,
  When at last these words they heard:
'The sentence on this young prisoner
  Is for the present deferred."
And no one blamed him or wondered
  When he went to her and smiled,
And tenderly led from the court-room,
  Himself, the "guilty" child.

THE IDIOT BOY.

Southey.

IT had pleased Heaven to form poor Ned a thing of idiot-mind;
Yet to the poor unreasoning man, Heaven had not been unkind.
Old Sarah loved her helpless child, when helplessness made dear;
And life was happiness to him, who had no hope or fear.

She knew his wants, she understood each articulate call;
And he was everything to her, and she to him was all.
And so for many a year they dwelt, nor knew a wish beside;
But age at length on Sarah came, and she fell sick and died.

He tried, in vain, to 'waken her; he called her o'er and o'er;
They told him, she was dead; the sound to him no import bore.
They closed her eyes and shrouded her, and he stood wondering by,
And when they bore her to the grave, he followed silently.
They laid her in her narrow house, they sang the funeral stave;
But when the funeral train dispersed he loitered by the grave.

The rabble boys, who used to jeer, whene'er they saw poor Ned,
Now stood and watched him at the grave, and not a word they said.
They came and went, and came again, till night at last drew on;
And still he loitered by the grave, till all the rest were gone.

And when he found himself alone, he swift removed the clay;
And raised the coffin up in haste, and bore it swift away.
And when he reached his hut, he laid the coffin on the floor;
And with the eagerness of joy, he barred the cottage door.

And out he took his mother's corpse, and placed it in a chair;
And then he heaped the hearth, and blew the kindling fire with care;
He placed his mother in a chair, and in her wonted place;
And blew the kindling fire, that shone reflected on her face.

And pausing now, her hand would feel, and now her face behold;
"Why, mother, do you look so pale? and why are you so cold?"
—It had pleased Heaven, from the poor wretch his only friend to call;
But Heaven was kind to him, and soon in death restored him all.

Poems about Man.

ELEGY, WRITTEN IN A COUNTRY CHURCHYARD.

Gray.

THE curfew tolls the knell of parting day,
  The lowing herds wind slowly o'er the lea,
The ploughman homewards plods his weary way,
  And leaves the world to darkness and to me.

Now fades the glimm'ring landscape on the sight,
  And all the air a solemn stillness holds,
Save where the beetle wheels his droning flight,
  And drowsy tinklings lull the distant folds;

Save that from yonder ivy-mantled tower,
  The moping owl does to the moon complain
Of such, as wandr'ing near her secret bow'r,
  Molest her ancient solitary reign.

Beneath those rugged elms, that yew tree's shade,
  Where heaves the turf in many a mouldering heap,
Each in his narrow cell for ever laid,
  The rude forefathers of the hamlet sleep.

The breezy call of incense-breathing morn,
  The swallow twittering from her straw-built shed,
The cock's shrill clarion, or the echoing horn,
  No more shall rouse them from their lowly bed.

For them no more the blazing hearth shall burn,
  Or busy housewife ply her evening care;
No children run to lisp their sire's return
  Or climb his knees the envied kiss to share.

Oft did the harvest to their sickle yield;
  Their furrow oft the stubborn glebe has broke:
How jocund did they drive their team afield!
  How bow'd the woods beneath their sturdy stroke!

Let not ambition mock their useful toil,
  Their homely joys and destiny obscure;
Nor Grandeur hear, with a disdainful smile,
  The short and simple annals of the poor.

The boast of Heraldry, the pomp of Power,
  And all that Beauty, all that Wealth e'er gave,
Await alike the inevitable hour:
  The paths of Glory lead—but to the grave.

Nor you, ye Proud, impute to these the fault,
  If memory o'er their tomb no trophies raise,
Where through the long-drawn aisle and fretted vault,
  The pealing anthem swells the note of praise.

Can storied urn, or animated bust,
  Back to its mansion call the fleeting breath?
Can Honour's voice provoke the silent dust,
  Or Flattery soothe the dull cold ear of death?

Perhaps, in this neglected spot, is laid
  Some heart once pregnant with celestial fire;
Hands that the rod of Empire might have sway'd,
  Or waked to ecstacy the living lyre:

But Knowledge to their eyes her ample page,
  Rich with the spoils of time, did ne'er unroll
Chill Penury repressed their noble rage,
  And froze the genial current of the soul!

Full many a gem of purest ray serene,
  The dark unfathom'd caves of Ocean bear;
Full many a flower is born to blush unseen,
  And waste its sweetness on the desert air!

Some village Hampden, that, with dauntless breast,
  The little tyrant of his fields withstood;
Some mute inglorious Milton here may rest—
  Some Cromwell, guiltless of his country's blood.

The applause of listening senates to command,
  The threats of pain and ruin to despise,
To scatter plenty o'er a smiling land,
  And read their history in a nation's eyes,

Their lot forbade; nor circumscribed alone
  Their glowing virtues, but their crimes confined—
Forbade to wade through slaughter to a throne,
  And shut the gates of mercy on mankind;

The struggling pangs of conscious truth to hide;
  To quench the blushes of ingenuous shame;
Or heap the shrine of luxury and pride,
  With incense kindled at the Muse's flame.

Far from the madding crowd's ignoble strife,
  Their sober wishes never learned to stray:
Along the cool sequester'd vale of life
  They kept the noiseless tenor of their way!

Yet e'en these bones from insult to protect,
  Some frail memorial, still erected nigh,
With uncouth rhymes and shapeless sculpture deck'd,
  Implores the passing tribute of a sigh.

Their name, their years, spell'd by the unletter'd muse,
  The place of fame and elegy supply;
And many a holy text around she strews,
  To teach the rustic moralist to die.

For who, to dumb Forgetfulness a prey,
  This pleasing, anxious being e'er resign'd—
Left the warm precincts of the cheerful day,
  Nor cast one longing, lingering look behind?

On some fond breast the parting soul relies,
  Some pious drops the closing eye requires:
E'en from the tomb the voice of Nature cries,
  E'en in our ashes live their wonted fires!

For thee, who, mindful of the unhonour'd dead,
  Dost in these lines their artless tale relate,
If, 'chance, by lonely Contemplation led,
  Some kindred spirit shall enquire thy fate.

Haply, some hoary-headed swain may say,
  "Oft have we seen him at the peep of dawn,
Brushing with hasty steps the dew away,
  To meet the sun upon the upland lawn.

"There at the foot of yonder nodding beech,
  That wreathes its old fantastic roots so high,
His listless length at noontide would he stretch,
  And pore upon the brook that babbles by.

"Hard by yon wood, now smiling as in scorn,
  Muttering his wayward fancies, he would rove;
Now drooping, woful, wan, like one forlorn,
  Or crazed with care, or crossed in hopeless love.

"One morn I missed him on the accustomed hill,
  Along the heath, and near his favourite tree;
Another came, nor yet beside the rill,
  Nor up the lawn, nor at the wood, was he.

"The next, with dirges due in sad array,
  Slow through the churchway path we saw him borne;
Approach and read (for thou canst read) the lay
  'Graved on the stone beneath yon aged thorn."

THE EPITAPH.

Here rests his head upon the lap of earth,
  A youth to fortune and to fame unknown;
Fair Science frowned not on his humble birth,
  And Melancholy marked him for her own.

Large was his bounty, and his soul sincere,
  Heav'n did a recompense as largely send;
He gave to Misery all he had—a tear;
  He gained from Heav'n ('twas all he wished) a friend.

No farther seek his merits to disclose,
  Or draw his frailties from their dread abode;
(There they alike in trembling hope repose),
  The bosom of his Father and his God.

THE COMMON LOT.

James Montgomery.

ONCE, in the flight of ages past,
There lived a man—and WHO WAS HE !
Mortal! howe'er thy lot be cast,
That man resembled thee.

Unknown the region of his birth,
The land in which he died unknown :
His name has perished from the Earth ;
This truth survives alone :—

That joy and grief, and hope and fear,
Alternate triumphed in his breast ;
His bliss and woe,—a smile, a tear !—
Oblivion hides the rest.

The bounding pulse, the languid limb,
The changing spirits' rise and fall,—
We know that these were felt by him,
For these are felt by all.

He suffered,—but his pangs are o'er ;
Enjoyed,—but his delights are fled ;
Had friends,—his friends are now no more ;
And foes,—his foes are dead.

He loved,—but whom he loved, the grave
Hath lost in its unconscious womb :
Oh, she was fair! but naught could save
Her beauty from the tomb.

He saw—whatever thou hast seen ;
Encountered—all that troubles thee ;
He was—whatever thou hast been ;
He is—what thou shalt be.

The rolling seasons, day and night,
Sun, moon, and stars, the earth and main,
Erewhile his portion, life and light,
To him exist in vain.

The clouds and sunbeams, o'er his eye
That once their shade and glory threw,
Have left in yonder silent sky
No vestige where they flew.

The annals of the human race,
Their ruins since the world began,
Of HIM afford no other trace
Than this—THERE LIVED A MAN !

THE BRIDGE.

Longfellow.

I STOOD on the bridge at midnight,
As the clocks were striking the hour,
And the moon rose o'er the city,
Behind the old church tower.

I saw her bright reflection
In the waters under me,
Like a golden goblet falling
And sinking into the sea.

And far in the hazy distance
Of that lovely night in June,
The blaze of the flaming furnace
Gleamed redder than the moon.

Among the long black rafters
The wavering shadows lay,
And the current that came from the ocean
Seemed to lift and bear them away ;

As sweeping and eddying through them,
Rose the belated tide,
And, streaming into the moonlight,
The seaweed floated wide.

And like those waters rushing
Among the wooden piers,
A flood of thoughts came o'er me
That filled my eyes with tears.

How often, O how often,
In the days that had gone by,
I had stood on that bridge at midnight,
And gazed on that wave and sky !

How often, O how often,
I had wished that the ebbing tide
Would bear me away on its bosom,
O'er the ocean wild and wide !

For my heart was hot and restless,
And my life was full of care,
And the burden laid upon me
Seemed greater than I could bear.

But now it has fallen from me,
It is buried in the sea ;
And only the sorrow of others
Throws its shadows over me.

Yet, whenever I cross the river
On its bridge with wooden piers,
Like the odour of brine from the ocean
Come the thoughts of other years.

And I think how many thousands
Of care-encumbered men,
Each bearing his burden of sorrow,
Have crossed the bridge since then.

I see the long procession
Still passing to and fro ;
The young heart light and restless,
And the old subdued and slow.

And for ever and for ever,
As long as the river flows ;
As long as the heart has passions,
As long as life has woes ;

The moon and its broken reflection,
And its shadows shall appear
As the symbol of love in heaven,
And its wavering image here.

THE WANTS OF MAN.

John Quincy Adams.

Man wants but little here below,
Nor wants that little long.—GOLDSMITH.

"MAN wants but little here below,
Nor wants that little long."
'Tis not with me exactly so,
But 'tis so in the song.
My wants are many, and if I told
Would number many a score;
And were each wish a mint of gold,
I still should long for more.

What first I want is daily bread,
And canvas-backs and wine;
And all the realms of nature spread
Before me when I dine;
With four choice cooks from France, beside,
To dress my dinner well;
Four courses scarcely can provide
My appetite to quell.

What next I want, at heavy cost,
Is elegant attire:
Black sable furs for winter's frost,
And silks for summer's fire.
And Cashmere shawls, and Brussels lace
My bosom's front to deck,
And diamond rings my hands to grace,
And rubies for my neck.

And then I want a mansion fair,
A dwelling house in style,
Four stories high, for wholesome air—
A massive marble pile:
With halls for banquetting and balls,
All furnished rich and fine;
With high blood studs in fifty stalls,
And cellars for my wine.

I want a garden and a park,
My dwelling to surround—
A thousand acres (bless the mark!)
With walls encompass'd round—
Where flocks may range and herds may low,
And kids and lambkins play,
And flowers and fruit commingled grow,
All Eden to display.

I want when summer's foliage falls,
And Autumn strips the trees,
A house within the city's walls,
For comfort and for ease;
But here as space is somewhat scant,
And acres somewhat rare,
My house in town I only want
To occupy—a square.

I want a steward, butler, cooks:
A coachman, footman, grooms;
A library of well-bound books,
And picture-garnish'd rooms;
Correggio's Magdalen, and Night,
The Matron of the Chair;
Guido's fleet coursers, in their flight,
And Claudes at least a pair.

I want a cabinet profuse
Of medals, coins, and gems;
A printing press for private use,
Of fifty thousand ems;
And plants, and minerals, and shells;
Worms, insects, fishes, birds;
And every beast on earth that dwells
In solitude or herds.

I want a board of burnish'd plate,
Of silver and of gold;
Tureens, of twenty pounds in weight,
And sculpture's richest mould:
Plateaus with chandeliers and lamps,
Plates, dishes—all the same;
And porcelain vases, with the stamps
Of Sèvres and Angoulême.

And maples of fair glossy stain,
Must form my chamber doors,
And carpets of the Wilton grain
Must cover all my floors;
My walls with tapestry bedeck'd,
Must never be outdone;
And damask curtains must protect
Their colours from the sun.

And mirrors of the largest pane
From Venice must be brought;
And sandal-wood and bamboo-cane,
For chairs and tables bought;
On all the mantel-pieces, clocks
Of thrice gilt bronze must stand,
And screens of ebony and box
Invite the stranger's hand.

I want (who does not want?) a wife,
Affectionate and fair,
To solace all the woes of life,
And all its joys to share;
Of temper sweet, of yielding will,
Of firm yet placid mind,
With all my faults to love me still,
With sentiment refined.

And as time's car incessant runs,
And fortune fills my store,
I want of daughters and of sons
From eight to half a score.
I want (alas! can mortal dare
Such bliss on earth to crave?)
That all the girls be chaste and fair—
The boys all wise and brave.

And when my bosom's darling sings,
With melody divine,
A pedal harp of many strings
Must with her voice combine.
Piano, exquisitely wrought,
Must open stand, apart,
That all my daughters may be taught
To win the stranger's heart.

My wife and daughters will desire
Refreshment from perfumes,
Cosmetics for the skin require,
And artificial blooms.
The civet fragrance shall dispense
And treasured sweets return;
Cologne revive the flagging sense,
And smoking amber burn.

And when at night my weary head
Begins to droop and doze,
A chamber south to hold my bed,
For nature's soft repose;
With blankets, counterpanes, and sheet,
Mattress, and sack of down,
And comfortables for my feet,
And pillows for my crown.

I want a warm and faithful friend,
To cheer the adverse hour,
Who ne'er to flattery will descend,
Nor bend the knee to power;
A friend to chide me when I'm wrong,
My inmost soul to see;
And that my friendship prove as strong
For him, as his for me.

I want a kind and tender heart,
For others' wants to feel;
A soul secure from fortune's dart,
And bosom arm'd with steel;
To bear Divine chastisement's rod,
And, mingling in my plan,
Submission to the will of God,
With charity to man.

I want a keen observing eye,
An ever-listening ear,
The truth through all disguise to spy,
And wisdom's voice to hear;
A tongue, to speak at virtue's need,
In heaven's sublimest strain;
And lips the cause of man to plead,
And never plead in vain.

I want uninterrupted health,
Throughout my long career,
And streams of never-failing wealth,
To scatter far and near—
The destitute to clothe and feed,
Free bounty to bestow,
Supply the helpless orphan's need,
And soothe the widow's woe.

I want the genius to conceive,
The talents to unfold,
Designs, the vicious to retrieve,
The virtuous to uphold;
Inventive power, combining skill,
A persevering soul,
Of human hearts to mould the will,
And reach from pole to pole.

I want the seals of power and place,
The ensigns of command,
Charged by the people's unbought grace,
To rule my native land;
Nor crown, nor sceptre would I ask
But for my country's will,
By day, by night, to ply the task
Her cup of bliss to fill.

I want the voice of honest praise
To follow me behind,
And to be thought, in future days,
The friend of human kind;
That after-ages as they rise,
Exulting may proclaim,
In choral union to the skies,
Their blessings on my name.

These are the wants of mortal man;
I cannot need them long,
For life itself is but a span,
And earthly bliss a song.
My last great want, absorbing all,
Is, when beneath the sod,
And summoned to my final call—
The mercy of my God.

And oh! while circles in my veins
Of life the purple stream,
And yet a fragment small remains
Of nature's transient dream,
My soul, in humble hope unscared,
Forget not thou to pray,
That this THY WANT may be prepared
To meet the Judgment-Day.

Poems about Women.

LEDYARD'S PRAISE OF WOMEN.

Aikin.

Through many a land and clime a ranger,
With toilsome steps I've held my way,
A lonely, unprotected stranger,
To all the stranger's ills a prey.

While steering thus my course precarious,
My fortune still had been to find
Men's hearts, and dispositions various,
But gentle Woman ever kind.

Alive to ev'ry tender feeling,
To deeds of mercy ever prone,
The wounds of pain and sorrow healing
With soft compassion's sweetest tone.

No proud delay, no dark suspicion,
Stints the free bounty of their heart;
They turn not from the sad petition,
But cheerful aid at once impart.

Formed in benevolence of nature,
Obliging, modest, gay, and mild,
Woman's the same endearing creature
In courtly town and savage wild.

When parched with thirst, with hunger wasted,
Her friendly hand refreshment gave;
How sweet the coarsest food has tasted!
What cordial in the simple wave.

Her courteous looks, her words caressing,
Shed comfort on the fainting soul:
Woman's the stranger's general blessing,
From sultry India to the Pole.

THE PRAISE OF WOMEN.

Mackay.

Woman may err—Woman may give her mind,
To evil thoughts, and lose her pure estate.
But for *one* woman who affronts her kind
By wicked passions and remorseless hate,
A thousand make amends in age and youth,
By heavenly Pity, by sweet Sympathy,
By Patient Kindness, by enduring Truth,
By Love, supremest in adversity.
Theirs is the task to succour the distress'd,
To feed the hungry, to console the sad,
To pour the balm upon the wounded breast.
And find dear pity, even for the bad.
Blessings on women! In the darkest day
Their love shines brightest; in the perilous hour
Their weak hands glow with strength our feuds to stay.
Blessings upon them! and if man would shower
His condemnation on the few that err,
Let him be calm, and cease his soul to vex:
Think of his mother, and for sake of her
Forgive them all, and bless their gentle sex.

WOMAN'S LOVE.

When man is waxing frail,
And his hand is thin and weak;
And his lips are parch'd and pale;
And wan and white his cheek;
Oh, then doth woman prove
Her constancy and love!

She sitteth by his chair,
And holds his feeble hand;
She watcheth ever there,
His wants to understand;
His yet unspoken will
She hasteneth to fulfil.

She leads him, when the moon
Is bright o'er dale and hill,
And all things save the tune
Of the honey bees, are still,
Into the garden's bowers
To sit 'midst herbs and flowers.

And when he goes not there,
To feed on breath and bloom,
She brings the posy rare
Into his darkened room;
And 'neath his weary head
The pillow smooth doth spread.

Until the hour when death
His lamp of life doth dim,
She never wearieth,
She never leaveth him;
Still near him night and day,
She meets his eye alway.

And when the trial is o'er,
And the turf is on his breast,
Deep in her bosom's core
Lies sorrow unexprest.
Her tears, her sighs are weak,
Her settled grief to speak.

And though there may arise
Balm for her spirit's pain;
And though her quiet eyes
May sometimes smile again,
Still, still, she must regret;
She never can forget.

THE FIRST GREY HAIR.

T. H. Bayley.

THE matron at her mirror, with her hand upon her brow,
Sits gazing on her lovely face—ay, lovely even now;
Why doth she lean upon her hand with such a look of care?
Why steals that tear across her cheek?—She sees her first grey hair.

Time from her form hath ta'en away but little of its grace;
His touch of thought hath dignified the beauty of her face;
Yet she might mingle in the dance where maidens gaily trip,
So bright is still her hazel eye, so beautiful her lip.

The faded form is often mark'd by sorrow more than years;
The wrinkle on the cheek may be the course of secret tears;
The mournful lip may murmur of a love it ne'er confest,
And the dimness of the eye betray a heart that cannot rest.

But she hath been a happy wife;—the lover of her youth
May proudly claim the smile that pays the trial of his truth;
A sense of slight—of loneliness—hath never banish'd sleep;
Her life hath been a cloudless one; then, wherefore doth she weep?

She look'd upon her raven locks;—what thoughts did they recall?
Oh! not of nights when they were deck'd for banquet or for ball;—
They brought back thoughts of early youth; ere she had learnt to check,
With artificial wreaths, the curls that sported o'er her neck.

She seem'd to feel her mother's hand pass lightly through her hair,
And draw it from her brow, to leave a kiss of kindness there;
She seem'd to view her father's smile, and feel the playful touch
That sometimes feigned to steal away the curls she prized so much.

And now she sees her first grey hair! oh, deem it not a crime
For her to weep—when she beholds the first footmark of Time!
She knows that, one by one, those mute mementoes will increase,
And steal youth, beauty, strength away, till life itself shall cease.

'Tis not the tear of vanity for beauty on the wane—
Yet though the blossom may not sigh to bud, and bloom again.
It cannot but remember with a feeling of regret,
The Spring for ever gone—the Summer sun so nearly set.

Ah, Lady! heed the monitor! thy mirror tells the truth,
Assume the matron's folded veil, resign the wreath of youth;
Go—bind it on thy daughter's brow, in her thou'lt still look fair;
'Twere well would all learn wisdom who behold the first grey hair!

WOMAN.

Ebenezer Elliott.

What highest prize hath woman won
  In science or in art?
What mightiest work by woman done,
  Boasts city, field, or mart?
"She hath no Raphael," Painting saith,
  "No Newton," Learning cries:
Shows us her Steam-ship! her Macbeth!
  Her thought-won victories!

Hail, boastful man! though worthy are
  Thy deeds when thou art true.
Things worthier still and holier far
  Our sister yet will do;
For this the worth of women shows,
  On every peopled shore,
That still as man in wisdom grows,
  He honours her the more.

Oh, not for wealth, or fame, or power,
  Hath man's weak angel striven,
But silent as the growing flower,
  To make of earth a heaven!
And in her garden of the sun
  Heaven's brightest rose shall bloom,
For woman's best is unbegun!
  Her advent yet to come.

WOMAN'S MISSION.

H. J. Johnson.

Though she may not in the battle
  Bravely lead men to the fight—
Though she may not wield the sabre
  For the right against the might;
She can hover near the bedside
  Where the wounded soldier lies—
She can cheer his dying moments,
  Watch beside him till he dies.

Though she may not guide the voyage
  Of the staunch old "Ship of State,"
Steer it from the rocks and breakers
  Where its foes in anguish wait;
She may wield a mightier influence
  Over those who rule the land;
She may be the silent power
  That shall nerve the statesman's hand.

Though she may not in the council
  Of the nation, raise her voice—
Though she may not, by their ballots,
  Be proclaimed the people's choice—
She can teach the little children
  To be brave and firm, and true—
True to manhood, God, and country,
  More than this no *man* can do.

Though she may not from the pulpit,
  Speak the words of truth and love,
Warning them of death and judgment,
  Pointing them to God above,
She can speak to some poor sinner—
  Tell him Christ for him was given—
She may, by some kind words spoken,
  Win a soul for God and Heaven.

In the battle, in the pulpit,
  In the councils of the land,
On Fame's high and dizzy summit,
  Woman's form may never stand;
But more holy is her mission—
  Noblest work that God has given!
Hers to lift with hands so tender,
  Our poor world up nearer Heaven.

Poems about Woman's Rights.

THE RIGHTS OF WOMEN.

The rights of women, what are they?
The rights to love and work each day;
The right to weep when others weep,
The right to wake when others sleep.

The right to dry the falling tear,
The right to stay the rising fear;
The right to smooth the brow of care,
And whisper comfort to despair.

The right to watch *the parting breath,*
To soothe and cheer the bed of death;
The right, when earthly hopes all fail,
To point to that within the veil.

The right the wanderer to reclaim,
And win the lost from paths of shame;
The right to comfort and to bless
The widow and the fatherless.

The right the little ones to guide,
To teach them truth and nought beside;
With earnest love and gentle praise,
To bless and cheer their youthful days.

The right to live for those we love,
The right to die that love to prove;
The right to brighten earthly homes
With pleasant smiles and gentle tones.

Are these thy rights? Then use them [well;
Thy silent influence none can tell.
If these are thine, why ask for more—
Thou hast enough to answer for.

WOMEN'S RIGHTS.

Yes, God has made me a woman,
  And I'm content to be
Just what He meant, not reaching out
  For other things since He
Who knows me best and loves me most
  Has ordered this for me.

A woman, to live my life out
  In quiet, womanly ways,
Hearing the far-off battle,
  Seeing as through a haze
The crowding struggling world of men
  Fight through their busy days.

I am not strong and valiant,
  I would not join the fight,
Or jostle with crowds in the highways,
  To sully my garments white;
But I have rights as a woman,
  And here I claim my right.

The right of a rose to bloom
  In its own sweet separate way,
With none to question its perfumed pink,
  And none to utter nay
If it reaches a root or points a thorn,
  As even a rose-tree may.

The right of a lady birch to grow,
  To grow as the Lord shall please,
By never a sturdy oak rebuked,
  Denied nor sun nor breeze.
For all its pliant slenderness,
  Kin to the stronger trees.

The right to a life of my own—
  Not merely a casual bit
Of somebody else's life, flung out,
  That, taking hold of it
I may stand as a cypher does
  After a numeral writ.

The right to gather and glean
  What food I need and can,
From the garnered store of knowledge,
  Which man has heaped for man.
Taking with free hands freely,
  And after an ordered plan.

The right—ah, best and sweetest,
  To stand all undismayed,
Whenever sorrow or want or sin
  Call for a woman's aid.
And none to cavil or question,
  By never a look gainsaid.

I ask not for a ballot;
  Though life were at a stake,
I would beg for a nobler justice,
  That men for manhood's sake
Should give ungrudgingly, nor withhold
  Till I must fight and take.

The fleet foot and the feeble foot
  Both seek the selfsame goal.
The weakest soldier's name is writ
  On the great army-roll.
And God, who made man's body strong,
  Made, too, the woman's soul.

Poems about Love.

IF 'TIS LOVE TO WISH YOU NEAR.

Dibdin.

If 'tis love to wish you near,
To tremble when the wind I hear,
  Because at sea you floating rove;
If of you to dream at night,
To languish when you're out of sight,—
  If this be loving, then I love.

If, when you're gone, to count each hour,
To ask of every tender power
  That you may kind and faithful prove;
If void of falsehood and deceit,
I feel a pleasure when we meet,—
  If this be loving, then I love.

To wish your fortune to partake,
Determined never to forsake;
  Though low in poverty we strove;
If, so that me your wife you'd call,
I offer you my little all,—
  If this be loving, then I love.

I LOVE THEE! I LOVE THEE!

Hood.

I love thee! I love thee!
  'Tis all that I can say:—
It is my vision in the night,
  My dreaming in the day;
The very echo of my heart,
  The blessing when I pray,
I love thee! I love thee!
  Is all that I can say.

I love thee! I love thee!
  Is ever on my tongue;
In all my proudest poesy,
  That chorus still is sung.
It is the verdict of my eyes
  Amidst the gay and young;
I love thee! I love thee!
  A thousand maids among.

I love thee! I love thee!
  Thy bright and hazel glance,
The mellow lute upon those lips
  Whose tender tones entrance.
But most, dear heart of hearts, thy proofs,
  That still these words enhance;
I love thee! I love thee!
  Whatever be thy chance.

THE PASSIONATE SHEPHERD TO HIS LOVE.

Marlowe.

Come, live with me, and be my love,
And we will all the pleasures prove
That valleys, groves, or hill or field,
Or woods and steepy mountains yield;

Where we will sit upon the rocks,
And see the shepherds feed their flocks,
By shallow rivers, to whose falls
Melodious birds sing madrigals.

And I will make thee beds of roses,
And then a thousand fragrant posies,
A cap of flowers, and a kirtle,
Embroidered all with leaves of myrtle;

.. gown made of the finest wool,
Which from our pretty lambs we pull;
Slippers, lined choicely for the cold,
With buckles of the purest gold.

A belt of straw and ivy-buds,
With coral clasps and amber studs:
And if these pleasures may thee move,
Come live with me and be my love.

Thy silver dishes, for thy meat,
As precious as the gods do eat,
Shall, on an ivory table, be
Prepared each day for thee and me.

The shepherd swains will dance and sing
For thy delight each May morning,
If these delights thy mind may move,
Come live with me and be my love.

I'LL NEVER LOVE THEE MORE.

Marquis of Montrose.

My dear and only love, I pray
  That little world of thee
Be governed by no other sway
  But purest monarchy:
For if confusion have a part,
  Which virtuous souls abhor,
I'll call a synod in my heart,
  And never love thee more.

As Alexander I will reign.
  And I will reign alone;
My thoughts did ever more disdain
  A rival on my throne.
He either fears his fate too much,
  Or his deserts are small,
Who dares not put it to the touch,
  To gain or lose it all.

But I will reign and govern still,
  And always give the law,
And have each subject at my will,
  And all to stand in awe;
But 'gainst my batteries if I find
  Thou storm or vex me sore,
As if thou set me as a blind,
  I'll never love thee more.

And in the empire of thy heart,
  Where I should solely be,
If others do pretend a part,
  Or dare to share with me:
Or committees if thou erect,
  Or go on such a score,
I'll smiling mock at thy neglect,
  And never love thee more.

But if no faithless action stain
  Thy love and constant word,
I'll make thee famous by my pen,
  And glorious by my sword.
I'll serve thee in such noble ways
  As ne'er was known before:
I'll deck and crown thy head with bays,
  And love thee more and more.

LOVE ME LITTLE—LOVE ME LONG.

Love me little, love me long,
Is the burden of my song,
Love that is too hot and strong
    Burneth soon to waste.
Still I would not have thee cold,
Not too backward or too bold:
Love that lasteth till 'tis old
    Fadeth not in haste.

If thou lovest me too much,
It will not prove as true as touch;
Love me little, more than such,
    For I fear the end.
I am with little well content,
And a little from thee sent
Is enough with true intent,
    To be steadfast friend.

Say thou lov'st me while thou live,
I to thee my love will give,
Never dreaming to deceive
    While that life endures.
Nay, and after death in sooth,
I to thee will keep my truth,
As now when in my may of youth,
    This my love assures.

Constant love is moderate ever,
And it will through life persever;
Give me that, with true endeavour
    I will it restore.
A suit of durance let it be,
For all weathers, that for me,
For the land or for the sea,
    Lasting evermore.

Winter's cold or summer's heat,
Autumn's tempests on it beat,
It can never know defeat,
    Never can rebel.
Such the love that I would gain,
Such the love I tell thee plain,
Thou must give or woo in vain;
    So to thee farewell.

TRUE LOVE.

Richard Sharp.

True love wealth cannot buy—vice never knows;
Pure are the countless sources whence it flows;
From faith long tried, from lives that blend in one
From many a soft word spoken, kind deed done,
Too small, perhaps, for each to have a name,
Too oft recurring much regard to claim;
As in fair constellations may combine
The stars that, singly undistinguished shine.
Love, too, is proud, and will not be controlled;
Timid, and must be rather guessed than told;
Would be divined, but then by only one,
And fain the notice of all else would shun.
It stays not to forgive; it cannot see
The failings from which none, alas! are free;
Blind but to faults, quick sighted to descry
Merit oft hid from a less searching eye;
Ever less prone to doubt than to believe;
Ever more glad to give than to receive:
Constant as kind, though changing nature, name;
Many, yet one; another, yet the same:
'Tis Friendship, Pity, Joy, Grief, Hope, nay Fear;
Not the least tender when in form severe.
It dwells with every rank, in every clime,
And sets at naught the malice e'en of Time!
In youth more rapturous, but in age more sure,
Chief blessing of the rich—sole comfort of the poor.

LOVE.

Robert Southey.

They sin who tell love can die:
With all other passions fly,
All others are but vanity.
In Heaven ambition cannot dwell,
Nor avarice in the vaults of Hell;
Earthly these passions, as of Earth,
They perish where they have their birth.
  But Love is indestructible;
Its holy flame for ever burneth,
From Heaven it came, to Heaven returneth.
Too oft on earth a troubled guest,
At times deceived, at times opprest;
  It here is tried and purified,
And hath in Heaven its perfect rest.
It soweth here with toil and care,
But the harvest time of love is there
Oh! when a mother meets on high
The babe she lost in infancy,
Hath she not then for pains and fears,
  The day of woe, the anxious night,
For all her sorrow, all her tears,
  An over-payment of delight!

MAUD MULLER.

Whittier.

MAUD MULLER, on a summer's day,
Raked the meadow sweet with hay.

Beneath her torn hat glowed the wealth
Of simple beauty and rustic health.

Singing, she wrought, and her merry glee
The mock-bird echoed from his tree.

But, when she glanced to the far-off town,
White from its hill-slope looking down,

The sweet song died, and a vague unrest
And a nameless longing filled her breast—

A wish, that she hardly dared to own,
For something better than she had known.

The Judge rode slowly down the lane,
Smoothing his horse's chestnut mane.

He drew his bridle in the shade
Of the apple trees, to greet the maid,

And asked a draught from the spring that flowed
Through the meadows across the road.

She stooped where the cool spring bubbled up,
And filled for him her small tin cup,

And blushed as she gave it, looking down
On her feet so bare, and her tattered gown.

"Thanks!" said the Judge, "a sweeter draught
From a fairer hand was never quaffed."

He spoke of the grass, and flowers and trees,
Of the singing birds and the humming bees;

Then talked of the haying, and wondered whether
The cloud in the west would bring foul weather.

And Maud forgot her briar-torn gown;
Her graceful ankles bare and brown;

And listened, while a pleased surprise
Looked from her long-lashed hazel eyes.

At last, like one who for delay
Seeks a vain excuse, he rode away.

Maud Müller looked and sighed: "Ah, me!
That I the Judge's bride might be!

"He would dress me up in silks so fine,
And praise and toast me at his wine.

"My father should wear a broadcloth coat,
My brother should sail a painted boat.

"I'd dress my mother so grand and gay,
And the baby should have a new toy each day.

"And I'd feed the hungry, and clothe the poor,
And all should bless me who left our door."

The Judge looked back as he climbed the hill,
And saw Maud Müller standing still.

"A form more fair, a face more sweet,
Ne'er hath it been my lot to meet.

"And her modest answer and graceful air,
Show her wise and good as she is fair.

"Would she were mine, and I to-day,
Like her a harvester of hay:

"No doubtful balance of rights and wrongs
And weary lawyers with endless tongues.

"But low of cattle and song of birds,
And health of quiet and loving words."

But he thought of his sisters, proud and cold,
And his mother, vain of her rank and gold.

So closing his heart, the Judge rode on,
And Maud was left in the field alone.

But the lawyers smiled that afternoon.
When he hummed in court an old love tune;

And the young girl mused beside the well,
Till the rain on the unraked clover fell.

He wedded a wife of richest dower,
Who lived for fashion as he for power.

Yet oft in his marble hearth's bright glow
He watched a picture come and go.

And sweet Maud Müller's hazel eyes
Looked out in their innocent surprise.

Oft when the wine in his glass was red,
He longed for the wayside well instead;

And closed his eyes on his garnished rooms,
To dream of meadows and clover blooms.

And the proud man sighed with a secret pain:
"Ah, that I were free again!

"Free as when I rode that day,
Where the barefoot maiden raked her hay."

She wedded a man unlearned and poor,
And many children played round her door.

But care and sorrow, and child-birth pain
Left their traces on heart and brain,

And oft when the summer sun shines hot
On the new-mown hay in the meadow lot,

And she heard the little spring-brook fall
Over the roadside, through the wall,

In the shade of the apple-tree again
She saw a rider draw his rein:

And, gazing down with timid grace,
She felt his pleased eyes read her face.

Sometimes her narrow kitchen walls
Stretched away into stately halls,

The weary wheel to a spinnet turned,
The tallow candle an astral burned,

And for him who sat by the chimney lug.
Dozing and grumbling o'er pipe and mug,

A manly form at her side she saw,
And joy was duty, and love was law,

Then she took up her burden of life again,
Saying only, "It might have been!"

Alas! for maiden, alas! for Judge,
For rich repiner and household drudge!

God pity them both! and pity us all,
Who vainly the dreams of youth recall,

For of all sad words of tongue or pen,
The saddest are these: "It might have been!"

Ah, well! for us some sweet hope lies
Deeply buried from human eyes;

And, in the hereafter, angels may
Roll the stone from its grave away!

GENEVIEVE.

Coleridge.

All thoughts, all passions, all delights,
Whatever stirs this mortal frame,
All are but ministers of Love,
And feed his sacred flame.

Oft in my waking dreams do I
Live o'er again that happy hour,
When midway on the mount I lay,
Beside the ruined tower.

The moonshine, stealing o'er the scene,
Had blended with the lights of eve;
And she was there, my hope, my joy,
My own dear Genevieve.

She leaned against the armèd man,
The statue of the armed knight;
She stood and listened to my lay,
Amid the lingering light.

Few sorrows hath she of her own,
My hope! my joy! my Genevieve!
She loves me best whene'er I sing
The songs that make her grieve.

I played a soft and doleful air,
I sang an old and moving story—
An old rude song that suited well
That ruin wild and hoary.

She listened with a flitting blush,
With downcast eyes and modest grace;
For well she knew I could not choose
But gaze upon her face.

I told her of the knight that wore
Upon his shield a burning brand;
And that for ten long years he wooed
The Lady of the Land.

I told her how he pined: and ah!
The deep, the low, the pleading tone
With which I sang another's love
Interpreted my own.

She listened with a flitting blush,
With downcast eyes, and modest grace;
And she forgave me that I gazed
Too fondly on her face?

But when I told the cruel scorn
That crazed that bold and lovely knight
And that he crossed the mountain woods,
Nor rested day nor night;

That sometimes from the savage den,
And sometimes from the darksome shade,
And sometimes starting up at once
In green and sunny glade,—

Then came and looked him in the face
An angel beautiful and bright;
And that he knew it was a fiend;
This miserable knight!

And that, unknowing what he did,
He leaped amid a murderous band,
And saved from outrage worse than death
The Lady of the Land.

And how she wept and clasped his knees;
And how she tended him in vain—
And ever strove to expiate
The scorn that crazed his brain;—

And that she nursed him in a cave;
And how his madness went away,
When on the yellow forest-leaves
A dying man he lay;—

His dying words—but when I reached
That tenderest strain of all the ditty,
My faltering voice and pausing harp
Disturbed her soul with pity.

All impulses of soul and sense
Had thrilled my guileless Genevieve:
The music and the doleful tale,
The rich and balmy eve;

And hopes and fears that kindle hope,
An undistinguishable throng,
And gentle wishes long subdued,
Subdued and cherished long.

She wept with pity and delight,
She blushed with love and virgin shame,
And like the murmur of a dream,
I heard her breathe my name;

Her bosom heaved—she stepped aside,
As conscious of my looks she stept—
Then suddenly, with timorous eye
She fled to me and wept.

She half enclosed me with her arms,
She pressed me with a meek embrace;
And, bending back her head, looked up,
And gazed upon my face.

'Twas partly love and partly fear,
And partly 'twas a bashful art,
That I might rather feel than see
The swelling of heart.

I calmed her fears, and she was calm,
And told her love with virgin pride;
And so I won my Genevieve,
My bright and beauteous bride.

HER LETTER.

Bret Harte.

I'M sitting alone by the fire,
  Dressed just as I came from the dance,
In a robe even *you* would admire—
  It cost a cool thousand in France;
I'm bediamonded out of all reason,
  My hair is done up in a cue:
In short, sir, "the belle of the season"
  Is wasting an hour upon you.

A dozen engagements I've broken;
  I left in the midst of a set;
Likewise a proposal half spoken,
  That waits—on the stairs—for me yet.
They say he'll be rich—when he grows up—
  And then he adores me indeed,
And you, sir, are turning your nose up,
  Three thousand miles off, as you read.

"And how do I like my position?"
  "And what do I think of New York?"
"And now, in my higher ambition,
  With whom do I waltz, flirt, or talk?"
"And isn't it nice to have riches;
  And diamonds, and silks, and all that?"
"And isn't it a change to the ditches
  And tunnels of Poverty Flat?"

Well, yes—if you saw us out driving
  Each day in the park, four in hand—
If you saw poor dear mamma contriving
  To look supernaturally grand—
If you saw papa's picture, as taken
  By Brady, and tinted at that—
You'd never suspect he sold bacon
  And flour at Poverty Flat.

And yet, just this moment, when sitting
  In the glare of the grand chandelier—
In the bustle and glitter befitting
  The "finest *soirée* of the year,"
In the midst of a *gaze de Chambery*,
  And the hum of the smallest of talk—
Somehow, Joe, I thought of the "Ferry,"
  And the dance that we had on "The Fork."

Of Harrison's barn with its muster
  Of flags festooned over the wall;
Of the candles that shed their soft lustre,
  And tallow on head-dress and shawl;
Of the steps that we took to one fiddle;
  Of the dress of my queer *vis-à-vis*;
And how I once went down the middle
  With the man that shot Sandy McGee;

Of the moon that was quietly sleeping
  On the hill when the time came to go;
Of the few baby peaks that were peeping
  From under their bedclothes of snow;
Of that ride—that to me was the rarest;
  Of—the something you said at the gate;
Ah, Joe, then I wasn't an heiress
  To "the best-paying lead in the State."

Well, well, it's all past; yet it's funny
  To think, as I stood in the glare
Of fashion and beauty and money,
  That I should be thinking, right there,
Of some one who breasted high water,
  And swam the North Fork, and all that,
Just to dance with old Folinsbee's daughter,
  The lily of Poverty Flat.

But goodness! what nonsense I'm writing!
  (Mamma says my taste still is low);
Instead of my triumphs reciting,
  I'm spooning on Joseph—heigh-ho!
And I'm to be "finished" by travel—
  Whatever's the meaning of that?
Oh, why did papa strike pay gravel
  In drifting on Poverty Flat!

Good night! here's the end of my paper;
  Good night! if the longitude please—
For maybe, whilst wasting my taper,
  Your sun's climbing over the trees,
But know, if you haven't got riches,
  And are poor, dearest Joe, and all that,
That my heart's somewhere there in the ditches,
  And you've struck it—on Poverty Flat.

Poems about Devoted Love.

FAITHFUL.

Rose Terry Cooke.

A LONG bare ward in the hospital;
  A dying girl in the narrow bed;
A nurse whose footsteps lightly fall,
  Soothing softly that restless head.

Slain by the man she learned to love,
  Beaten, murdered, and flung away;
None beheld it but God above,
  And she who bore it. And there she lay.

"A little drink of water, dear?"
  Slowly the white lips gasp and sip,
"Let me turn you over, so you can hear,
  While I let the ice on your temple drip."

A look of terror disturbs her face;
  Firm and silent those pale lips close;
A stranger stands in the nurse's place;
  "Tell us who hurt you, for no one knows."

A glitter of joy is in her eye;
  Faintly she whispers, "Nobody did."
And one tear christens the loving lie
  From the heart in that wounded bosom hid.

"Nobody did it," she says again,
  "Nobody hurt me!" her eyes grow dim;
But in that spasm of mortal pain,
  She says to herself, "I've saved you, Jim!"

Day by day, as the end draws near,
  To gentle question or stern demand,
Only that one response they hear,
  Though she lift to heaven her wasted hand.

"Nobody hurt me!" they see her die.
  The same word still on her latest breath:
With a tranquil smile she tells her lie,
  And glad goes down to the gates of death.

Beaten, murdered, but faithful still,
  Loving above all wrong and woe,
If she has gone to a world of ill,
  Where, oh! saint, shall we others go?

Even I think that evil man
  Has hope of a better life in him,
When she so loved him her last words ran,
  "Nobody hurt me! I've saved you, Jim!"

THE DEVOTED.

STERN faces were around her bent,
  And eyes of vengeful ire.
And fearful were the words they spake,
  Of torture, stake and fire;
Yet calmly in the midst she stood,
  With eye undimmed and clear,
And though her lip and cheek were white,
  She wore no signs of fear.

"Where is thy traitor spouse?" they said:
  A half formed smile of scorn,
That curled upon her haughty lip,
  Was back for answer borne;
"Where is thy traitor spouse?" again,
  In fiercer tones they said,
And sternly pointed to the rack,
  All rusted o'er with red!

Her heart and pulse beat firm and free—
  But in a crimson flood
O'er pallid lip, and cheek, and brow,
  Rushed up the burning blood;
She spake, but proudly rose her tones,
  As when in hall or bower,
The haughtiest chief that round her stood
  Had meekly owned their power.

"My noble lord is placed within—
  A safe and sure retreat"—
"Now tell us where, thou lady bright:
  As thou wouldst mercy meet,
Nor deem thy life can purchase his;
  He cannot 'scape our wrath,
For many a warrior's watchful eye
  Is placed o'er every path.

"But thou may'st win his broad estates,
  To grace thine infant heir,
And life and honour to thyself,
  So thou his haunts declare."
She laid her hand upon her heart,
  Her eye flashed proud and clear,
And firmer grew her haughty tread—
  "My lord is hidden *here!*

"And if ye seek to view his form,
  Ye first must tear away,
From round his secret dwelling-place
  These walls of living clay!"
They quailed beneath her haughty glance,
  They silent turned aside,
And left her all unharmed amidst
  Her loveliness and pride.

EDWIN AND EMMA.

Mallet.

Far in the windings of a vale,
  Fast by a shelt'ring wood,
The safe retreat of health and peace,
  A humble cottage stood.

There beauteous Emma flourish'd fair
  Beneath her mother's eye,
Whose only wish on earth was now
  To see her blest, and die.

The softest blush that nature spreads
  Gave colour to her cheek;
Such orient colour smiles through Heav'n
  When May's sweet mornings break.

Nor let the pride of great ones scorn
  The charmers of the plains;
That sun which bids their diamonds blaze
  To deck our lily deigns.

Long had she fired each youth with love,
  Each maiden with despair,
And though by all a wonder own'd,
  Yet knew not she was fair;

Till Edwin came, the pride of swains,
  A soul that knew no art;
And from whose eyes, serenely mild,
  Shone forth the feeling heart.

A mutual flame was quickly caught,
  Was quickly too reveal'd,
For neither bosom lodged a wish
  Which virtue keeps conceal'd.

What happy hours of heartfelt bliss
  Did love on both bestow!
But bliss too mighty long to last,
  Where fortune proves a foe.

His sister, who, like Envy form'd,
  Like her in mischief joy'd,
To work them harm with wicked skill
  Each darker art employ'd.

The father, too, a sordid man,
  Who love nor pity knew,
Was all unfeeling as the rock
  From whence his riches grew.

Long had he seen their mutual flame,
  And seen it long unmoved;
Then with a father's frown at last
  He sternly disapproved.

In Edwin's gentle heart a war
  Of diff'ring passions strove;
His heart, which durst not disobey,
  Yet could not cease to love.

Denied her sight, he oft behind
  The spreading hawthorn crept,
To snatch a glance, to mark the spot
  Where Emma walk'd and wept.

Oft, too, in Stanemore's wintry waste,
  Beneath the moonlight shade,
In sighs to pour his softened soul,
  The midnight mourner stray'd.

His cheeks, where love with beauty glow'd,
  A deadly pale o'ercast;
So fades the fresh rose in its prime
  Before the northern blast.

The parents now with late remorse
  Hung o'er his dying bed,
And wearied Heav'n with fruitless pray'rs,
  And fruitless sorrows shed.

"'Tis past," he cried, "but if your souls
  Sweet mercy yet can move,
Let these dim eyes once more behold
  What they must ever love."

She came; his cold hand softly touch'd,
  And bathed with many a tear.
Fast falling o'er the primrose pale,
  So morning dews appear.

But oh, his sister's jealous care,
  (A cruel sister, she!)
Forbade what Emma came to say,
  "My Edwin, live for me."

Now homeward as she hopeless went,
  The churchyard path along,
The blast blew cold, the dark owl scream'd
  Her lover's fun'ral song.

Amid the falling gloom of night,
  Her startling fancy found
In ev'ry bush his hov'ring shade,
  His groan in ev'ry sound.

Alone, appall'd, thus had she pass'd
  The visionary vale,
When lo! the death-bell smote her ear,
  Sad sounding in the gale.

Just then she reach'd with trembling steps
  Her aged mother's door;
"He's gone," she cried, "and I shall see
  That angel face no more.

"I feel, I feel this breaking heart
  Beat high against my side!"
From her white arm down sunk her head,
  She shiver'd, sigh'd, and died.

EDWIN AND ANGELINA.

Goldsmith.

"Turn, gentle hermit of the dale,
And guide my lonely way
To where yon taper cheers the vale
With hospitable ray.

"For here forlorn and lost I tread,
With fainting steps and slow,
Where wilds, unmeasurably spread,
Seem lengthening as I go."

"Forbear, my son," the hermit cries,
"To tempt the dangerous gloom;
For yonder faithless phantom flies
To lure thee to thy doom.

"Here to the houseless child of want
My door is open still;
And though my portion is but scant,
I give it with good will.

"Then turn to night, and freely share
Whate'er my cell bestows;
My rushy couch and frugal fare,
My blessing and repose.

"No flocks that range the valley free
To slaughter I condemn.
Taught by that power that pities me,
I learn to pity them.

"But from the mountain's grassy side
A guiltless feast I bring.
A scrip with herbs and fruit supplied,
And water from the spring.

"Then, pilgrim, turn, thy cares forego,
All earth-born cares are wrong;
Man wants but little here below,
Nor wants that little long."

Soft as the dew from heaven descends,
His gentle accents fell;
The modest stranger lowly bends,
And follows to the cell.

Far in a wilderness obscure
The lonely mansion lay;
A refuge to the neighbouring poor,
And strangers led astray.

No stores beneath its humble thatch
Required a master's care;
The wicket, opening with a latch,
Received the harmless pair.

And now, when busy crowds retire
To take the evening rest,
The hermit trimmed his little fire,
And cheered his pensive guest;

And spread his vegetable store,
And gaily press'd and smiled;
And, skill'd in legendary lore,
The lingering hours beguiled.

Around in sympathetic mirth,
Its tricks the kitten tries;
The cricket chirrups in the hearth;
The crackling faggot flies.

But nothing could a charm impart
To soothe the stranger's woe;
For grief was heavy at his heart,
And tears began to flow.

His rising cares the hermit spied,
With answering care opprest.
"And whence, unhappy youth," he cried,
"The sorrows ot thy breast?

"From better habitations spurn'd,
Reluctant dost thou roam?
Or grieve for friendship unreturn'd,
Or unregarded love?

"Alas! the joys that fortune brings
Are trifling, and decay;
And those who prize the paltry things,
More trifling still than they.

"And what is friendship but a name,
A charm that lulls to sleep,
A shade that follows wealth and fame,
And leaves the wretch to weep?

"And love is still an emptier sound,
The modern fair one's jest;
On earth unseen, or only found
To warm the turtle's nest.

"For shame, fond youth! thy sorrows hush,
And spurn the sex," he said;
But while he spoke, a rising blush
His love-lorn guest betrayed.

Surprised he sees new beauties rise
Swift mantling to the view—
Like colours o'er the morning skies,
As bright, as transient too.

The bashful look, the rising breast,
Alternate spread alarms;
The lovely stranger stands confest
A maid in all her charms.

"And ah! forgive a stranger rude,
A wretch forlorn," she cried,
"Whose feet unhallowed thus intrude
Where Heaven and you reside.

"But let a maid thy pity share,
Whom love has taught to stray—
Who seeks for rest, but finds despair
Companion of her way.

"My father lived beside the Tyne,
A wealthy lord was he;
And all his wealth was marked as mine,
He had but only me.

"To win me from his tender arms
Unnumbered suitors came,
Who praised me for imputed charms,
And felt, or feigned, a flame.

"Each hour a mercenary crowd
With richest proffers strove;
Among the rest young Edwin bowed,
But never talked of love.

"In humble, simplest habit clad,
No wealth nor power had he;
Wisdom and worth were all he had—
But these were all to me.

"And when, beside me in the dale,
He carolled lays of love,
His breath lent fragrance to the gale
And music to the grove.

"The blossom opening to the day,
The dews of heaven refined,
Could nought of purity display
To emulate his mind.

"The dew, the blossom on the tree,
With charms inconstant shine;
Their charms were his; but woe is me!
Their constancy was mine.

"For still I tried each fickle art,
Importunate and vain;
And while his passion touched my heart,
I triumphed in his pain;

"Till quite dejected with my scorn,
He left me to my pride;
And sought a solitude forlorn,
In secret, where he died.

"But mine the sorrow, mine the fault,
And well my life shall pay;
I'll seek the solitude he sought,
And stretch me where he lay;

"And there, forlorn, despairing, hid,
I'll lay me down and die;
'Twas so for me that Edwin did,
And so for him will I."

"Forbid it, Heaven!" the hermit cried,
And clasped her to his breast:
The wondering fair one turned to chide—
'Twas Edwin's self that pressed!

"Turn, Angelina, ever dear!
My charmer, turn to see
Thy own, thy long-lost Edwin here,
Restored to love and thee.

"Thus let me hold thee to my heart
And every care resign;
And shall we never, never part,
My life, my all that's mine?

"No, never from this hour to part,
We'll live and love so true;
The sigh that rends thy constant heart,
Shall break thy Edwin's too."

WILLY REILLY.

Old Ballad.

"Oh! rise up, Willy Reilly, and come along with me,
I mean for to go with you and leave this counterie,
To leave my father's dwelling, his houses and free lands—"
And away goes Willy Reilly and his dear Cooleen Bawn.

They go by hills and mountains, and by yon lonesome plain,
Through shady groves and valleys all dangers to refrain;
But her father followed after with a well chosen band,
And taken was poor Reilly and his dear Cooleen Bawn.

It's home then she was taken, and in her closet bound,
Poor Reilly all in Sligo jail lay on the stony ground;
Till at the bar of justice before the Judge he'd stand,
For nothing but the stealing of his dear Cooleen Bawn.

"Now in the cold, cold iron, my hands and feet are bound,
I'm handcuffed like a murderer, and tied unto the ground;
But all this toil and slavery I'm willing for to stand,
Still hoping to be succoured by my dear Cooleen Bawn."

The jailor's son to Reilly goes, and thus to him did say,
"Oh! get up, Willy Reilly, you must appear this day,
For great Squire Folliard's anger you never can withstand;
I'm afear'd you'll suffer sorely for your dear Cooleen Bawn.

"This is the news, young Reilly, last night that I did hear,
The lady's oath will hang you, or else will set you clear."
"If that be so," says Reilly, "her pleasure I will stand,
Still hoping to be succoured by my dear Cooleen Bawn."

Now Willy's drest from top to toe all in a suit of green,
His hair hangs o'er his shoulders most glorious to be seen;
He's tall and straight and comely as any could be found.
He's fit for Folliard's daughter, was she heiress to a crown.

The Judge he said, "This lady being in her tender youth,
If Reilly has deluded her, she will declare the truth."
Then, like a moving beauty bright, before him she did stand.
"You're welcome there my heart's delight and dear Cooleen Bawn."

"Oh, gentlemen," Squire Folliard said, "with pity look on me,
This villain came amongst us to disgrace our family,
And by his base contrivances this villany was planned;
If I don't get satisfaction I will quit this Irish land."

The lady with a tear began, and thus replied she,
"The fault is none of Reilly's, the blame lies all on me;
I forced him for to leave his place and come along with me;
I loved him out of measure, which has wrought our destiny."

Then out bespoke the noble Fox, at the table he stood by,
"Oh! gentlemen, consider on this extremity,
To hang a man for love is a murder you may see,
So spare the life of Reilly, let him leave this counterie."

"Good my Lord, he stole from her her diamonds and her rings,
Gold watch and silver buckles and many precious things,
Which cost me in bright guineas, more than five hundred pounds,
I will have the life of Reilly should I lose ten thousand pounds."

"Good my Lord, I gave them him as tokens of true love;
And when we are a-parting I will them all remove;
If you have got them, Reilly, pray send them home to me;
They're poor compared to that true heart which I have given to thee.

"There is a ring among them I allow yourself to wear,
With thirty locket diamonds well set in silver fair;
And as a true love token wear it on your right hand,
That you may think on my broken heart when you're in a foreign land."

Then out spoke noble Fox, "You may let the prisoner go,
The lady's oath has cleared him, as the Jury all may know;
She has released her own true love, she has renewed his name,
May her honour bright gain high estate, and her offspring rise to fame."

IN THE MINING TOWN.

Rose Hartwick Thorpe.

"'Tis the last time, darling," he gently said,
As he kissed her lips like the cherries red,
While a fond look shone in his eyes of brown!
"My own is the prettiest girl in town!
To-morrow the bell from the tower will ring
A joyful peal. Was there ever a king
So truly blest, on his royal throne,
As I shall be when I claim my own!"

'Twas a fond farewell; 'twas a sweet good-bye,
But she watched him go with a troubled sigh,
So, into the basket that swayed and swung
O'er the yawning abyss, he lightly sprung.
And the joy of her heart seemed turned to woe
As they lowered him into the depths below,
Her sweet, young face, with its tresses brown,
Was the fairest face in the mining town.

Lo! the morning came: but the marriage bell,
High up in the tower, rang a mournful knell
For the true heart buried 'neath earth and stone,
Far down in the heart of the mine—alone.
A sorrowful peal on their wedding-day,
For the breaking heart and the heart of clay.
And the face that looked from her tresses brown
Was the saddest face in the mining town.

Thus time rolled along on its weary way,
Until fifty years, with their shadows grey,
Had darkened the light of her sweet eyes' glow,
And had turned the brown of her hair to snow.
Oh! never the kiss from the husband's lips
Or the clasps of a child's sweet finger tips
Had lifted one moment the shadows brown
From the saddest heart in the mining town.

Far down in the depths of the mine one day,
In the loosened earth they were digging away,
They discovered a face, so young, so fair;
From the smiling lip to the bright brown hair,
Untouched by the finger of Time's decay,
When they drew him up to the light of day,
The wondering people gathered 'round
To gaze at the man thus strangely found.

Then a woman came from among the crowd,
With her long white hair and her slight form bowed.
She silently knelt by the form of clay,
And kissed the lips that were cold and grey.
Then, the sad old face, with its snowy hair
On this youthful bosom lay pillowed there,
He had found her at last, his waiting bride,
And the people buried them side by side.

TWO LOVES AND A LIFE.

William Sawyer.

To the scaffold's foot she came;
Leaped her black eyes into flame,
Rose and fell her panting breast,—
There a pardon closely pressed.

She had heard her lover's doom,
Traitor death and shameful tomb,—
Heard the price upon his head,
"I will save him," she had said.

"Blue-eyed Annie loves him too,
She will weep, but Ruth will do;
Who should save him, sore distress'd,
Who but she who loves him best!"

To the scaffold now she came,
On her lips there rose his name,—
Rose, and yet in silence died,—
Annie nestled by his side.

Over Annie's face he bent,
Round her waist his fingers went:
"Wife" he called—called her "wife!"
Simple word to cost a life!

In Ruth's breast the pardon lay;
But she coldly turned away:—
"He has sealed his traitor fate,
I can love, and I can hate."

"Annie is his wife," they said.
"Be it wife, then, to the dead;
Since the dying she will mate;
I can love, and I can hate!"

"What their sin? They do but love;
Let this thought thy bosom move."
Came the jealous answer straight,—
"I can love and I can hate!"

"Mercy!" still they cried. But she,
"Who has mercy upon me?
Who? My life is desolate—
I can love, and I can hate!"

From the scaffold stairs she went,
Shouts the noonday silence rent,
All the air was quick with cries,—
"See the traitor! see, he dies!"

Back she looked, with stifled scream,
Saw the axe upswinging gleam;
All her woman's anger died.—
"From the King!" she faintly cried—

"From the King. His name—behold!"
Quick the parchment she unrolled,
Paused the axe in upward swing,—
"He is pardoned!" "Live the King!"

Glad the cry, and loud and long;
All about the scaffold throng,—
There entwining, fold in fold,
Raven tresses, locks of gold.

There against Ruth's tortured breast
Annie's tearful face is pressed.
While the white lips murmuring move—
"I can hate—but I can love!"

"CURFEW MUST NOT RING TO-NIGHT."

Rose Hartwick Thorpe.

In the time of Cromwell, a young soldier, for some offence, was condemned to die, and the time of his death was fixed "at the ringing of the curfew." Naturally, such a doom would be fearful and bitter to one in the years of his hope and prime, but to this unhappy youth death was doubly terrible, since he was soon to have been married to a beautiful lady whom he had long loved.

The lady, who loved him ardently in return, had used her utmost efforts to avert his fate, pleading with the judges, and even with Cromwell himself, but all in vain. In her despair she tried to bribe the old sexton not to ring the bell, but she found that impossible. The hour drew near for the execution. The preparations were completed. The officers of the law brought forth the prisoner, and waited, while the sun was setting, for the signal from the distant bell-tower. To the wonder of everybody it did not ring. Only one person at that moment knew why. The poor girl herself, half wild with the thought of her lover's peril, had rushed unseen up the winding stairs, and climbed the ladders into the belfry loft and seized the tongue of the bell. The old sexton was in his place, prompt to the fatal moment. He threw his weight upon the rope and the bell, obedient to his practised hand, reeled and swung to and fro in the tower. But the brave girl kept her hold, and no sound issued from the metallic lips. Again and again the sexton drew the rope, but with desperate strength the young heroine held on. Every moment made her position more and more fearful, every sway of the bell's huge weight threatened to fling her through the high tower window, but she would not let go. At last the sexton went away. Old and deaf, he had not noticed that the curfew gave no peal. The brave girl descended from the belfry, wounded and trembling. She hurried from the church to the place of execution. Cromwell himself was there, and was just sending to demand why the bell was silent. She made her appearance before him, fell at his feet, told her story, showed her hands all bruised and torn. Cromwell's eyes lit up with pity, and he cried, "Go! Your lover lives. Curfew shall not ring to-night."

Slowly England's sun was setting o'er the hill-tops far away,
Filling all the land with beauty at the close of one sad day,
And the last rays kissed the foreheads of a man and maiden fair,
He with footsteps slow and weary—she with sunny, floating hair;
He with bowed head, sad and thoughtful, she with lips all cold and white,
Struggling to keep back the murmur,—"Curfew must not ring to-night."

"Sexton," Bessie's white lips faltered, pointing to the prison old,
With its turrets tall and gloomy, with its walls dark, damp, and cold,
"I've a lover in that prison, doomed this very night to die
At the ringing of the curfew, and no earthly help is nigh!
Cromwell will not come till sunset," and her lips grew strangely white
As she breathed the husky whisper,—"Curfew must not ring to-night."

"Bessie," calmly spoke the sexton,—every word pierced her young heart
Like the piercing of an arrow, like a deadly poison dart—
"Long, long years I've rung the curfew from that gloomy, shadowed tower;
Every evening, just at sunset, it has told the twilight hour;
I have done my duty ever, tried to do it just and right,
Now I'm old I still must do it; curfew, it must ring to-night."

Wild her eyes and pale her features, stern and white her thoughtful brow,
And within her secret bosom Bessie made a solemn vow.
She had listened while the judges read without a tear or sigh,
"At the ringing of the curfew Basil Underwood must die."
And her breath came fast and faster, and her eyes grew large and bright;
In an undertone she murmured, "Curfew must not ring to-night."

She with quick steps bounded forward, sprang within the old church door,
Left the old man threading slowly paths so oft he'd trod before.
Not a moment paused the maiden, but with eye and cheek aglow
Mounted up the gloomy tower, where the bell swung to and fro,
As she climbed the dusty ladder on which fell no ray of light—
Up and up, her white lips saying, "Curfew shall not ring to-night."

She has reached the topmost ladder; o'er her hangs the great dark bell;
Awful is the gloom beneath her, like the pathway down to hell!
Lo! the ponderous tongue is swinging, 'tis the hour of curfew now,
And the sight has chilled her bosom, stopped her breath, and paled her brow.
Shall she let it ring? No, never! flash her eyes with sudden light,
And she springs and grasps it firmly—"Curfew shall not ring to-night."

Out she swung, far out—the city seemed a speck of light below,
'Twixt Heaven and earth her form suspended, as the bell swung to and fro!
And the sexton at the bell-rope, old and deaf, heard not the bell,
But he thought it still was ringing fair young Basil's funeral knell.
Still the maiden clung more firmly, and with trembling lips and white,
Said, to hush her heart's wild beating, "Curfew shall not ring to-night."

It was o'er; the bell ceased swaying; and the maiden stepped once more
Firmly on the dark old ladder, where for a hundred years before
Human foot had not been planted. The brave deed that she had done
Should be told long ages after, as the rays of setting sun
Should illume the sky with beauty; aged sires, with heads of white,
Long should tell the little children curfew did not ring that night.

O'er the distant hills came Cromwell; Bessie sees him, and her brow,
Full of hope and full of gladness, has no anxious traces now.
At his feet she tells her story, shows her hands all bruised and torn;
And her face, so sweet and pleading, yet with sorrow pale and worn,
Touched his heart with sudden pity, lit his eye with misty light:
"Go! your lover lives," said Cromwell; "Curfew shall not ring to-night."

THE WITTY WIVES OF WEINSBERG.

Burger.

WHICH way to Weinsberg? Neighbour, say!
'Tis sure a famous city.
It must have cradled in its day,
Full many a maid of noble clay,
And matrons, wise and witty;
And if ever marriage should happen to me,
A Weinsberg dame my wife shall be.

King Conrad once, historians say,
Fell out with this good city.
So down he came, one luckless day—
Horse, foot, dragoons, in stern array—
And cannon—more's the pity!
Around the walls the artillery roared,
And bursting bombs their fury poured.

But nought the little town could scare;—
Then, red with indignation,
He bade the herald straight repair
Up to the gates and thunder there
The following proclamation:
"Rascals! when I your town do take,
No living thing shall save its neck!"

Now when the herald's trumpet sent
These tidings through the city,
To every house the death-knell went;
Such murder-cries the hot air rent
Might move the stones to pity.
Then bread grew dear; but good advice
Could not be had for any price.

Yet oft when counsel, deed, and prayer
Had all proved unavailing;
When hope hung trembling on a hair,
How oft has woman's wit been there,
A refuge never failing!
For woman's wit and papal fraud
Of olden time were famed abroad.

A youthful dame; praised be her name
Last night had seen her plighted:
Whether in waking hour or dream
Conceived a rare and novel scheme
Which all the town delighted;
Which you, if you think otherwise,
Have leave to laugh at and despise.

At midnight hour, when culverin
And gun and bomb were sleeping,
Before the camp, with mournful mien,
The loveliest embassy were seen
All kneeling low and weeping.
So sweetly plaintively they prayed,
But no reply save this was made:

"The women have free leave to go,
Each with her choicest treasure,
But let the knaves their husbands know
That unto them the King will show
The weight of his displeasure."
With these sad terms the lovely train
Stole weeping from the camp again.

But when the morning gilt the sky,
What happened? Give attention:
The city gates wide open fly,
And all the wives came trudging by,
Each bearing—need I mention?—
Her own dear husband on her back,
All snugly seated in a sack.

Full many a sprig of court, the joke
Not relishing, protested,
And urged the king; but Conrad spoke—
"A monarch's word must not be broke,"
And there the matter rested.
"Bravo!" he cried, "ha, ha! Bravo!
Our lady guessed it would be so."

JEANIE MORRISON.

William Motherwell.

I'VE wander'd east, I've wander'd west,
Through mony a weary way;
But never, never, can forget
The luve o' life's young day
The fire that's blawn on Beltane e'en,
May weel be black gin Yule;
But blacker fa' awaits the heart
Where first fond love grows cule.

O dear, dear Jeanie Morrison,
The thochts o' bygane years
Still fling their shadows ower my path
And blind my e'en wi' tears:
They blind my e'en wi' saut, saut tears,
And sair and sick I pine,
As memory idly summons up
The blithe blinks of o' langsyne.

'Twas then we luvit ilk ither weel;
'Twas then we 'swa did part;
Sweet time—sad time! twa bairns at schule,
Twa bairns, and but ae heart!
'Twas then we sat on a laigh bink,
To lier ilk ither lear;
And tones, and looks and smiles, were shed,
Remember'd ever mair.

I wonder, Jeanie, often yet,
When sitting on that bink,
Cheek touchin' cheek, loof lock'd in loof,
What our wee heads could think?
When baith went doun ower ae braid page
Wi' ae buik on our knee,
Thy lips were on thy lesson; but
My lesson was in thee.

Oh mind ye how we hung our heads,
How cheeks brent red wi' shame,
Whene'er the schule-weins, laughin' said,
We cleek'd together hame?
And mind ye o' the Saturdays,
(The school then skail't at noon)
When we ran aff to speel the brae,—
The broomy braes o' June?

My head rins round and round about,
My heart flows like a sea,
As ane by ane the thochts rush back
O' schule time and o' thee.
Oh, mornin' life! Oh, mornin' luve!
Oh, lichtsome days and lang,
When hinnied hopes around our hearts,
Like simmer blossoms sprang.

O mind ye, luve, how aft we left
The deavin' dinsome toun,
To wander by the green burnside,
And hear the water croon;
The simmer leaves hung ower our heads,
The flowers burst round our feet,
And in the gloamin' o' the wud
The throssil whusslit sweet.

The throssil whusslit in the wud,
The burn sung to the trees,
And we, with Nature's heart in tune,
Concerted harmonies;
And on the knowe abune the burn,
For hours thegither sat
In the silentness o' joy, till baith
Wi' very gladness grat!

Aye, aye, dear Jeanie Morrison.
Tears trinkled down your cheek,
Like dew beads on a rose, yet nane
Had ony power to speak.
That was a time, a blessed time,
When hearts were fresh and young,
When freely gushed all feelings forth,
Unsyllabled—unsung!

I marvel, Jeanie Morrison,
Gin I ha'e been to thee
As closely twined wi' earliest thochts
As ye ha'e been to me?
Oh! tell me gin their music fills
Thine ear as it does mine;
Oh! say gin o'er your heart grows grit
Wi' dreamings o' langsyne?

I've wandered east, I've wandered west,
I've borne a weary lot;
But in my wanderings far or near,
Ye never were forgot.
The fount that first burst frae this heart,
Still travels on its way;
And channels deeper as it rins
The luve o' life's young day.

O dear, dear Jeanie Morrison,
Since we were sinder'd young,
I've never seen your face, nor heard
The music o' your tongue;
But I could hug all wretchedness,
And happy could I die,
Did I but ken your heart still dream'd
O' bygane days and me!

TO MARY IN HEAVEN.

This has been generally esteemed as the most BEAUTIFUL of the lyrics of ROBERT BURNS.

THOU lingering star with lessening ray,
  That lov'st to greet the early morn,
Again thou usherest in the day
  My Mary from my soul was torn.
Oh, Mary! dear departed shade!
  Where is thy place of blissful rest?
See'st thou thy lover lowly laid?
  Hear'st thou the groans that rend his breast?

That sacred hour can I forget?
  Can I forget the hallowed grove
Where by the winding Ayr we met
  To live one day of parting love?
Eternity will not efface
  Those records dear of transports past!
Thy image at our last embrace—
  Ah! little thought we 'twas our last;

Ayr, gurgling, kiss'd his pebbled shore,
  O'erhung with wild woods thickening green,
The fragment birch, and hawthorn hoar,
  Twined amorous round the raptured scene.
The flowers sprung wanton to be press'd,
  The birds sung love on every spray,
Till too, too soon, the glowing west
  Proclaim'd the speed of wingèd day.

Still o'er these scenes my memory wakes,
  And fondly broods with miser care;
Time but the impression deeper makes,
  As streams their channels deeper wear.
My Mary! dear departed shade!
  Where is thy place of blissful rest?
See'st thou thy lover lowly laid?
  Hear'st thou the groans that rend his breast?

THE DEATH OF MARY.

Charles Wolfe

IF thou wouldst stay, e'en as thou art,
  All cold and all serene,
I still might press thy silent heart,
  And where thy smile has been,

While e'en thy chill bleak corse I have,
  Thou seemest still mine own,
But there—I lay thee in the grave,
  And now—I am alone.

I do not think where'er thou art,
  Thou hast forgotten me;
And I perhaps may soothe this heart
  In thinking still of thee!

Yet there was round thee such a dawn,
  Of light ne'er seen before,
As fancy never could have drawn,
  And never can restore.

If I had thought thou could'st have died,
  I might not weep for thee;
But I forgot, when by thy side,
  That thou could'st mortal be:

It never through my mind had pass'd,
  That time would e'er be o'er—
When I on thee should look my last,
  And thou should'st smile no more.

And still upon that face I look,
  And think 'twill smile again;
And still the thought I will not brook,
  That I must look in vain;

But when I speak thou dost not say
  What thou ne'er left'st unsaid;
And now I feel, as well I may,
  Sweet Mary, thou art dead.

THE DAY WHEN YOU'LL FORGET ME.

Morgan.

You call me sweet and tender names,
  And softly smoothe my tresses,
And all the while my happy heart
  Beats time to your caresses.
You love me in your tender way
  I answer as you let me,
But, ah! there comes another day,
  The day when you'll forget me.

I know that ev'ry fleeting hour
  Is marked by thoughts I bring you,
I know there dwells a subtle pow'r
  In the sweet songs I sing you.
I do not fear the darkest way
  With those dear arms about me;
Ah, no! I only dread the day
  When you can live without me.

And still you call me tender names,
  And softly smoothe my tresses,
And still my happy answ'ring heart
  Beats time to your caresses.
Hush! let me put that touch away,
  And clasp your hands above me,
So, while I ask to die that day,
  The day you will not love me.

You need not check the thoughts that rise
  With darkness wrapt about them,
For, gazing in your earnest eyes,
  My heart can almost doubt them.
Yet, hush my whispers as you may,
  Such chidings do not fret me;
Ah, no! I only fear that day,
  The day when you'll forget me.

FORGET THEE!

Rev. John Moultrie.

"FORGET thee!"—If to dream by night, and muse on thee by day,
If all the worship deep and wild a poet's heart can pay,
If prayers in absence, breathed for thee to Heaven's protecting power,
If wingèd thoughts that flit to thee, a thousand in an hour,
If busy Fancy blending thee with all my future lot—
If this thou call'st "forgetting," thou indeed shalt be forgot!

"Forget thee!"—Bid the forest birds forget their sweetest tune!
"Forget thee!"—Bid the sea forget to swell beneath the moon;
Bid the thirsty flowers forget to drink the eve's refreshing dew;
Thyself forget thine own dear land" and its "mountains wild and blue,"
Forget each old familiar face, each long remember'd spot—
When these things are forgot by thee, then thou shalt be forgot!

Keep, if thou wilt, thy maiden peace still calm and fancy free;
For God forbid thy gladsome heart should grow less glad for me:
Yet, while that heart is still unwon, oh, bid not mine to rove,
But let it muse its humble faith and uncomplaining love:
If these preserved for patient years at last avail me not,
Forget me then;—but ne'er believe that thou canst be forgot!

COLIN AND LUCY.

Tickell.

Of Leinster, famed for maidens fair,
Bright Lucy was the grace;
Nor e'er did Liffey's limpid stream
Reflect so fair a face.

Till luckless love and pining care
Impair'd her rosy hue,
Her coral lip, and damask cheek.
And eyes of glossy blue.

Oh! have you seen a lily pale,
When beating rains descend?
So droop'd the slow-consuming maid;
Her life now near its end.

By Lucy warn'd of flattering swains
Take heed, ye easy fair;
Of vengeance due to broken vows,
Ye perjured swains beware.

Three times all in the dead of night,
A bell was heard to ring;
And at her window, shrieking thrice,
The raven flapp'd his wing.

Too well the love-lorn maiden knew
The solemn boding sound;
And thus, in dying words, bespoke
The virgins weeping round:

"I hear a voice you cannot hear,
Which says, I must not stay:
I see a hand you cannot see,
Which beckons me away.

"By a false heart, and broken vows,
In early youth I die.
Am I to blame, because his bride
Is thrice as rich as I?

"Ah, Colin! give not her thy vows;
Vows due to me alone:
Nor thou, fond maid, receive his kiss,
Nor think him all thy own.

"To-morrow in the church to wed,
Impatient, both prepare;
But know, fond maid, and know, false man,
That Lucy will be there.

"Then, bear my corse, ye comrades, bear,
The bridegroom blithe to meet;
He in his wedding trim so gay,
I in my winding-sheet."

She spoke, she died;—her corse was borne,
The bridegroom blithe to meet;
He in his wedding-trim so gay,
She in her winding-sheet.

Then what were perjured Colin's thoughts?
How were those nuptials kept?
The bride-men flocked round Lucy dead,
And all the village wept.

Confusion, shame, remorse, despair,
At once his bosom swell:
The damps of death bedew'd his brow,
He shook, he groaned, he fell.

From the vain bride (ah, bride no more!)
The varying crimson fled,
When stretched before her rival's corse,
She saw her husband dead.

Then to his Lucy's new-made grave,
Convey'd by trembling swains,
One mould with her, beneath one sod,
For ever he remains.

Oft at their grave the constant hind
And plighted maid are seen;
With garlands gay, and true-love knots,
They deck the sacred green.

But, swain forsworn, whoe'er thou art,
This hallow'd spot forbear;
Remember Colin's dreadful fate,
And fear to meet him there.

Poems about Proposing.

A WOMAN'S ANSWER.

Selected by Mrs. E. W. Cole.

Do you know you have asked for the costliest thing
E'er made by the hand above ?
A woman's heart and a woman's life,
And a woman's wonderful love ?

Do you know you have asked for this priceless thing
As a child might ask for a toy ?
Demanding what others have died to win,
With the reckless dash of a boy ?

You have written my lesson of duty out ;
Manlike you have questioned me ;
Now stand at the bar of my woman's soul,
Until I shall question thee.

You require your mutton shall always be hot,
Your socks and your shirts be whole ;
I require your heart to be true as God's stars,
And as true as His Heaven your soul.

You require a cook for your mutton and beef ;
I require a far greater thing ;
A seamstress you're wanting for socks and for shirts,
I look for a man and a king.

A king for the beautiful realm called home,
A man that the Maker, God.
Shall look upon as he did on the first,
And say " It is very good."

I am fair and young, but the rose will fade
From my soft young cheek one day :
Will you love me then, 'mid the falling leaves,
As you did 'mid the blooms of May ?

Is your heart an ocean so strong and deep,
I may launch my all on its side ?
A loving woman finds heaven or hell
On the day she becomes a bride.

I require all the things that are grand and true,
All things that a man should be ;
If you give this all I would stake my life
To be all you demand of me.

If you cannot be this, a laundress and cook
You can hire, and a little to pay ;
But a woman's heart and a woman's life
Are not to be won in that way.

Poems about Marriage.

THE FORCED BRIDAL.

I saw her on the bridal night:
  Rich jewels decked her hair;
But in her eye—once sparkling bright—
  I marked a yearning care.
Before the altar, side by side,
  Without a smile or word,
They stood—the bridegroom and the bride—
  The victim and her lord!

Upon her cold and pallid brow
  There hung a single gem;
It needed but her passive vow
  To gain a diadem!
That vow was uttered—still the bride
  Before the altar stands;
With heightened form and seeming pride,
  She listens to the banns.

Her hair fell o'er her angel face,
  In glowing wreaths of jet;
Upon her head, her lord would place
  His jewelled coronet.
Why shrank he back? A stolid look
  His guilty eye did meet;
He gazed—the tightened heart-strings broke—
  A corpse was at his feet!

In haste around the prostrate bride
  Her lord's attendants crowd,
And scores of friends are at her side
  With notes of pity loud.
They loose her robe—the star has set!
  Her shining locks they part—
Her temples chafe—but all too late—
  The wound's A BROKEN HEART!

WIDOW AT HER DAUGHTER'S BRIDAL.

L. H. Sigourney.

Deal gently thou, whose hand hath won
  The young bird from its nest away.
Where careless, 'neath the vernal sun,
  She gaily carolled day by day.
The haunt is lone, the heart must grieve,
  From whence her timid wing doth soar,
They pensive list at hush of eve,
  Yet hear her gushing song no more.

Deal gently with her; thou art dear,
  Beyond what vestal lips have told,
And, like a lamb from fountains clear,
  She turns confiding to thy fold;
She, round thy sweet domestic bower,
  The wreaths of changeless love shall twine,
Watch for thy step at vesper hour,
  And blend her holiest prayer with thine.

Deal gently, thou, when far away,
  'Mid stranger scenes her foot shall rove.
Nor let thy tender care decay—
  The soul of woman lives in love;
And shouldst thou, wondering, mark a tear,
  Unconscious, from her eyelids break,
Be pitiful, and soothe the fear
  That man's strong heart may ne'er partake.

A mother yields her gem to thee,
  On thy true breast to sparkle rare;
She places 'neath thy household tree
  The idol of her fondest care;
And by thy trust to be forgiven
  When Judgment wakes in terror wild;
By all thy treasured hopes of heaven,
  Deal gently with the widow's child!

Poems about Unfortunates.

VILLAGE-BORN BEAUTY.

SEE the star-breasted villain,
To yonder cot bound,
Where the sweet honeysuckle
Entwines it round,
Yet sweeter, far sweeter,
Than flower e'er seen,
Is the poor hedger's daughter,
The pride of the green.
But more, never more,
Will she there please all eyes
Her peace of mind withers,
Her happiness flies!
She pauses, sighs, trembles,
And yet dares to roam,
The village-born beauty's
Seduced from her home.

From a post-chaise and four
She's in London set down,
Where robbed of her virtue,
She's launched on the town;
Her carriage, her servants,
And jewels so gay,
Tell how high she is kept,
And o'er all bears the sway.
At the opera—the playhouse,
The parks or elsewhere,
Her beauty outrivals
Each beauty that's there;
And while, big with envy,
Her downfall they tell,
The village-born beauty
O'er all bears the belle.

But soon from indifference,
Caprice, or what not—
She's turned on the world—
By her keeper forgot;
Yet, fond to be flattered,
And fettered in vice,
She's this man's or that,
As he comes to her price;
At length, growing stale,
All her finery sold,
In the bloom of her youth,
Through disease looking old,
Forsook by her lovers,
And sought for no more,
The village-born beauty,
Becomes quite impure.

Up lanes and through alleys
She now takes her way,
Exposed to all weathers
By night and by day:
Cold, houseless, and shivering,
And wet to the skin,
With glass after glass
Drowns her sorrows in gin;
Distress'd, sore, and ragged,
Sad, friendless, and poor,
She's borne to some garret,
Or workhouse obscure;
Breathes a prayer hope to heaven
A sinner to save!
When the village-born beauty
Is laid in the grave.

Then pity, ye fair ones,
Nor be too severe,
And give a frail sister
The boon of a tear!
When prone to condemn them,
Reflect, think awhile—
That the heart often bleeds
When the face wears a smile.
Think, too, how to beauty
They oft owe their fall,
And what may through vice
Be the fate of you all;
And O, while sweet innocence
Bears the proud sway,
May hell seize the villain
That smiles to betray.

MARY. *Kitchner.*

BRIGHTLY dawns the day as Mary
Leaves her rustic village home,
Tripping lightly as a fairy,
Heedless of the trials to come;
For sweet Mary's heart is captured
By a gentleman "so grand"—
He declared he was enraptured
As he clasped her tiny hand.

Mary on her way is singing
In the fulness of her heart,
Knowing not that fate is bringing
Troubles that will ne'er depart
While within her life is beating,
Leaving there much grief and pain;
Then there will be no retreating
On the path she'll tread again.

Now through verdant meadows walking,
Singing soft with air so gay,
With the birds and flowers talking,
Just to pass the time away!
Thinking of the pleasant meeting
Near the rustic farmhouse, when
She, her heart with rapture beating,
Thought him "handsomest of men."

Now the maid is shyly talking,
While a man with haughty air
Praises her while he is walking,
Winning smiles so rich and fair,
Using all the daring cunning
Found within such men as he.
While the maid is swiftly running
To fulfil her destiny.

He his love for her confessing,
Will she fly away with him?
Surely she can want no pressing?
Why, her eyes are growing dim!
"Mary, I am softly asking:
Leave your home, and come with me!
'Neath your smiles I'll e'er be basking,
Come, and you shall happy be."

Thus the gentle maid consented,
Leaving all kind friends behind;
But how greatly she repented,
When she was no longer blind.
Left, forsaken and discarded
By the man she loved so well,
And for aye must be regarded
As an erring one who fell.

Mary then comes as a pleader
For affection's early dawn.
Pause and ponder, gentle reader;
Does she yet deserve thy scorn?
Think of sisters in their brightness
Of rare purity and worth;
Would they justify your lightness,
If they revelled in your mirth?

LOUISE ON THE DOORSTEP.

Mackay.

Half-past three in the morning!
  And no one in the street
But me on the sheltering door-step
  Resting my weary feet;
Watching the rain-drops patter
  And dance where the puddles run,
As bright in the flaring gaslight
  As dew-drops in the sun.

There's a light upon the pavement—
  It shines like a magic glass,
And there are faces in it
  That look at me and pass.
Faces—ah! well remembered
  In the happy Long Ago,
When my garb was white as lilies,
  And my thoughts as pure as snow.

Faces! ah, yes! I see them—
  One, two, and three—and four—
That come in the gust of tempests,
  And go on the winds that bore.
Changeful and evanescent,
  They shine 'mid storm and rain,
Till the terror of their beauty
  Lies deep upon my brain.

One of them frowns; *I* know him,
  With his thin long snow-white hair,—
Cursing his wretched daughter
  That drove him to despair.
And the other, with wakening pity
  In her large tear-streaming eyes,
Seems as she yearned towards me,
  And whispered "Paradise."

They pass,—they melt in the ripples,
  And I shut mine eyes, that burn,
To escape another vision—
  That follows where'er I turn—
The face of a false deceiver
  That lives and lies; ah, me!
Though I see it in the pavement,
  Mocking my misery!

They are gone!—all three!—quite vanished,
  Let nothing call them back!
For I've had enough of phantoms,
  And my heart is on the rack!
God help me in my sorrow;
  But *there*,—in the wet, cold stone,
Smiling in heavenly beauty,
  I see my lost, mine own!

There, on the glimmering pavement,
  With eyes as blue as morn,
Floats by the fair-haired darling
  Too soon from my bosom torn.
She clasps her tiny fingers—
  She calls me sweet and mild,
And says that my God forgives me
  For the sake of my little child.

I will go to her grave to-morrow,
  And pray that I may die;
And I hope that my God will take me
  Ere the days of my youth go by.
For I am old in anguish,
  And long to be at rest,
With my little babe beside me,
  And the daisies on my breast.

BEAUTIFUL SNOW.

Wm. Andrew Sigourney.

"SEVERAL nice little romances have been given in connection with the beautiful poem bearing the above title. The true story however is quite different, and we now give it with the entire poem as it first appeared, all but the last stanza, in the *Galaxy* for July, 1869, signed 'WILLIAM ANDREW SIGOURNEY,' and dated 'Ivy Glen, December, 1853.'

"In 1850, W. A. Sigourney, a nephew of the late Mrs. L. H. Sigourney, married a wealthy and accomplished young lady in New York City. They soon after went to Europe, where they remained two years, and where she yielded to the tempter and lost her purity and fidelity. On her return home her parents discarded her, and, being shunned and disgraced, she plunged headlong into vice and dissipation. Her husband, as charitable and kind as he was devoted, tried every means to reclaim her to duty, without avail. She sank deeper and deeper in vice, until she was arrested as a common outcast, and sent to the work-house. Being liberated by a well known magistrate, she promised to reform, and for a short time lived with her husband; but in the autumn of 1853 she returned to her old haunts, began to drink to excess, and thus continued until one stormy night of December, when she died in White Street, and was found in the morning nearly covered with snow. She was buried by her husband in Greenwood."

BEAUTIFUL snow, beautiful snow;
Falling so lightly,—Daily and nightly,
All round the dwellings of the lofty and low:
Horses are prancing,—Cheerily dancing,
Stirred by the spirit that comes with the snow.

Beautiful snow, beautiful snow!
Up at day dawning,—In the cold morning,
Children exult, though the winds fiercely blow;
Hailing the snow-flakes,—Falling as day breaks,—
Joyful they welcome the beautiful snow.

Beautiful snow, beautiful snow!
Childhood's quick glances,—See the bright fancies,
Decking the window-panes softly and slow;
Forest and city,—Figure so pretty,
Left by the magical fingers of snow.

Beautiful snow, beautiful snow!
Atmosphere chilling,—Carriage wheels stilling,
Warming the cold earth and kindling the glow
Of Christian pity—For the great city
Of wretched creatures, who starve 'mid the snow.

Beautiful snow, beautiful snow!
Fierce winds are blowing,—Thickly 'tis snowing;
Night gathers round us—How warm then the glow
Of the fire so bright,—On the cold winter night,
As we draw in the curtains to shut out the snow.

Beautiful snow, beautiful snow!
Round the dear fireside,—In the sweet eventide,
Closely we gather, though the keen winds blow;
Safely defended,—Kindly befriended,
Pity the homeless exposed to the cold, icy snow.

OH! the snow, the beautiful snow,
Filling the sky, and earth below
Over the housetops, over the street,
Over the heads of the people you meet:
Dancing—flirting—skimming along—
Beautiful snow! it can do no wrong;
Flying to kiss a fair lady's cheek,
Clinging to lips in frolicsome freak;
Beautiful snow from heaven above,
Pure as an angel, gentle as love!

Oh! the snow, the beautiful snow;
How the flakes gather, and laugh as they go,
Whirling about in maddening fun;
Chasing—laughing—hurrying by,
It lights on the face, and it sparkles the eye;

And the dogs, with a bark and a bound,
Snap at the crystals as they eddy around;
The town is alive, and its heart in a glow,
To welcome the coming of beautiful snow.

How wild the crowd goes swaying along,
Hailing each other with humour and song;
How the gay sleighs like meteors flash by,
Bright for the moment, then lost to the eye;
Ringing—swinging—dashing they go,
Over the crust of the beautiful snow;
Snow so pure when it falls from the sky,
To be trampled and tracked by thousands of feet,
Till it blends with the filth in the horrible street.

Once I was pure as snow, but I fell,
Fell like the snow-flakes from heaven to hell;
Fell to be trampled as filth on the street,
Fell to be scoffed, and spit on, and beat;
Pleading—cursing—dreading to die,
Selling my soul to whoever would buy;
Dealing in shame for a morsel of bread,
Hating the living and fearing the dead.
Merciful God, have I fallen so low?
And yet I was once like the beautiful snow.

Once I was fair as the beautiful snow,
With an eye like a crystal, a heart like its glow;
Once I was loved for my innocent grace—
Flattered and sought for the charms of my face!
Fathers—mothers—sisters—all—
God and myself I have lost by my fall.
The veriest wretch that goes shivering by
Will make a wide sweep lest I wander too nigh;
For all that is on or above me I know,
There is nothing so pure as the beautiful snow.

How strange it should be that this beautiful snow
Should fall on a sinner with nowhere to go!
How strange it should be when the night comes again,
If the snow and the ice struck my desperate brain!
Fainting—freezing—dying alone,
Too wicked for prayer, too weak for a moan
To be heard in the streets of the crazy town,
Gone mad in the joy of snow coming down;
To be and to die in my terrible woe,
With a bed and a shroud of the beautiful snow.

Helpless and foul as the trampled snow,
Sinner, despair not: Christ stoopeth low
To rescue the soul that is lost in sin,
And raise it to life and enjoyment again.
Groaning—bleeding—dying for thee,
The Crucified hung on the cursed tree;
His accents of mercy fall soft on thine ear—
"Is there mercy for me? Will he heed my weak prayer?"
Oh God! in the stream that for sinners did flow,
Wash me, and I shall be whiter than snow.

THE BRIDGE OF SIGHS.

Thomas Hood.

One more unfortunate
  Weary of breath,
Rashly importunate,
  Gone to her death!
Take her up tenderly,
  Lift her with care;
Fashioned so slenderly—
  Young and so fair!

Look at her garments,
Clinging like cerements,
Whilst the wave constantly
  Drips from her clothing:
Take her up instantly,
  Loving, not loathing.

Touch her not scornfully!
Think of her mournfully,
  Gently and humanly—
Not of the stains of her;
All that remains of her
  Now is pure womanly.

Make no deep scrutiny
Into her mutiny,
  Rash and undutiful;
Past all dishonour,
Death has left on her
  Only the beautiful.

Still, for all slips of hers—
  One of Eve's family,—
Wipe those poor lips of hers
  Oozing so clammily.
Loop up her tresses
  Escaped from the comb,—
Her fair auburn tresses,—
Whilst wonderment guesses,
  Where was her home?

  Who was her father?
  Who was her mother?
  Had she a sister?
  Had she a brother?
Or was there a dearer one
Still, and a nearer one
  Yet, than all other?

Alas! for the rarity
Of Christian charity
  Under the sun!
Oh, it was pitiful!
Near a whole city full,
  Home she had none.

Sisterly, brotherly,
Fatherly, motherly
  Feelings had changed,—
Love, by harsh evidence,
Thrown from its eminence;
Even God's providence
  Seeming estranged.

Where the lamps quiver
So far in the river,
  With many a light
From window and casement,
From garret to basement,
She stood with amazement,
  Houseless by night.

The bleak wind of March
  Made her tremble and shiver;
But not the dark arch,
  Or the black, flowing river;
Mad from life's history,
Glad to death's mystery,
  Swift to be hurled—
Anywhere, anywhere
  Out of the world!

In she plunged boldly,
No matter how coldly
  The rough river ran,—
Over the brink of it!
Picture it,—think of it,
  Dissolute man!
Lave in it, drink of it
  Then if you can!

Take her up tenderly,
  Lift her with care,
Fashioned so slenderly,
  Young, and so fair!
Ere her limbs, frigidly,
Stiffen too rigidly,
  Decently, kindly,
Smooth and compose them;
And her eyes, close them,
  Staring so blindly;—
Dreadfully staring
  Through muddy impurity,
As when the daring
Last look of despairing
  Fixed on futurity.

Perishing gloomily,
Spurred by contumely,
Cold inhumanity,
Burning insanity,
  Into her rest!
Cross her hands humbly,
As if praying dumbly,
  Over her breast!
Owning her weakness,
  Her evil behaviour,
And leaving, with meekness,
  Her sins to her Saviour!

SOCIETY'S DISGRACE.

W. C. Smith.

A LONELY woman wandered by,
With crouching form and averted eye;
In her arms she carried an infant fair,
In her heart she carried a grim despair.
And close to her heaving aching breast,
Her child of shame she closely pressed.
The night grew dark as she wandered on,
Still closer pressing her little one;
Her step grows feeble as she goes
Down to the river that darkly flows.
Then with a wail of wild despair,
She plunges in with her baby fair.
Time rolls on,—but the waters fail
To hide the bodies that tell the tale.
The state steps in—too late to save,
She tosses them into a pauper's grave.
Then come forward—the pulpit and press
To moralize—they can't do less.
Their fate's discussed by a Christian World,
And an orthodox verdict has them hurled
Down as deep as they can go,
Into Theology's fire below.
Piously quoting with virtuous breath,
The wages of sin is surely death.
A gent of fashion goes walking by,
A cane in his hand, a glass to his eye;
Gracefully bows to the ladies fair,
As he lifts his hat from his curly hair;
Causing many a flutter and sigh
In the ladies' hearts as he saunters by.
Courted at *clubs* and at festive scenes.
King of *Hearts* among beauty's Queens;
He plays his hand with a graceful ease,
And seems to win whene'er he please.
And many a damsel's hand is played
To get his *diamond* upon her *spade*.
Although 'twas known he meant to snare
That trusting maiden pure and fair;
And swore by all in Heaven above,
No other damsel he could love;
And vowed that she his wife should be,
If she would trust implicitly.
Although 'twas known he was to blame,
For bringing that poor girl to shame;
Although 'twas known she bore his child,
She's voted base—he only wiled.
Although 'twas known he caused her death,
Against him there is not a breath.
And this is in a Christian land,
Where justice is boasted on every hand.
Prompt to punish the hungry thief,
Who steals a loaf to get relief:
But the seducer with villainous wiles,
In safety can bask in Society's smiles.

MY HEID IS LIKE TO REND.

William Motherwell.

My heid is like to rend, Willie,
  My heart is like to break—
I'm wearin' aff my feet, Willie,
  I'm dyin' for your sake!
Oh lay your cheek to mine, Willie,
  Your hand on my briest-bane—
Oh say ye'll think on me, Willie,
  When I am deid and gane!

It's vain to comfort me, Willie,
  Sair grief maun ha'e its will—
But let me rest upon your briest,
  To sab and greet my fill.
Let me sit on your knee, Willie,
  Let me shed by your hair,
And look into the face, Willie,
  I never shall see mair!

I'm sitting on your knee, Willie,
  For the last time in my life—
A puir heart-broken thing, Willie,
  A mither, yet nae wife.
Ay, press your hand upon my heart,
  And press it mair and mair—
Or it will burst the silken twine
  Sae strong is its despair!

Oh wae's me for the hour, Willie,
  When we thegither met—
Oh wae's me for the time, Willie,
  That our first tryst was set!
Oh wae's me for the loamin' green
  Where we were wont to gae—
And wae's me for the destinie,
  That gart me luve thee sae!

Oh! dinna mind my words, Willie,
  I downa seek to blame—
But oh! its hard to live, Willie,
  And dree a warld's shame!
Het tears are hailin' ower your cheek,
  And hailin' ower your chin:
Why weep ye sae for worthlessness,
  For sorrow and for sin?

I'm weary o' this warld, Willie,
  And sick wi' a' I see—
I canna live as I ha'e lived,
  Or be as I should be.
But fauld unto your heart, Willie,
  The heart that still is thine—
And kiss ance mair the white, white cheek,
  Ye said was red langsyne.

A stoun' gaes through my heid, Willie,
  A sair stoun' through my heart—
Oh, haud me up and let me kiss
  Thy brow ere we twa pairt.
Anither, and anither yet:
  How fast my life-strings break.
Farewell, farewell! through yon kirk yard
  Step lichtly for my sake.

The lav'rock in the lift, Willie,
  That lilts far ower our heid,
Will sing the morn as merrilie
  Abune the clay-cauld deid;
And this green turf we're sittin' on,
  With dew-draps shimmerin' sheen,
Will hap the heart that luvit thee,
  As warld has seldom seen.

But oh, remember me, Willie,
  On land where'er ye be—
And oh, think on the leal, leal heart
  That ne'er luvit ane but thee.
And oh, think on the cauld, cauld mools,
  That file my yellow hair—
That kiss the cheek, and kiss the chin,
  Ye never sall kiss mair.

ANNIE GRAY.

Rev. Charles Jefferys.

Of all our village beauties
  The first was Annie Gray;
With her the years of childhood
  Pass'd like a summer's day:
When o'er her brow the orange wreath
  Was braided with her hair—
Within the holy fane she stood,
  And seem'd an angel there:
O heartful were the blessings
  Of that eventful day.
Young and old their prayers united
  In their love for Annie Gray.

But ah! the bridegroom came not,
  They sought him far and wide,—
By mill-stream and thro' forest,
  And by the steep hill-side:
His panting steed was trembling there,
  But riderless was he;
The loving heart lay cold beneath
  The old, old trysting tree:
O heartfelt were the sorrows
  Of that eventful day.
Young and old their griefs united
  For the love-lorn Annie Gray.

She spoke not, and she wept not,
  But wasting day by day,
We knew her gentle spirit
  Ere long would pass away.
One haven only could be found
  For her poor stricken breast;
And we had not the hope, or wish
  To keep her from her rest:—
Yet heartfelt was the anguish
  Of that eventful day;
Young and old their tears commingled
  O'er the tomb of Annie Gray.

SONG OF THE SHIRT.

Hood.

WITH fingers weary and worn,
With eyelids heavy and red,
A woman sat, in unwomanly rags,
Plying her needle and thread,—
Stitch! stitch! stitch!
In poverty, hunger and dirt,
And still, with a voice of dolorous pitch,
She sang the "Song of the Shirt."

"Work! work! work!
While the cock is crowing aloof!
And work—work—work,
Till the stars shine through the roof!
It's oh! to be a slave
Along with the barbarous Turk,
Where woman has never a soul to save,
If this is Christian work!

"Work—work—work,
Till the brain begins to swim,
Work—work—work,
Till the eyes are heavy and dim!
Seam, and gusset, and band,
Band, and gusset, and seam,
Till over the buttons I fall asleep,
And sew them on in a dream!

"Oh! men with sisters dear!
Oh! men with mothers and wives!
It is not linen you're wearing out,
But human creatures' lives!
Stitch—stitch—stitch,
In poverty, hunger, and dirt,
Sewing at once, with a double thread,
A shroud as well as a shirt.

"But why do I talk of death,
That phantom of grisly bone?
I hardly fear his terrible shape,
It seems so like my own,—
It seems so like my own,
Because of the fasts I keep.
O God! that bread should be so dear,
And flesh and blood so cheap!

"Work—work—work,
My labour never flags;
And what are its wages? A bed of straw,
A crust of bread,—and rags,—
That shattered roof—and this naked floor—
A table—a broken chair—
And a wall so blank, my shadow I thank
For sometimes falling there!

Work—work—work!
From weary chime to chime!
Work—work—work,
As prisoners work for crime!
Band, and gusset, and seam,
Seam, and gusset, and band,
Till the heart is sick and the brain benumbed,
As well as the weary hand.

Work—work—work,
In the dull December light,
And work—work—work,
When the weather is warm and bright—
While underneath the eaves
The brooding swallows cling,
As if to show me their sunny backs,
And twit me with the Spring.

"Oh! but to breathe the breath
Of the cowslip and primrose sweet—
With the sky above my head
And the grass beneath my feet;
For only one sweet hour
To feel as I used to feel,
Before I knew the woes of want,
And the walk that costs a meal;

"Oh! but for one short hour!
A respite, however brief!
No blessed leisure for love or hope,
But only time for grief!
A little weeping would ease my heart,
But in their briny bed
My tears must stop, for every drop
Hinders needle and thread!"

With fingers weary and worn,
With eyelids heavy and red,
A woman sat in unwomanly rags,
Plying her needle and thread—
Stitch! stitch! stitch!
In poverty, hunger and dirt,
And still, with a voice of dolorous pitch—
Would that its tone could reach the rich!—
She sang this "Song of the Shirt."

THE RUINED COTTAGE.

Mrs. Maclean, "L.E.L."

None will dwell in that cottage, for they say
Oppression reft it from an honest man.
And that a curse clings to it; hence the vine
Trails its green weight of leaves upon the ground;
Hence weeds are in that garden; hence the hedge,
Once sweet with honeysuckle, is half dead;
And hence the grey moss on the apple tree.
Once one dwelt there, who had been in his youth
A soldier; and when many years had passed
He sought his native village, and sat down
To end his days in peace. He had one child—
A little, laughing thing, whose large dark eyes,
He said were like the mother's he had left
Buried in strange lands. And time went on
In comfort and content, and that fair girl
Had grown far taller than the red rose tree,
Her father planted her first English birthday;
And he had trained it up against an ash
Till it became his pride;—it was so rich
In blossom and in beauty, it was called
The tree of Isabel! 'Twas an appeal
To all the better feelings of the heart
To mark their quiet happiness,—their home,
In truth a home of love; and, more than all,
To see them on the Sabbath; when they came
Among the first to church; and Isabel
With her bright colour, and her clear glad eyes,
Bowed down so meekly in the house of prayer;
And in the hymn her sweet voice audible;
Her father look'd so fond of her, and then
From her looked up so thankfully to heaven;
And their small cottage was so very neat;
Their garden fill'd with fruits, and herbs, and flowers;
And in the winter there was no fireside
So cheerful as their own. But other days
And other fortunes came—an evil power!

They bore against it cheerfully, and hoped
For better times, but ruin came at last;
And the old soldier left his own dear home,
And left it for a prison. 'Twas in June,
One of June's brightest days—the bee, the bird,
The butterfly were on their brightest wings;
The fruits had their first tinge of summer light
The sunny sky, the very leaves seemed glad,
And the old man looked back upon his cottage
And wept aloud. They hurried him away,
And the dear child that would not leave his side.
They led him from the sight of the blue heaven
And the green trees into a low dark cell,
The windows shutting out the blessed sun
With iron grating; and for the first time
He threw him on his bed, and could not hear
His Isabel's "good-night!" But the next morn
She was the earliest at the prison gate,
The last on whom it closed; and her sweet voice,
And sweeter smile, made him forget to pine.
She brought him every morning fresh wild flowers;
But every morning could he see her cheek
Grow paler and more pale, and her low tones
Get fainter and more faint, and a cold dew
Was on the hand he held. One day he saw
The sun shine through the grating of his cell,
Yet Isabel came not; at every sound
His heart-beat took away his breath, yet still
She came not near him. But one sad day
He marked the dull street through the iron bars
That shut him from the world;—at length he saw
A coffin carried carelessly along,
And he grew desperate—he forced the bars;
And he stood on the street, free and alone!
He had no aim, no wish for liberty—
He had only felt one want, to see the corpse
That had no mourners. When they set it down.
Or e'er 'twas lowered into the new dug grave,
A rush of passion came upon his soul,
And he tore off the lid, and saw the face
Of Isabel, and knew he had no child!
He lay down by the coffin quietly—
His heart was broken!

MARY, THE MAID OF THE INN.

Southey.

Who is yonder poor maniac, whose wildly-fixed eyes
 Seem a heart overcharged to express?
She weeps not, yet often and deeply she sighs:
She never complains, but her silence implies
 The composure of settled distress.

No aid, no compassion the maniac will seek:
 Cold and hunger awake not her care.
Through her rags do the winds of the winter blow bleak
On her poor wither'd bosom half bare, and her cheek
 Has the deathly-pale hue of despair.

Yet cheerful and happy, nor distant the day,
 Poor Mary the maniac has been;
The traveller remembers who journeyed this way,
No damsel so lovely, no damsel so gay,
 As Mary, the maid of the inn.

Her cheerful address fill'd her guests with delight
 As she welcomed them in with a smile.
Her heart was a stranger to childish affright,
And Mary would walk by the abbey at night,
 When the wind whistled down the dark aisle.

She loved; and young Richard had settled the day,
 And she hoped to be happy for life;
But Richard was idle and worthless, and they
Who knew him would pity poor Mary, and say
 That she was too good for his wife.

'Twas in autumn, and stormy and dark was the night,
 And fast were the windows and door;
Two guests sat enjoying the fire that burnt bright,
And, smoking in silence with tranquil delight,
 They listen'd to hear the wind roar.

"'Tis pleasant," cried one, "seated by the fireside,
 To hear the wind whistle without."
"A fine night for the abbey!" his comrade replied.
"Methinks a man's courage would now be well tried
 Who should wander the ruins about.

"I myself, like a school-boy, would tremble to hear
 The hoarse ivy shake over my head:
And could fancy I saw, half persuaded by fear,
Some ugly old abbot's white spirit appear—
 For this wind might awaken the dead!"

"I'll wager a dinner," the other one cried,
 "That Mary would venture there now."
"Then wager, and lose!" with a sneer he replied;
"I'll warrant she'd fancy a ghost by her side,
 And faint if she saw a white cow."

"Will Mary this charge on her courage allow?"
 His companion exclaimed with a smile;
"I shall win,—for I know she will venture there now,
And earn a new bonnet by bringing a bough
 From the elder that grows in the aisle."

With fearless good-humour did Mary comply,
And her way to the abbey she bent;
The night it was dark, and the wind it was high,
And as hollowly howling it swept through the sky,
She shiver'd with cold as she went.

O'er the path so well known still proceeded the maid,
Where the abbey rose dim on the sight.
Through the gateway she enter'd, she felt not afraid;
Yet the ruins were lonely and wild, and their shade
Seemed to deepen the gloom of the night.

All around her was silent, save when the rude blast
Howl'd dismally round the old pile;
Over weed-cover'd fragments still fearless she passed.
And arrived at the innermost ruin at last,
Where the elder-tree grew in the aisle.

Well pleased did she reach it, and quickly drew near
And hastily gather'd the bough;
When the sound of a voice seemed to rise on her ear:
She paused, and she listen'd all eager to hear,
And her heart panted fearfully now.

The wind blew, the hoarse ivy shook over her head,
She listen'd—naught else could she hear.
The wind ceased; her heart sunk in her bosom with dread,
For she heard in the ruins distinctly the tread
Of footsteps approaching her near.

Behind a wide column, half breathless with fear
She crept, to conceal herself there:
That instant the moon o'er a dark cloud shone clear,
And she saw in the moonlight two ruffians appear,
And between them a corpse did they bear.

Then Mary could feel her heart-blood curdle cold!
Again the rough wind hurried by,—
It blew off the hat of the one, and behold
Even close to the feet of poor Mary it roll'd—
She felt, and expected to die.

"Curse the hat!" he exclaimed; "Nay, come on here and hide
The dead body," his comrade replies.
She beholds them in safety pass on by her side,
She seizes the hat, fear her courage supplied,
And fast through the abbey she flies.

She ran with wild speed, she rush'd in at the door,
She gazed horribly eager around,
Then her limbs could support their faint burden no more,
And, exhausted and breathless, she sunk on the floor,
Unable to utter a sound.

Ere yet her pale lips could the story impart,
For a moment the hat met her view;
Her eyes from that object convulsively start,
For—O God! what cold horror then thrilled through her heart
When the name of her Richard she knew!

Where the old abbey stands on the common hard by,
His gibbet is now to be seen;
His irons you still from the road may espy,
The traveller beholds them, and thinks, with a sigh,
Of poor Mary, the maid of the inn.

THE MANIAC.

Matthew Gregory Lewis.

STAY, gaoler! stay, and hear my woe!
  He is not mad who kneels to thee;
For what I'm now, too well I know,
  And what I was, and what should be!
I'll rage no more in proud despair—
  My language shall be mild, though sad,
But yet I'll firmly, truly swear,
  I am not mad! I am not mad!

My tyrant foes have forged the tale,
  Which chains me in this dismal cell;
My fate unknown my friends bewail—
  Oh! gaoler, haste that fate to tell!
Oh! haste my father's heart to cheer,
  His heart at once 'twill grieve and glad,
To know, though chained a captive here,
  I am not mad! I am not mad!

He smiles in scorn—he turns the key—
  He quits the grate—I knelt in vain!
His glimmering lamp still, still I see—
  'Tis gone—and all is gloom again!
Cold, bitter cold!—no warmth, no light!
  Life, all thy comforts once I had!
Yet here I'm chained this freezing night,
  Although not mad! no, no—not mad!

'Tis sure some dream—some vision vain!
  What! I—the child of rank and wealth—
Am I the wretch who clanks this chain,
  Bereft of freedom, friends, and health?
Ah! while I dwell on blessings fled,
  Which never more my heart must glad,
How aches my heart, how burns my head,
  But 'tis not mad! it is not mad!

Hast thou, my child, forgot ere this
  A parent's face, a parent's tongue?
I'll ne'er forget thy parting kiss,
  Nor round my neck how fast you clung!
Nor how with me you sued to stay,
  Nor how that suit my foes forbade;
Nor how—I'll drive such thoughts away—
  They'll make me mad! they'll make me mad!

Thy rosy lips, how sweet they smiled!
  Thy mild blue eyes, how bright they shone!
None ever saw a lovelier child!
  And art thou now for ever gone?
And must I never see thee more,
  My pretty, pretty, pretty lad?
I *will* be free!—Unbar the door!
  I am not mad! I am not mad!

Oh, hark! what mean those yells and cries!
  His chain some furious madman breaks!
He comes! I see his glaring eyes!
  Now, now, my dungeon-grate he shakes!

Help! help!—he's gone!—O fearful woe!
  Such screams to hear, such sights to see!
My brain, my brain! I know, I know
  I am not mad—but soon shall be!

Yes, soon! for, lo, now, while I speak,
  Mark how yon demon's eye-balls glare!
He sees me!—now with dreadful shriek
  He whirls a serpent high in air!
Horror! the reptile strikes his tooth
  Deep in my heart, so crushed and sad!
Ay, laugh, ye fiends! I feel the truth!
  Your task is done—I'm mad! I'm mad!

THE PAUPER'S DEATH-BED.

Mrs. Southey

TREAD softly, bow the head—
  In reverent silence bow—
No passing-bell doth toll,
Yet an immortal soul
    Is passing now.

Stranger, however great,
  With lowly reverence bow;
There's one in that poor shed,
One by that paltry bed,
    Greater than thou.

Beneath that beggar's roof,
  Lo! Death doth keep his state.
Enter—no crowds attend—
Enter—no guards defend
    This palace-gate.

That pavement damp and cold
  No smiling courtiers tread.
One silent woman stands,
Lifting with meagre hands,
    A dying head.

No mingling voices sound;
  An infant wail alone.
A sob suppressed—again
That short deep gasp—and then
    The parting groan.

Oh, change! oh, wondrous change!
  Burst are the prison bars!
This moment *there*, so low,
So agonised—and now
    Beyond the stars!

Oh, change! stupendous change!
  There lies the soulless clod;
The sun eternal breaks,
The new Immortal wakes,
    Wakes with his God.

Poems about Tears.

THE TEAR OF SYMPATHY.

How lovely shines the liquid pearl,
  Which, trickling from the eye,
Pours in a suffering brother's wound
  The tear of sympathy!

Its beams a fairer lustre yield
  Than richest rubies give;
Golconda's gems, though bright, are cold—
  It cheers, and bids us live.

Softer the tones of Friendship's voice,
  Its word more kindly flows;
More grateful in its simplest sound
  Than all which art bestows.

When torturing anguish racks the soul,
  When sorrow points its dart,
When Death, unerring, aims the blow
  Which cleaves a brother's heart—

Then, Sympathy! 'tis thine to lull
  The sufferer's soul to rest—
To feel each pang, to share each throb,
  And ease his troubled breast.

'Tis thine to aid the sinking frame;
  To raise the feeble hand;
To bind the heart by anguish torn,
  With sweet affection's band.

'Tis thine to cherish Hope's fond smile,
  To chase Affliction's gloom,
To mitigate the pains that wait
  Our passage to the tomb.

Then give me, Heaven, the soul to feel,
  The hand to Mercy prone,
The eye with kindly drops that flows
  For sorrows not my own.

Be mine the cause of Misery's child—
  Be mine the wish sincere
To pluck the sting that wounds his breast,
  And heal it with a tear.

VERSES ON A TEAR.

Rogers.

Oh! that the Chemist's magic art
  Could crystallize this sacred treasure!
Long should it glitter near my heart,
  A secret source of pensive pleasure.

The little brilliant, ere it fell,
  Its lustre caught from Chloe's eye!
Then, trembling, left its coral cell—
  The spring of Sensibility!

Sweet drop of pure and pearly light,
  In thee the rays of Virtue shine;
More calmly clear, more mildly bright,
  Than any gem that gilds the mine.

Benign restorer of the soul!
  Who ever fly'st to bring relief,
When first she feels the rude control
  Of Love or Pity, Joy or Grief.

The Sage's and the Poet's theme,
  In ev'ry clime, in ev'ry age;
Thou charm'st in Fancy's idle dream,
  In Reason's philosophic page.

That very law which moulds a tear,
  And bids it trickle from its source,
That law preserves the earth a sphere,
  And guides the planets in their course.

PEARL OF THE UNIVERSE.

Darwin.

No radiant pearl which crested fortune wears,
No gem, that twinkling hangs from beauty's ears;
Not the bright stars, which night's blue arch adorn,
Nor rising sun, that gilds the vernal morn;
Shine with such lustre as the tear that flows
Down virtue's manly cheek for others' woes.

ONLY A TEAR.

Cottager and Artisan.

OF all the teachers whose temper was tried,
Whose patience was taxed, and whose rule was defied
By the giddiest set of troublesome boys—
Who gloried in fun and revelled in noise;
Who hated restraint, and loved a good game,
And never confessed to the slightest of shame!—
Poor Dominie Price was most to be pitied,
He seemed to be born to be "done" and outwitted!

The most troublesome one of that troublesome lot
Without any doubt was Timothy Spot.
He would sit in the school with a good-humoured face
And assist every boy to get into—disgrace!
He could use with success ventriloquial powers,
And startled the master with pea-shooting showers;
Would caricature the old man on a slate,
Would run away early, and always came late!

Put the clock on an hour, cut the cane into bits,
And startle with crackers poor Price into fits!
Now Dominie Price, 'tis our duty to add,
Was a kind-hearted man, and he felt quite sad
When he thought of young Tim and his rackety ways,
And knew he would be a dunce all his days;
It grieved him to think the boy was so wild—
For in spite of his faults he loved the child.

One day Master Spot was unusually gay—
He'd been playing his tricks the whole of the day!
And Dominie Price though unusually kind,
To thrash the young rascal had made up his mind.
He was hoisted aloft—his back was laid bare,
And the rod set a-swinging above in the air!
When—no!—the kind heart of the master would not
Allow it to fall on Timothy Spot.

The boy thus let off looked up in surprise,
And saw a large *tear* in the schoolmaster's eye!
Yes—ONLY A TEAR—large, glistening, round,
It rolled down his cheek and fell on to the ground.
Master Spot never spoke, but gazed on that tear,
His heart seemed to swell with love, not with fear;
And a tear to match that which had fallen before
Now lay side by side on the school-house floor.

Slowly back to his seat young Timothy went,
And in *thinking* the rest of that day was spent;
And when the duties of school were done,
Instead of scampering off for fun,
He went to the master and said, "From this day
I will try to act in a different way.
'Twas the tear, not the birch, I couldn't withstand."
And the master grasped the pupil's hand!

Then, over a cup of excellent tea,
The pair were as happy as happy could be;
But, ere the boy arose to go,
The Bible was brought, and clear and low
The master read from the Holy Writ
Some words of wisdom as they sat;
He read of times to laugh and to cry,
Of a time to be born and a time to die.

Ere wishing good-bye at the cottage door,
"My boy," said he, "I have one word more;
Remember it well, for my locks are hoary:
''Tis only the wise that inherit glory!'"

The boy went home, but not to sleep,
For the word of God had fallen deep;
"The wise!" "The wise!" rang in his ears,
And again he saw the old man's tears,
And again he heard, "For my locks are hoary:
''Tis only the wise that inherit glory!'"

Years passed away, and the old man's face
Is no more seen in its well-known place;
But the boy is a preacher of great renown,
Who courts not favour nor dreads a frown;
And he loves to tell, and men love to hear,
The story of love, and that fallen tear.

Poems about God.

ODE TO THE ALMIGHTY.

Derzhavin.

O THOU Eternal One! whose presence bright
  All space doth occupy—all motion guide:
Unchanged through Time's all-devastating flight;
  Thou only God! there is no God beside:
Being above all beings! Three in One!
  Whom none can comprehend, and none explore:
Who fill'st existence with THYSELF alone,
  Embracing all,—supporting—ruling o'er,—
  Being whom we call God—and know no more!

In its sublime research, Philosophy
  May measure out the ocean deep—may count
The sands, or the sun's rays—but, God! for Thee
  There is no weight nor measure: none can mount
Up to Thy mysteries: Reason's brightest spark,
  Though kindled by Thy light, in vain would try
To trace Thy counsels, infinite and dark;
  And Thought is lost ere Thought can soar so high,
  E'en like past moments in Eternity.

Thou, from primæval nothingness, didst call
  First chaos, then existence:—Lord! on Thee
Eternity had its foundation; all
  Sprang forth from Thee—of light, joy, harmony,
Sole origin:—all life, all beauty Thine.
  Thy word created all, and doth create;
Thy splendour fills all space with rays divine.
  Thou art, and wert, and shalt be! Glorious! Great!
  Light-giving, life-sustaining Potentate!

Thy chains the unmeasured universe surround:
  Upheld by Thee, by Thee inspired with breath!
Thou the beginning with the end hast bound,
  And beautifully mingled life and death!
As sparks mount upward from the fiery blaze,
  So suns are born, so worlds spring forth from Thee;
And as the spangles in the sunny rays
  Shine round the silver snow, the pageantry
Of heaven's bright army glitters in Thy praise.

A million torches lighted by Thy hand,
  Wander, unwearied, through the blue abyss:
They own thy power, accomplish Thy command;
  All gay with life—all eloquent with bliss.
What shall we call them? Piles of crystal light—
  A glorious company of golden streams—
Lamps of celestial ether, burning bright—
  Suns, lighting systems with their joyous beams?
But Thou to these art as the moon to night!

Yes! as a drop of water in the sea,
All this magnificence in Thee is lost:
What are ten thousand worlds compared to Thee?
And what am *I*, then? Heaven's unnumber'd host,
Though multiplied by myriads and array'd
In all the glory of sublimest thought,
Is but an atom in the balance weigh'd
Against Thy greatness! Is a cipher brought
Against infinity! What am I, then? Nought.

Nought; but the effluence of Thy light divine,
Pervading worlds, hath reach'd my bosom too:
Yes! in my spirit doth Thy spirit shine,
As shines the sunbeam in a drop of dew.
Nought! but I live, and on Hope's pinions fly
Eager towards Thy presence; for in Thee
I live, and breathe, and dwell; aspiring high,
Even to the Throne of Thy divinity.
I am, O God! and surely Thou must be.

Thou art! directing, guiding all,—Thou art!
Direct my understanding then, to Thee!
Control my spirit, guide my wandering heart!
Though but an atom 'midst immensity,
Still I am something, fashion'd by Thy hand:
I hold a middle rank 'twixt heaven and earth,—
On the last verge of mortal being stand,
Close to the realms where angels have their birth,
Just on the boundaries of the spirit-land!

The chain of being is complete in me,
In me is matter's last gradation lost,
And the next step is spirit—Deity!
I can command the lightning, and am dust!
A monarch and a slave, a worm, a god!
Whence came I here, and how so marvellously
Constructed and conceived? unknown! this clod
Lives surely through some higher energy;
For from itself alone it could not be!

Creator, yes. Thy wisdom and Thy word
Created me, Thou Source of life and good!
Thou Spirit of my spirit, and my Lord,
Thy light, Thy love, in their bright plenitude
Filled me with an immortal soul, to spring
Over the abyss of death, and bade it wear
The garments of eternal day, and wing
Its heavenly flight beyond this little sphere,
Even to its source—to Thee—its Author there.

O thoughts ineffable! O visions blest!
Though worthless our conceptions all of Thee
Yet shall Thy shadowed image fill our breast,
And waft its homage to Thy Deity.
God! thus alone my lowly thoughts can soar,
Thus seek Thy presence—Being wise and good!
'Midst Thy vast works admire, obey, adore;
And when the tongue is eloquent no more,
The soul shall speak in tears of gratitude.

THE ORDER OF PROVIDENCE.

Pope.

All are but parts of one stupendous whole,
Whose body Nature is, and God the soul;
That, changed through all, and yet in all the same,
Great in the earth, as in th' ethereal frame;
Warms in the sun, refreshes in the breeze,
Glows in the stars, and blossoms in the trees;
Lives through all life, extends through all extent;
Spreads undivided, operates unspent;
Breathes in our soul, informs our mortal part,
As full, as perfect, in a hair as heart;
As full, as perfect, in vile man that mourns,
As the rapt seraph that adores and burns;
To him no nigh, no low, no great, no small;
He fills, he bounds, connects, and equals all.

Cease, then, nor order imperfection name:
Our proper bliss depends on what we blame.
Know thine own point: This kind, this true degree
Of blindness, weakness, Heaven bestows on thee.
Submit.—In this or any other sphere,
Secure to be as bless'd as thou canst bear,
Safe in the hand of one disposing power,
Or in the natal, or the mortal hour.
All nature is but art, unknown to thee;
All chance, direction, which thou canst not see;
All discord, harmony, not understood;
All partial evil, universal good.

WISDOM IN NATURE.

There's not a tint that paints the rose
Or decks the lily fair,
Or marks the humblest flower that grows,
But God has placed it there.

There's not of grass a simple blade,
Or leaf of lowliest mien,
Where heav'nly skill is not displayed,
And heav'nly goodness seen.

There's not a star whose twinkling light
Illumes the spreading earth;
There's not a cloud, so dark or bright,
But wisdom gave its birth.

There's not a place on earth's vast round,
In ocean's deep or air,
Where love and beauty are not found,
For God is everywhere.

THE UNIVERSAL PRAYER.

Pope.

FATHER of ALL! in every age,
  In every clime adored,
By saint, by savage, and by sage,
  Jehovah, Jove, or Lord!

Thou great FIRST CAUSE, least understood,
  Who all my sense confined
To know but this, that thou art good,
  And that myself am blind;

Yet gave me, in this dark estate,
  To see the good from ill;
And, binding nature fast in fate,
  Left free the human will.

What conscience dictates to be done,
  Or warns me not to do,
This teach me more than hell to SHUN,
  That, more than heaven PURSUE.

What blessings Thy free bounty gives
  Let me not cast away;
For God is paid when man receives,—
  To enjoy is to obey.

Yet not to earth's contracted span
  Thy goodness let me bound;
Or think thee Lord alone of man,
  When thousand worlds are round.

Let not this weak, unknowing hand
  Presume Thy bolts to throw,
And deal damnation round the land
  On each I judge Thy foe.

If I am right, Thy grace impart
  STILL IN THE RIGHT TO STAY;
If I am WRONG, *O, teach my heart*
  TO FIND THAT BETTER WAY.

Save me alike from foolish pride,
  Or impious discontent
At aught Thy wisdom has denied,
  Or aught Thy goodness lent.

Teach me to feel another's woe;
  To hide the fault I see;
That mercy I to others show
  THAT MERCY *show to me.*

Mean though I am, not wholly so,
  Since quickened by Thy breath;
Oh, lead me, wheresoe'er I go,—
  Through this day's life or death.

This day be bread and peace my lot;
  All else beneath the sun
Thou know'st if best bestowed or not,
  And let Thy will be done.

To Thee, Whose temple is all space,
  Whose altar, earth, sea, skies!
ONE CHORUS LET ALL BEING RAISE!
  ALL NATURE'S INCENSE RISE!

THE ETERNAL GOODNESS.

Whittier.

I DIMLY guess from blessings known
  Of greater out of sight,
And with the chastised Psalmist, own
  His judgments, too, are right.

I long for household voices gone,
  For vanished smiles I long;
But God hath led my dear ones on,
  And he can do no wrong.

I know not what the future hath
  Of marvel or surprise,
Assured alone that life and death
  His mercy underlies.

No offering of my own I have,
  No works my faith to prove;
I can but give the gifts He gave,
  And plead His love for love.

And so beside the Silent Sea
  I wait the muffled oar;
No harm from Him can come to me,
  On ocean or on shore.

I know not where His islands lift
  Their fronded palms in air;
I only know I cannot drift
  Beyond His love and care.

Poems about Religion.

THE CREEDS OF THE BELLS.

By George W. Bungay.

How sweet the chime of Sabbath bells;
Each one its creed in music tells,
In tones that float upon the air,
As soft as song, as pure as prayer;
And I will put in simple rhyme,
The language of the golden chime.
My happy heart with rapture swells,
Responsive to the bells—sweet bells.

"In deeds of love, excel, excel,"
Chimed out from ivied towers a bell;
"This is the church not built on sands,
Emblem of one not built with hands;
Its forms and sacred rights revere—
Come worship here, come worship here;
In ritual and faith excel, excel,"
Chimed out the Episcopalian bell.

"Oh, heed the ancient landmarks well!"
In solemn tones exclaimed a bell;
"No progress made by mortal man
Can change the just, eternal plan,
With God there can be nothing new—
Ignore the false, embrace the true,
While all is well, is well, is well,"
Pealed out the good old Dutch church bell.

"Ye purifying waters swell,"
In mellow tones rang out the bell;
"Though faith alone in Christ can save
Man must be plunged beneath the wave,
To show the world unfaltering faith,
In what the sacred Scripture saith.
Oh, swell, ye rising waters swell!"
Pealed out the clear-toned Baptist bell.

"Not faith alone, but works as well,
Must test the soul," said a soft bell;
"Come here and cast aside your load,
And work your way along the road,
With faith in God, and faith in man,
And hope in Christ, where hope began;
Do well, do well, do well, do well,"
Pealed forth a Unitarian bell.

"Farewell, farewell, base world, farewell,"
In warning notes exclaimed a bell;
"Life is a boon to mortals given,
To fit the soul for bliss in Heaven.
Do not invoke the avenging rod,
Come here and learn the will of God.
Say to the world, farewell, farewell,"
Pealed out the Presbyterian bell.

"In after life there is no hell!"
In raptures rang a cheerful bell.
"Look up to Heaven this holy day,
Where angels wait to cheer the way;
There are no fires, no fiends to blight
The future life; be just and right.
No hell! no hell! no hell! no hell!"
Rang out the Universalist bell!

"The pilgrim fathers heeded well
My cheerful voice," pealed forth a bell;
"No fetters here to clog the soul;
No arbitrary creeds control
The free heart and progressive mind
That leave the dusty path behind.
Speed well, speed well, speed well, speed well!"
Pealed out the Independent bell.

"No Pope, no Pope to doom to hell
The Protestant," rang out a bell;
"Great Luther left his fiery zeal
Within the hearts that truly feel,
That loyalty to God will be
The fealty that makes men free.
No images where incense fell!"
Rang out old Martin Luther's bell.

"All hail, ye saints in Heaven that dwell
Close by the Cross," exclaimed a bell;
"Lean o'er the battlements of bliss,
And deign to bless a world like this;
Let mortals kneel before this shrine—
Adore the water and the wine.
All hail, ye saints, the chorus swell!"
Chimed in the Roman Catholic bell.

"To all the truth we tell, we tell,"
Shouted in ecstasies a bell,
"Come all ye weary wanderers, see,
Our Lord has made salvation free;
Repent, believe; have faith, and then
Be saved, and praise the Lord. Amen!
Salvation's free, we tell, we tell,"
Shouted the Methodistic bell.

RELIGION.

John Critchely Prince.

My religion is love—'tis the noblest and purest;
And my temple the universe—widest and surest,
I worship my God through his works, which are fair,
And the joy of my heart is perpetual prayer.

I wake to new life at the coming of spring,
When the lark is aloft with a fetterless wing;
When the thorn and the woodbine are bursting with buds,
And the throstle is heard in the depths of the woods;
When the verdure grows bright where the rivulets run,
And the primrose and daisy look up to the sun;
When the iris of April expands o'er the plain,
And a blessing comes down in the drops of the rain;
When the skies are as pure, and the breezes as mild,
As the smile of my wife, and the kiss of my child.

When the summer in fulness of beauty is born,
I love to be out with the first blush of morn;
And to pause in the field where the mower is blithe,
Keeping time with a song to the sweep of his scythe.

At meridian I love to revisit the bowers
'Mid the murmur of bees and the breathing of flowers;
And there, in some sylvan and shadowy nook,
To lay myself down on the brink of the brook;
Where the coo of the ring-dove sounds soothingly near,
And the light laugh of childhood comes sweet to my ear.

I love, too, at evening, to rest in the dell
Where the tall fern is drooping above the green well;
When the vesper star burns—when the zephyr-wind blows,
When the lay of the nightingale ruffles the rose;
When silence is round me, below and above,
And my heart is imbued with the spirit of love;
When the things that I gaze on grow fairer, and seem
Like the fancy-wrought shapes of some young poet's dream.

In the calm reign of autumn I'm happy to roam,
When the peasant exults in a full harvest home;
When the boughs of the orchard with fruitage incline,
And the clusters are ripe on the stem of the vine;
When nature puts on the last smiles of the year,
And the leaves of the forest are scatter'd and sere;
When the lark quits the sky, and the linnet the spray,
And all things are clad in the garb of decay.

Even winter to me hath a thousand delights,
With its short gloomy days, and its long, starry nights;
And I love to go forth ere the dawn, to inhale
The health-breathing freshness that floats in the gale;
When the sun riseth red o'er the crest of the hill,
And the trees of the woodland are hoary and still!
When the motion and sound of the streamlet are lost
In the icy embrace of mysterious frost;
When the hunter is out on the shelterless moor,
And the robin looks in at the cottager's door;
When the spirit of nature hath folded his wings,
To nourish the seeds of all glorious things,
Till the herb and the leaf, and the fruit and the flower,
Shall awake in the fulness of beauty and power.

There's a harvest of knowledge in all that I see,
For a stone or a leaf is a treasure to me;
There's the magic of music in every sound,
And the aspect of beauty encircles me round:
While the fast gushing joy that I fancy and feel
Is more than the language of song can reveal.
Did God set His fountains of light in the skies,
That man should look up with the tears in his eyes?
Did God make this earth so abundant and fair,
That man should look down with a groan of despair?
Did God fill the world with harmonious life,
That man should go forth with destruction and strife?
Did God scatter freedom o'er mountain and wave,
That man should exist as a tyrant and slave?
Away with so hopeless—so joyless a creed,
For the soul that believes it is darken'd indeed.

THE VILLAGE PASTOR.

Goldsmith.

NEAR yonder copse, where once the garden smiled,
And still where many a garden flower grows wild;
There, where a few torn shrubs the place disclose,
The village preacher's modest mansion rose.
A man he was to all the country dear,
And passing rich with forty pounds a year;
Remote from towns he ran his godly race,
Nor e'er had changed, nor wished to change his place;
Unskilful he to fawn, or seek for power,
By doctrines fashion'd to the varying hour:
For other aims his heart had learn'd to prize,
More bent to raise the wretched than to rise.
His house was known to all the vagrant train,
He chid their wand'rings, but relieved their pain;
The long remember'd beggar was his guest,
Whose beard descending swept his aged breast.
The ruin'd spendthrift, now no longer proud,
Claim'd kindred there, and had his claims allowed.
The broken soldier, kindly bade to stay,
Sat by his fire, and talk'd the night away;
Wept o'er his wounds, or, tales of sorrow done,
Shoulder'd his crutch, and show'd how fields were won.
Pleased with his guests, the good man learn'd to glow,
And quite forgot their vices in their woe;
Careless their merits or their faults to scan,
His pity gave ere charity began.

Thus to relieve the wretched was his pride,
And e'en his failings lean'd to virtue's side;
But in his duty prompt at every call,
He watch'd and wept, he pray'd and felt for all;
And, as the bird each fond endearment tries
To tempt his new-fledged offspring to the skies,
He tried each art, reproved each dull delay,
Allured to brighter worlds, and led the way.

At church, with meek and unaffected grace,
His looks adorned the venerable place;
Truth from his lips prevail'd with double sway,
And fools, who came to scoff, remained to pray.
The service past, around the pious man,
With ready zeal, each honest rustic ran;
E'en children follow'd, with endearing wile,
And pluck'd his gown, to share the good man's smile.
His ready smile a parent's warmth exprest,
Their welfare pleased him, and their cares distrest;
To them his heart, his love, his griefs were given,
But all his serious thoughts had rest in heaven.
As some tall cliff that lifts its awful form,
Swells from the vale, and midway leaves the storm,
Though round its breast the rolling clouds are spread,
Eternal sunshine settles on its head.

Poems about a Future State.

HAMLET ON IMMORTALITY.

Shakespeare.

To be, or not to be, that is the question :—
Whether 'tis nobler in the mind to suffer
The slings and arrows of outrageous fortune :
Or to take arms against a sea of troubles,
And, by opposing, end them ? To die,—to sleep,—
No more ;—and, by a sleep, to say we end
The heart-ache, and the thousand natural shocks
That flesh is heir to : 'tis a consummation
Devoutly to be wished. To die ;—to sleep ;—
To sleep! perchance to dream ;—ay, there's the rub!
For in that sleep of death what dreams may come,
When we have shuffled off this mortal coil,
Must give us pause. There's the respect
That makes calamity of so long life :
For who would bear the whips and scorns of time,
The oppressor's wrong, the proud man's contumely,
The pangs of despised love, the law's delay,
The insolence of office, and the spurns
That patient merit of the unworthy takes,
When he himself might his quietus make
With a bare bodkin ? Who would fardels bear,
To grunt and sweat under a weary life,
But that the dread of something after death,—
The undiscovered country, from whose bourn
No traveller returns,—puzzles the will,
And makes us rather bear those ills we have,
Than fly to others that we know not of ?
Thus conscience does make cowards of us all ;
And thus the native hue of resolution
Is sicklied o'er with the pale cast of thought ;
And enterprises of great pith and moment,
With this regard, their currents turn awry,
And lose the name of action.

CATO ON IMMORTALITY.

Addison.

It must be so—Plato, thou reason'st well!
Else, whence this pleasing hope, this fond desire,
This longing after immortality ?
Or, whence this secret dread, and inward horror,
Of falling into nought ? Why shrinks the soul
Back on herself, and startles at destruction ?—
'Tis the Divinity that stirs within us,
'Tis heaven itself, that points out an hereafter,
And intimates Eternity to man.
Eternity! thou pleasing—dreadful thought!
Through what variety of untried being,
Through what new scenes and changes must we pass!
The wide, the unbounded prospect lies before me ;
But shadows, clouds, and darkness, rest upon it.
Here will I hold : If there's a Power above us—
And that there is, all nature cries aloud
Through all her works—He must delight in virtue ;
And that which he delights in, must be happy,
But when ? or where ? This world was made for Cæsar.
I'm weary of conjectures—this must end them.
(*Laying his hand on his sword.*)
Thus I am doubly armed. My death, my life,
My bane and antidote, are both before me.
This—in a moment, brings me to an end,
But this—informs me I shall never die!
The soul, secured in her existence, smiles
At the drawn dagger, and defies its point.—
The stars shall fade away, the sun himself
Grow dim with age, and nature sink in years ;
But thou shalt flourish in immortal youth,
Unhurt amidst the war of elements,
The wreck of matter, and the crash of worlds!

WE ARE SEVEN.

Wordsworth.

A SIMPLE child
That lightly draws its breath,
And feels its life in every limb,
What should it know of death?

I met a little cottage girl;
She was eight years old, she said;
Her hair was thick with many a curl
That clustered round her head.

She had a rustic, woodland air,
And she was wildly clad;
Her eyes were fair, and very fair;
—Her beauty made me glad.

"Sisters and brothers, little maid,
How many may you be?"
"How many? Seven in all," she said.
And wondering looked at me.

"And where are they? I pray you tell,"
She answered, "Seven are we;
And two of us at Conway dwell,
And two are gone to sea.

"Two of us in the churchyard lie,
My sister and my brother;
And, in the churchyard cottage, I
Dwell near them with my mother."

"You say that two at Conway dwell,
And two are gone to sea.
Yet ye are seven!—I pray you tell,
Sweet maid, how this may be?"

Then did the little maid reply,
"Seven boys and girls are we;
Two of us in the churchyard lie,
Beneath the churchyard tree."

"You run about, my little maid,
Your limbs they are alive;
If two are in the churchyard laid,
Then ye are only five."

"Their graves are green, they may be seen,"
The little maid replied,
"Twelve steps or more from my mother's door,
And they are side by side.

"My stockings there I often knit,
My kerchief there I hem;
And there upon the ground I sit—
I sit and sing to them.

"And often after sunset, Sir,
When it is light and fair,
I take my little porringer,
And eat my supper there.

"The first that died was little Jane;
In bed she moaning lay,
Till God released her of her pain:
And then she went away.

"So in the churchyard she was laid;
And all the summer dry,
Together round her grave we played,
My brother John and I.

"And when the ground was white with snow,
And I could run and slide,
My brother John was forced to go,
And he lies by her side."

"How many are you, then," said I,
"If they two are in heaven?"
The little maiden did reply,
"O master! we are seven."

"But they are dead: those two are dead;
Their spirits are in heaven!"
'Twas throwing words away, for still
The little maid would have her will,
And said, "Nay, we are seven!"

THE NEW NURSERY.

Susan Coolidge.

In the old familiar nursery
 The children were busy at play,
So busy they scarcely noticed
 When now and again, all day,
Mother or nursey entered
 And carried something away.

A chair or a tiny table,
 A pillow from off a bed,
The blankets and the coverlets
 They took, but they nothing said:
The pretty picture from off the wall,
 The table-cloth bright and red.

The cribs and then the cradle
 Rolled through the open door,
The bread-and-milk basins vanished,
 The carpet from the floor;
Then one by one the playthings went,
 At last there was nothing more.

And the little ones ceased their playing,
 And sat with solemn surprise,
Watching mamma and nursey,
 For they could not at all surmise
Why they should carry the toys away
 And hide them from their eyes.

The old familiar nursery
 Seemed lonely now and bare,
They missed the little snow-white beds,
 And every table and chair,
And the red lips quivered with crying
 While the grieved blue eyes did stare.

Then suddenly someone opened
 A carefully guarded door,
And they saw a large new nursery
 They had never seen before,
All gay and bright and beautiful,
 With sunshine on the floor.

There were the chairs and tables,
 And the pictures from the wall,
And the little beds all neatly spread,
 Each with its pillow small,
And every plaything they had missed,
 There were they, one and all.

And puzzle and sorrow forgotten,
 The joyous little crew
Left the bare, lonely room behind,
 And ran the doorway through;
And they did not miss the old at all,
 So pleasant was the new

And I thought as I saw them going,
 Of lives grown dull and bare,
Stripped of the sweet accustomed things
 Which made them dear and fair,
And only a puzzled patience left
 For the hearts that waited there.

And how shall suddenly open
 Some day, with a heavenly key,
A closely guarded invisible door,
 And the happy eyes shall see
Where, set in the glory of sunshine,
 The vanished and dear things be.

And they will laugh for pleasure,
 And scarcely believe it true,
And hasten to pass the portal;
 And, once they are safely through,
Forget the old sad and lonely life
 In the happiness of the new.

BRIGHT BE THE PLACE OF THY SOUL.

Byron on Kirke White.

Bright be the place of thy soul!
 No lovelier spirit than thine
E'er burst from its mortal control,
 In the orbs of the blessed to shine.

On earth thou wert all but divine.
 As thy soul shall immortally be;
And our sorrow may cease to repine,
 When we know that thy God is with thee.

Light be the turf of thy tomb!
 May its verdure like emeralds be;
There should not be the shadow of gloom
 In aught that reminds us of thee.

Young flowers and an evergreen tree
 May spring from the spot of thy rest;
But no cypress nor yew let us see;
 For why should we mourn for the blest?

THERE IS NO DEATH.

J. S. A.

We do not die—we cannot die;
 We only change our state of life
When these earth-temples fall and lie
 Unmoving 'mid the world's wild strife.

There is no death in God's wide world;
 But one eternal scene of change:
The flag of life is never furled,
 It only taketh wider range.

And when the spirit leaves its frame,
 Its home in which it long hath dwelt
It goes, a life that's real to claim,
 As if in this it had but slept.

Then let us not speak of "the dead,"
 For none are dead—all live, all love:
Our friends have only changed—have sped
 From lower homes to homes above.

OVER THERE.

Oh, the spacious grand plantation,
Over there!
Shining like a constellation,
Over there!
Holy with a consecration,
From all tears and tribulation,
From all crime and grief and care,
To all uses good and fair,
Over there!
Always brooding warm and golden,
Shines the mellow sunshine olden,
Over there!
Never blighting shadow passes
O'er the silken star-eyed grasses,
Waving wide their flowing hair
In the clear, translucent air,
Over there!
Oh, the grand encamping mountains,
Over there!
Oh, the sheeny, spouting fountains,
Over there!
Oh, the boundless starlit arches,
Where the sun in glory marches,
On a road for ever tending
Through bright angel worlds unending.
Over there!
Brilliant blossoms breathe and burn
Over there!
Nectar drunken drops the fern
By the tulip's early urn,
Over there!
Orange-buds and passion-flowers
Lattice sweet hymeneal bowers,
Over there!
All the heavenly creatures born
Of the breeze, the dew, the morn,
In the divinest beauty grow,
Drape their purple, drift their snow,
Don their crimson, sheen their gold,
Shed their odours manifold
On the palpitating air,
On the flower-laden air,
Over there!
Oh, the royal forests growing,
Over there!
Breath of balsam ever flowing,
Over there!
Pine-trees sing their breezy chime,
Palm-trees lift their plumy prime
In the ever Eden time,
Over there!
And a passionate perfume
Fills the deep delicious gloom;
While through forest arcades ringing
Lustrous birds are floating, singing,
Over there!
No salt tears the ground are drenching,
Over there!
Faint with toil no thin forms blenching,
Over there!
No more burdened backs are aching,
No more hearts are breaking, breaking,
Over there!
No more lifted hands outreaching
With a frantical beseeching;
No more desperate endeavours;
No more separating evers;
No more desolating nevers,
Over there! Over there!

THE BETTER LAND.

Mrs. Hemans

Child. I hear thee speak of the Better Land.
Thou callest its children a happy band.
Mother, oh, where is that radiant shore?
Shall we not seek it, and weep no more?
Is it where the flower of the orange blows,
And the fireflies glance through the myrtle boughs?—
Mother. Not there, not there, my child.

Child. Is it where the feathery palm-trees rise,
And the date grows ripe under sunny skies?
Or 'midst the green islands of glittering seas,
Where fragrant forests perfume the breeze,
And strange bright birds on their starry wings
Bear the rich hues of all glorious things?
Mother. Not there, not there, my child.

Child. Is it far away in some region old,
Where the rivers wander o'er sands of gold;
Where the burning rays of the ruby shine,
And the diamond lights up the secret mine,
And the pearl gleams forth from the coral strand,
Is it there, sweet mother, that better land?
Mother. Not there, not there, my child.

Mother. Eye hath not seen it, my gentle boy,
Ear hath not heard its deep songs of joy,
Dreams cannot picture a world so fair,
Sorrow and death may not enter there;
Time doth not breathe on its fadeless bloom,
For beyond the clouds, for beyond the tomb—
It is there, it is there, my child.

THE LAND OF LOVE.

THERE is a land of love,
Where every wind breathes soft, and glad, and free;
And every silvery, rippling stream exhales
Heart-joyous melody.

There sweetest, fairest flowers
Ope their love-tinted petals to the sun,
And gently breathe their ravishing perfume
The wayworn heart upon.

No burning sorrows there;
No broken, bleeding hearts can there abide,
No silent, yearning, unrequited love;
All, all are satisfied.

SHALL WE KNOW THE LOVED ONES THERE?

W. W. Hebbard.

And shall we know the loved ones there,
In yon bright world of love and bliss,
When on the wings of ambient air,
Our spirits soar away from this?
Or must we feel the ceaseless pain
Of absence in that glorious sphere,
And search through heaven's bright hosts in vain
The sainted forms we've cherished here?

Will not their hearts demand us there,—
Those hearts, whose fondest throbs were given
To us on earth, whose every prayer
Petitioned for our ties in heaven?
Whose love outlived the story past,
And closer twined around us here,
And deeper grew until the last—
Say, will they not demand us there?

Will they not wander lonely o'er
Those fields of light and life above,
If spirits they have loved of yore
Respond not to the call of love?
And though the glory of the skies,
And seraphs glittering crowns they wear,
Though heaven's full radiance greet their eyes,
Still, will they not demand us there?

It must be so; for heaven is home,
Where severed spirits re-unite;
And from the basement to its dome
Are altars sacred to the rite;
And joy doth strike her golden strings,
And holier seems that home of bliss,
As some reft heart from earth upsprings
To meet in that the loved of this.

AFTER DEATH.

Oh, where exists the spirit world
Which we must some day surely see?
Oh, where abides the Paradise
In which no death can be?

That mystic, solemn, sacred world
Where every eye is free from tears,
And every hand is true and good,
No fallings and no fears?

The world where we may hold for aye
Treasures far dearer than we lost;
Live on in blithe eternal peace,
Be no more tempest-tost?

Will there be tranquil meadow-trees,
Broad-bowering in their leafy calm?
And gentle winds that sleep through noon,
And wake for evening psalm?

Will there be sunshine on vast hills,
And rivers in the spreading vales,
And wealth of flowers and dewy leaves,
Where flute the nightingales?

Will there be gardens whose sweet fruit
Ripens and reddens all the day,
And homes where clustering roses cling,
And do not fade away?

We know not. But the weary fight
Is over when that life shall be,
And changed the aching of the soul
To calm felicity.

SHALL WE KNOW EACH OTHER THERE?

When we hear the music ringing
In the bright celestial dome—
When sweet angels' voices singing
Gladly bid us welcome home
To the land of ancient story,
Where the spirit knows no care;
In that land of life and glory—
Shall we know each other there?

When the holy angels meet us,
As we go to join their band,
Shall we know the friends that greet us
In that glorious spirit land?
Shall we see the same eyes shining
On us as in days of yore?
Shall we feel the dear arms twining
Fondly round us as before?

Yes, my earth-worn soul rejoices,
And my weary heart grows light,
For the thrilling angel voices,
And the angel faces bright,
That shall welcome us in heaven
Are the loved of long ago;
And to them 'tis kindly given
Thus their mortal friends to know.

Oh, ye weary, sad, and tossed ones,
Droop not, faint not by the way!
Ye shall join the loved and just ones
In that land of perfect day.
Harp-strings, touched by angel fingers,
Murmured in my raptured ear;
Evermore their sweet song lingers—
"We *shall* know each other there."

NO SECTS IN HEAVEN.

Talking of sects till late one eve,
Of various doctrines the saints believe,
That night I stood in a troubled dream,
By the side of a darkly flowing stream.

And a "Churchman" down to the river came,
When I heard a strange voice call his name,
"Good father, stop; when you cross the tide,
You must leave your robes on the other side."

But the aged father did not mind;
And his long gown floated out behind,
As down to the stream his way he took,
His pale hands clasping a gilt-edged book.

"I'm bound for heaven, and when I'm there,
Shall want my Book of Common Prayer;
And, though I put on a starry crown,
I should feel quite lost without my gown."

Then he fixed his eyes on the shining track,
But his gown was heavy and held him back,
And the poor old father tried in vain
A single step in the flood to gain.

I saw him again on the other side,
But his silk gown floated on the tide;
And no one asked in that blissful spot,
Whether he belonged to the "Church" or not.

Then down to the river a Quaker strayed;
His dress of a sombre hue was made.
"My coat and hat must all be gray—
I cannot go any other way."

Then he buttoned his coat straight up to his chin,
And staidly, solemnly waded in.
And his broad-brimmed hat he pulled down tight,
Over his forehead so cold and white.

But a strong wind carried away his hat;
A moment he silently sighed over that;
And then, as he gazed to the further shore,
The coat slipped off and was seen no more.

As he entered heaven his suit of gray
Went quietly sailing away, away;
And none of the angels questioned him
About the width of his beaver's brim.

Next came Dr. Watts with a bundle of psalms
Tied nicely up in his aged arms,
And hymns as many, a very wise thing,
That the people in heaven all round might sing.

But I thought that he heaved an anxious sigh,
And he saw that the river ran broad and high,
And looked rather surprised as one by one
The psalms and hymns in the wave went down.

And after him, with his MSS.,
Came Wesley, the pattern of goodliness;
But he cried, "Dear me! what shall I do?
The water has soaked them through and through."

And there on the river far and wide,
Away they went down the swollen tide;
And the saint, astonished, passed through alone,
Without his manuscripts, up to the throne.

Then gravely walking, two saints by name
Down to the stream together came;
But, as they stopped at the river's brink,
I saw one saint from the other shrink.

"Sprinkled or plunged? may I ask you, friend,
How you attained to life's great end?"
"*Thus*, with a few drops on my brow."
"But *I* have been dipped as you see me now.

"And I really think it will hardly do,
As I'm 'close communion,' to cross with you;
You're bound, I know, to the realms of bliss,
But you must go that way, and I'll go this."

Then straightway plunging with all his might,
Away to the left—his friend to the right.
Apart they went from this world of sin,
But at last together they entered in.

And now, when the river was rolling on,
A Presbyterian Church went down;
Of women there seemed an innumerable throng,
But the men I could count as they passed along.

And concerning the road they could never agree,
The *old* or the *new* way, which it could be,
Nor ever a moment paused to think
That both would lead to the river's brink.

And a sound of murmuring, long and loud,
Came ever up from the moving crowd;
"You're in the old way, and I'm in the new;
That is the false and this is the true"—
Or, "I'm in the old way, and you're in the new;
That is the false, and *this* is the true."

But the *brethren* only seemed to speak;
Modest the sisters walked and meek,
And if ever one of them chanced to say
What troubles she met with on the way,
How she longed to pass to the other side,
Nor feared to cross over the swelling tide,

A voice arose from the brethren then,
"Let no one speak but the 'holy men;'
For have ye not heard the words of Paul,
'Oh, let the women keep silence all'?"

I watched them long in my curious dream,
Till they stood by the borders of the stream;
Then, just as I thought, the two ways met:
But all the brethren were talking yet,
And would talk on till the heaving tide
Carried them over side by side—
Side by side, for the way was one;
The toilsome journey of life was done;
And all who in Christ the Saviour died,
Came out alike on the other side.

No forms of crosses or books had they;
No gowns of silk or suits of gray;
No creeds to guide them, or MSS.,
For all had put on Christ's righteousness.

FOOTSTEPS OF ANGELS.

Longfellow.

When the hours of Day are numbered,
 And the voices of the Night
Wake the better soul, that slumbered,
 To a holy, calm delight;

Ere the evening lamps are lighted,
 And, like phantoms grim and tall,
Shadows from the fitful fire-light
 Dance upon the parlour wall;

Then the forms of the departed
 Enter at the open door;
The beloved, the true-hearted,
 Come to visit me once more.

He, the young and strong, who cherished
 Noble longings for the strife,
By the road-side fell and perished,
 Weary with the march of life!

They, the holy ones and weakly,
 Who the cross of suffering bore,
Folded their pale hands so meekly,
 Spake with us on earth no more!

And with them the Being Beauteous,
 Who unto my youth was given,
More than all things else to love me,
 And is now a saint in heaven.

With a slow and noiseless footstep
 Comes that messenger divine,
Takes the vacant chair beside me,
 Lays her gentle hand in mine.

And she sits and gazes at me
 With those deep and tender eyes,
Like the stars so still and saint-like,
 Looking downward from the skies.

Uttered not, yet comprehended,
 Is the spirit's voiceless prayer,
Soft rebukes in blessings ended,
 Breathing from her lips of air.

O, though oft depressed and lonely,
 All my fears are laid aside,
If I but remember only
 Such as these have lived and died!

RESIGNATION.

Longfellow.

There is no flock, however watched and tended,
 But one dead lamb is there!
There is no fireside, howsoe'er defended,
 But has one vacant chair!

The air is full of farewells to the dying,
 And mournings for the dead;
The heart of Rachel, for her children crying,
 Will not be comforted!

Let us be patient! These severe afflictions
 Not from the ground arise,
But oftentimes celestial benedictions
 Assume this dark disguise.

We see but dimly through the mists and vapours
 Amid these earthly damps;
What seem to us but sad, funereal tapers,
 May be heaven's distant lamps.

There is no death! What seems so is transition;
 This life of mortal breath
Is but a suburb of life elysian,
 Whose portal we call death.

She is not dead—the child of our affection—
 But gone unto that school
Where she no longer needs our poor protection,
 And Christ himself doth rule.

In that great cloister's stillness and seclusion,
 By guardian angels led,
Safe from temptation, safe from sin's pollution,
 She lives whom we call dead.

Day after day we think what she is doing
 In those bright realms of air;
Year after year her tender steps pursuing,
 Behold her grown more fair.

Thus do we walk with her, and keep unbroken
 The bond which nature gives,
Thinking that our remembrance, though unspoken,
 May reach her where she lives.

Not as a child shall we again behold her;
 For when with raptures wild
In our embraces we again enfold her,
 She will not be a child;

But a fair maiden in her Father's mansion,
 Clothed with celestial grace;
And beautiful with all the soul's expansion
 Shall we behold her face.

And though at times impetuous with emotion,
 And anguish long suppressed,
The swelling heart heaves moaning like the ocean,
 That cannot be at rest,—

We will be patient, and assuage the feeling
 We may not wholly stay;
By silence sanctifying, not concealing,
 The grief that must have way.

WHISTLING IN HEAVEN.

W. S. Ralph.

YOU'RE surprised that I ever should say so?
Just wait till the reason I've given
Why I say I sha'n't care for the music,
Unless there is whistling in heaven.
Then you'll think it no very great wonder,
Nor so strange, nor so bold a conceit,
That unless there's a boy there a-whistling,
Its music will not be complete.

It was late in the autumn of '40;
We had come from our far Eastern home
Just in season to build us a cabin,
Ere the cold of the winter should come;
And we lived all the while in our wagon
That husband was clearing the place
Where the house was to stand; and the clearing
And building it took many days.

So that our heads were scarce sheltered
In under its roof, when our store
Of provisions was almost exhausted,
And husband must journey for more,
And the nearest place where he could get them
Was yet such a distance away,
That it forced him from home to be absent
At least a whole night and a day.

You see, we'd but two or three neighbours,
And the nearest was more than a mile,
And we hadn't found time yet to know them,
For we had been busy the while.
And the man who had helped at the raising
Just stayed till the job was well done;
And as soon as his money was paid him,
Had shouldered his axe and had gone.

Well, husband just kissed me and started—
I could scarcely suppress a deep groan
At the thought of remaining with baby
So long in the house all alone;
For, my dear, I was childish and timid,
And braver ones might well have feared,
For the wild wolf was often heard howling,
And savages sometimes appeared.

But I smothered my grief and my terror
Till husband was off on his ride,
And then in my arms I took Josey,
And all the day long sat and cried,
As I thought of the long dreary hours
When the darkness of night should fall,
And I was so utterly helpless,
With no one in reach of my call.

And when the night came with its terrors,
To hide ev'ry ray of light,
I hung up a quilt by the window,
And almost dead with affright,
I kneeled by the side of the cradle,
Scarce daring to draw a full breath,
Lest the baby should wake, and its crying
Should bring us a horrible death.

There I knelt until late in the evening,
And scarcely an inch had I stirred,
When suddenly, far in the distance,
A sound as of whistling I heard.
I started up dreadfully frightened,
For fear 'twas an Indian's call;
And then very soon I remembered
The red man ne'er whistles at all.

And when I was sure 'twas a white man,
  I thought, were he coming for ill,
He'd surely approach with more caution—
  Would come without warning, and still.
Then the sounds, coming nearer and nearer,
  Took the form of a tune light and gay,
And I knew I needn't fear evil
  From one who could whistle that way.

Very soon I heard footsteps approaching,
  Then came a peculiar dull thump,
As if someone was heavily striking
  An axe in the top of a stump:
And then, in another brief moment,
  There came a light tap on the door,
When quickly I undid the fast'ning,
  And in stepped a boy, and before

There was either a question or answer,
  Or either had time to speak.
I just threw my arms around him,
  And gave him a kiss on the cheek.
Then I started back, scared at my boldness,
  But he only smiled at my fright,
As he said, "I'm only your neighbour's boy, Elick,
  Come to tarry with you through the night.

"We saw your husband go eastward,
  And made up our minds where he'd gone,
And I said to the rest of our people,
  'That woman is there all alone.
And I venture she's awfully lonesome,
  And though she may have no great fear,
I think she would feel a bit safer
  If only a boy were but near.'

"So, taking my axe on my shoulder,
  For fear that a savage might stray
Across my path and need scalping,
  I started right down this way;
And coming in sight of the cabin,
  And thinking to save you alarm,
I whistled a tune just to show you
  I didn't intend any harm.

"And so here I am, at your service;
  But if you don't want me to stay,
Why, all you need do is to say so,
  And should'ring my axe I'll away."
I dropped in a chair and near fainted,
  Just at thought of his leaving me then,
And his eye gave a knowing bright twinkle,
  As he said, "I guess I'll remain."

And then I just sat there and told him
  How terribly frightened I'd been,
How his face was to me the most welcome
  Of any I ever had seen:
And then I lay down with the baby,
  And slept all the blessed night through,
For I felt I was safe from all danger
  Near so brave a young fellow and true.

So now, my dear friend, do you wonder,
  Since such a good reason I've given,
Why I say I sha'n't care for the music,
  Unless there is whistling in heaven?
Yes, often I've said so in earnest,
  And now what I've said I repeat,
That unless there's a boy there a-whistling,
  Its music will not be complete.

Poems about Conscience.

THE DREAM OF EUGENE ARAM.

Hood.

'TWAS in the prime of summer-time,
An evening calm and cool,
And four-and-twenty happy boys
Came bounding out of school:
There were some that ran, and some that leapt
Like troublets in a pool.

Away they sped with gamesome minds,
And souls untouched by sin;
To a level mead they came, and there
They drave the wickets in.
Pleasantly shone the setting sun
Over the town of Lynn.

Like sportive deer they coursed about,
And shouted as they ran,
Turning to mirth all things of earth,
As only boyhood can;
But the ushers at remote from all,
A melancholy man.

His hat was off, his vest apart,
To catch heaven's blessed breeze;
For a burning thought was in his brow,
And his bosom ill at ease:
So he leaned his head on his hands, and read
The book upon his knees.

Leaf after leaf he turned it o'er,
Nor ever glanced aside,
For the peace of his soul he read that book
In the golden eventide.
Much study had made him very lean,
And pale and leaden-eyed.

At last he shut the ponderous tome,—
With a fast and fervent grasp
He strained the dusky covers close,
And fixed the brazen hasp:
"O God! could I so close my mind,
And clasp it with a clasp!"

Then leaping on his feet upright,
Some moody turns he took,—
Now up the mead, then down the mead,
And past a shady nook,—
And lo! he saw a little boy
That pored upon a book.

"My gentle lad, what is't you read—
Romance or fairy fable?
Or is it some historic page
Of kings and crowns unstable?"
The young boy gave an upward glance:
"It is 'The Death of Abel.'"

The usher took six hasty strides,
As smit with sudden pain,—
Six hasty strides beyond the place,
Then slowly back again;
And down he sat beside the lad,
And talked with him of Cain;

And, long since then, of bloody men,
Whose deeds tradition saves;
Of lonely folk cut off unseen
And hid in sudden graves;
Of horrid stabs, in groves forlorn,
And murders done in caves;

And how the sprites of injured men
Shriek upward from the sod,—
Ay, how the ghostly hand will point
To show the burial clod;
And unknown facts of guilty acts
Are seen in dreams from God!

He told how murderers walk the earth
Beneath the curse of Cain,—
With crimson clouds before their eyes,
And flames about their brain;
For blood has left upon their souls
Its everlasting stain!

"And well," quoth he, "I know for truth
Their pangs must be extreme,—
Woe, woe, unutterable woe,—
Who spill life's sacred stream.
For why? Methought last night I wrought
A murder—in a dream.

"One that had never done me wrong—
A feeble man and old;
I led him to a lonely field,—
The moon shone clear and cold;
Now here, said I, this man shall die,
And I will have his gold.

"Two sudden blows with a ragged stick,
And one with a heavy stone,
One hurried gash with a hasty knife,
And then the deed was done:
There was nothing lying at my foot
But lifeless flesh and bone.

"Nothing but lifeless flesh and bone,
  That could not do me ill;
And yet I feared him all the more
  For lying there so still;
There was a manhood in his look
  That murder could not kill!

"And, lo! the universal air
  Seemed lit with ghastly flame—
Ten thousand thousand dreadful eyes,
  Were looking down in blame:
I took the dead man by the hand,
  And called upon his name!

"O God, it made me quake to see
  Such sense within the slain!
But when I touched the lifeless clay,
  The blood gushed out amain!
For every clot a burning spot
  Was scorching in my brain!

"And now from forth the frowning sky,
  From the heaven's topmost height,
I heard a voice—the awful voice
  Of the blood-avenging sprite:
"Thou guilty man! take up thy dead,
  And hide it from my sight!

"I took the dreary body up,
  And cast it in a stream—
A sluggish water, black as ink,
  The depth was so extreme.
My gentle boy, remember this
  Is nothing but a dream.

"Down went the corpse with a hollow [plunge,
  And vanished in the pool;
Anon I cleansed my bloody hands,
  And washed my forehead cool,
And sat among the urchins young
  That evening in the school.

"That night I lay in agony,
  In anguish dark and deep;
My fevered eyes I dared not close,
  But stared aghast at Sleep;
For Sin had rendered unto her
  The keys of hell to keep.

"All night I lay in agony,
  From weary chime to chime,
With one besetting horrid hint,
  That racked me all the time—
A mighty yearning like the first
  Fierce impulse unto crime.

"One stern tyrannic thought, that made
  All other thoughts its slave;
Stronger and stronger every pulse
  Did that temptation crave—
Still urging me to go and see
  The dead man in his grave.

"Heavily I rose up—as soon
  As light was in the sky—
And sought the black accursed pool
  With a wild misgiving eye;
And I saw the dead in the river bed,
  For the faithless stream was dry.

"Merrily rose the lark, and shook
  The dewdrop from its wing;
But I never marked its morning flight,
  I never heard it sing:
For I was stooping once again
  Under the horrid thing.

"With breathless speed, like a soul in chase
  I took him up and ran—
There was no time to dig a grave
  Before the day began:
In a lonesome wood, with heaps of leaves,
  I hid the murdered man!

"And all that day I read in school,
  But my thought was other where!
As soon as the mid-day task was done,
  In secret I was there:
And a mighty wind had swept the leaves
  And still the corpse was bare!

"Then down I cast me on my face
  And first began to weep;
For I knew my secret then was one
  That earth refused to keep;
Or land or sea, though he should be
  Ten thousand fathoms deep!

"So wills the fierce avenging sprite,
  Till blood for blood atones!
Ay, though he's buried in a cave,
  And trodden down with stones,
And years have rotted off his flesh,
  The world shall see his bones!

"O God! that horrid, horrid dream
  Besets me now awake!
Again—again, with dizzy brain,
  The human life I take;
And my red right hand grows raging hot
  Like Cranmer's at the stake.

"And still no peace for the restless clay
  Will wave or mould allow;
The horrid thing pursues my soul,—
  It stands before me now!"
The fearful boy looked up, and saw
  Huge drops upon his brow.

That very night, while gentle sleep
  The urchin eyelids kissed,
Two stern-faced men set out from Lynn,
  Through the cold and heavy mist;
And Eugene Aram walked between,
  With gyves upon his wrist.

THE UNCLE.

Henry Glassford Bell.

I HAD an uncle once—a man of threescore years and three ;—
And, when my reason's dawn began, he'd take me on his knee ;
And often talk, whole winter nights, things that seemed strange to
me.

He was a man of gloomy mood, and few his converse sought ;
But, it was said, in solitude his conscience with him wrought ;
And there, before his mental eye, some hideous vision brought.

There was not one in all the house who did not fear his frown,
Save I, a little careless child—who gambolled up and down ;
And often peeped into his room, and plucked him by the gown.

I was an orphan and alone—my father was his brother ;
And all their lives I knew that they had fondly loved each other ;
And in my uncle's room there hung the picture of my mother.

There was a curtain over it—'twas in a darkened place,
And few or none had ever looked upon my mother's face,
Or seen her pale expressive smile of melancholy grace.

One night—I do remember well—the wind was howling high,
And through the ancient corridors it sounded drearily—
I sat and read at that old hall ; my uncle sat close by.

I read—but little understood the words upon the book ;
For, with a sidelong glance, I marked my uncle's fearful look,
And saw how all his quivering frame in strong convulsions shook.

A silent terror o'er me stole, a strange, unusual dread ;
His lips were white as bone—his eyes sunk far down in his head ;
He gazed on me, but 'twas the gaze of the unconscious dead !

Then, suddenly, he turned him round, and drew aside the veil
That hung before my mother's face ; perchance my eyes might fail,
But, ne'er before, that face to me had seemed so ghastly pale !

"Come hither, boy !" my uncle said,—I started at the sound ;
'Twas choked and stifled in his throat, and hardly utterance found :—
"Come hither, boy !" then fearfully he cast his eyes around.

"That lady was thy mother once—thou wert her only child ;
Oh boy ! I've seen her when she held thee in her arms and smiled,—
She smiled upon thy father, boy, 'twas that which drove me wild !

"He was my brother, but his form was fairer far than mine;
I grudged not that;—he was the prop of our ancestral line,
And manly beauty was of him a token and a sign.

"Boy! I had loved her, too,—nay, more, 'twas I who loved her first;
For months—for years—the golden thought within my soul was nursed!
He came—he conquered—they were wed; my air-blown bubble burst!

"Then on my mind a shadow fell, and evil hopes grew rife;
The madd'ning thought stuck in my heart, and cut me like a knife,
That she, whom all my days I loved, should be another's wife!

"I left my home—I left the land—I crossed the raging sea;—
In vain—in vain!—where'er I turned, my memory went with me;—
My whole existence, night and day, in memory seemed to be.

"I came again—I found them here:—he died—no one knew how;
The murdered body ne'er was found, the tale is hushed up now;
But there was one who rightly guessed the hand that struck the blow.

"It drove *her* mad—yet not his death—no—not his death alone:
For she had clung to hope, when all knew well that there was none;
No, boy! it was a sight she saw that froze her into stone!

"I am thy uncle, child,—why stare so frightfully aghast?—
The arras waves,—but know'st thou not 'tis nothing but the blast?
I, too, have had my fears like these, but such vain fears are past.

"I'll show thee what thy mother saw,—I feel 'twill ease my breast,
And this wild tempest-laden night suits with the purpose best.
Come hither—thou hast often sought to open this old chest.

"It has a secret spring; the touch is known to me alone;
Slowly the lid is raised, and now—what see you that you groan
So heavily?—That thing is but a bare-ribbed skeleton."

A sudden crash—the lid fell down—three strides he backwards gave.
"Oh, Fate, it is my brother's self returning from the grave!
His grasp of lead is on my throat—will no one help, or save?"

That night they laid him on his bed, in raving madness tossed;
He gnashed his teeth, and with wild oaths blasphemed the Holy Ghost;
And, ere the light of morning broke, a sinner's soul was lost!

Poems about Duty.

THEN DO RIGHT.

WOULD'ST thou lead a useful life,
Would'st thou miss a world of strife,
Have thy bark serenely glide
Smoothly down life's earthly tide,
See the bright and sunny side?
Then do right!

Would'st thou have of men good-will,
Find a good in every ill,
Pass along in goodly cheer,
Never held in coward fear,
Have a mind and conscience clear?
Then do right!

Would'st thou save thy earthly form
From diseases' blight and storm,
Prosper without selfish end,
Find in all a brother, friend,
Each a helping hand to lend?
Then do right.

Would'st thou truest friendship know,
Would'st thou pure and holy grow,
Every tempter wisely scan,
Hold thy passions under ban,
Rise a truer, higher man?
Then do right!

THE WORLD IS FULL OF BEAUTY.

Gerald Massey.

THERE lives a voice within me, a guest-angel of my heart;
And its sweet lispings win me till the tears a-trembling start.
Up evermore it springeth, like some magic melody,
And evermore it singeth this sweet song of songs to me:
This world is full of beauty, as other worlds above;
And, if we did our duty, it might be full of love.

If faith, and hope, and kindness passed, as coin 'twixt heart and heart,
How through the eyes' tear-blindness should the sudden soul upstart!
The dreary, dim, and desolate should wear a sunny bloom,
And love should spring from buried hate like flowers from winter's tomb.
This world is full of beauty, as other worlds above;
And, if we did our duty, it might be full of love.

Were truth our uttered language, angels might talk with men,
And, God-illumined, earth should see the golden age again;
The burdened heart should soar in mirth, like morn's young prophet-lark,
And misery's last tear wept on earth quench hell's last cunning spark.
This world is full of beauty, as other worlds above;
And, if we did our duty, it might be full of love.

The leaf-tongues of the forest, and the flower-lips of the sod,
The happy birds that hymn their raptures in the ear of God,
The summer wind that bringeth music over land and sea,
Have each a voice that singeth this sweet song of songs to me:
This world is full of beauty, as other worlds above;
And, if we did our duty, it might be full of love.

SCATTER THE GERMS OF THE BEAUTIFUL.

Mrs. L. A. Cobb.

SCATTER the germs of the beautiful!
  By the wayside let them fall,
That the rose may spring by the cottage gate,
  And the vine on the garden wall;
Cover the rough and the rude of earth
  With a veil of leaves and flowers,
And mark with the opening bud and cup
  The march of summer hours.

Scatter the germs of the beautiful
  In the holy shrine of home,
Let the pure and fair and the graceful there
  In their loveliest lustre come;
Leave not a trace of deformity
  In the temple of the heart,
But gather about its hearth the gems
  Of nature and of art.

Scatter the germs of the beautiful
  In the temple of our God,
Of the God who starred the uplifted sky,
  And who flowered the trampled sod;
Building a temple for himself
  And a home for every race;
He reared each arch in symmetry,
  And curved each line in grace.

Scatter the germs of the beautiful
  In the depth of every soul;
They shall bud and blossom and bear the fruit
  While the endless ages roll;
Plant with the flowers of charity
  The portals of the tomb,
And truth, love, joy about your path
  In Paradise, shall bloom.

HASTE NOT! REST NOT!

Goethe.

WITHOUT haste, and without rest!
Bind the motto to thy breast;
Bear it with thee as a spell;
Storm and sunshine guide it well;
Heed not flowers that round thee bloom,
Bear it onward to the tomb.

Haste not! let no thoughtless heed
Mar for aye the spirit's speed;
Ponder well and know the right,
Onward then, with all thy might;
Haste not! years can ne'er atone
For one reckless action done.

Rest not! life is sweeping by,
Go and dare before you die;
Something mighty and sublime
Leave behind and conquer time;
Glorious 'tis to live for aye,
When these forms have passed away.

Haste not! rest not! calmly wait;
Meekly bear the storms of fate;
Duty be thy proper guide,
Do the right whate'er betide;
Haste not! rest not! conflicts past,
God shall crown thy work at last.

THREE WORDS OF STRENGTH.

Schiller.

THERE are three lessons I would write,—
  Three words as with a burning pen,
In tracings of eternal light,
  Upon the hearts of men.

Have HOPE. Though clouds environ now,
  And gladness hides her face in scorn,
Put thou the shadow from thy brow,—
  No night but hath its morn.

Have FAITH. Where'er thy bark is driven,—
  The calm's disport, the tempest's mirth,—
Know this,—God rules the hosts of heaven,
  Th' inhabitants of earth.

Have LOVE. Not love alone for one,—
  But man, as man, thy brothers call,
And scatter like the circling sun
  Thy charities on all.

Thus grave these lessons on thy soul,—
  Hope, Faith, and Love, and thou shalt find
Strength, when life's surges rudest roll,
  Light, when thou else wert blind.

THE HERITAGE.

Lowell.

THE rich man's son inherits lands,
 And piles of brick, and stones, and gold,
And he inherits soft, white hands,
 And tender flesh that feels the cold,
 Nor dares to wear the garment old;
A heritage, it seems to me,
One scarce would wish to hold in fee.

The rich man's son inherits cares:
 The bank may break, the factory burn,
A breach may burst his bubble shares,
 And soft white hands could hardly earn
 A living that would serve his turn;
A heritage, it seems to me,
One scarce would wish to hold in fee.

The rich man's son inherits wants,
 His stomach craves for daily fare;
With sated heart, he hears the pants
 Of toiling hinds with brown arms bare,
 And wearies in his easy chair!
A heritage, it seems to me,
One scarce would wish to hold in fee.

What doth the poor man's son inherit?
 Stout muscles and a sinewy heart,
A hardy frame, a hardier spirit;
 King of two hands, he does his part
 In every useful toil and art;
A heritage, it seems to me,
A king might wish to hold in fee.

What doth the poor man's son inherit?
 Wishes o'erjoyed with humble things,
A rank adjudged by toil-worn merit,
 Content that from employment springs,
 A heart that in its labour sings;
A heritage, it seems to me,
A king might wish to hold in fee.

What doth the poor man's son inherit?
 A patience learned by being poor,
Courage, if sorrow come, to bear it;
 A fellow-feeling that is sure
 To make the outcast bless his door;
A heritage, it seems to me,
A king might wish to hold in fee.

Oh, rich man's soul! there is a toil,
 That with all others level stands;
Large charity doth never soil,
 But only whiten soft, white hands—
 This is the best crops from thy lands;
A heritage, it seems to me,
Worth being rich to hold in fee.

Oh, poor man's son! scorn not thy state!
 There is worse weariness than thine,
In merely being rich and great!
 Toil only gives the soul to shine,
 And makes rest fragrant and benign;
A heritage, it seems to me,
Worth being poor to hold in fee.

Both, heirs to some six feet of sod,
 Are equal in the earth at last;
Both, children of the same dear God,
 Prove title to your heirship vast
 By record to a well-filled past;
A heritage, it seems to me,
Well worth a life to hold in fee.

LIVE TO SOME PURPOSE.

Procter.

THEY err who measure life by years,
 With false or thoughtless tongue:
Some hearts grow old before their time;
 Others are always young.

'Tis not the number of the lines
 On life's fast-filling page,
'Tis not the pulse's added throbs,
 Which constitute their age.

Some souls are serfs among the free,
 While others nobly thrive;
They stand just where their fathers stood;
 Dead, even while they live.

Others, all spirit, heart, and sense,
 Theirs the mysterious power
To live in thrills of joy or woe,
 A twelvemonth in an hour!

Seize, then, the minutes as they pass:
 The woof of life is thought!
Warm up the colours! let them glow
 With fire of fancy fraught.

Live to some purpose; make thy life
 A gift of use to thee:
A joy, a good, a golden hope,
 A heavenly argosy.

PROCRASTINATION.

THERE'S a little mischief-maker,
  That is stealing half our bliss;
Sketching pictures in a dream-land
  That are never seen in this;
Dashing from the lips the pleasures
  Of the present while we sigh:
You may know this mischief-maker
  For his name is By-and-By.

He is sitting by your hearthstones,
  With his sly, bewitching glance,
Whispering of the coming morrow
  As the social hours advance:
Loitering 'mid our calm reflections,
  Hiding forms of beauty nigh:
He's a smooth deceitful fellow,
  This enchanter, By-and-By.

You may know him by his winning,
  By his careless, sportive air;
By his sly, obtrusive presence,
  That is straying everywhere:
By the trophies that he gathers
  Where his sombre victims lie;
For a bold determined fellow
  Is the conquerer, By-and-By.

When the calls of duty haunt us,
  And the present seems to be
All the time that ever mortals
  Snatch from dark eternity,
Then a fairy hand seems painting
  Pictures on a painted sky;
For a cunning little artist
  Is the fairy, By-and-By.

'By-and-By,' the wind is singing,
  'By-and-By,' the heart replies;
But the phantom just above us
  Ere we grasp it ever flies.
List not to the idle charmer,
  Scorn the very specious lie—
Do not e'er believe or trust in
  This deceiver, By-and-By.

TO-DAY AND TO-MORROW.

Carpenter.

Don't tell me of to-morrow,
  Give me the man who'll say,
That when a good deed's to be done,
  "Let's do the deed to-day."
We may all command the present,
  If we act and never wait;
But repentance is the phantom
  Of a past that comes too late.

Don't tell me of to-morrow,
  There is much to do to-day
That can never be accomplished,
  If we throw the hours away.
Every moment has its duty,
  Who the future can foretell?
Then, why put off till to-morrow,
  What to-day can do as well?

Don't tell me of to-morrow,
  If we look upon the past,
How much that we have left to do,
  We cannot do at last;
To-day it is the only time
  For all on this frail earth;
It takes an age to form a life,
  A moment gives it birth.

ANIMAL EXISTENCE.

Watts

THERE are a number of us creep
Into this world, to eat and sleep;
And know no reason why we're born,
But only to consume the corn,
Devour the cattle, fowl and fish,
And leave behind an empty dish.
The crows and ravens do the same,
Unlucky birds of hateful name;
Ravens or crows might fill their places,
And swallow corn and carcases,
Then if their tombstone, when they die,
Be n't taught to flatter and to lie,
There's nothing better will be said
Than that 'they've eat up all their bread,
Drunk up their drink, and gone to bed.'

NOTHING TO DO.

Rev. W. J. Mathams.

Nothing to do! in a world like this,
  With thousands round us dying;
Nothing to do! when at every turn
  Children for bread are crying.

Nothing to do! while widows weep
  O'er those now past returning!
With helpless little lives to keep,
  Too little to be earning.

Nothing to do! while men can dare
  To spill the blood of brothers!
And on battle plains lie wounded boys
  Of broken-hearted mothers.

Nothing to do! while the burning tongue
  Of him in fever raging,
Cries out for water thou couldst bring,
  His inward fires assuaging.

Nothing to do! while God's dear love
  Is spurned for the sake of gold;
And the souls of men in His Church
  Like cattle are bought and sold.

Nothing to do! while the drunken fool
  Reels back to his cheerless home,
And smites the face which once he kissed,
  And in murder seals his doom.

Nothing to do! while banks do break,
  And thieves are great and high;
And the simple souls who trusted them
  In penury weep and die.

Nothing to do! while heathens wait
  For words of the better life,
To steel the gloom from eternity,
  And end their years of strife.

Nothing to do! are men so weak
  As not to feel their blindness?
As not to bless the hand that seeks
  To do a deed of kindness?

Nothing to do! oh, basest lie
  Which blasts the lips with a curse;
For he who these evils passeth by
  Himself shall suffer worse.

Nothing to do! say, wilt thou dare,
  With the judgment-throne in view,
To utter these words of guilt and shame,
  "Oh God, I had nothing to do?"

TO A WEARIED WORKER

J. M. W.

"Rest?—Thou must not seek for rest,
  Until thy task be done;
Thou must not lay thy burden down
  Till setting of the sun.

Thou must not weary of the life,
  Nor scorn thy lowly lot,
Nor cease to work, because such work
  Thy neighbour prizeth not.

Thou must not let thy heart grow cold,
  Nor hush each generous tone,
Nor veil the bright love in thine eye;
  Thou must not *live alone.*

When others strive, thou too, must help,
  And answer when they call;
The power to love God gave to thee,
  Thou must employ for all.

"Freedom and Rest" thou wouldest have:
  Freedom is service meet;
And rest of soul is but a name
  For toil amid life's heat.

Unmoved to gaze upon the strife,
  Is not true liberty;
To others thou must minister,
  Wouldst thou be truly free.

In the outward world 'tis vain to seek
  The Eden thou wouldst win:
That ancient paradise is gone—
  Thine Eden is within.

THE GOLDEN RULE OF PYTHAGORAS.

Written in Greece 2,400 years ago.

Let not soft slumber close thine eyes,
Before thou recollectest thrice
Thy train of actions through the day—
'Where have my feet found out the way?
What have I learned, where'er I've been,
From all I've heard, from all I've seen?
What know I more that's worth the
  knowing?
What have I done that's worth the doing?
What have I sought that I should shun?
What duties have I left undone?
Or into what new follies run?
These self enquiries are the road
That leads to virtue—leads to good.

HE LIVETH LONG WHO LIVETH WELL.

Dr. Bonar.

He liveth long who liveth well!
All other life is short and vain;
He liveth longest who can tell
Of living most for heavenly gain.

He liveth long who liveth well!
All else is being flung away;
He liveth longest who can tell
Of true things truly done each day.

Waste not thy being; back to Him,
Who freely gave it, freely give,
Else is that being but a dream,
'Tis but to *be*, and not to *live*.

Be wise, and use thy wisdom well:
Who wisdom *speaks* must *live* it too;
He is the wisest who can tell
How first he *lived*, then *spoke*, the true.

Fill up each hour with what will last;
Buy up the moments as they go;
The life above, when this is past,
Is the ripe fruit of life below.

Sow truth, if thou the true wouldst reap;
Who sows the false shall reap the vain:
Erect and sound thy conscience keep,
From hollow words and deeds refrain.

Sow love, and taste its fruitage pure:
Sow peace, and reap its harvest bright;
Sow sunbeams on the rock and moor,
And find a harvest-home of light.

WORK FOR HEAVEN.

"Household Words."

If thou hast thrown a glorious thought
Upon life's common ways,
Should other men the gain have caught,
Fret not to lose the praise.

Great thinker! often shalt thou find,
While folly plunders fame,
To thy rich store the crowd is blind,
Nor knows thy very name.

What matter that? if thou uncoil
The soul that God has given—
Not in the world's mean eye to toil,
But in the sight of Heaven?

If thou art true, yet in thee lurks
For fame a human sigh,
To nature go and see how works
That handmaid of the sky.

Her own deep bounty she forgets,
Is full of germs and seeds;
Nor glorifies herself, nor sets
Her flowers above her needs.

She hides the modest leaves between;
She loves untrodden roads;
Her richest treasures are not seen
By any eye but God's.

Accept the lesson—look not for
Reward—from out thee chase
All selfish ends; and ask no more
Than to fulfil thy place.

BE TRUE

Dr. Bonar

Thou must be true thyself,
If thou the truth wouldst teach;
Thy soul must overflow, if thou
Another's soul wouldst reach!
It needs the overflow of heart
To give the lips full speech.

Think truly, and thy thoughts
Shall the world's famine feed;
Speak truly, and each word of thine
Shall be a fruitful seed;
Live truly, and thy life shall be
A great and noble creed.

Poems about Justice.

ETERNAL JUSTICE.

Mackay.

THE man is thought a knave or fool,
Or bigot plotting crime,
Who, for the advancement of his kind,
Is wiser than his time.
For him the hemlock shall distil—
For him the axe be bared—
For him the gibbet shall be built,
For him the stake prepared!
Him shall the scorn and wrath of man
Pursue with deadly aim,
And malice, envy, spite, and lies
Shall desecrate his name:
But truth shall conquer at the last,
As round and round we run—
The right shall yet come uppermost,
And justice shall be done.

Pace through thy cell, old Socrates,
Cheerily to and fro;
Trust to the impulse of thy soul,
And let the poison flow.
They may shatter to earth the lamp of clay
That holds a light divine,
But they cannot quench the fire of thought
By any such deadly wine.
They cannot blot thy spoken words
From the memory of man
By all the poison ever was brew'd
Since time its course began.
To-day abhorr'd, to-morrow adored,
So round and round we run;
And ever the truth comes uppermost,
And ever is justice done.

Plod in thy cave, gray anchorite;
Be wiser than thy peers;
Augment the range of human power,
And trust to coming years.
They may call thee wizard, and monk accursed,
And load thee with dispraise;
Thou wert born five hundred years too soon
For the comfort of thy days;
But not too soon for humankind,
Time hath reward in store;
And the demons of our sires become
The saints that we adore.
The blind can see, the slave is lord,
So round and round we run;
And ever the wrong is proved to be wrong
And ever is justice done.

Keep, Galileo, to thy thought,
And nerve thy soul to bear:
They may gloat o'er the senseless words they wring
From the pangs of thy despair;
They may veil their eyes, but they cannot hide
The sun's meridian glow;
The heel of a priest may tread thee down,
And a tyrant work thee woe;
But never a truth has been destroy'd:
They may curse it and call it a crime;
Pervert and betray, or slander and slay,
Its teachers for a time;
But the sunshine aye shall light the sky,
As round and round we run;
And the truth shall ever come uppermost,
And justice shall be done.

And live there now such men as these—
With thoughts like the great of old?
Many have died in their misery,
And left their thought untold;
And many live, and are rank'd as mad,
And placed in the cold world's ban,
For sending their bright far-seeing souls
Three centuries in the van.
They toil in penury and grief;
Unknown, if not malign'd;
Forlorn, forlorn, hearing the scorn
Of the meanest of mankind!
But yet the world goes round and round,
And the genial seasons run;
And ever the truth comes uppermost,
And ever is justice done.

THE KING AND THE COTTAGER.

A PERSIAN LEGEND.

John G. Saxe.

Pray list unto a legend
 The ancient poets tell;
'Tis of a mighty monarch
 In Persia once did dwell;
A mighty queer old monarch
 Who ruled his kingdom well.

"I must build another palace,"
 Observed this mighty king;
"For this is getting shabby
 Along the southern wing;
And, really for a monarch,
 It isn't quite the thing."

So he travelled o'er his kingdom;
 A proper site to find,
Where he might build a palace
 Exactly to his mind,
All with a pleasant prospect
 Before it and behind.

Not long with this endeavour
 The King had travelled round,
Ere, to his royal pleasure;
 A charming spot he found;
But an ancient widow's cabin
 Was standing on the ground.

"Ah, here," exclaimed the monarch,
 "Is just the proper spot,
If this woman would allow me
 To remove her little cot."
But the beldam answered plainly,
 She had rather he would not!

"Within this lonely cottage,
 Great Monarch, I was born;
And only from this cottage
 By Death will I be torn:
So spare it, in your justice,
 Or spoil it in your scorn!"

Then all the courtiers mocked her,
 With cruel words and jeers:—
"'Tis plain her royal master
 She neither loves nor fears:
We would knock her ugly hovel
 About her ugly ears!

But to her deep amazement,
 His Majesty replied;
"Good woman, never heed them,
 The *King* is on your side:
Your cottage is your castle,
 And here you shall abide.

"To raze it in a moment,
 The power is mine I grant;
My absolute dominion
 A hundred poets chant;
For being *Khan* of Persia,
 There's nothing that I *can't!*"

('Twas in this pleasant fashion
 The mighty monarch spoke;
For kings have merry fancies
 Like other mortal folk;
And none so high and mighty
 But loves his little joke.)

"But power is scarcely worthy
 Of honour or applause,
That in its dominion
 Contemns the widow's cause,
Or perpetrates injustice
 By trampling on the laws.

"That I have wronged the meanest
 No honest tongue may say:
So bide you in your cottage,
 Good woman, while you may!
What's yours by deed and purchase
 No man may take away.

"And I will build beside it,
 For though your cot may be
In such a lordly presence
 No fitting thing to see,
If it honour not my castle,
 It will surely honour me!

"For so my loyal people.
 Who gaze upon the sight,
Shall know that in oppression
 I do not take delight;
Nor hold a king's convenience
 Before a subject's right!"

Now from his spoken purpose
 The King departed not;
He built the royal dwelling
 Upon the chosen spot,
And there they stood together,
 The palace and the cot!

Long, long he ruled his kingdom
 In honour and renown;
But danger ever threatens
 The head that wears a crown,
And Fortune, tired of smiling,
 For once put on a frown.

And so two wicked courtiers,
 Who long had strove in vain
By craft and evil counsels
 To mar the monarch's reign
Contrived a scheme infernal
 Whereby he should be slain!

To plan their wicked treason,
 They sought a lonely spot
Behind the royal palace,
 Hard by the widow's cot,
Who heard their machinations,
 And straight revealed the plot.

"I see," exclaimed the Persian,
 "*The just are wise alone;*
Who spares the rights of others
 May chance to guard his own;
The widow's humble cottage
 Has propped a monarch's throne!"

Poems about Charity.

HAVE CHARITY.

Burns.

THEN gently scan your brother man,
  Still gentler sister woman;
Though they may gang a kennin' wrang,
  To step aside is human.
One point must still be greatly dark,
  The moving why they do it:
And just as lamely can ye mark
  How far perhaps they rue it.

Who made the heart, 'tis He alone
  Decidedly can try us;
He knows each chord,—its various tone,
  Each spring,—its various bias:
Then at the balance let's be mute,
  We never can adjust it;
What's done we partly may compute,
  But know not what's resisted.

I DARE NOT SCORN.

Nicol.

I MAY not scorn the meanest thing
  That on the earth doth crawl;
The slave who dares not burst his chain,
  The tyrant in his hall,

The vile oppressor, who hath made
  The widow'd mother mourn,
Though, worthless, he before me stand—
  I cannot, dare not scorn.

The darkest night that shrouds the sky,
  Of beauty hath a share;
The blackest heart hath signs to tell
  That God still lingers there.

I pity all that evil are—
  I pity, and I mourn;
But the Supreme hath fashion'd all,
  And, oh! I dare not scorn.

IF WE KNEW.

Mrs. Charles.

IF we knew the cares and crosses,
  Crowded round our neighbour's way;
If we knew the little losses,
  Sorely grievous day by day,
Would we then so often chide him
  For the lack of thrift and gain,
Leaving on his heart a shadow,
  Leaving on our lives a stain;

If we knew the clouds above us
  Held by gentle blessing there,
Would we turn away, all trembling,
  In our blind and weak despair?
Would we shrink from little shadows,
  Lying on the dewy grass,
While 'tis only birds of Eden
  Just in mercy flitting past?

If we knew the silent story
  Quivering through the heart of pain,
Would our manhood dare to doom it
  Back to haunts of vice and shame?
Life is many a tangled crossing,
  Joy has many a break of woe,
And the cheeks tear-washed are whitest,
  And the blessed angels know.

Let us reach within our bosoms
  For the key to other lives,
And with love to erring nature,
  Cherish good that still survives;
So that when our disrobed spirits
  Soar to realms of light again,
We may say, "Dear Father! judge us
  As we judged our fellow men."

HOW LITTLE WE KNOW OF EACH OTHER!

How little we know of each other!
 As we pass through the journey of life,
With its struggles, its fears and temptations,
 Its heart-breaking cares and its strife.
We can only see things on the surface,
 For few people glory in sin;
And an unruffled face is no index
 To the tumult which rages within.

How little we think of each other;
 The man who to-day passes by,
Blessed with fortune, and honour, and titles,
 And holding his proud head on high,
May carry a dread secret with him,
 Which makes of his bosom a hell,
And he sooner or later a felon,
 May writhe in a prisoner's cell.

How little we know of each other!
 That woman of fashion, who sneers
At the poor girl betray'd and abandon'd,
 And left to her sighs and her tears,
May, ere the sun rises to-morrow,
 Have the mask rudely torn from her face,
And sink from the height of her glory
 To the dark shades of shame and disgrace.

How little we know of each other!
 Of ourselves too little we know,
We are all weak when under temptation,
 All subject to error and woe.
Then let blessed charity rule us,
 Let us put away envy and spite,
Or the skeleton grim in our closet
 May some day be brought to the light.

FREELY GIVE.

Go forth among the poor;
 Thy pathway leadeth there;
Thy gentle voice may soothe their pain,
 And blunt the thorns of care.
Go forth with earnest zeal,
 Nor from the duty start,
Speak to them words of gracious love,—
 Blest are the pure in heart.

Go forth among the sad,
 Lest their dark cup o'erflow;
They have on earth a heritage
 Of weariness and woe,
Tears dim their daily toil
 And sighs break out from sleep;
Change darkness into holy light,
 Blest are the eyes that weep.

Go forth through all the earth,
 There waiteth work for you,
The harvest truly seems most fair,
 But labourers are few;
With tireless, hopeful love
 Fulfil your lofty part,
And yours shall be the blessing too,—
 Blest are the pure in heart.

TWO CHURCH-BUILDERS.

John G. Saxe.

A FAMOUS king would build a church,
 A temple vast and grand;
And that the praise might be his own,
 He gave a strict command
That none should add the smallest gift
 To aid the work he planned.

And when the mighty dome was done,
 Within the noble frame,
Upon a tablet broad and fair,
 In letters all aflame
With burnished gold, the people read
 The royal builder's name.

Now when the king, elate with pride,
 That night had sought his bed,
He dreamed he saw an angel come
 (A halo round his head),
Erase the royal name, and write
 Another in its stead.

What could it be? Three times that night
 That wondrous vision came;
Three times he saw that angel hand
 Erase the royal name,
And write a woman's in its stead
 In letters all aflame.

Whose could it be? He gave command
 To all about his throne
To seek the owner of the name
 That on the tablet shone;
And so it was, the courtiers found
 A widow poor and lone.

The king enraged at what he heard,
 Cried, "Bring the culprit here!"
And to the woman trembling sore,
 He said, "'Tis very clear
That thou hast broken my command;
 Now let the truth appear!"

"Your majesty," the widow said,
 "I can't deny the truth;
I love the Lord—my Lord and yours—
 And so in simple sooth,
I broke your Majesty's command
 (I crave your royal ruth).

"And since I had no money, Sire,
 Why I could only pray
That God would bless your Majesty;
 And when along the way
The horses drew the stones, I gave
 To one a wisp of hay!"

"Ah! now I see," the king exclaimed,
 "Self-glory was my aim:
The woman gave for love of God,
 And not for worldly fame—
'Tis my command the tablet bear
 The pious widow's name

THE SILVER PLATE.

Margaret J. Preston.

THEY passed it along from pew to pew,
And gathered the coins, now fast, now few,
That rattled upon it: and every time
Some eager fingers would drop a dime
On the silver plate with a silver sound.
A boy, who sat in the aisle, looked round
With a wistful look—"Oh, if only he
Had a dime to offer how glad he'd be!"
He fumbled his pockets, but didn't dare
To hope he should find a penny there;
And much as he searched, when all was done,
He hadn't discovered a single one.

He had listened with wide-set earnest eyes,
As the minister, in a plaintive wise,
Had spoken of children all abroad
The world who had never heard of God;
Poor pitiful Pagans, who didn't know,
When they came to die, where their souls would go:
And who shrieked with fear when their mothers made
Them kneel to an idol god—afraid
He might eat them up—so fierce and wild,
And horrid he seemed to the frightened child,
"How different," murmered the boy, while his
Lips trembled, "How different Jesus is!"

And the more the minister talked, the more
The boy's heart ached to its inner core;
And the nearer to him the silver plate
Kept coming, the harder seemed his fate,
That he hadn't a penny (had that sufficed)
To give that the heathen might hear of Christ.
But all at once, as the silver sound
Just tinkled beside him, the boy looked round,
And he blushed as his eyes began to swim.

Then bravely turning as if he knew
There was nothing better that he could do,
He spoke in a voice that held a tear—
"Put the plate on the bench, beside me here."
And the plate was placed, for they thought he meant
To empty his pockets of every cent.
But he stood straight up, and he softly put
Right square in the midst of the plate—his foot,
And he said with a sob controlled before,
"I will give myself—I have nothing more!"

Poems about Kindness.

GENTLE WORDS.

A gentle word hath a magic power
  The weary breast to beguile;
It gladdens the eye, and lightens the brow,
  And changes the tear to a smile.

In the genial sunshine it sheds around,
  The shadows of care depart;
And we feel in its gentle and soothing tone,
  There's a balm for the wounded heart.

O watch, thou, then, that thy lips ne'er breathe
  A bitter, ungentle word;
For that which is lightly and idly said,
  Is often too deeply heard;

And though for a moment it leaves no trace,
  For pride will its woes conceal,—
Remember the spirit that's calm and still,
  Is always the first to feel.

It may not be in thy power, perchance,
  To secure a lofty place,
Or blazon thy name on history's page,
  As a friend of the human race;

For oft in the daily tasks of life,
  Though the world behold thee not,
A gentle and kindly word may soothe
  A brother's desponding lot.

Since life is a thorny and difficult path,
  Where toil is a portion of man,
We all should endeavour while passing along,
  To make it as smooth as we can.

Then let us learn to live in love,
  Where'er our fortunes call;
With a generous heart, a cheerful smile,
  And a gentle word for all.

THE GENTLE WORD.

Frances S. Osgood.

It came when pain and sorrow bowed
  A soul too much alone;
Like music came that kindly word,
  From one I ne'er have known.

Too sensitive to praise or blame,
  My childish heart I know:
And lightly yields my fragile frame
  To touch of joy or woe.

It brought a glow of glad surprise
  To pallid cheek and brow;
It brought the tears to drooping eyes,
  It brings them even now.

'Twas but a word—a little word—
  'Twas one I often meet!
Yet uttered then, so far away,
  It sounded passing sweet.

For well I know some friendly heart,
  I dreamed not of before,
First *thought* for me that little word—
  Nay, maybe thought of more!

Ah, *if* the clarion tones of fame
  Shall ever ring for me,
They shall not drown—my *heart* shall hear
  The praise I won for thee.

A NEW JOY.

F. W. Faber.

I met a child and kissed it; who shall say
  I stole a joy in which I had no part?
The happy creature from that very day
  Hath felt the more his little human heart.
Now when I pass he runs away and smiles,
And tries to seem afraid with pretty wiles.
  I am a happier and a richer man,
Since I have sown this new joy in the earth;
'Tis no small thing for us to reap stray mirth
  In every sunny wayside where we can.
It is a joy to me to be a joy,
  Which may in the most lonely heart take root;
And it is gladness to that little boy
  To look out for me at the mountain foot.

COMPASSION.

Miss Aiken.

AROUND the fire one wintry night,
The farmer's rosy children sat;
The fagot lent its blazing light,
And jokes went round in careless chat;

When, hark! a gentle hand they hear
Low tapping at the bolted door,
And thus, to gain their willing ear,
A feeble voice was heard implore:—

"Cold blows the blast across the moor,
The sleet drives hissing in the wind;
Yon toilsome mountain lies before—
A dreary, treeless waste behind.

My eyes are weak, and dim with age,
No road, no path can I descry;
And these poor rags ill stand the rage
Of such a keen, inclement sky.

So faint I am, these tottering feet
No more my palsied frame can bear;
My freezing heart forgets to beat.
The drifting snows my tomb prepare.

Open your hospitable door,
And shield me from the biting blast:
Cold, cold it blows across the moor—
The weary moor that I have passed!"

With hasty steps the farmer ran,
And close beside the fire they place
The poor half-frozen beggar-man,
With shaking limbs and pale-blue face.

The little children flocking came,
And chafed his frozen hand in theirs;
And busily the good old dame
A comfortable mess prepares.

Their kindness cheered his drooping soul,
And slowly down his wrinkled cheek
The big round tears were seen to roll,
Which told the thanks he could not speak.

The children then began to sigh,
And all their merry chat was o'er;
And yet they felt, they knew not why,
More glad than they had done before.

KINDNESS TO THE POOR.

'WE cannot always be giving;
The woman has come again;
She has such a whining story
Of hunger, or cold, or pain;
She wearies with petitions;
Her Johnny is out of a place,
Her children are sick with hunger—
I tire of her listless face.'

Grand Philip sat lazily reading;
The crimson gas-light shook,
From a shade that was ruby tinted,
Its red flakes over his book.
I thought that he did not notice;
But suddenly, sweet and low,
He said, with the voice of a dreamer,
'Don't let the woman go.'

And then, with his smile so royal,
So sweet with pity and pain,
He call'd her to the study,
Out of the merciless rain.
'Sit down, my friend,' and he gave her
The best chair in the place;
And I saw a quick blush brighten
Her haggard and listless face.

And then, in tones like music,
He sounded her frozen heart,
Till the thrill of a gentle question
Sunder'd its ice apart;
And tears, and sobs, and passion
Came thick as the midnight rain;
And she told such a pitiful story,
My own heart throbb'd with pain.

'You see,' said Philip, softly,
'She is greater than you or I;
She has struggled and conquer'd where we, love,
Would maybe sink down and die:
She has fought in the dark with demons,
With evil on every side;
And Satan hath tried to strip her
Even of her womanly pride.

'Love, let us be very tender;
The lowliest soul may be
A temple of priceless treasure,
That only a God can see.'
So the woman left our study,
With the face of an angel of light;
And she is my noblest pattern
Who came as a beggar that night.

GOOD TEMPER.

Charles Swain.

There's not a cheaper thing on earth,
 Nor yet one half so dear;
'Tis worth more than distinguish'd birth,
 Or thousands gain'd a year;
It lends the day a new delight;
 'Tis virtue's firmest shield;
And adds more beauty to the night
 Than all the stars may yield.

It maketh poverty content,
 To sorrow whispers peace;
It is a gift from Heaven sent
 For mortals to increase:
It meets you with a smile at morn;
 It lulls you to repose;
A flower for peer and peasant born,
 An everlasting rose.

A charm to banish grief away,
 To snatch the frown from care;
Turn tears to smiles, make dulness gay—
 Spread gladness everywhere:
And yet 'tis cheap as summer dew,
 That gems the lily's breast;
A talisman for love, as true
 As ever man possess'd.

As smiles the rainbow through the cloud
 When threatening storm begins—
As music 'mid the tempest loud,
 That still its sweet way wins—
As spring an arch across the tide,
 Where waves conflicting foam,
So comes this seraph to our side,
 This angel of our home.

What may this wondrous spirit be,
 With power unheard before—
This charm, this bright divinity?
 Good temper—nothing more!
Good temper!—'tis the choicest gift
 That woman homeward brings,
And can the poorest peasant lift
 To bliss unknown to kings.

SPEAK GENTLY.

D. Bates.

Speak gently! it is better far
To rule by love than fear;
Speak gently! let not harsh words mar
The good we might do here.

Speak gently! Love doth whisper low
The vows that true hearts bind,
And gently Friendship's accents flow,
Affection's voice is kind.

Speak gently to the little child;
Its love be sure to gain;
Teach it in accents soft and mild
It may not long remain.

Speak gently to the aged one,
Grieve not the care-worn heart;
The sands of life are nearly run;
Let such in peace depart.

Speak gently to the young, for they
Will have enough to bear;
Pass through this life as best they may,
'Tis full of anxious care.

Speak gently, kindly, to the poor,
Let no harsh tones be heard:
They have enough they must endure
Without an unkind word.

Speak gently to the erring; know
They may have toil'd in vain;
Perchance unkindness made them so;
Oh! win them back again.

Speak gently! He who gave His life
To bend man's stubborn will,
When elements were in fierce strife
Said to them, 'Peace, be still!'

Speak gently! 'tis a little thing
Dropp'd in the heart's deep well;
The good, the joy, which it may bring,
Eternity shall tell.

SPEAK GENTLY TO THE ERRING.

Woodman.

Speak gently to the erring—
Ye know not all the power
With which the dark temptation came
In some unguarded hour:
Ye may not know how earnestly
They struggled, or how well,
Until the hour of weakness came,
And sadly thus they fell!

Speak gently of the erring—
Oh! do not thou forget,
However darkly stain'd by sin,
He is thy brother yet.
Heir of the self-same heritage,
Child of the self-same God,
He hath but stumbled in the path
Thou hast in weakness trod.

Speak kindly to the erring—
For is it not enough
That innocence and peace are gone,
Without thy censure rough?
It surely is a weary lot
That sin-crushed heart to bear;
And they who share a happier fate
Their chidings well may spare.

Speak kindly to the erring—
Thou yet may'st lead him back,
With holy words, and tones of love,
From Misery's thorny track:
Forget not thou hast often sinn'd,
And sinful yet must be;
Deal kindly with the erring one,
As God has dealt with thee.

BLEST.

"Christian at Work."

BLEST be the tongue that speaks no ill,
  Whose words are always true,
That keeps the "law of kindness" still,
  Whatever others do.

Blest be the ears that will not hear
  Detraction's envious tale:
'Tis only through the list'ning ear
  That falsehood can prevail.

Blest be the heart that knows no guile,
  That feels no wish unkind,
Forgetting provocation while
  Good deeds are kept in mind.

Blest be the hands that toil to aid
  The great world's ceaseless need—
The hands that never are afraid
  To do a kindly deed.

Blest be the thoughtful brain that schemes
  A beautiful ideal; [dreams,
Mankind grows great through noble
  And time will make them real.

Do good in thought. Some future day
  'Twill ripen into speech;
And words are seeds that grow to deeds:
  None know how far they reach.

Like thistle-down upon the breeze,
  Swift scattered here and there,
So words will travel far, and these
  A fruitful harvest bear.

Where goodness dwells in heart and mind
  Both words and deeds will be
Like cords that closer draw mankind,
  In peace and charity.

PORTIA'S SPEECH ON MERCY.

Shakespeare.

THE quality of mercy is not strain'd;
It droppeth as the gentle dew from heaven
Upon the place beneath; it is twice blessed—
It blesseth him that gives, and him that takes;
'Tis mightiest in the mightiest; it becomes
The thronèd monarch better than his crown;
His sceptre shows the force of temporal power,
The attribute to awe and majesty,
Wherein doth sit the dread and fear of kings;
But mercy is above this sceptred sway—
It is enthroned in the hearts of kings,
It is an attribute of God himself;
And earthly power doth then show likest God's
When mercy seasons justice. Therefore, Jew,
Though justice be thy plea, consider this—
That in the course of justice, none of us
Should see salvation; we do pray for mercy;
And that same prayer doth teach us all
To render the deeds of mercy.

THINGS THAT NEVER DIE.

THE pure, the bright, the beautiful,
  That stirred our hearts in youth,
The impulse to a wordless prayer,
  The dreams of love and truth;
The longings after something lost,
  The spirit's yearning cry,
The strivings after better hopes—
  These things can never die.

The timid hand stretched forth to aid
  A brother in his need,
The kindly word in grief's dark hour
  That proves a friend indeed;
The plea for mercy gently breathed
  When justice threatens high,
The sorrow of a contrite heart—
  These things shall never die,

The memory of a clasping hand,
  The pressure of a kiss,
And all the trifles, sweet and frail,
  That make up love's first bliss;
If with a firm unchanging faith,
  And holy trust on high, [met—
Those hands have clasped, those lips have
  These things shall never die.

The cruel and the bitter word,
  That wounded as it fell;
The chilling want of sympathy,
  We feel but never tell;
The hard repulse that grieves the heart
  Whose hopes were bounding high,
In an unfading record kept—
  These things shall never die.

Let nothing pass, for every hand
  Must find some work to do;
Lose not a chance to waken love—
  Be firm, and just, and true:
So shall a light that cannot fade
  Beam on thee from on high,
And angel-voices say to thee—
  "These things shall never die."

SPEAK NOT HARSHLY.

SPEAK not harshly—much of care
Every human heart must bear;
Enough of shadows sadly play
Around the very sunniest way;
Enough of sorrows darkly lie,
Veiled within the merriest eye.
By thy childhood's gushing tears—
By thy griefs of after years—
By the anguish thou dost know—
Add not to another's woe.

Speak not harshly—much of sin
Dwelleth every heart within;
In its closely covered cells
Many a wayward passion dwells.
By the many hours misspent—
By the thoughts to folly lent—
By the wrong thou didst not shun—
By the good thou hast not done—
With a lenient spirit scan
The weakness of thy brother man.

KIND WORDS.

Whittier.

A LITTLE word in kindness spoken,
A motion or a tear,
May heal a spirit broken,
And make a friend sincere.

A word, or look, has crushed to earth
Oft many a budding flower,
Which, had a smile but owned its birth,
Would have blest life's latest hour.

Then deem it not an idle thing
A kindly word to speak;
The face you wear, the smile you bring,
May soothe a heart or break.

THERE'S NO DEARTH OF KINDNESS.

Gerald Massey.

THERE'S no dearth of kindness
In this world of ours;
Only in our blindness
We gather thorns for flowers!
Outward, we are spurning—
Trampling one another!
While we are inly yearning
At the name of "Brother!"

There's no dearth of kindness
Or love among mankind,
But in darkling loneness
Hooded hearts grow blind
Full of kindness tingling,
Soul is shut from soul,
When they might be mingling
In one kindred whole.

There's no dearth of kindness,
Though it be unspoken,
From the heart it buildeth
Rainbow-smiles in token—
That there be none so lowly,
But have some angel-touch:
Yet, nursing loves unholy,
We live for self too much.

As the wild rose bloweth,
As runs the happy river,
Kindness freely floweth
In the heart for ever.
But if men will hanker
Ever for golden dust,
Kingliest hearts will canker,
Brightest spirits rust.

There's no dearth of kindness
In this world of ours;
Only in our blindness
We gather thorns for flowers!
Oh, cherish God's best giving,
Falling from above;
Life were not worth living,
Were it not for Love.

THE UNKIND WORD.

Major Calder Campbell.

The strongest love hath yet, at times,
  A weakness in its power;
And latent sickness often sends
  The madness of an hour!
To her I loved, in bitterness
  I said a cruel thing:
Ah me! how much of misery
  From idle words may spring!

I loved her then—I love her still;
  But there was in my blood
A growing fever, that did give
  Its frenzy to my mood;
I sneer'd because another's sneers
  Had power my heart to wring:
Ah me! how much of misery
  From idle words may spring!

And when, with tears of wonder, she
  Look'd up into my face,
I coldly turn'd away mine eyes,
  Avoiding her embrace:
Idly I spake of idle doubts,
  And many an idle thing:
Ah me! how much of misery
  From idle words may spring!

Twas over soon, the cause,—not soon
  The sad effects pass'd by!
They rule beneath the winter's sun,
  And 'neath the summer's sky!
I sought forgiveness,—she forgave,
  But kept the lurking sting:
Alas! how much of misery
  From idle words may spring!

Month after month, year after year,
  I strove to win again
The heart an idle word had lost,
  But strove, alas! in vain.
Oh! ye who love, beware lest thorns
  Across Love's path ye fling:
Ye little know what misery
  From idle words may spring.

FRIENDS.

Swain.

If thou hast lost a friend
  By hard or hasty word,
Go call him to thy heart again;
  Let pride no more be heard.
Remind him of those happy days,
  Too beautiful to last;
Ask, if a word should cancel years
  Of truth and friendship past.
Oh! if thou'st lost a friend
  By hard or hasty word,
Go call him to thy heart again;
  Let pride no more be heard.

Oh! tell him, from thy thought
  The light of joy hath fled;
That, in thy sad and silent breast,
  Thy lonely heart seems dead:
That mount and vale, each path ye trod
  By morn or evening dim,
Reproach you with their frowning gaze,
  And ask your soul for him.
Then, if thou'st lost a friend
  By hard or hasty word,
Go call him to thy heart again;
  Let pride no more be heard.

GENTLE WORDS.

Each gentle word is a bird of love
That wings its way through the sky above,
To sing a song on the golden strand,
To give thee joy in the summer-land.

Each gentle word is a blooming vine,
That winds its way 'mid the stars that
  shine,
To weave a wreath on the golden strand,
To give thee joy in the summer-land.

Each gentle word is a music tide
That passes on to the other side,
To chant a lay on the golden strand,
To give thee joy in the summer-land.

Each gentle word is a sweet guitar
That blends its notes with the harps afar,
That angels touch on the golden strand,
To give thee joy in the summer-land.

All gentle words are the silver bells
That echo forth from the heart's deep
  wells,
To ring a chime on the golden strand,
To give thee joy in the summer-land.

BE KIND TO THE LOVED ONES AT HOME.

J. B. Woodbury.

Be kind to thy father, for when thou wert young,
Who loved thee so fondly as he?
He caught the first accents that fell from thy tongue,
And joined in thy innocent glee.
Be kind to thy father for now he is old,
His locks intermingled with grey;
His footsteps are feeble, once fearless and bold,
Thy father is passing away.

Be kind to thy mother, for, lo! on her brow,
May traces of sorrow be seen;
Oh, well may'st thou cherish and comfort her now,
For loving and kind hath she been.
Remember thy mother, for thee will she pray,
As long as God giveth her breath;
With accent of kindness then cheer her lone way,
E'en to the dark valley of death.

Be kind to thy brother, his heart will have mirth,
While he thinks he is not left alone;
The flowers of feeling would fade at their birth,
If the dew of affection were gone.
Be kind to your brother wherever you are.
The love of a brother shall be
An ornament purer and richer by far,
Than pearls from the depths of the sea.

Be kind to thy sister, not many may know
The depth of true sisterly love:
The wealth of the ocean lies fathoms below
The surface that sparkles above.
Be kind to thy father, once fearless and bold;
Be kind to thy mother so near;
Be kind to thy brother, nor show thy heart cold;
Be kind to thy sister so dear.

BE KIND.

Be kind to the old man, while strong in thy youth—
Be kind, not in seeming alone, but in truth;
He once was as young and as hopeful as thou,
With a bosom as light, as unwrinkled a brow!

Be kind to the poor man, and give of thy bread,
With shelter and pillow to comfort his head;
His lot and thine own may be one ere he dieth,
Or neighbour to thine the low grave where he lieth!

Be kind to the crooked, the lame, and the blind;
What's lacked in the body they feel in the mind;
And while virtue through trial and pain cometh forth,
In the mind, not the body, is man's truest worth.

Be kind to the fallen who lives but to mourn;
Be kind to the outcast who seeks to return;
Be kind to the hardened who never hath prayed;
Be kind to the timid who still is afraid!

The injured, who down by oppression is borne;
The slighted who withers; the victim of scorn;
The flattered who topples aloft but to fall;
The wronger and wronged—oh, be kindly to all!

SAY A KIND WORD WHEN YOU CAN.

WHAT were life without someone to cheer us,
  With a word or a smile on our way—
A friend who is faithfully near us,
  And heeds not what others may say;
The bravest of spirits have often
  Half failed in the race that they ran,
For a kind word life's hardships to soften,
  So say a kind word when you can.

Each one of us owns to some failing,
  Though some may have more than the rest;
But there's no good in heedlessly railing
  'Gainst those that are striving their best.
Remember, a word spoke complaining,
  May blight ev'ry effort and plan,
Which a kind word would help in attaining,
  So say a kind word when you can.

Oh! say a kind word then, whenever
  'Twill make the heart cheerful and glad,
But, chiefly, forget it oh never,—
  To the one that is hopeless and sad.
For there's no word so easy in saying;
  So begin, if you have not began,—
And never in life be delaying,
  To say a kind word when you can.

SEEDS OF KINDNESS.

LET us gather up the sunbeams
  Lying all around our path:
Let us keep the wheat and roses,
  Casting out the thorns and chaff;
Let us find our sweetest comfort
  In the blessings of to-day,
With a patient hand removing
  All the briars from the way.

  Then scatter seeds of kindness,
   For our reaping by-and-by.

If we knew the baby fingers,
  Pressed against the window pane,
Would be cold and stiff to-morrow—
  Never trouble us again—
Would the bright eyes of our darling
  Catch the frown upon our brow?—
Would the prints of rosy fingers
  Vex us then as they do now?

Ah! those little ice-cold fingers,
  How they point our memories back
To the hasty words and actions
  Strewn along our backward track!
How those little hands remind us,
  As in snowy grace they lie,
Not to scatter thorns—but roses,
  For our reaping by-and-by.

SCATTER BLESSINGS AS YOU GO.

SCATTER blessings, little darling,
  Life for you has just begun,
Let your smiles be bright and kindly
  As the rays of setting sun;
Hearts will lighten at your coming;
  Tears be dried and cease to flow
If you scatter on your pathway
  Kindly blessings as you go.

Scatter blessings, gentle maiden,
  They are better far than arts
Practised only for the moment
  On some unsuspecting hearts;
But the blessings last for ever!
  After you are old and grey
Some fond heart will love and cherish
  Words that never fade away.

Scatter blessings, white hair'd mother;
  Don't forget the shadow'd life
That has naught of joy and sunlight,
  Only mingled woe and strife
Scatter blessings, welcome blessings,
  On your pathway here below,
They will never be forgotten,
  Scatter blessings as you go.

THERE ARE KIND HEARTS EVERYWHERE.

O CALL it not a desert bare,
  This beauteous world below;
Nor say no flow'r of sympathy
  For anguish, for anguish here doth grow;
Affliction may have tried thee—
  Thy lot been hard to bear,
Yet speak not so untruly,
  There are kind hearts ev'rywhere;
Yet speak not so untruly,
  There are kind hearts ev'rywhere.

This world might be a Paradise,
  And life made bright with love,
Could each the other try to serve,
  And friendship, and friendship seek to prove.
Be patient, ever patient,
  And joy will be thy share;
So judge not too severely,
  There are kind hearts ev'rywhere;
So judge not too severely,
  There are kind hearts ev'rywhere.

O call it not a mockery,
  This beauteous world of ours;
Though full of lovely hopes that bloom
  To perish, to perish like its flow'rs;
Though dark clouds gather o'er thee,
  Ne'er yield thee to despair;
This life hath still its sunshine,
  There are kind hearts ev'rywhere;
This life hath still its sunshine,
  There are kind hearts ev'rywhere.

Poems about Humanity.

SOMEBODY'S DARLING.

Mrs. Lacoste.

Into the ward of the white-washed hall,—
Where the dead and dying lay,
Wounded by bayonet, shell, or ball,—
"Somebody's Darling" was borne one day:
"Somebody's Darling," so young and so brave,
Wearing yet, on his pale, sweet face,
Soon to be hid by the dust of the grave,
The lingering light of his boyhood's grace.

Matted and damp are the curls of gold,
Kissing the snow of that fair young brow;
Pale are the lips of delicate mould—
"Somebody's Darling" is dying now.
Back from his beautiful blue-veined brow,
Brush all the wandering waves of gold;
Cross his hands on his bosom now,—
"Somebody's Darling" is still and cold.

Kiss him once for "Somebody's" sake,
Murmur a prayer soft and low;
One bright curl from its fair mates take,
They were "Somebody's" pride, you know;
"Somebody's" hand had rested there—
Was it a mother's, soft and white?
And have the lips of a sister fair
Been baptised in these waves of light?

God knows best! he had "Somebody's" love;
"Somebody's" heart enshrined him there;
"Somebody" wafted his name above,
Night and morn, on the wings of prayer.
"Somebody" wept when he marched away,
Looking so handsome, brave, and grand;
"Somebody's" kiss on his forehead lay,
"Somebody" clung to his parting hand.

'Somebody's" waiting and watching for him
Yearning to hold him again to the heart;
And there he lies with his blue eyes dim,
And the smiling childlike lips apart!
Tenderly bury the fair young dead,
Pausing, to drop on his grave a tear!
Carve, on the wooden slab at his head,—
"'Somebody's Darling' slumbers here."

ONE OF THE LITTLE ONES.

George L. Catlin.

'Twas a crowded street, and a cry of joy
Came from a ragged, barefoot boy—
A cry of eager and glad surprise,
And he opened wide his great black eyes,
As he held before him a coin of gold
He had found in a heap of rubbish old
By the curb-stone there.
The passers-by
Paused at hearing that joyous cry,
As if 'twere a Heavenly chime that rung,
Or a note from some angel song had been sung
There, in the midst of the hurry and din
That raged in the city's heart within:
And they wondered to hear that song of grace
Sung in such strange, unusual place.
As ofttimes into a dungeon deep
Some ray of sunlight perchance will creep,
So did that innocent, childish cry
Break on the musings of passers-by
Bidding them all at once forget
Stocks, quotations, and tare and tret,
And the thousand cares with which are rife
The daily rounds of a business life.
"How it sparkles," the youngster cried,
As the golden piece he eagerly eyed.
"Oh, see it shine," and he laughed aloud,
Little heeding the curious crowd
That gathered 'round. "Hurrah," said he,
"How glad my poor old mother'll be;
I'll buy her a brand-new Sunday hat,
And a pair of shoes for Nell, at that.
And baby sister shall have a dress—
There'll be enough for all, I guess;
And then I'll——"
"Here," said a surly voice,
"That money's mine. You can take your choice
Of giving it up or going to jail;"
The youngster trembled, and then turned pale,
As he looked, and saw before him stand
A burly drayman with outstretched hand;
Rough and uncouth was the fellow's face,
And without a single line or trace
Of the goodness that makes the world akin.
"Come, be quick, or I'll take you in,"
Said he.
"For shame," said the listening crowd.
"The money is mine," he blustered out;
"I lost it yesterday hereabout.
I don't want nothin' but what's my own,
And I'm goin' to have it."
The lad alone
Was silent. A tear stood in his eye,
But he brushed it away, he *would not* cry,
"Here, master," he answered, "take it then;
If it's yours, it's yours; if it hadn't been—"
A sob told all he would have said,
Of the hope now so suddenly raised, now dead;
And then with a sigh which volumes told,
He dropped the glittering piece of gold
Into the other's hand. Once more
He sighed—and his dream of wealth was o'er.
But no. Humanity hath a heart
Always ready to take the part
Of childish sorrow wherever found.
"Let's make up a purse"—the word went 'round
Through the kindly crowd, and a hat was passed,
And the coins came falling thick and fast,
"Here, sonny, take this," they said. Behold,
Full twice as much as the piece of gold
He had given up was in the hand
Of the urchin. He could not understand
It all. The tears came thick and fast,
And his grateful heart found voice at last.
But, lo, when he spoke, the crowd had gone—
Left him, in gratitude there alone.
Who'll say there is not some sweet good-will
And kindness left in this cold world still?

THE FIREMAN.

R. T. Conrad.

[Written at the request of the Association for the Relief of Disabled Firemen, Philadelphia.]

THE city slumbers. O'er its mighty walls,
Night's dusky mantle, soft and silent, falls;
Sleep o'er the world slow waves its wand of lead,
And ready torpors wrap each sinking head.
Stilled is the stir of labour and of life!
Hushed is the hum, and tranquillized the strife.
Man is at rest with all his hopes and fears;
The young forget their sports, the old their cares:
The grave or careless, those who joy or weep,
All rest contented on the arm of sleep.
Sweet is the pillowed rest of beauty now,
And slumber smiles upon her tranquil brow;
Her bright dreams lead her to the moonlit tide,
Her heart's own partner wandering by her side.
'Tis summer's eve; the soft gales scarcely rouse
The low-voiced ripple and the rustling boughs;
And faint and far, some minstrel's melting tone
Breathes to her heart a music like its own.
When hark! Oh horror! what a crash is there!
What shriek is that which fills the midnight air?
'Tis fire! 'tis fire! She wakes to dream no more!
The hot blast rushes through the blazing door!
The dun smoke eddies round; and hark! that cry;
"Help! help! Will no one aid? I die—I die!"
She seeks the casement; shuddering at its height,
She turns again; the fierce flames mock her flight;
Along the crackling stairs they fiercely play,
And roar, exulting, as they seek their prey.
"Help! help! Will no one come?" She cries no more,
But, pale and breathless, sinks upon the floor.
Will no one save thee? Yes, there yet is one
Remains to save, when hope itself is gone;
When all hath fled, when all but he would fly,
The Fireman comes, to rescue or to die!
He mounts the stair—it wavers 'neath his tread!
He seeks the room—flames flashing round his head;
He bursts the door; he lifts her prostrate frame,
And turns again to brave the raging flame,
The fire blast smites him with its stifling breath;
The falling timbers menace him with death;
The sinking floors his hurried step betray;
And ruin crashes round his desperate way.
Hot smoke obscures—ten thousand cinders rise—
Yet still he staggers forward with his prize.
He leaps from burning stair to stair. On! on!
Courage! One effort more, and all is won!
The stair is passed—the blazing hall is braved!
Still on! Yet on! Once more! *Thank Heaven she's saved.*
The hardy seaman pants the storm to brave,
For beck'ning Fortune woos him from the wave;
The soldier battles 'neath his smoky shroud,
For Glory's bow is painted on the cloud;
The Fireman also dares each shape of death—
But not for fortune's gold nor glory's wreath.
No selfish throbs within their breasts are known;
No hope of praise or profit cheers them on.
They ask no meed, no fame; and only seek
To shield the suffering and protect the weak;
For this the howling midnight storm they woo;
For this the raging flames rush fearless through;
Mount the frail rafter—tread the smoky hall—
Or toil unshrinking, 'neath the tottering wall.
Nobler than they who, with fraternal blood,
Dye the dread field or tinge the shuddering flood—
O'er their firm ranks no crimson banners wave;
They dare—they suffer—not to slay—*but save!*
At such a sight, Hope smiles more heavenly bright;
Pale, pensive Pity trembles with delight;
And soft-eyed Mercy, stooping from above,
Drops a bright tear—a tear of joy and love!
And should the Fireman, generous, true, and brave,
Fall as he toils the weak to shield and save;
Shall no kind friend, no ministering hand be found
To pour the balm of comfort in his wound?
Or should he perish, shall his orphans say,
"He died for them—but what for us do they?"
Say, is it thus we should his toils requite?
Forbid it, Justice, Gratitude, and Right!
Forbid it, ye who dread what he endures;
Forbid it, ye whose slumbers he secures;
Forbid it, ye whose hoards he toils to save;
Forbid it, all, ye generous, just and brave!
And, above all, be you his friends, ye fair:
For you were ever his especial care!
Give to his cause your smiles, your gentle aid—
The Fireman's wounds are healed—the orphan's tears are stayed.

TRUE HUMANITY.

Dibdin.

WHEN once the din of war's begun
That heroes so delight in,
Armies are conquer'd, cities won,
By bloodshed and brave fighting.
The trumpet sounds! the columns march;
Friends from dear friends are sunder'd;
Prepared is the triumphal arch,
And the fallen foe are plunder'd.
All this I own deserves a name,
And truly in the roll of fame
Portrays a marking feature:
Yet give me bravery from the heart,
From self divested, and apart,
Exceeding mortal nature.
That rushes through devouring waves,
And, like a guardian angel, saves
A sinking fellow-creature.

In equal balance to maintain
The barriers of each nation,
Thus ever did stern Fate ordain
Slaughter should thin creation.
The trumpet sounds! his native land
Each tries to save from slavery:
While in the contest, hand to hand,
Walk clemency and bravery.
All this, I own, deserves a name,
And stands in the records of fame,
A truly marking feature;
Yet give me bravery from the heart,
From self divested, and apart—
Type of celestial nature,
That rushes through devouring waves,
And like a guardian angel, saves
A sinking fellow creature.

"WE'LL TAKE HER CHILDREN IN AMONGST OUR OWN."

Victor Hugo.

'Tis night. The cabin door is shut, the room,
  Though poor, is warm, and has a flickering light
By which you just distinguish through the gloom
  A shelf with row of plates that glimmer bright.
Some nets hung out to dry upon the wall,
And at the furthest end a curtained bedstead tall;
  Near it a mattress on rude benches spread—
A nest of souls—five children sleeping there;
  Upon the hearth some embers glowing red:
And by the bedside, wrapt in thought and prayer,
  The mother kneeling, anxious and alone,
While out of doors, with foaming breakers white
Unto the clouds, the winds, the rocks, the night,
  The gloomy ocean lifts its ceaseless moan.

Her husband is out fishing. From a lad,
  With chance and danger he has had to fight,
No matter what the weather—good or bad;
  The children hunger, and are thinly clad;
So in his little sailing boat each night
He must set off, however hard it blow,
His wife remains at home to wash and sew,
Prepare the bait, and mend the nets, and keep
  Watch o'er the herring broth—their only meal—
Till, all the children being put asleep,
  She can pray God for her dear husband's weal.
She prays, and praying hears the gulls' wild cry
  Sound as it mocked her, dismal shadows press
Into her mind—waves rolling mountains high,
  Fragments of wrecks, and sailors in distress,
And all the while, pent in its wooden frame,
The clock's impassive pulse beats on the same;
Each beat a summons countless souls obey,
To enter life or pass from life away.

But Jenny thinks no case is like her own,—
Her husband in his boat is all alone,
Alone this bitter night, beneath that sky's black pall!
"No help!" she sighs, "the boys are all too small!"
  Poor mother! saying now, "Were they but men,
Their father is alone"—the day draws nigh
  When they will share their father s perils; then,
"Would they once more were children!" wilt thou cry

She takes her lantern and her cloak—maybe
He is returning; anyhow she'll see
If still the beacon light be burning clear,
And if the waves are less, and daybreak near.

She goes—too soon: 'tis dark and rainy too,
No line of light divides the sky and main—
Nothing so dreary as this early rain;
You'd say Day wept its birth as mortal children do.
She wanders on—no window shows a light;
Sudden her glance—intent to find her way—
Meets an old hovel, fallen to decay;
No fire within—'tis black and cold as night,
From the low roof the ragged thatch flies fast,
And the door rattles loosely in the blast.

"Ah! the poor widow—I forgot her quite!
My husband found her worse the other day,
I'll just look in, a friendly word to say;
Sick and alone—a dismal lot is hers!"
She knocks, she listens—no one speaks or stirs,
Jenny stands shiv'ring at the broken door;
"Sick and with such young children, sick and poor—
She has but two, but then her husband's dead."
She knocks and calls, "What, neighbour! all in bed?"
Still the same silence—"Well, she must sleep fast;
No use in calling." All at once the blast,
As though the elements did sometimes heed
And take compassion on our human need,
Beat on the door and blew it open wide.

She entered, and her lantern's feeble light
Revealed the hovel's bare and ruined plight;
The rain fell through the roof on every side.

In the far corner of the wretched room
An awful form appeared from out the gloom—
A woman motionless and stiff—feet bare,
Glazed eyes that seemed to threaten by their stare;
A corpse—a mother not long since, strong, active, gay—
The spectre of dead poverty to-day!
All that remains to prove how dire the strife
That paupers wage with want and cold for life!
From out the straw one livid arm hung down,
The hand already dark with hues of death;
The mouth wide open, and the forehead's frown
Told of the struggle for the latest breath,
And bore the impress of that awful cry
Of death which echoes through eternity!
Close by the bed on which their mother died
A cradle stood, and in it side by side
Two rosy infants smile in slumber sweet;
The mother, feeling her last hour draw near,
Had heaped on them the gown she used to wear,
And rolled her cloak about their little feet,
Hoping that covered thus by fold on fold
They would keep warm while she was growing cold.

But what has Jenny in that cabin done;
What is she bearing in her cloak away;
What is the fear that causes her to run,
With beating heart, in such a stealthy way;
What is it she, with troubled glance, has laid
Upon her bed, behind the curtain's shade?
The woman has been stealing, you would say.

When she got home it was the break of day,
She sat down pale and trembling, some regret
Seemed to be weighing on her mind, she let
The brow she clasped fall heavy on the bed
And in short broken sentences, she said,
"My husband! Heavens! What will the poor man say!
Such toil and trouble—what a thing I've done!

Five children on his hands already. None
Work harder than he does; and I must make
His burden heavier. How that door does shake!
I thought 'twas he. Well, if he scold outright,
Or even beat me, it will serve me right.
Is that his footsteps? No—not yet—I'm glad—
Why, what a shame! things must be getting bad
When I'm afraid to see him back again!"
And then she shuddered, and a gloomy train
Of thought absorbed her so, she heard no more
The shrieking sea-birds or the waves' dull roar.
  Sudden the door bursts open, lets a track
Of cold light in: upon the threshold stands,
Dragging his dripping net with both his hands,
  The fisher, calling gaily, "Well! I'm back."

"'Tis you!" cried Jenny, as she caught and prest
Her husband as a lover to her breast,
And kissed his very clothes in her delight;
While he kept saying, "Here I am,—all right!"
His manly face, lit by the turf-fire showed
How his true heart at sight of Jenny glowed.
  "The sea's a thief!" he cried, "I'm fairly done!"

"What weather?" "Bad." "What sort of haul?" "Why, none;
But now I hug my Jenny all seems bright,
Well! I've caught nothing! and my net is torn—
  There was a devil of a wind that blew,
And once I thought—'twas getting on toward morn—
  We should capsize—the cable broke in two
What were you doing then?" O'er Jenny's frame
A shudder passed before her answer came—
"I! nothing much—I sat and sewed—the sea
Roared so like thunder it quite frightened me.
The winter seems set in before its time."
Then trembling as if taken in a crime,
Jenny continued—"Oh! and by the way,
Our neighbour's lying dead—died yesterday,
I think—at least it was last evening late—
'Twas after you were gone at any rate.
She leaves two children—boy and girl—quite small—
Johnny begins to walk and Meg to crawl.
  The poor good soul was almost starved, I fear."
The man looked grave at once, and flung away
His close blue cap wet through with rain and spray;
  "Deuce take it!" he exclaimed, and rubbed his ear,
"This will make seven, and we had five before;
How shall we keep the wolf from off the door?
  Why, in bad weather, as it was, the fare
Often ran short—'tis hard to see one's way.
  Well! I can't help it—'tis the Lord's affair.
Why take the mother from such brats away?
Not bigger than my fists—what use to say,
'Work for your bread' to mites like those? No doubt
Men must be scholars to make these things out,
  They fairly bother me,—go fetch them, wife,
If they should wake and find themselves alone,
With mammy dead, 'twould scare them out of life.
Look you, the mother's knocking at our door,
We'll take her children in amongst our own;
  At evening they will play about our knees,
Just like the other five we had before,
  Brothers and sisters all. When the Lord sees
That we have got to feed and clothe two more,
He'll send more fish into our net. Besides,
I can drink water, and work double tides.
  That's settled—run and fetch them—'tis not far.
What! vexed? I never saw you move so slow before!"
  She turns and draws the curtains—"There they are!"

HOW JANE CONQUEST RANG THE BELL.

James Milne, of Newcastle.

'TWAS about the time of Christmas, a many years ago,
When the sky was black with wrath and rack, and the earth was white with snow.
When loudly rang the tumult of winds and waves at strife;
In her home by the sea, with her babe on her knee, sat Harry Conquest's wife.
And he was on the waters, she knew not, knew not where,
For never a lip could tell of the ship to lighten her heart's despair.
And her babe was dying, dying, the pulse in the tiny wrist
Was all but still, and the brow was chill, and pale as the white sea mist.
Jane Conquest's heart was hopeless, she could only weep, and pray
That the Shepherd mild would take the child painlessly away.
The night grew deep and deeper, and the storm had a stronger will,
And buried in deep and dreamless sleep lay the hamlet under the hill.
And the fire was dead on the hearthstone within Jane Conquest's room,
And still sat she with her babe on her knee, at prayer amid the gloom,
When, borne above the tempest, a sound fell on her ear,
Thrilling her thought, for well she knew 'twas a voice of mortal fear;
And a light lept in at the lattice, sudden and swift and red,
Crimsoning all the whited wall, and the floor and the roof o'erhead.
It shone with a radiant glory on the face of the dying child,
Like a fair first ray of the shadowless day of the land of the undefiled;
And it lit up the mother's features with a glow so strange and new,
That the white despair that had gathered there seemed changed to hope's own hue
For one brief moment, heedless of the babe upon her knee,
With the frenzied start of a frightened heart, up to her feet rose she;
And thro' the quaint old casement she looked upon the sea—
Thank God, that the sight she saw that night so rare a sight should be.
Hemm'd in by hungry billows, whose madness foam'd at lip,
Half a mile from the shore, or hardly more, she saw a gallant ship
Aflame from deck to topmast, aflame from stem to stern,
For there seemed no speck on all the wreck where the fierce fire did not burn.
And the night was like a sunset, and the sea like a sea of blood,
And the rocks and the shore were bathed all o'er as by some gory flood.

She looked and looked, till the terror crept cold thro' every limb, [dim,
And her breath came quick, and her heart turned sick, and her sight grew dizzy and
And her lips had lost their utterance; though she strove, she could not speak,
But her feeling found no channel of sound in prayer, or sob, or shriek.
Silent she stood and rigid, with her child to her bosom prest,
Like a woman of stone, with stiff arms thrown round a stony babe at breast;
Till once more that cry of anguish thrill'd thro' the tempest's strife,
And it stirr'd again in her heart and brain the active, thinking life;
And the light of an inspiration lept to her brightened eye,
And on lip and brow was written now a purpose pure and high.
Swiftly she turn'd and softly she crossed the chamber floor,
And faltering not, in his tiny cot she laid the babe she bore;
And then, with a holy impulse, she sank to her knees and made
A lowly prayer in the silence there, and this was the prayer she prayed:
"Christ, who didst bear the scourging, but now dost wear the crown,
I at Thy feet, O true and sweet, would lay my burden down.
Thou badest me love and cherish the babe Thou gavest me,
And I have kept Thy word, nor stept aside from following Thee;
And lo! the boy is dying, and vain is all my care,
And my burden's weight is very great! yea, greater than I can bear.
And, Lord, Thou know'st what peril doth threat these poor men's lives;
I, a lone woman, most weak and human, plead for their waiting wives.
Thou canst not let them perish; up, Lord, in Thy strength and save
From the scorching breath of this terrible death on the cruel winter wave.
Take Thou my babe and watch it, no care is like to Thine,
And let Thy power, in this perilous hour, supply what lack is mine."
And so her prayer she ended, and rising to her feet,
Turned one look to the cradle nook where the child's faint pulses beat;
And then with softest footsteps retrod the chamber floor,
And noiselessly groped for the latch, and oped and crossed the cottage door.
The snow lay deep, and drifted as far as sight could reach,
Save where alone the dank weed strewn did mark the sloping beach.
But, whether 'twas land or ocean, or rock, or sand, or snow,
Or sky o'erhead, on all was shed the same fierce, fatal glow.
And thro' the tempest bravely Jane Conquest fought her way,
By snowy deep and slippery steep, to where her goal lay.

And she gain'd it, pale and breathless, and weary, and sore, and faint,
But with soul possess'd with the strength, and zest, and ardour of a saint.
Silent and weird, and lonely amid its countless graves,
Stood the old grey church on its tall rock perch, secure from the flood's great waves.
And beneath its sacred shadow lay the hamlet safe and still,
For howsoever the sea and the wind may be, 'twas quiet under the hill.
Jane Conquest reached the churchyard, and stood by the old church door;
But the oak was tough, and had bolts enough, and her strength was frail and poor.
So she crept through a narrow window and climbed the belfry stair,
And grasp'd the rope, sole cord of hope for the mariners in despair.
And the wild wind help'd her bravely, and she wrought with an earnest will,
And the clamorous bell spake out right well to the hamlet under the hill.
And it roused the slumb'ring fishers, nor its warning task gave o'er
Till a hundred fleet and eager feet were hurrying to the shore;
And then it ceased its ringing, for the woman's work was done,
And many a boat that was now afloat showed man's work was begun.
But the ringer in the belfry lay motionless and cold,
With the cord of hope, the church-bell rope, still in her frozen hold.
How long she lay it boots not, but she woke from her swoon at last,
In her own bright room, to find the gloom and the grief of the peril past.
With a sense of joy within her, and the Christ's sweet presence near,
And friends around, and the cooing sound of her babe's voice in her ear;
And they told her all the story, how a brave and gallant few
O'ercame each check, and reached the wreck and saved the hapless crew;
And how the curious sexton had climbed the belfry stair,
And of his fright, when, cold and white, he found her lying there;
And how, when they had borne her back to her home again,
The child she left, with a heart bereft of hope, and wrung with pain,
Was found within its cradle in a quiet slumber laid,
With a peaceful smile on its lips the while, and the wasting sickness stay'd.
And she said 'twas Christ that watched it, and brought it safely through,
And she praised His truth, and His tender ruth, who had saved her darling too.
And then there came a letter across the surging foam,
And last the breeze that over the seas bore Harry Conquest home.
And they told him all the story that still their children tell,
Of the fearful sight on that winter night, and the ringing of the bell.

Human Brotherhood.

TWO OF THE NOBLEST POEMS IN THE WORLD.

WHAT I LIVE FOR.

G. Linnæus Banks.

I LIVE for those who love me,
  For those I know are true;
For the heaven that smiles above me
  And awaits my spirit, too;
For all human ties that bind me,
For the task my God assign'd me,
For the bright hopes left behind me,
  And the good that I can do.

I live to learn their story
  Who've suffered for my sake,
To emulate their glory,
  And follow in their wake;
Bards, martyrs, patriots, sages,
The noblest of all ages,
Whose deeds crown history's pages
  And time's great volume make.

I live to hail that season
  By gifted minds foretold,
When men shall live by reason
  And not alone for gold;
When man to man united,
And every wrong thing righted,
The whole world shall be lighted
  As Eden was of old.

I live to hold communion
  With all that is divine,
To feel that there is union
  'Twixt Nature's heart and mine;
To profit by affliction,
Reap truth from fields of fiction,
Grow wiser from conviction—
  Fulfilling God's design.

I live for those that love me,
  For those that know me true,
For the heaven that smiles above me
  And awaits my spirit, too;
For the wrong that needs resistance,
For the cause that needs assistance,
For the future in the distance,
  And the good that I can do.

YOU ASK ME HOW I LIVE.

Joseph Robbins.

LIVING friendly, feeling friendly,
  Acting fairly to all men,
Seeking to do that to others
  They may do to me again,
Hating no man, scorning no man,
  Wronging none by word or deed:
But forbearing, soothing, serving,
  Thus I live—and this my creed.

Harsh condemning, fierce contemning,
  Is of little Christian use,
One soft word of kindly peace
  Is worth a torrent of abuse;
Calling things bad, calling men bad,
  Adds but darkness to their night,
If thou would'st improve thy brother
  Let thy goodness be his light.

I have felt and known how bitter
  Human coldness makes the world,
Ev'ry bosom round me frozen,
  Not an eye with pity pearl'd:
Still my heart with kindness teeming
  Glad when other hearts are glad,
And my eyes a tear-drop findeth
  At the sight of others sad.

Ah! be kind—life hath no secret
  For our happiness like this;
Kindly hearts are seldom sad ones,
  Blessing ever bringeth bliss;
Lend a helping hand to others,
  Smile though all the world should frown,
Man is man—we all are brothers,
  Black or white or red or brown.

Man is man through all gradations,
  Little recks it where he stands,
How divided into nations,
  Scattered over many lands;
Man is man by form and feature,
  Man by vice and virtue too,
Man in all one common nature
  Speaks and binds us brothers true.

THE FATHERLAND.

Lowell.

WHERE is the true man's fatherland?
Is it where he by chance is born?
Doth not the yearning spirit scorn
In such scant borders to be spanned?
O yes! his fatherland must be
As the blue heaven wide and free!

Is it alone where freedom is,
Where God is God, and man is man?
Doth he not claim a broader span
For the soul's love of home than this?
O yes! his fatherland must be
As the blue heaven wide and free!

Where'er a human heart doth wear
Joy's myrtle-wreath or sorrow's gyves,
Where'er a human spirit strives
After a life more true and fair—
There is the true man's birthplace grand;
His is a world-wide fatherland!

Where'er a single slave doth pine,
Where'er one man may help another—
Thank God for such a birthright, brother—
That spot of earth is thine and mine!
There is the true man's birthplace grand;
His is a world-wide fatherland!

TRIUMPH OF FRATERNITY.

Gerald Massey.

'TIS coming up the steep of time,
And this old world is growing brighter;
We may not see its dawn sublime,
Yet high hopes make the heart throb lighter.
We may be sleeping in the ground
When it awakes the world in wonder;
But we have felt it gathering round,
And heard its voice in living thunder—
'Tis coming! yes, 'tis coming!

'Tis coming now, the glorious time
Foretold by seers and sung in story:
For which, when thinking was a crime,
Souls leapt to heaven from scaffolds gory!
They pass'd, nor see the work they wrought;
Now the crown'd hopes of centuries blossom!
But the live lightning of their thought
And daring deeds doth pulse earth's bosom—
'Tis coming! yes, 'tis coming!

Creeds, empires, systems rot with age,
But the great people's ever youthful!
And it shall write the future's page
To our humanity more truthful!
The gnarliest heart hath tender cords,
To waken at the name of 'brother;'
And time comes when brain-scorpion words
We shall not speak to sting each other.
'Tis coming! yes, 'tis coming!

Fraternity! Love's other name!
Dear, heaven-connecting link of being!
Then shall we grasp thy golden dream,
As souls, full-statured, grow far-seeing;
Then shall unfold our better part,
And in our life-cup yield more honey;
Light up with joy the poor man's heart
And Love's own world with smiles more sunny—
'Tis coming! yes, 'tis coming.

Ay, it must come! The tyrant's throne
Is crumbling, with our hot tears rusted:
The sword earth's mighty ones have leant on
Is canker'd, with our heart's blood crusted,
Room! for the men of mind make way!
Ye robber rulers, pause no longer,
Ye cannot stay the opening day!
The world rolls on, the light grows stronger—
The people's advent coming!

WHO IS MY NEIGHBOUR?

THY neighbour?—it is he whom thou
Hath power to aid and bless,
Whose aching heart and burning brow
Thy soothing hand may press.

Thy neighbour?—'tis the fainting poor,
Whose eye with want is dim,
Whom hunger sends from door to door—
Go thou, and succour him.

Thy neighbour?—'tis that weary man
Whose eyes are at their brim,
Bent low with sickness, cares, and pain—
Go thou, and comfort him.

Thy neighbour?—'tis the heart bereft
Of every earthly gem:
Widow and orphan, helpless left—
Go thou, and shelter them.

Thy neighbour?—yonder toiling slave,
Fetter'd in thought and limb,
Whose hopes are all beyond the grave—
Go thou, and ransom him.

Where'er thou meet'st a human form
Less favour'd than thine own,
Remember 'tis thy neighbour worm,
Thy brother or thy son.

Oh! pass not, pass not heedless by,
Perhaps thou canst redeem
The breaking heart from misery—
Go, share thy lot with him.

ARE WE NOT BROTHERS?

HUSHED be the battle's fearful roar,
The warrior's rushing call!
Why should the earth be drenched with gore?
Are we not brothers all?

Want, from the starving poor depart!
Chains, from the captive fall!
Great God, subdue th' oppressor's heart!
Are we not brothers all?

Sect, clan, and nation, oh, strike down
Each mean partition-wall!
Let love the voice of discord drown,—
Are we not brother's all?

Let love and truth and peace alone
Hold human hearts in thrall,
That heaven its work at length may own
And men be brothers all?

UNIVERSAL PATRIOTISM.

OH, the glory! Oh, the glory!
That shall come to our dear mother world,
When the lightning of truth bright'ning
With ages as they roll,
Pulsing tides of love from soul to soul,
Shall dissever all oppressions,
And destroy all false consessions
To a party, sect, or clan;
Shall abolish all relations
Of the boundaries of nations
That enslave our brother man.

Oh, the glory! Oh, the glory!
That shall come to our dear mother world,
When the spirit we inherit,
Striking valiant 'gainst the wrong,
Shouting, "Equal rights to all belong!"
Shall emancipate the races,
And shall consecrate all places
Holy in a common cause,
Till there is a heart communion,
Of Humanity in union.
Ruled at last by "higher laws!"

BOND OF BROTHERHOOD.

Lowell.

WHEN a deed is done for Freedom, through the broad earth's aching breast
Runs a thrill of joy prophetic, trembling on from east to west;
And the slave, where'er he cowers, feels the soul within him climb
To the awful verge of manhood, as the energy sublime
Of a century bursts full-blossom'd on the thorny stem of Time.
Through the walls of hut and palace shoots the instantaneous throe,
Where the travail of the Ages wrings earth's systems to and fro;
At the birth of each new Era, with a recognizing start,
Nation wildly looks to nation, standing with mute lips apart,
And glad Truth's yet mightier man-child leaps beneath the Future's heart.
So the Evil's triumph sendeth, with a terror and a chill,
Under continent to continent, the sense of coming ill,
And the slave where'er he cowers, feels his sympathies with God
In hot tear-drops ebbing earthward, to be drunk up by the sod,
Till a corpse crawls round unburied, delving in the nobler clod.
For mankind are one in spirit, and an instinct bears along,
Round the earth's electric circle, the swift flash of right or wrong;
Whether conscious or unconscious, yet Humanity's vast frame
Through its ocean-sunder'd fibres feels the gush of joy or shame;
In the gain or loss of one race all the rest have equal claim.

BROTHERHOOD OF ALL MANKIND.

Frances Wright.

Is there a thought can fill the human mind
More pure, more vast, more generous, more refin'd,
Than that which guides the enlightened patriot's toil:
Not he, whose view is bounded by his soil;
Not he, whose narrow heart can only shrine
The land—the people that he calleth *mine;*
Not he, who to set up that land on high,
Will make whole nations bleed, whole nations die;
Not he, who, calling that land's rights his pride,
Trampleth the rights of all the world beside;
No!—He it is, the just, the generous soul!
Who owneth brotherhood with either pole,
Stretches from realm to realm his spacious mind,
And guards the weal of all the human kind,
Holds freedom's banner o'er the earth unfurl'd,
And stands the guardian patriot of a world.

WHAT MIGHT BE DONE. *Mackay.*

What might be done if men were wise—
What glorious deeds, my suffering brother,
Would they unite,
In Love and Right,
And cease their scorn for one another?

Oppression's heart might be imbued
With kindling drops of loving-kindness,
And Knowledge pour,
From shore to shore,
Light on the eyes of mental blindness.

All Slavery, Warfare, Lies and Wrongs,
All Vice and Crime might die together;
And wine and corn,
To each man born,
Be free as warmth in summer weather.

The meanest wretch that ever trod,
The deepest sunk in guilt and sorrow,
Might stand erect,
In self-respect
And share the teeming world to-morrow.

What might be done? *This* might be done,
And more than *this*, my suffering brother,
More than the tongue
E'er said or sung,
If men were wise and loved each other.

ABOU BEN ADHEM AND THE ANGEL. *Leigh Hunt.*

Abou Ben Adhem (may his tribe increase!)
Awoke one night from a sweet dream of peace,
And saw within the moonlight in his room,
Making it rich, and like a lily bloom,
An angel writing in a book of gold:—
And to the presence in the room he said,
"What writest thou?"—The vision raised its head,
And with a look made of all sweet accord,
Answered, "The names of those who love the Lord."
"And is mine one?" said Abou, "Nay, not so,"
Replied the angel. Abou spoke more low,
But cheerly still; and said, "I pray thee then
Write me as one that loves his fellow-men."
The angel wrote and vanished. The next night
It came again with a great wakening light,
And showed the names whom love of God had blest,
And lo! Ben Adhem's name led all the rest.

Poems about Equality.

ALL MEN EQUAL.

Harriet Martineau.

ALL men are equal in their birth,
Heirs of the earth and skies;
All men are equal when that earth
Fades from their dying eyes.

'Tis man alone who difference sees,
And speaks of high and low,
And worships those, and tramples these,
While the same path they go.

Ye great! renounce your earth-born pride;
Ye low! your shame and fear:
Live, as ye worship, side by side;
Your brotherhood revere.

Dr. Watts.

WHY do the proud insult the poor,
And boast the large estates they have?
How vain are riches to secure
Their haughty owners from the grave!

* * * * *

WHY doth the man of riches grow
To insolence and pride,
To see his wealth and honours flow
With every rising tide!

Why doth he treat the poor with scorn,
Made of the self-same clay!
And boast, as though his flesh was born
Of better dust than they?

HUMAN EQUALITY.

STRUGGLER in life's weary battle,
Though misfortune's lot you know,
Though your task be hard and heavy,
Sink not tamely down in woe.

Boldly up and claim your birthright,
One of vast creation's heirs.
What though others be before you?
You've a right as great as theirs.

Right, by labour and exertion,
Onward, still, to work your way,
Right to view, though gloomy present,
Promise in the future day.

Right to call the golden harvests
From the ever willing land,
Right to wage the war with fortune,
Stout of heart and strong of hand.

Let not sloth delay your progress,
Let not error dim your sight,
Let not sneers at your endeavours
Turn you from the path of right.

Let not empty fears beset you,
Calmly every danger scan,
Only cowards shrink from duty,
Boldly dare to be a man.

What though others tower above you
With the wealth their fathers made,
Spreading out like forest monarchs,
Must you perish in their shade?

No. Continue your exertions,
Do not linger to despond,
Rather burst into the sunlight
Waiting for you far beyond!

If at you some wealthy witling
Turns his supercilious nose,.
Think, that FIFTY PALTRY DOLLARS
Make the difference in your clothes.

Think, would you exchange your manhood
And the hopes for which you strain,
For this creature's hoarded thousands,
Frozen heart and empty brain.

"Onward! Upward!" be your motto—
Let your gaze be fixed on high,
And, on Honor's bright'ning pathway,
Hope will bloom and Doubt shall die.

Poems about Nobility.

WHAT IS NOBLE?

Swain.

WHAT is noble?—to inherit
 Wealth, estate, and proud degree?
There must be some other merit
 Higher yet than these for me!
Something greater far must enter
 Into life's majestic span,
Fitted to create and centre
 True nobility in man.

What is noble? 'Tis the finer
 Portion of our mind and heart
Linked to something still diviner
 Than mere language can impart;
Ever prompting—ever seeing
 Some improvement yet to plan
To uplift our fellow-being,
 And, like man, to feel for man!

What is noble? Is the sabre
 Nobler than the human spade?
There's a dignity in labour
 Truer than e'er pomp arrayed.
He who seeks the mind's improvement
 Aids the world in aiding mind,
Every great commanding movement
 Serves not one, but all mankind.

O'er the forge's heat and ashes,
 O'er the engine's iron head,
Where the rapid shuttle flashes,
 And the spindle whirls its thread,
There is labour, lowly tending
 Each requirement of the hour—
There is genius, still extending
 Science, and its world of power.

'Mid the dust, and speed, and clamour
 Of the loom-shed and the mill;
'Midst the clink of wheel and hammer
 Great results are growing still.
Though too oft by fashion's creatures
 Work and workers may be blamed,
Commerce need not hide its features—
 Industry is not ashamed.

What is noble? That which places
 Truth in its enfranchised will,
Leaving steps, like angel-traces,
 That mankind may follow still.
E'en though scorn's malignant glances
 Prove him poorest of his clan,
He's the Noble who advances
 Freedom and the Cause of Man.

TRUE NOBILITY.

Robert Nicoll.

I ASK not for his lineage,
 I ask not for his name;
If manliness be in his heart,
 He noble birth may claim.

I care not though of world's wealth
 But slender be his part,
If *yes* you answer when I ask,
 "Hath he a true man's heart?"

I ask not from what land he came,
 Nor where his youth was nursed;—
If pure the spring, it matters not
 The spot from whence it burst.

The palace or the hovel
 Where first his life began,
I seek not of; but answer this—
 "Is he an honest man?"

THE NOBLEST WORK OF GOD.

Pope.

HONOUR and shame from no condition rise,
Act well your part, there all the honour lies.
Fortune to men has some small difference made—
One flaunts in rags, one flutters in brocade,

What differ more, you say, than crown and cowl?
I'll tell you, friend, a wise man and a fool!
You'll find, if once the monarch act the monk,
Or, cobbler like, the parson will be drunk,
Worth makes the man, the want of it the fellow;
The rest is all but leather or prunella!

Who noble ends by noble means obtains,
Or, failing, smiles in exile and chains;
Like great Aurelius let him reign, or bleed
Like Socrates; that man is great indeed.
What's fame? a fancied life in other's breath—
A thing beyond us e'en before our death.
A wit's a feather, and a chief a rod;
An honest man's the noblest work of God!

A MAN'S A MAN FOR A' THAT.

Burns.

Is there for honest poverty,
That hangs his head, and a' that?
The coward slave, we pass him by.
And dare be be poor for a' that.
For a' that, and a' that;
Our toils obscure, and a' that;
The rank is but a guinea-stamp,
The man's the gowd for a' that.

What though on hamely fare we dine,
Wear hoddin gray, and a' that.
Gie fools their silks, and knaves their wine,
A man's a man for a' that.
For a' that, and a' that,
Their tinsel show, and a' that;
The honest man, though e'er so poor,
Is king o' men for a' that.

You see yon birkie, ca'd a lord.
Wha struts and stares, and a' that,
Though hundreds worship at his word,
He's but a coof for a' that.
For a' that, and a' that,
His riband, star, and a' that:
The man of independent mind
He looks and laughs at a' that.

A king can make a belted knight,
A marquis, duke, and a' that;
An honest man's aboon his might,
Gude faith, he maunna fa' that.
For a' that, and a' that,
Their dignities, and a' that,
The pith o' sense, and pride o' worth,
Are bigger ranks than a' that.

Then let us pray, that come it may,
And come it will for a' that,
That sense and worth, o'er a' the earth,
May bear the gree, and a' that.
For a' that, and a' that.
It's coming yet, for a' that,
That man to man, the wide warld o'er.
Shall brothers be for a' that.

QUEER.

From "Harper's Weekly."

I KNOW a woman who hath beauteous share
Of this world's wealth, and who is young and gay,
With not a care, save to bedeck herself
In finest silks or satins every day.
For her is spread the daintiest of fare;
On her commands the deftest servants wait;
No sounds of childish rompings vex her ear
When, to receive her friends she sits in state.
Goes she abroad, a carriage satin-lined
Bears her where'er she chooses that it should;
And yet to neither friend nor kin gives she
Aught to enhance their pleasure or their good.
Moths may des'roy, and want of sunshine fade,
She parts with nothing from her hoarded store:
On poverty she looks with scornful gaze.
And ne'er to beggar is unbarred her door.
Queer,
Isn't it, dear.

I know another; very poor is she,
And though not old, her brow is marked with care;
Eight children cluster round her, and 'tis hard
To find them food to eat and clothes to wear.
Sometimes the meal she serves is scant indeed;
Always her hours of sleep and rest are few;
She hath no help but little, willing hands
That though love guides them, can but little do.
And yet if poorer friends seek her, that friend
With outstretched hand and brightsome smile is met,
While with the best the cottage can afford
In kindly haste the humble board is set.
And from her door no beggar turns away
Without some help, if but a bit of bread;
And even homeless dogs about it throng
In simple trust that there they may be fed.
Queer,
Isn't it, dear!

ARE THE HEROES DEAD?

Anonymous.

THE winds that once the Argo bore
Have died by Neptune's ruined shrines;
And her hull is the drift of the deep sea-floor,
Though shaped of Pelion's tallest pines.

You may seek her crew on every isle
Fair in the foam of Ægean seas;
But out of their rest no charm can wile
Jason, and Orpheus, and Hercules.

And Priam's wail is heard no more
By windy Ilion's sea-built walls;
Nor great Achilles, stained with gore,
Shouts, "O ye Gods! 'tis Hector falls!"

On Ida's mount lies the shining snow,
But Jove has gone from its brow away;
And red on the plain the poppies grow
Where the Greek and the Trojan fought that day.

Mother Earth! are the heroes dead?
Do they thrill the soul of the years no more
Are the gleaming snows and the poppies red
All that is left of the brave of yore?

Are there none to fight as Theseus fought—
Far in the young world's misty dream?
Or to teach as the grey-haired Nestor taught?
Mother Earth! are the heroes gone?

Gone? in a grander form they rise.
Dead? we may clasp their hands in ours;
And catch the light of their clearer eyes,
And wreathe their brows with immortal flowers.

Whenever a noble deed is done,
'Tis the pulse of a hero's heart is stirred;
Whenever Right has a triumph won,
There are the heroes' voices heard.

Their armour rings on a fairer field
Than the Greek and the Trojan fiercely trod;
For Freedom's sword is the blade they wield,
And the light above is the smile of God.

So in his isle of calm delight
Jason may sleep the years away;
For the heroes live, and the sky is bright,
And the world is a braver world to-day.

FOR THOSE WHO FAIL.

Joaquin Miller.

"ALL honour to him who shall win the prize,"
The world has cried for a thousand years;
But to him who tries, and who fails and dies,
I give great honour and glory and tears.

Give glory and honour, and pitiful tears
To all who fail in their deeds sublime;
Their ghosts are many in the van of years;
They were born with Time in advance of Time.

Oh, great is the hero who wins a name;
But greater many and many a time
Some pale-faced fellow who dies in shame,
And lets God finish the thought sublime.

THE CONQUERED.

W. W. S. in Blackwood.

I SING the Hymn of the Conquered, who fell in the battle of life—
The hymn of the wounded, the beaten, who died overwhelmed in the strife;
Not the jubilant song of the victors, for whom the resounding acclaim
Of nations was lifted in chorus, whose brows wore the chaplet of fame,—
But the hymn of the low and the humble, the weary, the broken in heart,
Who strove and who failed, acting bravely a silent and desperate part;
Whose youth bore no flower on its branches, whose hopes burned in ashes away,
From whose hands slipped the prize they had grasped at; who stood at the dying of day
With the work of their life all around them, unpitied, unheeded, alone,
With death sweeping down o'er their failure, and all but their faith overthrown.

While the voice of the world shouts its chorus, its pæan for those who have won—
While the trumpet is sounding triumphant; and, high to the breeze and the sun
Gay banners are waving, hands clapping, and hurrying feet
Thronging after the laurel-crowned victors—I stand on the field of defeat
In the shadow, 'mongst those who are fallen, and wounded, and dying—and there
Chant a requiem low, place my hand on their pain-knotted brows, breathe a prayer,
Hold the hand that is helpless, and whisper, "They only the victory win,
Who have fought the good fight and have vanquished the demon that tempts us within;

Who have held to their faith unseduced by the prize that the world holds on high;
Who have dared for a high cause to suffer, resist, fight,—if need be, to die."
Speak, History! Who are life's victors? Unroll thy long annals and say—
Are they those whom the world calls the victors, who won the success of the day?
The Martyrs or Nero? The Spartans who fell at Thermopylæ's tryst
Or the Persians and Xerxes? His judges or Socrates? Pilate or Christ?

UNKNOWN HEROES.

Oh! 'mid the dazzle and the glare
  Of this world's fleeting show,
How many stout hearts sink beneath
  A weight of battered woe—
Heroes whose names are scarcely breathed
  Beyond home's humble hearth—
Who lived unknown—unreck'd-of die—
  The Brave Souls of the Earth!

And genius, glory, love to shed
  Around the warrior's name,
And in verse or story consecrate
  Their own bright sons of Fame;
Thus morn's glad halo hovers o'er
  Proud peaks that pierce the sky,
While shrouded in oblivion's gloom
  The lowly valleys lie.

Yet in the hidden vales of life
  Are battles fought and won—
Genius, though seeking not the blaze
  Of Fame's too partial sun;
There oft are Fortune's stern scowls met,
  Griefs uncomplaining borne—
With only God and Hope to cheer
  Lone hearts with sorrow worn.

There have I seen strong men grow pale
  Beneath the grip of Want,
Disease's famish'd phantom form
  The lowly dwelling haunt,
And Death the parent's fond hopes crush,
  Relentless, one by one,
While from the gloom the suff'rers look'd,
  And breathed, "Heaven's will be done!"

God knows, Wealth's favourites ne'er can know
  The fortitude sublime
That nerves the poor man's soul to keep
  Unstain'd by vice and crime;
When the partner of his wretchedness,
  The children of his heart,
In looks of misery bid the tears
  Of helpless sorrow start.

'Tis music to the soldier's soul
  When a nation's proud acclaim
Greets him the laurell'd conqueror
  In war's unhallow'd game;
But loftier joy that hero boasts,
  Who toiling up life's road,
By unseen triumphs wins the smiles
  Of conscience and of God!

Like the lonely bark that ploughs her way
  Far on the dreary deep,
And sinks (unmark'd by all save Heaven)
  Beneath the storm's wild sweep,
Earth's unknown heroes silently
  The world's rough tempest brave,
And gliding noteless o'er life's waste, sink
  To a fameless grave.

Yet, what though unknown, ye warriors, if
  Ye war for Truth and Love!
Unmarked below, your silent lives
  Are register'd above;
When the blood-bought laurels of the field
  Beneath Time's touch shall die.
Ye nameless ones of earth shall shine
  In Heaven eternally!

In that all-glorious land beyond
  The grave's dark wilderness,
Where titles, riches, sounding names,
  Sink into nothingness,
The wretched beggar's tattered garb,
  By honest virtue worn,
Shall laugh the crime-stain'd diadems
  Of guilty kings to scorn.

Poems about Nobleness.

JOHN MAYNARD.

'TWAS on Lake Erie's broad expanse,
One bright midsummer day,
The gallant steamer *Ocean Queen*
Swept proudly on her way.
Bright faces clustered on the deck,
Or, leaning o'er the side,
Watched carelessly the feathery foam
That flecked the rippling tide.

Ah, who beneath that cloudless sky,
That smiling bends serene,
Could dream that danger awful, vast,
Impended o'er the scene—
Could dream that e'er an hour had sped
That frame of sturdy oak
Would sink beneath the lake's blue waves,
Blackened with fire and smoke.

A seaman sought the captain's side,
A moment whispered low;
The captain's swarthy face grew pale,
He hurried down below.
Alas, too late! Though quick and sharp
And clear his orders came,
No human effort could avail
To quench the insidious flame.

The bad news quickly reached the deck,
It sped from lip to lip,
And ghastly faces everywhere
Looked from the doomèd ship.
"Is there no hope—no chance of life?"
A hundred lips implore;
"But one," the captain made reply,
"To run the ship on shore."

A sailor whose heroic soul
That hour should yet reveal,
By name John Maynard, eastern born,
Stood calmly at the wheel.
"Head her south-east!" the captain shouts,
Above the smothered roar,
"Head her south-east without delay!
Make for the nearest shore!"

No terror pales the helmsman's cheek,
Or clouds his dauntless eye,
As in a sailor's measured tone
His voice responds, "Ay, ay!"
Three hundred souls, the steamer's freight,
Crowd forward wild with fear;
While at the stern the dreadful flames
Above the deck appear.

John Maynard watched the nearing flames
But still with steady hand,
He grasped the wheel, and stedfastly
He steered the ship to land.
"John Maynard, can you still hold out?"
He heard the captain cry;
A voice from out the stifling smoke
Faintly responds, "Ay, ay!"

But half a mile! a hundred hands
Stretch eagerly to shore.
But half a mile! That distance sped,
Peril shall all be o'er.
But half a mile! Yet stay, the flames
No longer slowly creep,
But gather round the helmsman bold
With fierce, impetuous sweep.

"John Maynard," with an anxious voice
The captain cries once more,
"Stand by the wheel five minutes yet,
And we will reach the shore."
Through flame and smoke that dauntless heart
Responded firmly, still
Unawed, though face to face with death,
"With God's good help I will!"

The flames approached with giant strides,
They scorch his hands and brow;
One arm disabled seeks his side,
Ah, he is conquered now!
But no! his teeth are firmly set,
He crushes down the pain—
His knee upon the stanchion pressed,
He guides the ship again.

One moment yet! one moment yet!
Brave heart, thy task is o'er!
The pebbles grate beneath her keel,
The steamer touches shore.
Three hundred grateful voices rise
In praise to God, that He
Hath saved them from the fearful fire,
And from th' ingulfing sea.

But where is he, that helmsman bold?
The captain saw him reel—
His nerveless hands released their task,
He sunk beside the wheel.
The waves received his lifeless corpse,
Blackened with smoke and fire,
God rest him! Hero never had
A nobler funeral pyre!

THE STORY OF A STOWAWAY.

Clement Scott.

Come, my lad, and sit beside me; we have often talked before
Of the hurricane and tempest, and the storms on sea and shore:
When we read of deed and daring, done for dear old England's sake,
We have cited Nelson's duty, and the enterprise of Drake;
'Midst the fever'd din of battle, roll of drum, and scream of fife,
Heroes pass in long procession, calmly yielding up their life.
Pomps and pageants have their glory, in cathedral aisles are seen
Marble effigies; but seldom of the mercantile marine.
If your playmates love adventure, bid them gather round at school
Whilst you tell them of a hero, Captain Strachan of Liverpool.

Spite of storm and stress of weather, in a gale that lash'd the land,
On the *Cyprian* screw steamer, there the captain took his stand.
He was no fair-weather sailor, and he often made the boast
That the ocean safer sheltered than the wild Carnarvon coast.
He'd a good ship underneath him, and a crew of English form,
So he sailed from out the Mersey in the hurricane and storm.
All the luck was dead against him—with the tempest at its height,
Fires expired and rudders parted, in the middle of the night
Sails were torn and rent asunder. Then he spoke with bated breath:
"Save yourselves, my gallant fellows! we are drifting to our death!"

Then they looked at one another, and they felt the awful shock,
When, with a louder crash than tempest, they were dashed upon a rock.
All was over now and hopeless; but across those miles of foam
They could hear the shouts of people, and could see the lights of home.
"All is over!" screamed the Captain. "You have answered duty's call.
Save yourselves! I cannot help you! God have mercy on us all!"
So they rushed about like madmen, seizing belt, and oar, and rope—
For the sailor knows where life is, there's the faintest ray of hope—
Then, amidst the wild confusion, at the dreaded dawn of day,
From the hold of that doomed vessel crept a wretched Stowaway!

Who shall tell the saddened story of this miserable lad?
Was it wild adventure stirred him, was he going to the bad?
Was he thief, or bully's victim, or a runaway from school,
When he stole that fatal passage from the port of Liverpool?
No one looked at him, or kicked him, 'midst the paralysing roar
All alone he felt the danger, and he saw the distant shore.
Over went the gallant fellow, when the ship was breaking fast,
And the captain with his lifebelt—he prepared to follow last;
But he saw a boy neglected, with a face of ashy grey,
"Who are you?" roared out the Captain. "I'm the boy what stow'd away!"

There was scarce another second left to think what he could do,
For the fatal ship was sinking—Death was ready for the two.
So the Captain called the outcast—as he faced the tempest wild—
From his own waist took the lifebelt—and he bound it round the child!
"I can swim, my little fellow! Take the belt, and make for land.
Up, and save yourself!" The outcast humbly knelt to kiss his hand.
With the lifebelt round his body then the urchin cleared the ship;
Over went the gallant Captain, with a blessing on his lip.
But the hurricane howled louder than it ever howled before,
As the Captain and the stowaway were making for the shore!

When you tell this gallant story to your playfellows at school,
They will ask you of the hero, Captain Strachan, of Liverpool.
You must answer: They discovered, on the beach at break of day,
Safe—the battered, breathing body of the little Stowaway;
And they watched the waves of wreckage and they searched the cruel shore,
But the man who tried to save the little outcast—was no more.

. . . .

When they speak of English heroes, tell this story where you can,
To the everlasting credit of the bravery of man,
Tell it out in tones of triumph or with tears and quickened breath,
"Manhood's stronger far than storms, and Love is mightier than Death!"

THE FATHER'S SACRIFICE.

There is a law in France imposing military service on certain conditions, to which there are few exceptions, the principal one being that a widow's only son is exempt. A small provincial land-holder and his wife had one son on whom the mother doated with unutterable fondness. The time drew near for the boy to go to military service. To escape this the father attempted suicide, that the mother being widowed by his death might keep the loved son at home. The succeeding lines are founded on this perfectly veritable circumstance.

The family was small, indeed, but three
Were there in all, but any one could see
That father, mother, and the only son
Were in affection dwelling as but one.
The mother's heart was centered in her child,
From babyhood, his loving eyes beguiled.
The boy was bright, with laughter ringing clear;
And he won hearts residing far and near;
And with an opening manhood, promised well,
To make his deeds among his fellows tell.
No sister and no other son was there
Parental love so beautiful to share.
But let me tell you 'twas not in our land
Resided this united little band.
'Twas in fair France, the land described as gay,
Where blue skies smile upon the glowing day.
But though so many things combine to charm,
Quite free from England's atmospheric harm,
There was conscription's terrible command,
Unknown in this, our free old foggy land,
The mother knew that with increasing years,
Her eyes would fill with sorrow laden tears.
Because her only boy must leave her side,
The law of France must certainly divide;
And as the day drew near when her good son
Must leave the home for duty to be done,
Her brow grew sadder, and her step more slow,
'Twas the o'ershadowing of unbidden woe
Which introduced the thorn into the rose,
And frequently the sunniest smiling froze.
The father saw the sorrow she endured,
And knew stern grief could never be allured
From her fond bosom when the boy should go,
The duties of a soldier's life to know.

And long the father pondered to devise,
If possible to make some way arise
Whereby this doating wife might not be robbed
Of him for whom her faithful bosom throbbed.
He thought of this by night as well as day,
And so the seasons slowly ebbed away.
There was but *one* escape,—no *widow's* boy
Was ever borne away to war's employ;
So, if *he* died, the mother and the son
Might in the cottage dwell as only one.
This thought itself the more and more impressed,
It held him when he went to bed for rest;
In hours of darkness, with too active eyes,
This soul-absorbing thought would still arise.
And so, one evening hour, he sought the tide,
Of the home-river, standing on its side.
A message there was placed within his vest
Which simply sacrificial love confessed—
"She shall not lose her boy," it was but these
Few syllables, yet oh! what agonies
Were there in them, and yet a hope, a dream,
As with a plunge he sought the chilly stream:
But aid was near, a boat was on the tide,
Strong arms, in evening shadows, reach his side,
And almost in the grasp of craving death
They won him back into the vital breath.
They bore him to the cottage standing nigh,
The message, too attracted many an eye.
Long did he lie upon the snowy bed
With strangest wand'ring in his troubled head.
"She shall not lose her boy" was on his lips,
The legend of his imminent eclipse.
The mother and the son well knew the worth
Of him, yet providentially on earth,
The story was detailed o'er all the land,
The story of the small united band,
And 'twas decreed that such a sacrifice
The father who gave life as willing price,
To shield his wife and son should see that they
Were not divided by dread martial sway.
So, with a strength renewed and thankful heart,
He saw his boy take up a civic part,
To do his nation good, and the dear wife
Knew truest raptures in her love-gemmed life,
And not in all the spacious land was there
A happier home, with fortune's modest share.

THE GALLEY SLAVE.

Henry Abbey.

There lived in France, in days not long now dead,
A farmer's sons, twin brothers, like in face;
And one was taken in the other's stead
For a small theft, and sentenced in disgrace
To serve for years a hated galley-slave,
Yet said no word his prized good name to save.

Trusting remoter days would be more blessed,
He set his will to work the verdict out,
And knew most men are prisoners at best
Who some strong habit ever drag about.
Like chain and ball: then meekly prayed that he
Rather the prisoner he was should be.

But best resolves are of such feeble thread,
They may be broken in Temptation's hands.
After long toil the guiltless prisoner said:
"Why should I thus, and feel life's precious sands
The narrow of my glass, the present, run,
For a poor crime that I have never done?"

Such questions are like cups, and hold reply!
For when the chance swung wide the prisoner fled,
And gained the country road, and hastened by
Brown furrowed fields and skipping brooklets fed
By shepherd clouds, and felt 'neath sapful trees,
The soft hand of the mesmerizing breeze.

Then, all that long day having eaten naught,
He at a cottage stopped, and of the wife
A brimming bowl of fragrant milk besought.
She gave it him; but as he quaffed the life,
Down her kind face he saw a single tear
Pursue its wet and sorrowful career.

Within the cot he now beheld a man
And maiden, also weeping. "Speak," said he,
"And tell me of your grief; for if I can,
I will disroot the sad tear-fruited tree."
The cotter answered: "In default of rent
We shall to-morrow from this roof be sent."

Then said the galley-slave: whoso returns
A prisoner escaped may feel the spur
To a right action, and deserves and earns
Proffered reward. I am a prisoner!
Bind these my arms, and drive me back my way,
That your reward the price of home may pay."

Against his wish the cotter gave consent,
And at the prison-gate received his fee,
Though some made it a thing for wonderment
That one so sickly and infirm as he,
When stronger would have dared not to attack,
Could capture this bold youth and bring him back.

Straightway the cotter to the mayor hied
And told him all the story, and that lord
Was much affected, dropping gold beside
The pursed sufficient silver of reward;
Then wrote his letter in authority,
Asking to set the noble prisoner free.

There is no nobler, better life on earth
Than that of conscious, meek self-sacrifice.
Such life our Saviour, in his lowly birth
And holy work, made his sublime disguise,
Teaching this truth, still rarely understood
'Tis sweet to suffer for another's good.

HEROES.

CHILDREN, when you sat wishing,
Down last night on the sands,
Beckoning moments of glory,
With little helpless hands,
I heard you saying and sighing,
As the wind went over the seas,
"There never will come knights errant,
To common days like these."

I heard you sighing and saying,
"The beautiful time is gone
When heroes hunted for monsters,
And conquer'd them one by one;
And now there is nothing noble,
And we all lie safe at night,
But we would not mind a monster,
If we could have a knight!"

Then taking breath for a moment,
You all stood up and said,
"Remember Garibaldi!
Not all the knights are dead:
A chief for men to follow,
Who never lingers nor halts;
A king for women and children,
Because he has no faults.

"But he is nothing to England!
There is the thought that smarts;
We want an English hero,
To trouble all our hearts."
Ah, children! who could tell you
That hearts grow sick and cold,
Without the healing trouble
That touch'd the waters of old!

Shake not your heads at England,
Her soil is still of worth;
It cannot lose the habit
Of bringing heroes forth.
I met one yesterday evening,
And when you hear his tale,
You'll not be sighing and saying
That times are feeble and pale.

The wind was soft and heavy,
  Where African palm-trees tower,
Hardly stirring the river,
  Hardly shaking a flower;
The night was grave and splendid,
  A dead queen lying in state,
With all her jewels upon her,
  And trumpets at her gate.

The wild notes waved and linger'd
  And fainted along the air,
Sometimes like defiance,
  And sometimes like despair,
When down the moonlit mountain
  And beside the river-calms,
The line of a dismal procession
  Unwound between the palms.

A train of driven captives,
  Weary, weak, amazed,—
Eighty hopeless faces,
  Never once upraised;
Bleeding from the journey,
  Longing for the grave:
Men and women and children,
  Every one a slave.

Lash'd and crying and crouching,
  They pass'd, suspecting not
There were three or four English
  Whose hearts grew very hot,—
Men who had come from a distance,
  Whose lives were in their hands,
To tell the love of Jesus
  About the heathen lands.

Studious men and gentle,
  But not in the least afraid;
With fire enough amongst them
  To furnish a crusade.
And when they saw the slave-troop
  Come hurrying down the hill,
Each man looked at the other,
  Unable to be still.

They did not care for treaties,
  And death they did not fear;
One great wrong would have roused them,—
  There were eighty here.
They were not doing man's work,
  They were doing the Lord's,
So they went and stopp'd the savages
  With these amazing words:—

"We are three or four English,
  And we CANNOT LET THIS BE,—
Get away to your mountains,
  And set the people free!"
You should have seen the black men,
  How grey their faces turn;
They think the name of England
  Is something that will burn.

They break, they fly like water
  In a rushing mighty wind:
The slaves stretch out uncertain hands,
  By long despair made blind,
Till in a wonderful moment
  The gasp of freedom came,
Like the leap of a tropical sunrise,
  That sets the world aflame.

A blast of weeping and shouting
  Cleansed all the guilty place;
And God was able to undraw
  The curtain from His Face.
A hundred years of preaching
  Could not proclaim the creed
Of Love and Power and Pity
  So well as that one deed.

A glorious gift is Prudence;
  And they are useful friends
Who never make beginnings
  Till they can see the ends;
But give us now and then a man,
  That we may make him king,
Just to scorn the consequence
  And just to DO THE THING.

BOB RAINS.

I aren't a cove as tells yarns well,
Cos why? I ain't the brains;
But I seed a thing done t'other day
By a pal o' mine, Bob Rains.

'Twas a bully sort of thing to do,
And made me kinder skeered.
But first I'll tell you who Bob was,
No doubt you never heerd.

A sort of good-for-nothing chap,
And often on the spree,
And if he'd got enough for beer,
He wouldn't work, not he;

He'd swear and rip like anything,
Was first man in a fight,
And sometimes got the horrors bad,
When days he had been tight.

He'd often been in chokey too,
For that he didn't care—
No single bobby tackled him,
There wasn't one as dare.

A rum kind o' cuss, and awful bad,
But still a jovial pal;
Always square with them he liked,
And never whopped his gal.

Well, t'other day I walked with Bob
To dinner down the lines,
Just talking of this thing and that,
And the beastly bad hard times.

When I heerd an engine whistle,
And I jumped off the track.
But Bob, he turned round quickest,
And then he set off back.

I wondered why at first, d'ye see,
I couldn't make it out—
Then I seed what made me sick,
And I tried to raise a shout.

A little kid, 'bout three years old,
Was in the six-foot way;
How he got there I couldn't tell,
It's more nor I could say.

I seed a woman, white and skeered,
Just looking awful wild;
I heerd her shout, Bob heerd it, too—
"O save, O save my child!"

The kid just laughed, as tho' 'twas fun,
Bob grabbed him by the arm,
And threw him far out on the grass—
I looked in wild alarm.

There wasn't time for Bob to run,
The engine knocked him flat,
And then I looked the other way—
I couldn't look at that.

I heard a yell, a shriek, a groan,
And then I turned me round—
The train was stopped, I rushed to Bob,
Laid mangled on the ground.

He just spoke once: "I saved the kid!"
I answered with a nod!
And then he smiled and closed his eyes,
And went to see his God.

I don't know much about such things,
So of course I cannot tell,
But I think it is a burning shame
If Bob don't now do well.

A FACT.

From *Good Words.*

It was on an English summer day,
Some six or seven years ago,
That a pointsman before his cabin paced,
With a listless step and slow.
He lit his pipe—there was plenty of time—
In his work was nothing new:
Just to watch the signals and shift the points
When the next train came in view.

He leant 'gainst his cabin and smoked away—
He was used to lounge and wait;
Twelve hours at a stretch he must mind those points,
And down-trains were mostly late.
A rumble—a roar—"She is coming now—
She's truer to time to-day!"
He turns—and not far off, between the rails,
Sees his youngest boy at play!

Not far, *but too far!* The train is at hand,
And the child is crawling there,
And patting the ground with crows of delight—
And not a moment to spare!
His face was dead white, but his purpose firm,
As straight to his post he trod,
And shifted the points, and saved the down-train
And trusted his child to God!

There's a rush in his ears, though the train has passed;
He gropes, for he cannot see,
To the place where the laughing baby crawled,
Where the mangled limbs must be.
But he hears a cry that is only of fear—
His joy seems too great to bear.
For, his duty done, God saw to his son—
The train had not touched a hair!

THE MAN OF ROSS.

Pope.

——ALL our praises why should lords engross?
Rise, honest Muse! and sing the Man of Ross:
Pleased Vaga echoes through the winding bounds,
And rapid Severn hoarse applause resounds.
Who hung with woods yon mountain's sultry brow?
From the dry rock who bade the waters flow?
Not to the skies in useless columns tost,
Or in proud falls magnificently lost?
But clear and artless, pouring through the plain
Health to the sick, and solace to the swain,
Whose causeway parts the vale with shady rows?
Whose seats the weary traveller repose?
Who taught that heaven-directed spire to rise?
"The Man of Ross," each lisping babe replies.
Behold the market-place with poor o'erspread!
The Man of Ross divides the weekly bread:
He feeds yon almshouse, neat, but void of state,
Where age and want sit smiling at the gate:
Him portioned maids, apprenticed orphans blessed,
The young who labour and the old who rest.
Is any sick? the Man of Ross relieves,
Prescribes, attends, the medicine makes and gives.
Is there a variance? enter but his door,
Baulked are the courts, and contest is no more.
Despairing quacks with curses fled the place,
And vile attorneys, now a useless race.
  Thrice happy man! enabled to pursue
What all so wish, but want the power to do!
Oh say! what sums that generous hand supply?
What mines to swell that boundless charity?
  Of debts and taxes, wife and children clear,
This man possessed five hundred pounds a year,
Blush, Grandeur; blush! proud Courts, withdraw your blaze!
Ye little stars, hide your diminished rays!
  And what! no monument, inscription, stone?
His race, his form, his name almost unknown?
  Who builds a church to God, and not to fame,
Will never mark the marble with his name.

BET GRAHAM.

John Bedford Leno.

I HAVE heard a great deal about battles,
And honours pluckt out of the strife;
But I know there be often more courage
Displayed in the battle of life.
More courage, more honour—less *murder*,
And barely a tithe of the wrong,
So I'll take for example a woman—
Contrasting her deeds with the strong.

Bet Graham lived down at Kimburton—
A village devoted to peace,
Just as much as its bit of a common
Was devoted to asses and geese.
She was dressed in a queer sort of manner,
In a hood that was faded and old,
With a thick pair of heavy nailed shoes on,
And a man's coat to keep out the cold.

Bet's husband was laid up with sickness,
And had been for many a day—
A-shaking, like Fear, with the ague,
That took him while stacking some hay:
He was fretful, and peevish, and stupid,
Or else he was moody and sad,
And at other times, wild and excited,
As though he'd gone stark, staring mad.

In the wide, open fields in the winter,
Unmindful of frost, sleet and snow,
With the icicles clinging about her,
With courage unfailing she'd go!
She was never behindhand when wanted,
She'd trudge it through wet and through dry,
And, armed with a sickle in autumn,
Toil on till the stars lit the sky.

Bet Graham was oftentimes called on
When doctors had tested their skill,
And confessed that their patients were dying,
In spite of mixed potion and pill:
She'd a rare lot of faith in ground ivy,
In dockroot, and burdoch, and yew,
In groundmoss, and goose-grass, and hyssop,
In ragwort, and garlic, and rue.

For whooping-cough, borax and honey;
For corns and for bunions, a charm;
In measles she trusted to saffron,
And spices to cheer and to warm;
But in all things, to words kindly spoken,
Good nursing and sisterly care,
To cheer up their spirits when drooping,
And banish all thoughts of despair.

When a neighbour was taken with fever,
And friends shunned the sufferer's bed,
She would hover about like an angel,
And watch till the spirit had fled;
Or else till the stricken and wounded
Had beaten the terrible foe,
And then to her husband and children
She'd wearily, cheerily go.

She would say that the lifeless look pretty—
To comfort the robbed ones who wept;
That the once little rosy-faced infant
Lay just all the world as it slept;
While she talked to its sisters and brothers
As though it would come back again,
And join in the sports of their childhood,
Devoid of affliction and pain.

When a poacher was lugged off to prison
For catching a rabbit or hare,
She would fly to his wife and his children,
And seek their misfortune to share;
She would comfort the weak and down-hearted,
And bid them take courage once more;
And tell them the Saviour they worshipped
Was hungry, and naked, and poor!

They may talk about courage and daring,
Of towns sacked and burned to the ground,
Of kings who have fought and have vanquished,
And victors with high honours crowned:
They may tell us of charm'd flags and banners
That waved 'mid the rack and the flame,
But 'twill take all their fine bits of bunting
To cover and wipe out their shame.

I know when our deeds are looked over,
And the righteous are picked from the wrong,
That full many a kingly chaplet
Will fall from the brow of the strong;
And I know that the lowly Bet Graham
Will rank with the just and the right,
For the hundreds of poor stricken neighbours
She lifted from darkness to light.

THE LEAK IN THE DIKE

Phœbe Cary.

THE good dame looked from her cottage
  At the close of the pleasant day,
And cheerily called to her little son
  Outside the door at play;
"Come, Peter, come! I want you to go
  While there is light to see,
To the hut of the blind old man who lives
  Across the dike, for me;
And take these cakes I made for him,—
  They are hot and smoking yet;
You have time enough to go and come
  Before the sun is set."

Then the good wife turned to her labour,
  Humming a simple song,
And thought of her husband, working hard
  At the sluices all day long;
And set the turf a-blazing,
  And brought the coarse black bread;
That he might find a fire at night,
  And find the table spread.

And Peter left the brother,
  With whom all day he had played,
And the sister who had watched their sports
  In the willow's tender shade;
And told them they'd see him back before
  They saw a star in sight,
Though he wouldn't be afraid to go
  In the very darkest night!

For he was a brave, bright fellow,
  With eye and conscience clear;
He could do whatever a boy might do,
  And he had not learned to fear.
Why, he wouldn't have robbed a bird's nest,
  Nor brought a stork to harm,
Though never a law in Holland
  Had stood to stay his arm!

And now, with his face all glowing,
  And eyes as bright as the day,
With the thoughts of his pleasant errand,
  He trudged along the way;
And soon his joyous prattle
  Made glad a lonesome place—
Alas! if only the blind old man
  Could have seen that happy face!
Yet he somehow caught the brightness
  Which his voice and presence lent;
And he felt the sunshine come and go
  As Peter came and went.

And now, as the day was sinking,
  And the winds began to rise,
The mother looked from her door again,
  Shading her anxious eyes;

And saw the shadows deepen,
  And birds to their homes come back,
But never a sign of Peter
  Along the level track.
But she said: "He will come at morning,
  So I need not fret or grieve,—
Though it isn't like my boy at all
  To stay without my leave."

But where was the child delaying?
  On the homeward way was he,
And across the dike while the sun was up
  An hour above the sea.
He was stooping now to gather flowers,
  Now listening to the sound,
As the angry waters dashed themselves
  Against their narrow bound.
"Ah! well for us," said Peter,
  "That the gates are good and strong,
And my father tends them carefully,
  Or they would not hold you long!
You're a wicked sea," said Peter;
  "I know why you fret and chafe;
You would like to spoil our lands and homes;
  But our sluices keep you safe!"

But hark! through the noise of waters
  Comes a low, clear, trickling sound;
And the child's face pales with terror,
  And his blossoms drop to the ground.
He is up the bank in a moment,
  And, stealing through the sand,
He sees a stream not yet so large
  As his slender, childish hand.
'*Tis a leak in the dike!* He is but a boy,
  Unused to fearful scenes;
But, young as he is, he has learned to know
  The dreadful thing that means.
A leak in the dike! The stoutest heart
  Grows faint that cry to hear,
And the bravest man in all the land
  Turns white with mortal fear.
For he knows the smallest leak may grow
  To a flood in a single night;
And he knows the strength of the cruel sea
  When loosed in its angry might.

And the boy! he has seen the danger,
  And, shouting a wild alarm,
He forces back the weight of the sea
  With strength of his single arm!
He listens for the joyful sound
  Of a footstep passing nigh;
And lays his ear to the ground, to catch
  The answer to his cry.
And he hears the rough wind blowing,
  And the waters rise and fall,
But never an answer comes to him,
  Save the echo of his call.

He sees no hope, no succour—
His feeble voice is lost;
Yet what shall he do but watch and wait,
Though he perish at his post!

So, faintly calling and crying
Till the sun is under the sea;
Crying and moaning till the stars
Come out for company;
He thinks of his brother and sister,
Asleep in their safe warm bed;
He thinks of his father and mother,
Of himself as dying—and dead;
And of how, when the night is over,
They must come and find him at last;
But he never thinks he can leave the place
Where duty holds him fast.

The good dame in the cottage
Is up and astir with the light,
For the thought of her little Peter
Has been with her all night.
And now she watches the pathway,
As yester eve she had done;
But what does she see so strange and black
Against the rising sun?
Her neighbours are bearing between them
Something straight to her door—
The child is coming home, but not
As he ever came before!

"He is dead!" she cries; "my darling!"
And the startled father hears,
And comes and looks the way she looks,
And fears the thing she fears:
Till a glad shout from the bearers
Thrills the stricken man and wife,—
"Give thanks, for your son has saved our land,
And God has saved his life!"
So, there in the morning sunshine
They knelt about the boy;
And every head was bared and bent
In tearful reverent joy.

'Tis many a year since then; but still,
When the sea roars like a flood,
Their boys are taught what a boy can do
Who is brave and true and good.
For every man in that country
Takes his son by the hand,
And tells him of little Peter,
Whose courage saved the land.

They have many a valiant hero.
Remembered through the years;
But never one whose name so oft
Is named with loving tears.
And his deed shall be sung by the cradle,
And told to the child on the knee,
So long as the dikes of Holland
Divide the land from the sea!

Poems about Moral Courage.

MORAL WORTH.

I LOVE the man who scorns to be,
  To name or sect a slave;
Whose soul is like the sunshine, free—
  Free as the ocean wave;

Who, when he sees oppression, wrong,
  Speaks out in thunder tones;
Who feels with truth that he is strong
  To grapple e'en with thrones.

I love the man who shuns to do
  An action mean or low;
Who will a nobler course pursue,
  To stranger, friend, or foe;

Who seeks for justice not for gain,
  Is merciful and kind;
Who will not cause a needless pain
  In body or in mind.

TRUE HEROISM.

W. D. Galagher.

HE who seeks the truth and trembles
  At the dangers he must brave
Is not fit to be a freeman;
  He at best is but a slave.

Speak! no matter what betide thee,
  Let them strike but make them hear:
Be thou like the noble Jesus,
  Scorn the threat that bids thee fear.

Be thou like the first apostles;
  Never fear, thou shalt not fall.
If a free thought seek expression,
  Speak it boldly! Speak it all!

Face thine enemies, accusers;
  Scorn the prison, rack, or rod!
And if thou hast truth to utter,
  Speak, and leave the rest to God!

TRUE HEROISM.

LET others tell of battles fought
  On bloody, ghastly fields,
Where honour greets the man who wins
  And death the man who yields;
But I will speak of him who fights
  And vanquishes his sins,
Who struggles on through weary years
  Against himself and wins.

He is a hero, staunch and brave,
  Who fights an unseen foe,
Who puts at last beneath his feet
  His passions base and low;
And stands erect in manhood's might,
  Undaunted, undismayed—
The bravest man that drew a sword
  In foray or in raid.

It calls for something more than brawn
  Or muscle to o'ercome,
An enemy who marcheth not
  With banner, plume and drum—
A foe, for ever lurking nigh,
  With silent stealthy tread,
For ever near your board by day,
  At night beside your bed.

All honour, then to each brave heart,
  Though poor or rich he be,
Who struggles with his baser part—
  Who conquers and is free.
He may not wear a hero's crown,
  Or fill a hero's grave;
But truth will place his name among
  The bravest of the brave.

DARE TO STAND ALONE.

Be firm, be bold, be strong, be true,
And dare to stand alone;
Stand for the right whate'er ye do,
Though helpers there be none.

Nay, bend not to the swelling surge
Of popular sneer and wrong;
'Twill bear thee on to ruin's verge,
With current wild and strong.

Stand for the right! Humanity
Implores, with groans and tears,
Thine aid to break the festering links
That bind her toiling years.

Stand for the right! Though falsehood reign,
And proud lips coldly sneer,
A poisoned arrow cannot wound
A conscience pure and clear.

Stand for the right and with clean hands
Exalt the truth on high;
Thou'lt find warm sympathising hearts
Among the passers-by.

Men who have seen, and thought and felt,
And yet could hardly dare
The battle's brunt, but by thy side
Will every danger share.

Stand for the right, proclaim it loud:
Thou'lt find an answering tone
In honest hearts, and thou no more
Be doomed to stand alone.

TRUST IN GOD AND DO THE RIGHT.

Norman MacLeod.

Courage brother! do not stumble,
Though thy path is dark as night;
There's a star to guide the humble—
Trust in God and do the right.

Let the road be long and dreary,
And its ending out of sight;
Foot it bravely—strong or weary—
Trust in God and do the right.

Perish policy and cunning,
Perish all that fears the light;
Whether losing, whether winning,
Trust in God and do the right.

Trust no party, church, or faction,
Trust no leader in the fight;
But in every word and action
Trust in God and do the right.

Trust no forms of guilty passion—
Fiends can look like angels bright;
Trust no custom, school, or fashion—
Trust in God and do the right.

Some will hate thee, some will love thee;
Some will flatter, some will slight:
Cease from man and look above thee—
Trust in God and do the right—

Firmest rule and safest guiding,
Inward peace and inward light;
Star upon our path abiding—
Trust in God and do the right.

Poems about Work.

A CHEER FOR THE WORKERS.

J. Richardson, in "Cassell's Working Man's Friend."

HURRAH for the men that work!
Whatever may be their trade;
Hurrah for the men who wield the pen,
And they who use the spade!
Who earn their daily bread
By the sweat of an honest brow;
Hurrah for the men who dig and delve,
And they who reap and plough!

Hurrah for the sturdy arm!
Hurrah for the sturdy will!
Hurrah for the worker's strength!
Hurrah for the worker's skill!
Hurrah for the arm that guides the plough,
And the hand that drives the quill!
Hurrah for the noble workers!
Hurrah for the young and old!
The men of worth all over the earth—
Hurrah for the workers bold!

Hurrah for the men that work,
And the trade that suits them best!
Hurrah for the six days' labour,
And the one of blessed rest!
Hurrah for the open heart!
Hurrah for the noble aim!
Hurrah for a quiet home!
Hurrah for an honest name!

Hurrah for the men who strive!
Hurrah for the men who save!
Who sit not down to sigh,
But struggle like the brave;
Hurrah for the men who *earn* their bread,
And will not stoop to *crave!*
Hurrah for the honest workers!
Hurrah for the young and old!
The men of worth all over the earth,—
Hurrah for the workers bold!

MUSIC OF LABOUR.

Mrs. F. D. Gage.

THE banging of the hammer,
The whirling of the plane,
The crashing of the busy saw,
The creeking of the crane,
The ringing of the anvil,
The grating of the drill,
The clattering of the turning-lathe,
The whirring of the mill,
The buzzing of the spindle,
The rattling of the loom,
The puffing of the engine,
The fan's continuous boom,
The clipping of the tailor's shears,
The driving of the awl,—
These sounds of honest industry
I love—I love them all.

The clicking of the magic type,
The earnest talk of pen,
The toiling of the giant press,
The scratching of the men,
The tapping of the yard-stick,
The tinkling of the scales,
The whistling of the needle
(When no bright cheek it pales),
The humming of the cooking-stove,
The surging of the broom,
The pattering feet of childhood,
The housewife's busy hum,
The buzzing of the scholars,
The teacher's kindly call,—
These sounds of active industry
I love—I love them all.

I love the ploughman's whistle,
The reaper's cheerful song,
The drover's oft repeated shout
Urging his stock along;
The bustle of the market man
As he hies him to the town,
The holloa from the tree-top
As the ripen'd fruit comes down;
The busy sound of reapers
That cut the ripen'd grain;
The thresher's joke and catch of glee
'Neath the moonlight on the plain,
The kind voice of the herdsman,
The shepherd's gentle call,—
These sounds of pleasant industry
I love—I love them all.

Oh, there's a good in labour,
If we labour but aright,
That gives vigour to the day-time,
And sweeter sleep at night;
A good that bringeth pleasure
Even to the toiling hours,
For duty cheers the spirit
As dew revives the flowers.
Then say not that Jehovah
Gave labour as a doom;
No' 'tis the richest mercy
From cradle to the tomb.
Then let us still be doing
Whate'er we find to do,
With a cheerful, hopeful spirit,
And free hand strong and true.

UNITED WORK.

Charles Mackay.

COME forth from the valley, come forth from the hill,
Come forth from the workshop, the mine and the mill,
From pleasure or slumber, from study or play
Come forth in your myriads and aid us to-day;
There's a word to be spoken, a deed to be done,
A truth to be uttered, a cause to be won.—

Come forth in your myriads, come forth every one!
Come youths in your vigor, come men in your prime,
Come age with experience, fresh gathered from time;
Come workers, you're welcome, come thinkers, you must,
Come thick as the clouds of the midsummer dust,
Or the waves of the sea, gleaming bright in the sun,—
There's a truth to be told, and a cause to be won,
Come forth in your myriads, come forth every one!

THE UNITY AND ETERNITY OF LABOUR.

Longfellow.

WHAT a glorious thing is human life:
How glorious man's destiny!
We behold all round about us, one vast union,
No man can labour for himself,
Without labouring at the same time for all others.
This truth becomes an inward benediction, lifting the soul mightily upward.
The feeling of our dignity and power grows strong when we say:
Being is not objectless and vain; we are all necessary links in the great chain which reaches forward into eternity.
All the great and wise and good whose names we read in the world's history have labored for us. We have entered into their harvest.
We tread in their footsteps, from which blessings grow.
We can undertake the sublime task which they once undertook;
We can try to make our common brotherhood wiser and happier;
We can build forward where they were forced to leave off,
And bring nearer to perfection the great edifice which they left incompleted.
And, at length, we, too, must leave it and go hence.
Oh! this is the sublimest thought of all,
We can never finish the noble task of life;
We can never cease to work—we can never cease to be.
What men call death cannot break off this task, which is never-ending.
No period is set to our being; we are eternal.

LIGHT FOR ALL.

From the German.

You cannot pay with money
 The million sons of toil—
The sailor on the ocean,
 The peasant on the soil,
The labourer in the quarry,
 The hewer of the coal;
Your money pays the hand,
 But it cannot pay the soul.
You gaze on the cathedral,
 Whose turrets meet the sky;
Remember the foundations,
 That in earth and darkness lie:
For, were not those foundations
 So darkly resting there,
Yon towers up could never soar
 So proudly in the air.
The workshop must be crowded
 That the palace may be bright;
If the ploughman did not plough,
 Then the poet could not write.
Then let every toil be hallow'd
 That man performs for man,
And have its share of honour,
 As part of one great plan.
See, light darts down from heaven,
 And enters where it may;
The eyes of all earth's people
 Are cheer'd with one bright day.
And let the mind's true sunshine
 Be spread o'er earth as free,
And fill the souls of men
 As the waters fill the sea.
The man who turns the soil
 Need not have an earthly mind;
The digger 'mid the coal
 Need not be in spirit blind:
The mind can shed a light
 On each worthy labour done—
As lowliest things are bright
 In the radiance of the sun.
What cheers the musing student,
 The poet, the divine?
The thought that for his fellows
 A brighter day will shine.
Let every human labourer
 Enjoy the vision bright—
Let the thought that comes from heaven
 Be spread like heaven's own light!
Ye men who hold the pen,
 Rise like a band inspired,
And poets, let your lyrics
 With hope for man be fired;
Till the earth becomes a temple,
 And every human heart
Shall join in one great service,
 Each happy in his part.

NO WORK THE HARDEST WORK.

Caroline F. Orne.

Ho! ye who at the anvil toil,
 And strike the sounding blow,
Where from the burning iron's breast
 The sparks fly to and fro,
While answering to the hammer's ring,
 And fire's intenser glow—
Oh! while ye feel 'tis hard to toil
 And sweat the long day through,
Remember it is harder still
 To have no work to do.

Ho! ye who till the stubborn soil,
 Whose hard hands guide the plough,
Who bend beneath the summer sun,
 With burning cheek and brow—
Ye deem the curse still clings to earth
 From olden time till now—
But while ye feel 'tis hard to toil
 And labour all day through,
Remember it is harder still
 To have no work to do.

Ho! ye who plough the sea's blue field—
 Who ride the restless wave,
Beneath whose gallant vessel's keel
 There lies a yawning grave,
Around whose bark the wintry winds
 Like fiends of fury rave—
Oh! while ye feel 'tis hard to toil
 And labour long hours through,
Remember it is harder still
 To have no work to do.

Ho! ye upon whose fever'd cheeks
 The hectic glow is bright,
Whose mental toil wears out the day
 And half the weary night,
Who labour for the souls of men
 Champions of truth and right—
Although ye feel your toil is hard,
 Even with this glorious view,
Remember it is harder still
 To have no work to do.

Ho! all who labour—all who strive—
 Ye wield a lofty power:
Do with your might, do with your strength,
 Fill every golden hour!
The glorious privilege to do
 Is man's most noble dower.
Oh! to your birthright and yourselves,
 To your own souls be true!
A weary, wretched life is theirs
 Who have no work to do.

LIVE FOR SOMETHING.

LIVE for something, be not idle—
Look about thee for employ!
Sit not down to useless dreaming—
Labour is the sweetest joy.
Folded hands are ever weary,
Selfish hearts are never gay,
Life for thee hath many duties—
Active be, then, while you may.

Scatter blessings in thy pathway!
Gentle words and cheering smiles
Better are than gold or silver,
With their grief-dispelling wiles,
As the pleasant sunshine falleth
Ever on the grateful earth,
So let sympathy and kindness
Gladden well the darkened heart.

Hearts there are oppressed and weary,
Drop the tear of sympathy,
Whisper words of hope and comfort,
Give and thy reward shall be
Joy unto thy soul returning,
From this perfect fountain head,
Freely, as thou freely givest,
Shall the grateful light be shed.

YE WORKERS ALL.

"Ye workers all, who toil so well to save
the race!"
Said a sweet bell,
"With varied badge and banner, come,—
Each brave heart beating like a drum;
Be royal men of noble deeds,
For love is holier than creeds;
In faith, hope, charity excel!"
Sang forth each creed—
Rang for each bell.

THE VILLAGE BLACKSMITH.

Longfellow.

UNDER a spreading chestnut tree
The village smithy stands;
The smith a mighty man is he,
With large and sinewy hands,
And the muscles of his brawny arms
Are strong as iron bands.

His hair is crisp, and black, and long,
His face is like the tan;
His brow is wet with honest sweat,
He earns whate'er he can;
And looks the whole world in the face,
For he owes not any man.

Week out, week in, from morn till night,
You can hear his bellows blow,
You can hear him swing his heavy sledge
With measured beat and slow,
Like sexton ringing the old kirk chimes
When the evening sun is low.

And children coming home from school
Look in at the open door:
They love to see the flaming forge,
And hear the bellows roar,
And catch the burning sparks that fly
Like chaff from a threshing floor.

He goes on Sunday to the church,
And sits among his boys,
He hears the parson pray and preach,
He hears his daughter's voice
Singing in the village choir,
And it makes his heart rejoice.

It sounds to him like her mother's voice
Singing in Paradise!
He needs must think of her once more,
How in her grave she lies,
And with his hard, rough hand he wipes
A tear from out his eyes.

Toiling, rejoicing, sorrowing,
Onward through life he goes;
Each morning sees some task begun,
Each evening sees its close;
Something attempted, something done,
Has earned a night's repose.

Thanks — thanks to thee, my worthy
friend,
For the lesson thou hast taught!
Thus at the sounding forge of life
Our fortunes must be wrought,—
Thus on its sounding anvil shap'd
Each burning deed and thought.

TO WORK IS TO PRAY.

Frances S. Osgood.

PAUSE not to dream of the future before us ;
Pause not to weep the wild cares that come o'er us ;
Hark, how Creation's deep musical chorus,
Unintermitting goes up into heaven !
Never the ocean wave falters in flowing ;
Never the little seed stops in its growing ;
More and more richly the rose-heart keeps glowing,
Till from its nourishing stem it is riven.

"Labour is *worship!*"—the robin is singing ;
"Labour is worship!"—the wild bee is ringing ;
Listen! that eloquent whisper unspringing
Speaks to thy soul from out Nature's great heart.
From the dark cloud flows the life-giving shower,
From the rough sod blows the soft-breathing flower ;
From the small insect, the rich coral bower :
Only man, in the plan, shrinks from his part.

Labour is *life!* 'Tis the still water faileth ;
Idleness ever despaireth, bewaileth ;
Keep the watch wound, for the dark rust assaileth ;
Flowers droop and die in the stillness of noon.
Labour is *glory!*—the flying cloud lightens ;
Only the waving wing changes and brightens ;
Idle hearts only the dark future frightens ;
Play the sweet keys, wouldst thou keep them in tune !

Labour is *rest* from the sorrows that greet us,
Rest from all petty vexations that meet us,
Rest from sin-promptings that ever entreat us !
Rest from world-sirens that lure us to ill.
Work—and pure slumbers shall wait on thy pillow ;
Work—thou shalt ride over Care's coming billow ;
Lie not down wearied 'neath Woe's weeping-willow ;
Work with a stout heart and resolute will !

Labour is *health!* Lo! the husbandman reaping,
How through his veins goes the life-current leaping !
How his strong arm, in its stalwart pride sweeping,
True as a sunbeam, the swift sickle guides !
Labour is *wealth*—in the sea the pearl groweth ;
Rich the queen's robe from the frail cocoon floweth :
From the fine acorn the strong forest bloweth ;
Temple and statue the marble block hides.

Droop not though shame, sin and anguish are round thee !
Bravely fling off the cold chain that hath bound thee !
Look to yon pure heaven smiling beyond thee ;
Rest not content in thy darkness—a clod !
Work—for some good, be it ever so slowly ;
Cherish some flower, be it ever so lowly ;
Labour—all labour is noble and holy ;
Let thy great deeds be thy prayer to thy God !

WORK IS PRAYER.

Duganne.

Brothers! be ye who ye may,
Sons of men, I bid you pray!
Pray unceasing, pray with might,
Pray in darkness, pray in light.
Life hath yet no hours to spare,
Life is toil, and toil is prayer.

Life is toil, and all that lives
Sacrifice of labour gives:
Water, fire, and air and earth,
Rest not, pause not, from their birth.
Sacred toil doth nature share:
Love and labour, work is prayer.

Patriot! toiling for thy kind,
Thou shalt break the chains that bind!
Shape thy thought and mould thy plan;
Toil for freedom, toil for man;
Sagely think and boldly dare:
Labour, labour! work is prayer.

Brother! round thee brothers stand,
Pledge thy truth, and give thy hand,
Raise the downcast, help the weak,
Toil for good, for virtue speak.
Let thy brother be thy care:
Labour, labour! work is prayer.

A WORD FOR THE POETS.

Sing, Poet! sing for the people,
For each and everywhere,
Like chimes in the old church steeple
That summon us all to prayer.

And clothe in language lowly—
The lessons you have to teach,
Words deep, and pure, and holy,
And found in the children's speech

Knock at the hearts of workers,
With a simple earnest song,—
A song of God's infinite mercy,
And not of man's infinite wrong.

There's enough of dark and dreary
In each one's work and life;
Let the poet's words be cheery,
To strengthen for the strife.

Aye! hopeful, not despairing,
Be the strains that onward urge;
Men march to death in battle,
Yet march not to a dirge.

Not a word of grief or repining,
But only of strength and cheer.
For the sun is always shining,
Though the clouds may hide it here.

THE LAW OF GREATNESS.

Edward Youl.

Brother, kneeling late and early,
Never working—praying ever—
Up and labour—work is prayer,
Worship is in best endeavour,

Days and nights not given to service
Turn thy life to sinful waste;
Be no laggard—be no sluggard,—
Live not like a man disgraced.

See—creation never resteth,
Ever God creates anew;
To be like Him is to labour,
To adore Him, is to do.

Do thy best, and do it bravely,
Never flag with under-zeal,—
This is writ with Scripture holy,
Thou must either work or steal.

None have mandate to be idle;
Folded hands are vilest crime;
God's command is labour-worship,
In thy youth and in thy prime.

For I preach the newest Gospel—
Work with hand and work with heart;
Work—the heavens are working alway,
Nature reads a text to Art.

Suns become the sires of systems,
Planets labour as they roll;
And the law of their celestial
Is a law within thy soul.

From thy nerves at each pulsation—
From the mystery of sleep,—
Comes a lesson, a monition,
Whose significance is deep,

Rightly read, and fitly heeded,
It will whisper to thy breast—
"Thou art clothed around with beauty,
And an angel is thy guest."

But the beauty, worketh, striveth,
And is leading thee apace
To a future whose foundations,
God hath planted not in space.

Oh, the angel—how he helpeth!
Hinder not by act of thine,
Lagging limbs or heart aweary,
Mar the work of the Divine.

Be a workman, oh, my brother;
Higher worship is there none,—
With its hymn of work-devotion,
Nature is one choral tone.

As I read the newest Gospel,—
When the spade divides the clod,
When the ploughshare turns the furrow,
Men in prayer strive with God.

Pray—"The early rain and latter,
Lord withhold not from our toil;
Fructify the seed we scatter,
With this worship, in the soil."

Say—"No slothful invocations
From our lips our lives profane;
We have kept the old commandment,
Taking not thy name in vain.

"But *they* break the old commandment,
And envoke Thy Name with sin,
Who, their idle hands uplifting,
Unearned good would garner in."

We have new interpretation
For the old instruction—ask
Best *he* asketh most who tasketh
Sinews to perform the task.

As I read the newest Gospel,
There is nothing fixed and still;
Constant only in mutation
Is God's law of good and ill.

Time was, when the tongue's petition
Wisely wrestled with the skies;
When the flames, that curled on altars,
Made accepted sacrifice.

Time was, when the crowd exalted
Priests above their fellow-men;—
But that worship is departed,
And doth not return again.

Ever working,—ever doing,—
Nature's law in space of time—
See thou heed it in thy worship;
Build thou up a life sublime.

Ever idleness blasphemeth,
In its prayer—in its praise;
How shall Heaven receive his incense
Who is idle all his days?

Be a workman, Oh, my brother;
Trust not worship to the tongue;
Pray with strenuous self-exertion;
Best by hands are anthems sung.

Everywhere the earth is hallowed,
Temples rise on every soil—
In the forest—in the city—
And their priest is daily toil.

Poems about Perseverance.

NEVER GIVE UP.

Tupper.

NEVER give up! It is wiser and better
Always to hope, than once to despair;
Fling off the load of doubt's cankering fetter,
And break the dark spell of tyrannical care.
Never give up! or the burden may sink you;
Providence kindly has mingled the cup;
And in all trials or troubles, bethink you,
The watch-word of life must be, "Never give up!"

Never give up! There are chances and changes
Helping the hopeful a hundred to one;
And, through the chaos, high Wisdom arranges
Ever success, if you'll only hope on.
Never give up! for the wisest is boldest,
Knowing that Providence mingles the cup;
And of all maxims, the best, as the oldest,
Is the true watch-word of, "Never give up!"

Never give up! Though the grape-shot may rattle,
Or the full thunder-cloud over you burst;
Stand like a rock, and the storm and the battle
Little shall harm you, though doing their worst.
Never give up! If adversity presses,
Providence wisely has mingled the cup;
And the best counsel, in all your distresses,
Is the stout watch-word of, "Never give up!"

NEVER SAY FAIL.

Keep pushing! 'tis wiser
  Than sitting aside,
And dreaming, and sighing,
  And waiting the tide;
In life's earnest battle
  They only prevail,
Who daily march onward,
  And never say fail.

With eyes ever open,
  And tongue that's not dumb,
And heart that will never
  To sorrow succumb.
You'll battle and conquer,
  Though thousands assail;
How strong and how mighty
  Who never say fail!

Ahead, then, keep pushing!
  And elbow your way,
Unheeding the envious,
  That would you betray.
All obstacles vanish,
  All enemies quail
Before the strong-hearted,
  Who never say fail!

In life's rosy morning,
  In manhood's firm pride,
Let this be your motto,
  Your footsteps to guide:
In storm or in sunshine,
  Whatever assail,
We'll onward and conquer!
  And never say fail!

PERSEVERE.

Drive the nail aright, boys,
  Hit it on the head;
Strike with all your might, boys,
  While the iron's red.

When you've work to do, boys,
  Do it with a will;
They who reach the top, boys,
  First must climb the hill.

Standing at the foot, boys,
  Gazing at the sky,
How can you get up, boys,
  If you never try?

Though you stumble oft, boys,
  Never be downcast;
Try and try again, boys,
  You'll succeed at last.

PERSEVERANCE.

We need not be ashamed to learn,
  And our first efforts show;
For in this world from little things
  The greatest often grow.
There's not a learned sage that lives,
  Whatever his degree,
Who did not at the first begin
  With simple A, B, C.

Then upward, onward, step by step,
  With perseverance rise;
Bend mind and will to every task,
  No first attempts despise.
'Tis idleness alone despairs,
  And never will aspire,
But industry still presses on
  With patience nought can tire.

Begin while life is bright and young,
  Work out each noble plan;
True knowledge lends a charm to youth.
  And dignifies the man.
Then upward, onward, step by step,
  With perseverance rise;
And emulate, with hearts of hope,
  The good, the great, the wise.

Two of the best and most encouraging poems in the world, one by a man and one by a woman.

A PSALM OF LIFE.

H. W. Longfellow.

Tell me not in mournful numbers,
  Life is but an empty dream!
For the soul is dead that slumbers,
  And things are not what they seem.

Life is real! Life is earnest!
  And the grave is not its goal;
Dust thou art, to dust returnest,
  Was not spoken of the soul.

Not enjoyment, and not sorrow,
  Is our destined end or way;
But to act, that each to-morrow,
  Finds us farther than to-day.

Art is long, and Time is fleeting,
  And our hearts though stout and brave,
Still like muffled drums are beating
  Funeral marches to the grave.

In the world's broad field of battle,
  In the bivouac of Life,
Be not like dumb, driven cattle!
  Be a hero in the strife!

Trust no Future, howe'er pleasant!
  Let the dead Past bury its dead!
Act,—act in the living present!
  Heart within, and God o'erhead!

Lives of great men all remind us
  We can make our lives sublime;
And, departing, leave behind us
  Footprints on the sands of time.

Footprints, that perhaps another,
  Sailing o'er life's solemn main,
A forlorn and shipwreck'd brother,
  Seeing, shall take heart again.

Let us, then, be up and doing,
  With a heart for any fate;
Still achieving, still pursuing,
  Learn to labour and to wait.

ONE BY ONE.

Miss Procter

One by one the sands are flowing,
  One by one the moments fall;
Some are coming, some are going,
  Do not strive to grasp them all.

One by one thy duties wait thee,
  Let thy whole strength go to each;
Let no future dreams elate thee,
  Learn thou first what those can teach.

One by one (bright gifts of Heaven),
  Joys are sent thee here below;
Take them readily when given,
  Ready, too, to let them go.

One by one thy griefs shall meet thee,
  Do not fear an armed band;
One will fade as others greet thee,
  Shadows passing through the land.

Do not look at life's long sorrow;
  See how small each moment's pain;
God will help thee for to-morrow,
  So each day begin again.

Every hour that fleets so slowly
  Has its task, to do or bear;
Luminous the crown and holy,
  When each gem is kept with care.

Do not linger with regretting,
  Or for passing hours despond;
Nor, the daily toil forgetting,
  Look too eagerly beyond.

Hours are golden links, God's token
  Reaching heaven; but one by one
Take them, lest the chain be broken
  Ere the pilgrimage be done.

Poems about Progress.

THE REFORMER.

Whittier.

All grim and soiled and brown with tan,
I saw a Strong One, in his wrath,
Smiting the godless shrines of man
Along his path.

The Church, beneath her trembling dome,
Essayed in vain her ghostly charm;
Wealth shook within his gilded home
With strange alarm.

Fraud from his secret chambers fled
Before the sunlight bursting in:
Sloth drew her pillow o'er her head
To drown the din.

"Spare," Art implored, "yon holy pile;
That grand, old, time-worn turret spare;"
Meek Reverence, kneeling in the aisle,
Cried out, "Forbear!"

Grey-bearded Use, who, deaf and blind,
Groped for his old accustom'd stone,
Lean'd on his staff, and wept to find
His seat o'erthrown.

Young Romance raised his dreamy eyes,
O'erhung with paly locks of gold:
"Why smite," he ask'd in sad surprise,
"The fair, the old?"

Yet louder rang the Strong One's stroke,
Yet nearer flash'd his axe's gleam;
Shuddering and sick of heart I woke,
As from a dream.

I look'd: aside the dust cloud roll'd—
The waster seem'd the builder too;
Up-springing from the ruin'd Old
I saw the New.

'Twas but the ruin of the bad—
The wasting of the wrong and ill;
Whate'er of good the old time had
Was living still.

Calm grew the brows of him I fear'd;
The frown which awed me pass'd away,
And left behind a smile which cheer'd
Like breaking day.

The grain grew green on battle-plains,
O'er swarded war-mounds grazed the cow;
The slave stood forging from his chains
The spade and plough.

Where frown'd the fort, pavilions gay
And cottage windows, flower entwined,
Look'd out upon the peaceful bay
And hills behind.

Through vine-wreathed cups with wine once red,
The lights on brimming crystal fell,
Drawn, sparkling, from the rivulet-head
And mossy well.

Through prison walls, like heaven-sent hope,
Fresh breezes blew and sunbeams stray'd,
And with the idle gallows-rope
The young child play'd.

Where the doomed victim in his cell
Had counted o'er the weary hours,
Glad school-girls, answering to the bell,
Came crown'd with flowers.

Grown wiser for the lesson given,
I fear no longer, for I know
That where the share is deepest driven,
The best fruits grow.

The outworn rite, the old abuse,
The pious fraud transparent grown,
The good held captive in the use
Of wrong alone—

These wait their doom from that great law
Which makes the past time serve to-day;
And fresher life the world shall draw
From their decay.

Oh! backward-looking son of time!—
The new is old, the old is new,
The cycle of a change sublime
Still sweeping through.

So wisely taught the Indian seer;
Destroying Seva, forming Brahm,
Who wake by turns earth's love and fear
Are one, the same.

Idly as thou, in that old day
Thou mournest, did thy sire repine;
So, in his time, thy child grown gray
Shall sigh for thine.

But life shall on and upward go;
Th' eternal step of Progress beats
To that great anthem, calm and slow,
Which God repeats.

Take heart!—the Waster builds again,—
A charmed life old Goodness hath;
The tares may perish,—but the grain
Is not for death.

God works in all things; all obey
His first propulsion from the night:
Wake thou and watch! the world is gray
With morning light!

THE GOOD TIME COMING.

Charles Mackay.

THERE'S a good time coming, boys,
  A good time coming;
We may not live to see the day,
But earth shall glisten in the ray
  Of the good time coming,
Cannon balls may aid the truth,
  But thought's a weapon stronger;
We'll win our battle by its aid;—
  Wait a little longer.

There's a good time coming, boys,
  A good time coming:
The pen shall supersede the sword,
And Right, not Might, shall be the lord,
  In the good time coming.
Worth, not Birth, shall rule mankind,
  And be acknowledg'd stronger;
The proper impulse has been given;—
  Wait a little longer.

There's a good time coming, boys,
  A good time coming:
War in all men's eyes shall be
A monster of iniquity,
  In the good time coming.
Nations shall not quarrel then,
  To prove which is the stronger;
Nor slaughter men for glory's sake;—
  Wait a little longer.

There's a good time coming, boys,
  A good time coming:
Hateful rivalries of creed
Shall not make their martyrs bleed
  In the good time coming.
Religion shall be shorn of pride,
  And flourish all the stronger;
And Charity shall trim her lamp;—
  Wait a little longer.

There's a good time coming, boys,
  A good time coming.
And a poor man's family,
Shall not be his misery
  In the good time coming;
Every child shall be a help,
  To make his right arm stronger;
The happier he, the more he has;—
  Wait a little longer.

There's a good time coming, boys,
  A good time coming:
Little children shall not toil,
Under, or above, the soil,
  In the good time coming.
But shall play in healthful fields
  Till limbs and mind grow stronger;
And every one shall read and write;—
  Wait a little longer.

There's a good time coming, boys,
  A good time coming:
The people shall be temperate.
And shall love instead of hate,
  In the good time coming.
They shall use, and not abuse,
  And make all virtue stronger;
The reformation has begun;—
  Wait a little longer.

There's a good time coming, boys,
  A good time coming:
Let us aid it all we can,
Every woman, every man,
  The good time coming.
Smallest helps, if rightly given,
  Make the impulse stronger;
'Twill be strong enough one day,
  Wait a little longer.

ONWARD.

James Montgomery.

HIGHER, higher will we climb
  Up the mount of glory,
That our names may live through time
  In our country's story:
Happy, when their welfare calls,
He who conquers, he who falls.

Deeper, deeper, let us toil
  In the mines of knowledge;
Nature's wealth and learning's spoil
  Win from school and college:
Delve we there for richer gems
Than the stars of diadems.

Onward, onward may we press
  Through the path of duty;
Virtue is true happiness,
  Excellence true beauty.
Minds are of celestial birth;
Make we, then, a heaven of earth.

Poems about Little Things.

LITTLE THINGS.

— *Mackay.*

A TRAVELLER through a dusty road
  Strewed acorns on the lea,
And one took root and sprouted up,
  And grew into a tree.
Love sought its shades at evening time
  To breathe its early vows,
And age was pleased, in heats of noon
  To bask beneath its boughs;
The dormouse loved its dangling twigs,
  The bird sweet music bore;
It stood a glory in its place,
  A blessing evermore!

A little spring had lost its way
  Amid the grass and fern;
A passing stranger scooped a well,
  Where weary men might turn;
He walled it in, and hung with care
  A ladle at the brink:
He thought not of the deed he did,
  But judged that toil might drink.
He passed again, and lo! the well,
  By summers never dried,
Had cooled ten thousand parching tongues,
  And saved a life beside!

A dreamer dropp'd a random thought,
  'Twas old, and yet was new;
A simple fancy of the brain,
  But strong in being true;
It shone upon a genial mind,
  And lo! its light became
A lamp of life, a beacon ray,
  A monitory flame.
The thought was small, its issue great,
  A watch-fire on the hill;
It sheds its radiance far adown,
  And cheers the valley still!

A nameless man amid a crowd
  That thronged the daily mart,
Let fall a word of hope and love,
  Unstudied from the heart;
A whisper on the tumult thrown,
  A transitory breath,
It raised a brother from the dust,
  It saved a soul from death.

LITTLE THINGS.

LETTERS join'd make words,
  And words to books may grow,
As, flake on flake descending,
  Forms an avalanche of snow.
A single utterance may good
  Or evil thoughts inspire;
One little spark enkindled,
  May set a town on fire.
What volumes may be written
  With little drops of ink!
How small a leak, unnoticed,
  A mighty ship will sink!
A tiny insect's labour
  Makes the coral strand,
And mighty seas are girdled
  With grains of golden sand.
A daily penny saved,
  A fortune may begin;
A daily penny squandered,
  May lead to vice and sin.
Our life is made entirely
  Of moments multiplied,
As little streamlets, joining,
  Form the ocean's tide.
Our hours and days, our months and years,
  Are in small moments given:
They constitute our time below,
  Eternity in Heaven.

LITTLE BY LITTLE.

DROP follows drop, and swells
  With rain the sweeping river;
Word follows word, and tells
  A truth that lives for ever.

Flake follows flake, like spirits
  Whose wings the winds dissever;
Thought follows thought, and lights
  The realm of mind for ever.

Beam follows beam, to cheer
  The cloud the bolt would shiver;
Throb follows throb, and fear
  Gives place to joy for ever.

The drop, the flake, the beam,
  Teach us a lesson ever;
The word, the thought, the dream,
  Impress the soul for ever.

VALUE OF LITTLE THINGS.

Cutler.

Scorn not the slightest word or deed,
Nor deem it void of power:
There's fruit in each wind-wafted seed,
That waits its natal hour.

What if the little rain should say,
"So small a drop as I
Can ne'er refresh those thirsty fields;
I'll tarry in the sky?"

What if a shining beam of noon
Should in its fountain stay,
Because its feeble light alone
Cannot create a day?

Doth not each rain-drop help to form
The cool refreshing shower?
And every ray of light to warm
And beautify the flower?

Go then and strive to do thy share:
One talent—less than thine—
Improved with steady zeal and care,
Would gain rewards divine.

LITTLE THINGS.

C. A. Mason.

We cannot all be heroes,
And thrill a hemisphere
With some great, daring venture,
Some deed that mocks at fear;
But we can fill a lifetime
With kindly acts and true.
There's always noble service
For noble souls to do.

We cannot all be preachers,
And sway with voice and pen,
As strong winds sway the forest,
The minds and hearts of men;
But we can be evangels
To souls within our reach.
There's always Love's own gospel
For loving hearts to preach.

We cannot all be martyrs,
And win a deathless name
By some divine baptism,
Some ministry of flame;
But we can live for Truth's sake,
Can do for her and dare.
There's always faithful witness
For faithful lives to bear.

DO YOUR BEST.

If you cannot on the ocean,
Sail among the swiftest fleet—
Rocking on the highest billows,
Laughing at the storms you meet—
You can stand among the sailors,
Anchored yet within the bay;
You can lend a hand to help them,
As they launch their boats away.

If you are too weak to journey
Up the mountains steep and high,
You can stand within the valley,
While the multitudes go by;
You can chant in happy measure
As they slowly pass along;
Though they may forget the singer,
They will not forget the song.

If you have not gold and silver
Ever ready to command—
If you cannot towards the needy
Reach an ever-open hand—
You can visit the afflicted,
O'er the erring you can weep:
You can be a helpful neighbour,
Eager Love's behests to keep.

LITTLE THINGS.

Do thy little, God hath made
Million leaves for forest shade;
Smallest stars their glory bring—
God employeth everything.

Do thy little, and when thou
Feelest on thy pallid brow,
Ere has fled the vital breath,
Cold and damp the sweat of death—

Then the little thou hast done,
Little battles thou hast won,
Little masteries achieved,
Little wants with care relieved,
Little words in love express'd,
Little wrongs at once confess'd,
Little favours kindly done.
Little toils thou didst not shun,
Little graces meekly worn,
Little slights with patience borne—

These shall crown the pillow'd head,
Holy light upon thee shed:
These are treasures that shall rise
Far beyond the smiling skies.

Poems about Humanity.

SENTIMENT OF A CONTENTED MIND.

Anon.

No glory I covet, no riches I want;
Ambition is nothing to me;
The one thing I beg of kind heaven to grant,
Is a mind independent and free.

With passion unruffled, untainted with pride,
By reason my life let me square:
The wants of my nature are cheaply supplied,
And the rest is but folly and care.

The blessings which Providence freely has lent,
I'll justly and gratefully prize;
While sweet meditation and cheerful content
Shall make me both healthful and wise.

In the pleasures the great man's possessions display,
Unenvied I'll challenge my part;
For every fair object my eyes can survey
Contributes to gladden my heart.

How vainly, through infinite trouble and strife,
The many their labours employ!
Since all that is truly delightful in life,
Is what all, if they please, may enjoy.

THE QUIET LIFE.

Pope.

Happy the man whose wish and care
A few paternal acres bound;
Content to breathe his native air
In his own ground.

Whose herds with milk, whose fields with bread,
Whose flocks supply him with attire;
Whose trees in summer yield him shade,
In winter, fire.

Blest, who can unconcern'dly find
Hours, days, and years slide soft away—
In health of body, peace of mind;
Quiet by day,

Sound sleep by night; study and ease
Together mix'd; sweet recreation;
And innocence, which most does please,
With meditation.

Thus let me live, unseen, unknown;
Thus unlamented let me die:
Steal from the world, and not a stone
Tell where I lie.

THE CHARACTER OF A HAPPY LIFE.

Sir Henry Wotton.

How happy is he born or taught,
That serveth not another's will:
Whose armour is his honest thought
And simple truth his highest skill:

Whose passions not his masters are;
Whose soul is still prepared for death;
Not ty'd unto the world with care
Of prince's ear, or vulgar breath.

Who has his life from rumours freed;
Whose conscience is his strong retreat;
Whose state can neither flatterers feed,
Nor ruin make oppressors great:

Who envies none, whom chance doth raise,
Or vice: who never understood
How deepest wounds are given with praise;
Nor rules of state, but rules of good:

Who God doth late and early pray
More of His grace than gifts to lend;
And entertains the harmless day
With a well chosen book or friend.

This man is freed from servile bands
Of hope to rise, or fear to fall;
Lord of himself, though not of lands;
And having nothing, yet hath all.

GOLDEN SIDE.

There is many a rest in the road of life,
If we only would stop to take it;
And many a tone from the better land,
If the querulous heart would make it!
To the sunny soul that is full of hope,
And whose beautiful trust ne'er faileth,
The grass is green and the flowers are bright,
Though the wintry storm prevaileth.

Better hope, though the clouds o'er you hang so low,
Ever keep the sad eyes still lifted;
The sweet sunny sky will be peeping through
When the ominous clouds are rifted!
There was ne'er a night but that had a day,
Or an evening without a morning;
The darkest hour, as the proverb goes,
Is the hour before the dawning.

There's many a gem in the path of life
Which we pass in our idle pleasure,
That's richer by far than the jewelled crown,
Or the miserly hoarded treasure;
It may be the love of a little child,
Or a dear mother's prayers to heaven,
Or some lone wanderer's grateful thanks
For a cup of water given.

Oh, 'tis better to weave in the web of life
The most beautiful golden filling,
To do all life's work with a cheerful heart
And with hands that are swift and willing, .
Than to snap the frail, tender minute threads
Of our curious lives asunder;
And then blame heaven for the tangled ends,
And still sit and grieve and wonder.

SOME MURMUR WHEN THEIR SKY IS CLEAR.

Archbishop Trench.

Some murmur when their sky is clear,
And wholly bright to view,
If but one speck of dirt appear
In their great heaven of blue;
And some with thankful love are filled
If but one streak of light,
One ray of God's good mercy, gild
The darkness of their night.

In palaces are hearts that ask,
In discontent and pride,
Why life is such a dreary task,
And all goods things denied;
And hearts in poorest huts admire
How Love has in their aid
(Love that never seems to tire)
Such rich provision made.

LOOK ON THE SUNNY SIDE.

Look always on the sunny side;
'Twill make us happier far,
Why should we try to find the cloud,
When brightly shines the star.

Some people only see the world,
As through a smoky glass,
They go half way to meet the woe,
And let the sunshine pass.

SORROW AND SERVICE.

If none were sick and none were sad
What service could we render?
I think if we were always glad,
We scarcely would be tender.
Did our beloved never need
Our patient ministration,
Earth would grow cold, and miss, indeed,
Its sweetest consolation,
If sorrow never claimed our heart,
And every wish were granted,
Patience would die and hope depart,
Life would be disenchanted.

Poems about Wishing.

WISHING.

John G. Saxe.

Of all amusements for the mind,
  From logic down to fishing,
There isn't one that you can find
  So very cheap as "wishing."
A very choice diversion, too,
  If we but rightly use it,
And not, as we are apt to do,
  Pervert it and abuse it.

I wish—a common wish indeed—
  My purse were somewhat fatter,
That I might cheer the child of need,
  And not my pride to flatter;
That I might make Oppression reel,
  As only gold can make it,
And break the Tyrant's rod of steel,
  As only gold can break it.

I wish—that Sympathy and Love,
  And every human passion,
That has its origin above,
  Would come and keep in fashion;
That Scorn, and Jealousy, and hate,
  And every base emotion,
Were buried fifty fathoms deep
  Beneath the waves of Ocean!

I wish—that friends were always true,
  And motives always pure;
I wish the good were not so few,
  I wish the bad were fewer;
I wish that parsons ne'er forgot
  To heed their pious teaching;
I wish that practising was not
  So different from preaching!

I wish—that modest worth might be
  Appraised with truth and candour;
I wish—that innocence were free
  From treachery and slander;
I wish that men their vows would mind,
  That women ne'er were rovers;
I wish that wives were always kind,
  And husbands always lovers!

I wish—in fine—that Joy and Mirth,
  And every good Ideal,
May come erewhile throughout the earth,
  To be the glorious Real;
Till God shall every creature bless
  With His supremest blessing,
And Hope be lost in Happiness,
  And Wishing in Possessing!

THE WISH.

I ask not golden stores of wealth,
  Or rank, and pomp, and state,
The noble's glittering coronet,
  The mansions of the great.
I care not that around my brow
  Fame's laurel leaf should twine,
Or, that on history's glowing page
  My name may proudly shine.

I envy not the calm retreat
  From worldly noise and strife—
The lowly cot—the flower-gemmed path—
  The simple joys of life.
I ask not that in soft repose
  My peaceful days may glide,
As the light bark is borne along
  The deep unruffled tide.

But *this* I ask; that while I live,
  I may not live in vain,
For I would cheer the aching heart,
  And soothe the mourner's pain—
Would wipe away grief's bitter tears,
  The poor man's struggles aid;
And guide the wanderer back, whose steps
  From virtue's path have strayed.

Then whether affluence and state
  Shall be my destined lot,
Or 'neath the humble cottage roof
  I dwell, it matters not.
If I, by self-denying love,
  Earth's weary ones can bless,
And deepen, as I pass along,
  The stream of happiness.

HIS AND MINE.

Rowland Brown.

Let her be his in the hours of pride, of pomp and revelry ;
Let her be his in courtly crowds of young frivolity !
Amidst the blaze of the banquet lights, in the halls of dance and song ;
I love her not for the admiring gaze of a gay and thoughtless throng.

Let her be his when exultant scorn shall beam from her eyes o' blue ;
Let her be his when her warm cheek glows with a strange unnatural hue ;
Let her be his when thoughtless words from thoughtless lips may fall ;
Let her be his when folly's lamps are alight in Vanity Hall.

Let her be his whilst the senseless crowd around her bow the knee ;
Let her be his (for I feel such scenes can awake no joy in me),
Let her be his for the transient hours such joys can charm the heart ;
But let her be mine when the dreams of night for the smiles of morn depart.

Let her be mine when mocking hands no fading garlands wreathe ;
Let her be mine when the scattered throngs no flattering incense breathe ;
Let her be mine when the thoughts of night are passed for the deeds of day ;
Let her be mine when the lips take heed of the tale the heart would say.

Let her be mine in that holy place, to set love's signet ring ;
Let her be mine in the blissful hour when the joy-bells merrily ring ;
Let her be mine when her spirit feels it cannot happier be
Than to rest in the home she has made in my heart, and to live and to die with me.

Let her be mine in the silent hour when angels hover by ;
Let her be mine when none are near to hear the bosom's sigh ;
Let her be mine when the light of heaven may rest on her placid brow ;
Let her be mine when God alone can hear the whisper'd vow :

Let her be mine through the battle of life with smiles love-deeds to crown ;
Let her be mine in the trying time when false friends on me frown ;
Let her be mine in the hour of death, to hear my last fond prayer ;
And let her be mine in the worlds of light to love and to bless me there.

WISHES OF HIGH AND LOW.

A man in his carriage was riding along,
A gaily dress'd wife by his side,
In satin and laces; she look'd like a queen,
And he like a king in his pride.

A wood-sawyer stood in the street as they pass'd;
The carriage and couple he eyed,
And said, as he work'd with a saw on a log,
"I wish I was rich and could ride."

The man in the carriage remark'd to his wife:
"One thing I would give if I could—
I'd give all my wealth for the strength and the health
Of the man that saweth the wood."

A pretty young maid with a bundle of work,
Whose face as the morning was fair,
Went tripping along with a smile of delight,
While humming a love-breathing air.

She looked on the carriage—the lady she saw,
Array'd in apparel so fine,
And said, in a whisper, "I wish from my heart
Those satins and laces were mine."

The lady look'd out on the maid with her work,
So fair in her calico dress,
And said, "I'd relinquish possession and wealth
Her beauty and youth to possess."

Thus, in this world, whatever our lot,
Our minds and our time we employ
In longing and sighing for what we have not,
Ungrateful for what we enjoy.

We welcome the pleasure for which we have sigh'd
The heart has a void in it still,
Growing deeper and wider the longer we live,
That nothing but Heaven can fill.

THE VANITY OF HUMAN WISHES.

WOLSEY.

Johnson

In full-blown dignity see Wolsey stand,
Law in his voice, and fortune in his hand:
To him the Church, the realm, their pow'rs consign,
Through him the rays of regal bounty shine;
Turn'd by his nod the stream of honour flows,
His smile alone security bestows;
Still to new heights his restless wishes tower,
Claim leads to claim, and power advances power;
Till conquest, unresisted, ceased to please,
And rights submitted left him none to seize.
At length his sovereign frowns—the train of state
Mark the keen glance, and watch the sign to hate.
Where'er he turns he meets a stranger's eye,
His suppliants scorn him, and his followers fly.
Now drops at once the pride of awful state,
The golden canopy, the glittering plate,
The regal palace, the luxurious board,
The liveried army, and the menial lord.

CHARLES XII.

Johnson.

On what foundation stands the warrior's pride,
How just his hopes, let Swedish Charles decide.
A frame of adamant, a soul of fire,
No dangers fright him, and no labours tire:
O'er love, o'er fear, extends his wide domain,
Unconquered lord of pleasure and of pain:
No joys to him pacific sceptres yield,
War sounds the trump, he rushes to the field:
Behold surrounding kings their powers combine,
And one capitulate, and one resign;
Peace courts his hand, but spreads her charms in vain;
"Think nothing gained," he cries, "till nought remain,
On Moscow's walls till Gothic standards fly,
And all be mine beneath the polar sky."
The march begins in military state,
And nations on his eye suspended wait;
Stern Famine guards the solitary coast,
And Winter barricades the realms of Frost.

He comes, nor want nor cold his course delay,—
Hide, blushing Glory, hide Pultowa's day!
The vanquished hero leaves his broken bands,
And shows his miseries in distant lands;
Condemned, a needy suppliant, to wait,
While ladies interpose and slaves debate.
But did not Chance at length her error mend?
Did not subverted empire mark his end?
Did rival monarch give the fatal wound?
Or hostile millions press him to the ground?
His fall was destined to a barren strand,
A petty fortress, and a dubious hand;
He left a name at which the world grew pale,
To point a moral, or adorn a tale.

Poems about Hope.

SWEET HOPE.

SWEET hope, thou art a sovereign balm
For hearts by sorrow wounded;
Thy smiles impart a tender calm,
E'en when by storms surrounded!
For, like the many tinted bow,
Grief's atmosphere thou cheerest,
And darker as the shadows grow,
The brighter thou appearest.

And though by every tongue reviled,
As treacherous, false, deceiving—
Who hath not dried his tears, and smiled,
Thy promises believing?
Then still I'll court thy soothing power,
And thy sweet influence cherish;
To thee I'll cling in life's last hour,
Nor quit thee till I perish.

HOPE ON, HOPE EVER.

Gerald Massey.

HOPE on, hope ever: though to-day be dark,
The sweet sunburst may smile on thee to-morrow;
Though thou art lonely, there's an eye will mark
Thy loneliness, and guerdon all thy sorrow.
Though thou must toil 'mong cold and sordid men,
With none to echo back thy thought or love thee,
Cheer up, poor heart, thou dost not beat in vain,
For God is over all, and heaven above thee;
Hope on, hope ever.

Hope on, hope ever; after darkest night,
Comes full of loving life the laughing morning.
Hope on, hope ever; Spring-tide flushed with light,
Aye crowns old Winter with her rich adorning.
Hope on, hope ever; yet the time shall come
When man to man shall be a friend and brother,
And this old world shall be a happy home,
And all Earth's family love one another.
Hope on, hope ever.

GARDEN OF THE HEART.

LEAF by leaf the roses fall,
Drop by drop the springs run dry,
One by one beyond recall,
Summer beauties fade and die;
But the roses bloom again,
And the springs will gush anew,
In the pleasant April rain,
And the summer's sun and dew.

So in hours of deepest gloom,
When the springs of gladness fail,
And the roses in their bloom
Droop like maidens wan and pale,
We shall find some hope that lies
Like a silent germ apart,
Hidden far from careless eyes
In the garden of the heart.

Some sweet hope to gladness wed,
That will spring afresh and new,
When grief's winter shall have fled,
Giving place to sun and dew;
Some sweet hope that breathes of spring,
Through the weary, weary time,
Budding for its blossoming,
In the spirit's silent clime.

HOPE ETERNAL.

S. F. Adams.

THE world may change from old to new,
From new to old again;
Yet hope and heaven, for ever true,
Within man's heart remain.

The dreams that bless the weary soul,
The struggles of the strong,
Are steps towards some happy goal,
The story of Hope's song.

Hope leads the child to plant the flower,
The man to sow the seed;
Nor leaves fulfilment to her hour,
But prompts again to deed.

And ere upon the old man's dust
The grass is seen to wave,
We look through falling tears,—to trust
Hope's sunshine on the grave.

THE PLEASURES OF HOPE.

Campbell.

At summer eve, when Heaven's ethereal bow
Spans with bright arch the glittering hills below,
Why to yon mountain turns the musing eye,
Whose bright summit mingles with the sky?
Why do those cliffs of shadowy tint appear
More sweet than all the landscape smiling near?—
'Tis distance lends enchantment to the view,
And robes the mountain in its azure hue.
Thus, with delight, we linger to survey
The promised joys of life's unmeasured way;
Thus, from afar, each dim-discovered scene
More pleasing seems than all the past hath been,
And every form, that Fancy can repair
From dark oblivion, glows divinely there.

* * * *

With thee, sweet Hope! resides the heavenly light
That pours remotest rapture on the sight;
Thine is the charm of life's bewildered way,
That calls each slumbering passion into play.
Waked by thy touch, I see the sister-band,
On tip-toe watching, start at thy command,
And fly where'er thy mandate bids them steer,
To Pleasure's path, or Glory's bright career.
Primeval Hope, the Aönian Muses say,
When Man and Nature mourned their first decay;
When every form of death, and every woe,
Shot from malignant stars to earth below:
When Murder bared her arm and rampant War
Yoked the red dragons of her iron car;
When Peace and Mercy, banished from the plain
Sprung on the viewless winds to Heaven again;
All, all forsook the friendless, guilty mind,
But Hope, the charmer, lingered still behind.

* * * *

Auspicious Hope! in thy sweet garden grow
Wreaths for each toil, a charm for every woe;,
Won by their sweets, in Nature's languid hour
The wayworn pilgrim seeks thy summer bower;
There, as the wild bee murmurs on the wing,
What peaceful dreams thy handmaid spirits bring!
What viewless forms th' Æolian organ play,
And sweep the furrowed lines of anxious thought away.

THE MARINER'S HOPE.

Angel of life! thy glittering wings explore
Earth's loneliest bounds, and Ocean's wildest shore.
Lo! to the wintry winds the pilot yields
His bark careering o'er unfathomed fields.

* * * *

Poor child of danger, nursling of the storm,
Sad are the woes that wreck thy manly form!
Rocks, waves, and winds, the shattered bark delay;
Thy heart is sad, thy home is far away.
But Hope can here her moonlight vigils keep,
And sing to charm the spirit of the deep:
Swift as yon streamer lights the starry pole,
Her visions warm the watchman's pensive soul,
His native hills that rise in happier climes,
The grot that heard his song of other times,
His cottage home, his bark of slender sail,
His glassy lake, and broomwood-blossomed vale,
Rush on his thought; he sweeps before the wind
Treads the loved shore he sighed to leave behind:
Meets at each step a friend's familiar face,
And flies at last to Helen's long embrace;
Wipes from her cheek the rapture-speaking tear
And clasps, with many a sigh, his children dear!
While long neglected, but at length caressed,
His faithful dog salutes the smiling guest,
Points to the master's eyes (where'er they roam)
His wistful face, and whines a welcome home.

THE SOLDIER'S HOPE.

Friend of the brave! in peril's darkest hour,
Intrepid Virtue looks to thee for power;
To thee the heart its trembling homage yields,
On stormy floods, and carnage-covered fields.
When front to front the bannered hosts combine,
Halt ere they close, and form the dreadful line.
When all is still on Death's devoted soil,
The march-worn soldier mingles for the toil;
As rings his glittering tube, he lifts on high
The dauntless brow, and spirit-speaking eye;
Hails in his heart the triumph yet to come,
And hears thy stormy music in the drum!

THE DISCOVERER'S HOPE.

Congenial Hope! thy passion-kindling power,
How bright, how strong, in youth's untroubled hour!
On yon proud height, with Genius hand-in-hand,
I see thee light, and wave thy golden wand,
"Go, child of Heaven! (thy wingèd words proclaim)
'Tis thine to search the boundless fields of fame!

Lo! Newton, priest of Nature, shines afar,
Scans the wide world, and numbers every star!"
Wilt thou, with him, mysterious rites apply,
And watch the shrine with wonder-beaming eye?
Yes, thou shalt mark, with magic art profound,
The speed of light, the circling march of sound;
With Franklin grasp the lightning's fiery wing,
Or yield the lyre of Heaven another string.

DOMESTIC HOPE.

PROPITIOUS Power! when rankling cares annoy
The sacred home of Hymenean joy;
When doomed to Poverty's sequestered dell,
The wedded pair of love and virtue dwell,
Unpitied by the world, unknown to fame,
Their woes, their wishes, and their hearts the same—
Oh, there, prophetic HOPE! thy smile bestow,
And chase the pangs that worth should never know—
There, as the parent deals his scanty store
To friendless babes, and weeps to give no more,
Tell, that his manly race shall yet assuage
Their father's wrongs, and shield his latter age.
What though for him no Hybla sweets distil,
Nor bloomy vines wave purple on the hill;
Tell, that when silent years have passed away,
That when his eye grows dim, his tresses grey,
These busy hands a lovelier cot shall build,
And deck with fairer flowers his little field,
And call from Heaven propitious dews to breathe
Arcadian beauty on the barren heath;
Tell, that while Love's spontaneous smile endears
The days of peace, the sabbath of his years,
Health shall prolong to many a festive hour
The social pleasures of his humble bower.

A MOTHER'S HOPE.

Lo! at the couch where infant beauty sleeps,
Her silent watch the mournful mother keeps;
She, while the lovely babe unconscious lies,
Smiles on her slumbering child with pensive eyes,
And weaves a song of melancholy joy—
"Sleep, image of thy father, sleep, my boy;
No lingering hour of sorrow shall be thine;
No sigh that rends thy father's heart and mine;
Bright as his manly sire the son shall be
In form and soul; but, ah! more blest than he!
Thy fame, thy worth, thy filial love at last,
Shall soothe his aching heart for all the past—
With many a smile my solitude repay,
And chase the world's ungenerous scorn away.
"And say, when summoned from the world and thee,
I lay my head beneath the willow tree,
Wilt *thou*, sweet mourner! at my stone appear,
And soothe my parted spirit lingering near?
Oh, wilt thou come at evening hour to shed
The tears of Memory o'er my narrow bed;
With aching temples on thy hand reclined,
Muse on the last farewell I leave behind,
Breathe a deep sigh to winds that murmur low,
And think on all my love, and all my woe?"

HOPE OF PROGRESS.

HOPE! when I mourn, with sympathising mind,
The wrongs of fate, the woes of human kind,
Thy blissful omens bid my spirit see
The boundless fields of rapture yet to be;
I watch the wheels of Nature's mazy plan,
And learn the future by the past of man.
Come, bright Improvement! on the car of Time,
And rule the spacious world from clime to clime?
Thy handmaid arts shall every wild explore,
Trace every wave, and culture every shore.
On Erie's banks, where tigers steal along,
And the dread Indian chants a dismal song,
Where human fiends on midnight errands walk,
And bathe in brains the murderous tomahawk,
There shall the flocks on thymy pasture stray,
And shepherds dance at Summer's opening day;
Each wandering genius of the lovely glen
Shall start to view the glittering haunts of men,
And silent watch, on woodland heights around,
The village curfew as it tolls profound.

* * * *

Where barbarous hordes on Scythian mountains roam,
Truth, Mercy, Freedom, yet shall find a home;
Where'er degraded Nature bleeds and pines,
From Guinea's coast to Sibir's dreary mines,
Truth shall pervade th' unfathomed darkness there,
And light the dreadful features of despair.—
Hark! the stern captive spurns his heavy load,
And asks the image back that Heaven bestowed!
Fierce in his eye the fire of valour burns,
And as the slave departs, the man returns.

DOWNFALL OF POLAND.

OH! sacred Truth! thy triumph ceased awhile,
And HOPE, thy sister, ceased with thee to smile
When leagued Oppression poured to Northern wars
Her whiskered pandoors and her fierce hussars,
Waved her dread standard to the breeze of morn,
Pealed her loud drum, and twanged her trumpet horn.
Tumultuous horror brooded o'er her van,
Presaging wrath to Poland—and to man!
Warsaw's last champion from her height surveyed,
Wide o'er the fields a waste of ruin laid,—
"O Heaven!" he cried, "my bleeding country save!—
Is there no hand on high to shield the brave?
Yet, though destruction sweep those lovely plains,
Rise, fellow-men! our country yet remains!

By that dread name, we wave the sword on high!
And swear for her to live!—with her to die!"
He said, and on the rampart-heights arrayed
His trusty warriors, few, but undismayed;
Firm-paced and slow, a horrid front they form,
Still as the breeze, but dreadful as the storm;
Low murmuring sounds along their banners fly,
Revenge, or death,—the watchword and reply;
Then pealed the notes, omnipotent to charm,
And the loud tocsin tolled their last alarm!—
In vain, alas! in vain, ye gallant few!
From rank to rank your volleyed thunder flew:—
Oh, bloodiest picture in the book of Time,
Sarmatia fell, unwept, without a crime;
Found not a generous friend, a pitying foe,
Strength in her arms, nor mercy in her woe!
Dropped from her nerveless grasp the shattered spear,
Closed her bright eye, and curbed her high career;—
Hope, for a season, bade the world farewell,
And Freedom shrieked—as Kosciusko fell!

HOPE OF LOVE.

In joyous youth, what soul hath never known
Thought, feeling, taste, harmonious to its own?
Who hath not paused while Beauty's pensive eye
Asked from his heart the homage of a sigh?
Who hath not known, with rapture-smitten frame
The power of grace, the magic of a name?

* * * * *

Who that would ask a heart to dullness wed,
The waveless calm, the slumber of the dead?
No; the wild bliss of Nature needs alloy,
And fear and sorrow fan the fire of joy?
And say, without our hopes, without our fears,
Without the home that plighted love endears,
Without the smile from partial beauty won,
Oh! what were man?—a world without a sun.

HOPE OF IMMORTALITY.

Unfading Hope! when life's last embers burn,
When soul to soul, and dust to dust return!
Heaven to thy charge resigns the awful hour!
Oh! then, thy kingdom comes! Immortal Power!
What though each spark of earth-born rapture fly
The quivering lip, pale cheek, and closing eye!
Bright to the soul thy seraph hands convey
The morning dream of life's eternal day—
Then, then, the triumph and the trance begin,
And all the phœnix spirit burns within!

* * * * *

Daughter of Faith, awake, arise, illume
The dread unknown, the chaos of the tomb;
Melt, and dispel, ye spectre-doubts, that roll
Cimmerian darkness o'er the parting soul!

* * * * *

What is the bigot's torch, the tyrant's chain?
I smile on death, if Heavenward Hope remain!

* * * * *

Cease, every joy, to glimmer on my mind,
But leave—oh! leave the light of Hope behind!
What though my winged hours of bliss have been,
Like angel-visits, few and far between,
Her musing mood shall every pang appease,
And charm—when pleasures lose the power to please!
Yes; let each rapture, dear to Nature, flee:
Close not the light of Fortune's stormy sea—
Mirth, Music, Friendship, Love's propitious smile,
Chase every care, and charm a little while,
Ecstatic throbs the fluttering heart employ,
And all her strings are harmonised to joy!—
But why so short is Love's delighted hour?
Why fades the dew on Beauty's sweetest flower?
Why can no hymned charm of music heal
The sleepless woes impassioned spirits feel?
Can fancy's fairy hands no veil create,
To hide the sad realities of fate?—
No! Not the quaint remark, the sapient rule,
Nor all the pride of Wisdom's worldly school,
Have power to soothe, unaided and alone,
The heart that vibrates to a feeling tone!
When stepdame Nature every bliss recalls,
Fleet as the meteor o'er the desert falls;
When, 'reft of all, yon widowed sire appears
A lonely hermit in the vale of years;
Say, can the world one joyous thought bestow
To Friendship, weeping at the couch of Woe?
No! but a brighter soothes the last adieu,—
Souls of impassioned mould, she speaks to you!
Weep not, she says, at Nature's transient pain,
Congenial spirits part to meet again!

* * * * *

Eternal Hope! when yonder spheres sublime
Pealed their first notes to sound the march of Time.
Thy joyous youth began—but not to fade.—
When all the sister planets have decayed;
When wrapt in fire the realms of ether glow,
And Heaven's last thunder shakes the world below.
Thou, undismayed, shalt o'er the ruins smile,
And light thy torch at Nature's funeral pile.

Poems about Education.

EDUCATION.

A Pleasurable Employment.

Thomson.

DELIGHTFUL task! to rear the tender thought,
To teach the young idea how to shoot,
To pour the fresh instruction o'er the mind,
To breath the enliv'ning spirit, and to fix
The generous purpose in the glowing breast.

EARLY DAWN OF EDUCATION.

Household Words.

MOTHER! watch the little hand
Picking berries by the way;
Making houses in the sand;
Tossing up the fragrant hay.
Never dare the question ask,—
Why to me this weary task?
The same little hands may prove
Messengers of light and love.

Mother! watch the little tongue
Prattling elegant and wild,
What is said and what is sung
By the happy, joyous child:
Catch the word while yet unspoken,
Stop the vow before 'tis broken:

Mother! watch the little heart
Beating soft and warm for you;
Wholesome lessons now impart,—
Keep, oh, keep that young heart true;
Extricating every weed,
Sowing good and precious seed;
Harvest rich you then may see,
Ripening then for eternity.

EDUCATION BY THE STATE.

Wordsworth.

O, FOR the coming of that glorious time
When, prizing knowledge as her noblest wealth
And best protection, this imperial realm,
While she exacts allegiance, shall admit
An obligation, on her part, to *teach*
Them who are born to serve her and obey;
Binding herself, by statute, to secure
For all the children whom her soil maintains,
The rudiments of letters, and inform
The mind with moral and religious truth,
Both understood and practised—so that none,
However destitute, be left to droop,
By timely culture unsustain'd; or run
Into a wild disorder; or be forced
To drudge through a weary life without the help
Of intellectual implements and tools;
A savage horde among the civilised,
A servile band among the lordly free.

CAPACITY FOR EDUCATION.

Bowring.

THE heart has tendrils like the vine,
Which round another's bosom twine,
Outspringing from the living tree
Of deeply planted sympathy;
Whose flowers are hope, its fruits are bliss,
Beneficence its harvest is.

There are some bosoms dark and drear,
Which an unwater'd desert are;
Yet there a curious eye may trace
Some smiling spot, some verdant place,
Where little flowers, the weeds between,
Spend their soft fragrance all unseen.

Despise them not—for wisdom's toil
Has ne'er disturb'd that stubborn soil:
Yet care and culture might have brought
The ore of truth from mines of thought;
And fancy's fairest flowers had bloom'd
Where truth and fancy lie entomb'd

Insult him not—his blackest crime
May, in his Maker's eye sublime,
In spite of all thy pride, be less
Than e'en thy daily waywardness;
Than many a sin and many a stain
Forgotten—and impress'd again.

There is in every human heart
Some not completely broken part,
Where seeds of truth and love might grow
And flowers of generous virtue blow:
To plant, to watch, to water there—
This, as our duty, be our care!

And sweet it is, the growth to trace,
Of worth, of intellect, of grace,
In bosoms where our labours first
Bid the young seed of spring-time burst
And lead it on from hour to hour,
To ripen into perfect flower.

THE VILLAGE SCHOOLMASTER.

Goldsmith.

Beside yon straggling fence that skirts the way, with blossom'd furze unprofitably gay,
There, in his noisy mansion, skill'd to rule, the village master taught his little school.
A man severe he was, and stern to view, I knew him well, and every truant knew;
Well had the boding tremblers learn'd to trace the day's disasters in his morning face;
Full well they laugh'd with counterfeited glee at all his jokes, for many a joke had he;
Full well the busy whisper circling round convey'd the dismal tidings when he frown'd;
Yet he was kind, or if severe in aught, the love he bore to learning was in fault.
The village all declared how much he knew, 'twas certain he could write and cipher too;
Lands he could measure, time and tide presage, and e'en the story ran that he could gauge;
In arguing, too, the master own'd his skill, for, e'en vanquish'd, he could argue still,
While words of learnèd length and thundering sound amazed the gazing rustics ranged around;
And still they gazed, and still the wonder grew that one small head could carry all he knew.

THE OLD SCHOOLMASTER.

L.O.H.

He sat at his desk at the close of day, for he felt the weight of his many years—
His form was bent and his hair was grey, and his eyes were dim with the falling tears.
The school was out and his task was done, and the house seemed now so strangely still,
As the red beam of the setting sun stole silently over the window-sill.

Stole silently into the twilight gloom, and the deepening shadows fell athwart
The vacant seats and the vacant room, and the vacant place in the old man's heart—
For his school had been all in all to him, who had no wife, children, land, nor gold;
But his frame was weak, and his eyes were dim, and the fiat was issued at last—"too old."

He bowed his head on his trembling hands a moment, as one might bend to pray;
"Too old!" they say, and the school demands a wiser and younger head to-day.
"Too old! too old!" these men forget it was I who guided their tender years;
Their hearts were hard, and they pitied not my trembling lips and my falling tears.

"Too old! too old!" it was all they said, I looked in their faces one by one,
But they turned away, and my heart was lead, "dear Lord, it is hard, but Thy will be done."
The night stole on and a blacker gloom was over the vacant benches cast;
The master sat in the silent room, but his mind was back in the days long past.

And he smiled as his kindly glances fell on the well beloved faces there—
John, Rob, and Will, and laughing Nell, and blue-eyed Bess, with golden hair,
And Tom, and Charley, and Ben, and Paul, who stood at the head of the spelling class—
All in their places—and yet they all were lying under the graveyard grass.

Thus all night long, till the morning came, and the darkness folded her robe of gloom,
And the sun looked in with his eye of flame, on the vacant seats of the silent room,
And the wind stole over the-window sill, and swept through the aisles in a merry rout;
But the face of the master was white and still—his work was finished, his school was out.

Poems about the Pen and Press.

THE Press—the Press—the glorious Press,
It makes the nations free?
Before it tyrants prostrate fall
And proud oppressors flee!
In what a state of wretchedness
Without it should we be;
And can we then too highly prize
The source of liberty?

The Press—the Press—the glorious Press,
It dissipates our gloom!
And sheds a ray of happiness
O'er victims of the tomb:
See, darkness from his ebon throne
Has fled to realms of night,
And o'er the world is now diffused
A flood of heavenly light.

The Press—the Press—the glorious Press,
What thanks are due to those,
Who all attempts to quench its beams,
Triumphantly oppose;
To them belongs the wreathe of fame!
The garland of renown!
The honour of a deathless name!
A never-fading crown!

The Press—the Press—the glorious Press,
Blessings by it abound!
It changes man, and makes him great,
Wherever man is found.
The idols of the heathen land,
And superstition's sway
And sceptres from the tyrants' hand,
Through it are cast away.

The Press—the Press—the glorious Press,
It makes the world anew;
And it will bring millennium on,
And give us then to view
The end of war, and lasting peace,
When sheathed shall be the sword;
And men shall call this hampered earth
The "Garden of the Lord."

THE PRESS. *G. W. Cutter.*

SOUL of the world! the Press! the Press,
What wonders hast thou wrought!
Thou rainbow realm of mental bliss;
Thou starry sky of thought!
As dew unto the thirsty flowers;
As the blessed light of heaven;
And widely as the summer showers,
Thy silent aid is given.

Yet canst thou flame upon the earth
Like the dread volcano's glow;
And tyrants tremble at thy birth
As at an earthquake's throe.
Hast thou not lit the darkest land,
And broke the fellest chain,
The despot's red accursed hand
Shall never forge again?

And priestly craft and kingly power
Have striven to bind thee down;
But ah, how low beneath thee cower
The mitre and the crown!
Thy nod can lop the proudest head;
The world thy sceptre owns;
The path thou dost to glory tread,
The path is paved with thrones.

Yet thou art gentle as the breeze—
The latest breath of day;
But chainless as the mighty seas,
In thy resistless sway.
At thy command the seals were broke
That bound the silent deep,
And liberty and truth awoke
From centuries of sleep.

Then first on every sinful shore,
That man in darkness trod,
Thy bright and speeding pinions bore
The beacon words of God.
The sage's lamp, the muses' lyre,
Thou brought'st o'er ocean's foam;
The stellar light of vestal fire;
The eloquence of Rome.

Thou flag of truth! thy folds have streamed
O'er many a field of blood;
And o'er the wreck of empires gleamed,
Like the rainbow o'er the flood;
The patriot's eye still turns to thee,
And hails thee from afar,
As the wanderer of the trackless sea
Hath hailed his guiding star.

While to the earth-stone of the hall,
And to the cottage hearth,
Thou bring'st a daily festival
Of nameless, priceless worth.
Thou lightest up the pallid cheek
Of the deserted poor,
And to the captive, worn and weak,
Openest the prison door.

O! ever in thy columns bright,
Let truth and virtue blend!
Be ever, ever in the right!
Be ever labour's friend.
His strong and honest arm shall be
Thy bulwark in distress;
God bless the land of liberty!
God save our country's press!

USE THE PEN.

J. E. Carpenter.

Use the pen! there's magic in it,
Never let it lag behind;
Write thy thought, the pen can win it
From the chaos of the mind.

Many a gem is lost for ever
By the careless passer by,
But the gems of thought should never
On the mental pathway lie.

Use the pen! reck not that others
Take a higher flight than thine,
Many an ocean cave still smothers
Pearls of price beneath the brine;

But the diver finds the treasure,
And the gem to light is brought;
So thy mind's unbounded measure
May give up some pearl of thought.

Use the pen! the day's departed
When the sword alone held sway,
Wielded by the lion-hearted,
Strong in battle. Where are they?

All unknown the deeds of glory
Done of old by mighty men—
Save the few who live in story,
Chronicled by sages' pen.

Use the pen! the sun above us
By whose light the chemist's art
Stamps the forms of those who love us,
Showing us their counterpart;

Cannot hold so high a power
As within the pen enshrined,
When, with genius for its dower,
It daguerreotypes the mind.

Use the pen! but let it never
Slander write, with death-black ink;
Let it be thy best endeavour
But to pen what good men think;

So thy words and thoughts, securing
Honest praise from wisdom's tongue,
May, in time, be as enduring
As the strains which Homer sung.

BOIL IT DOWN.

Whatever you have to say, my friend,
Whether witty, or grave, or gay,
Condense as much as ever you can,
And say in the readiest way;
And whether you write of rural affairs,
Or particular things in town,
Just take a word of friendly advice—
Boil it down.

For if you go spluttering over a page
When a couple of lines would do,
Your butter is spread so much, you see,
That the bread looks plainly through.
So when you have a story to tell,
And would like a little renown,
To make quite sure of your wish, my friend,
Boil it down.

When writing an article for the press,
Whether prose or verse just try
To utter your thoughts in the fewest of words,
And let them be crisp and dry.
And when it is finished, and you suppose
It's done exactly brown,
Just look over again, and then,
Boil it down.

For editors do not like to print
An article lazily long,
And the general reader does not care
For a couple of yards of a song,
So gather your wits in the smallest space
If you'd win the author's crown.
And every time you write, my friend,
Boil it down.

THE PRESS.

Allan Davenport.

HAIL! glorious offspring of the human mind,
Thou great regenerator of mankind!
With thee the march of intellect began:
To thee we owe that moral power of man,
Which, like the mighty current of the Thames,
Swells as it rolls, fed by a thousand streams;
That moral power which tyrants now must feel
Cannot be bound with chains, nor crushed by steel!
What greater gift to man could genius give?
What greater favour could mankind receive?
From thee all languages, the live and dead,
Receive the stamp which makes them easy read:
From the mental treasures of the soul
Receive their wings to fly from pole to pole!
What are the powers that be, who hold the rod,
Compared to thee, though but an iron god?
'Tis thou, omnipotent, must set us free;
What miracles have been performed by thee!
All hopes are in, all eyes are on the Press;
Let that be free, and who shall doubt success?
Arm'd with the scales of justice and the rod,
It lashes folly, tyranny, and fraud;
Repels oppression with the might of Jove,
Stamps immortality on honest fame,
And brands the villain with eternal shame.
The genius of the press shall yet prevail,
And conquer where the boldest armies fail;
For despots, whom no other powers distress,
Shrink when they hear the thunders of the Press
Roll through their kingdoms, in the civil storm,
Proclaiming justice, freedom, and reform.

THE VOICE OF THE PEN.

D. F. M'Carthy.

OH! the Orator's Voice is a mighty power
As it echoes from shore to shore,
And the fearless pen has more sway o'er men
Than the murderous cannon's roar.
What burst the chain from o'er the main,
And brightens the captive's den?
'Tis the fearless voice, and the Pen of power—
Hurrah! for the Voice and Pen!
Hurrah! hurrah! for the Voice and Pen!

The tyrant knaves who deny our rights,
And the cowards who blanch with fear,
Exclaim with glee, "No arms have ye—
Nor cannon, nor sword, nor spear!
Your hills are ours, with our forts and towers,
We are masters of mount and glen."
Tyrants, beware! for the arms we bear
Are, the Voice and the fearless Pen!

Though your horsemen stand with their bridles in hand,
And your sentinels walk around—
Though your matches flare in the midnight air,
And your brazen trumpets sound;
Oh! the orator's tongue shall be heard among
These listening warrior men;
And they'll quickly say, "Why should we slay
Our friends of the Voice and Pen?"

When the Lord created the earth and sea,
The stars and the glorious sun,
The Godhead SPOKE, and the universe woke—
And the mighty work was done!
Let a word be flung from the orator's tongue,
Or a drop from the fearless Pen,
And the chains accurs'd asunder burst,
That fettered the minds of men!

Oh! these are the swords with which we fight—
The arms in which we trust;
Which no tyrant hand will dare to brand,
Which time cannot dim or rust!
When these we bore, we triumphed before;
With these we'll triumph again;
And the world will say, "No power can stay
The voice and the fearless Pen!"
Hurrah! hurrah! for the Voice and Pen!

THE PEN AND THE PRESS.

J. C. Prince.

Young Genius walked out by the mountains and streams,
Entranced by the power of his own pleasant dreams,
Till the silent, the wayward, the wandering thing,
Found a plume that had fallen from a passing bird's wing;
Exulting and proud, like a boy at his play,
He bore the new prize to his dwelling away;
He gazed on awhile on it's beauties, and then
He cut it, and shaped it, and called it a Pen.

But its magical use he discovered not yet,
Till he dipped its bright lips in a fountain of jet;
And, oh! what a glorious thing it became.
For it spoke to the world in a language of flame;
While its master wrote on like a being inspired,
Till the hearts of the millions were melted or fired.
It came as a boon and a blessing to men,
The peaceful, the pure, the victorious Pen!

Young Genius went forth on his rambles once more,
The vast, sunless caverns of earth to explore;
He searched the rude rock, and with rapture found
A substance unknown, which he brought from the ground;
He fused it with fire, and rejoiced at the change,
As he moulded the ore into characters strange,
Till his thoughts and his efforts were crowned with success,
For an engine uprose, and he called it the Press.

The Pen and the Press, best alliance! combined
To soften the heart and enlighten the mind;
For *that* to the treasures of knowledge gave birth,
And *this* sent them forth to the ends of the earth:
Their battles for truth were triumphant indeed,
And the rod of the tyrant was snapped like a reed;
They were made to exhort us, to teach us, to bless,
Those invincible brothers, the Pen and the Press;

THE PRESS.

Thoughts flit and flutter through the mind,
As o'er the waves the shifting wind;
Trackless and traceless is their flight,
As falling stars of yesternight,
Or the old tide-marks on the shore
Which other tides have rippled o'er.

Yet heart by Genius trained and taught,
Arrests—records the fleeting thought,
Stamps on the minute or the hour
A lasting, an eternal power,
And to mind's passing shadows gives
An influence that for ever lives.

But mightiest of the mighty means,
On which the arm of Progress leans,
Man's noblest mission to advance,
His woes assuage, his weal enhance,
His rights enforce, his wrongs redress—
Mightiest of Mighty is the Press!

Poems about Books.

BOOKS.

Crabbe.

Books they give
New views to life, and teach us how to live;
They soothe the grieved, the stubborn they chastise;
Fools they admonish, and confirm the wise;
Their aid they yield to all; they never shun
The man of sorrow, nor the wretch undone;
Unlike the hard, the selfish, and the proud,
They fly not sullen from the suppliant crowd;
Nor tell to various people various things,
But show to subjects, what they show to kings.

Blest be the gracious Power, who taught mankind
To stamp a lasting image of the mind!
Beasts may convey, and tuneful birds may sing,
Their mutual feelings, in the opening spring
But man alone has skill and power to send
The heart's warm dictates to the distant friend;
'Tis his alone to please, instruct, advise
Ages remote, and nations yet to rise.

BOOKS.

Keats.

Bards of passion and of mirth,
Ye have left your souls on earth!
Have ye souls in heaven too,
Double-lived in regions new?
Thus ye live on high, and then
On the earth ye live again;
And the souls ye left behind you
Teach us here the way to find you
Where your other souls are joying,
Never slumber'd, never cloying.
Here your earth-born souls will speak
To mortals, of their little week;
Of their sorrows and delights;
Of their passions and their spite;
Of their glory and their shame;
What doth strengthen and what maim.
Thus ye teach us, every day,
Wisdom, though fled far away.
Bards of passion and of mirth,
Ye have left your souls on earth!
Ye have souls in heaven too,
Double-lived in regions new!

BOOKS.

Rantzau.

Golden volumes! richest treasures!
Objects of delicious pleasures!
You my eyes rejoicing please,
You my hands in capture seize.
Brilliant wits and musing sages,
Light who beamed through many ages,
Left to your conscious leaves their story;
And dared to trust you with their glory;
And now their hope of fame achieved,
Dear volumes!—you have not deceived.

BOOKS.

Bennock.

I love my books as drinkers love their wine,
The more I drink, the more they seem divine;
With joy elate my soul in love runs o'er,
And each fresh draught is sweeter than before!
Books bring me friends where'er on earth I be,
Solace of solitude—bonds of society!
I love my books! they are companions dear,
Sterling in worth, in friendship most sincere.
Here talk I with the wise in ages gone,
And with the noblygifted of our own;
If love, joy, laughter, sorrow please my mind,
Love, joy, grief, laughter in my books I find.

BOOKS.

Wordsworth.

. . . Books, we know,
Are a substantial world, both pure and good;
Round which, with tendrils strong as flesh and blood,
Our pastime and our happiness will grow.
. . . Books are yours;
Within whose silent chambers treasure lies
Preserved from age to age; more precious far
Than that accumulated store of gold
And orient gems, which for a day of need,
The Sultan hides deep in ancestral tombs,
These hoards of truth you can unlock at will.

BOOKS.

Southey.

My days among the dead are pass'd;
 Around me I behold,
Where'er these casual eyes are cast,
 The mighty minds of old;
My never-failing friends are they,
With whom I converse day by day.
With them I take delight in weal,
 And seek relief in woe;
And while I understand and feel
 How much to them I owe,
My cheeks have often been bedew'd
With tears of thoughtful gratitude.

BOOKS.

Daniel.

O Blessed Letters! that combine in one
All Ages past, and make one live with all,
By you we do confer with who are gone,
And the Dead-living unto Council call;
By you th' unborn shall have Communion
Of what we feel and what doth us befall.
Soul of the World, Knowledge without thee;
What hath the Earth that truly glorious is
. . . What Good is like to this,
To do worthy the writing, and to write
Worthy the Reading, and the World's Delight?

BOOKS.

Thompson.

In my cosy library "There studious let me sit,
And hold high converse with the mighty dead;
Sages of ancient time, as gods revered,
As gods beneficent, who bless'd mankind
With arts, with arms, and humanized a world."

BOOKS.

Byron.

But words are things, and a small drop of ink,
 Falling, like dew, upon a thought, produces
That which makes thousands, perhaps millions, think.

BOOKS.

Longfellow.

Books
Leave us heirs to ample heritages
Of all the best thoughts of the greatest sages,
And giving tongues unto the silent dead.

BOOKS.

Shakespeare.

Me, poor man, my library
Was dukedom large enough
. . . .
Knowing I loved my books, he furnished me
From my own library, with volumes that
I prize above my dukedom.—*Tempest* i.

BOOKS.

Bailey.

Worthy books
Are not my companions—they are solitudes;
We lose ourselves in them and all our cares.

BOOKS.

Dr. Dodd.

Books, dear books,
Have been, and are my comforts, morn and night;
Adversity, prosperity, at home,
Abroad, health, sickness,—good or ill report,
The same firm friends; the same refreshments rich,
And source of consolation.

BOOKS.

Mrs. Hale.

A blessing on the printer's art:—
Books are the mentors of the heart,
The burning soul, the burden'd mind,
In books alone companions find.

BOOKS.

Yriarte.

For every man of real learning
 Is anxious to increase his lore,
And feels, in fact, a greater yearning,
 The more he knows, to know the more.

BOOKS.

Overbury.

Books are a part of man's prerogative.
In formal ink they thoughts and voices hold,
That we to them our solitude may give,
And make time present travelled that of old.
I cannot think the glorious world of mind,
 Embalm'd in books, which I can only see
In patches, though I read my moments blind,
 Is to be lost to me.

THE BLESSEDNESS OF BOOKS.

E. W. Cole.

It may be thought presumptuous in me to insert this piece in praise of books amongst the poetic gems of the world. Some of my friends tell me it is not poetry, and the "London Saturday Review" calls it "a sort of hymn." But poetry or not poetry, one thing is certain, that every statement in it is true; and besides, it will advertise books. It is in praise of books, and I am fully convinced that books are the most precious of all earthly possessions—that they are destined to be the chief education, joy-makers, peace-makers, and federators of the world, and I cordially agree with Alcott when he says, "One cannot celebrate books sufficiently. After saying his best still something better remains to be spoken in their praise."

Books should be found in every house,
To form and feed the mind;
They are the best of luxuries
'Tis possible to find.

For all the books in all the world
Are man's most precious treasure;
They make him wise, and bring to him
His best, his choicest pleasure.

Books make his time pass happily,
Relieve his weary hours;
Amuse, compose, instruct his mind,
Enlarge his mental powers.

Books teach the boys and girls of earth
In twice two million schools:
Books make the difference between
Earth's learned and its fools.

Books teach ten million artisans
The proper way to take,
To find, to plan, to build, to mix,
And every product make.

Books teach schoolmasters, clergymen,
Of every rank and grade;
And doctors, lawyers, judges too—
Books are their tools of trade.

Books show man countries, cities, towns,
Manners and customs too;
Books show what all men eat and drink,
And everything they do.

Books give, beside descriptions of
This grand world of our own,
Vast knowledge of the starry worlds,
And point to worlds unknown.

Books give to man the history
Of each and every land;
Books show him human actions past—
The bad, the good, the grand.

Books show him human arts and laws
Of every time and place;
Books show the learnings and the faiths
Of all the human race.

Books give the choicest, noblest songs
Of every age and tongue;
Books give the grandest, sweetest tunes
That mankind ever sung.

Books give the best and greatest thoughts
Of all the good and wise;
Books treasure human knowledge up,
And thus it never dies.

Books show man all that men have done,
Have thought, have sung, have said;
Books show the deeds and wisdom of
The living and the dead.

Books show the joys, griefs, hopes, and fears
Of every race and clan;
Books show, by unity of thought,
The brotherhood of man.

Books show that men of every race,
Of colour, clime, and creed,
Have kindred feelings, passions, thoughts,
And brothers are indeed.

Books show that mankind's leading faiths
In morals are the same,
That in their main essentials
They differ but in name.

Books show that good men everywhere
Believe that war should cease;
And books will make that feeling grow,
And more and more increase.

Books thus will cause the flag of peace
Through earth to be unfurled—
Produce "the parliament of man,"
And federate the world.

Books give the reader vast delight
The bookless never know;
Books give him pleasure day and night
Wherever he may go.

Books please him in his lonely hours,
Wherever he may roam;
Books please when read aloud among
His loving friends at home.

Books, like strong drink, will drown man's cares
But do not waste his wealth;
Books leave him BETTER, drink the WORSE,
In character and health.

Books teach and please him when a child,
In youth, and in his prime;
Books give him soothing pleasure when
His health and strength decline.

Books give him hope beyond the grave
Of an immortal life;
Books teach that right, and truth, and love
Shall banish every strife.

Books give man knowledge while on earth,
Which makes him wiser here;
And, last, it serves as capital
To start with "Over There."

Books therefore are, of all man buys,
The choicest thing on earth;
Books have, of all his worldly goods,
The most intrinsic worth.

Books are the greatest blessing out,
The grandest thing we sell;
Books being more joy, Books do more good,
Than mortal tongue can tell.

Poems about Knowledge.

KNOWLEDGE.

The earth is large, O sons of men;
Her lands are broad and fair;
She teems with wealth hid from our ken,
In treasures rich and rare.

Like some fair palace filled with gold,
And all that man may need;
Adorned with beauties yet untold,
Our Earth is rich indeed.

But all her gates without are fast;
Thus guarded must she be;
None enter in to her repast,
Without the mystic key.

That key throws open door on door,
Each step new joys to see;
And ope's to all her goodly store,
And Knowledge is that key,

ART.

By Sprague.

When from the sacred garden driven,
Man fled before his Maker's wrath,
An angel left her place in heaven,
And cross'd the wanderer's sunless path.
'Twas Art! sweet Art! new radiance broke,
Where her light foot flew o'er the ground;
And thus with seraph voice she spoke,
"The curse a blessing shall be found."
She led him through the trackless wild,
Where noontide sunbeam never blazed:—
The thistle shrunk—the harvest smiled,
And nature gladen'd as she gazed.
Earth's thousand tribes of living things,
At Art's command to him are given,
The village grows, the city springs,
And point their spires of faith to heaven.

He rends the oak—and bids it ride,
To guard the shores its beauty graced;
He smites the rock—upheaved in pride,
See towers of strength, and domes of taste.
Earth teeming caves their wealth reveal,
Fire bears his banner on the wave,
He bids the mortal poison heal,
And leaps triumphant o'er the grave.

He plucks the pearls that stud the deep,
Admiring beauty's lap to fill:
He breaks the stubborn marble's sleep,
And mocks his own Creator's skill.
With thoughts that swell his glowing soul
He bids the ore illume the page,
And proudly scorning time's control,
Commerces with an unborn age.

In fields of air he writes his name,
And treads the chambers of the sky;
He reads the stars, and grasps the flame,
That quivers round the throne on high.
In war renown'd, in peace sublime,
He moves in greatness and in grace;
His power subduing space and time,
Links realm to realm, and race to race.

KNOWLEDGE.

James Montgomery.

THE lion o'er his wild domains
  Rules with the terror of his eye;
The eagle of the rock maintains
  By force his empire in the sky;
The shark, the tyrant of the flood,
  Reigns through the deep with quench-
    less rage;
Parent and young, unweaned from blood,
  Are still the same from age to age.

Of all that live, and move, and breathe,
  Man only rises o'er his birth;
He looks above, around, beneath,
  At once the heir of heaven and earth:
Force, cunning, speed, which Nature gave
  The various tribes throughout her plan,
Life to enjoy, from death to save,—
These are the lowest powers of man.

From strength to strength he travels on;
  He leaves the lingering brute behind;
And when a few short years are gone,
  He soars a disembodied mind
Beyond the grave his course sublime,
  Destined through nobler paths to run,
In his career the end of time
  Is but Eternity begun.

What guides him in his high pursuit,
  Opens, illumines, cheers his way,
Discerns the immortal from the brute,
  God's image from the mould of clay?
'Tis Knowledge:—Knowledge to the soul
  Is power, and liberty, and peace;
And while celestial ages roll,
  The joys of Knowledge shall increase.

HEIR OF THE AGES.

THOUGH small store of wealth I own,
  Though no rod of land have I;
Nor do towers of fretted stone
  Mark for me a mansion high.

Though I have no pearls or gold,
  Massive plate, or jewels rare;
Broidered silks of worth untold,
  Nor rich robes a queen might wear.

In my gardens narrow bound
  Flaunt not costly tropic blooms,
Ladening all the air around
  With a weight of rare perfumes.

Yet to an immense estate
  Am I heir, a child of God—
Richer, grander than doth wait
  Any earthly monarch's nod.

Heir of all the Ages, I—
  Heir of all that they have wrought,
All their store of empires high,
  All their wealth of precious thought.

Every golden deed of theirs
  Sheds its lustre on my way;
All their labors, all their prayers
  Sanctify this present day.

Heir of all the good, and more,
  Bought by labour, arm, and brain,
All accumulated lore,
  Deep and high and wide domain.

Heir of all that they have earned
  By their passion and their tears—
Heir of all that they have learned
  Through the weary toiling years.

Heir of all the faith sublime
  On whose wings they soared to heaven,
Heir of every hope that time
  To earth's fainting sons hath given.

Heir of all that earth can give,
  All the blessedness of time,
Heir of all for which I live,
  Heir of joys and hopes sublime.

Aspirations pure and high—
  Strength to dare and to endure—
Heir of all the Ages, I—
  Lo! I am no longer poor.

Heir am I and now possess,
  Earth and universe combine
Past and future all to bless,
  Lo! the infinite is mine.

Poems about Music.

MUSIC.

Collins.

O Music! sphere-descended maid,
Friend of pleasure, wisdom's aid!
Why, goddess, why to us denied,
Lay'st thou thy ancient lyre aside?
As, in that loved Athenian bower,
You learned an all-commanding power,
Thy mimic soul, O Nymph endeared
Can well recall what then it heard;
Where is thy native simple heart,
Devote to Virtue, Fancy, Art?
Arise, as in that elder time,
Warm, energetic, chaste, sublime!
Thy wonders, in that god-like age,
Fill thy recording sister's page—
'Tis said, and I believe the tale,
Thy humblest reed could more prevail,
Had more of strength, diviner rage,
Than all which charms this laggard age;
E'en all at once together found,
Cecilia's mingled world of sound—
O bid our vain endeavour cease;
Revive the just designs of Greece:
Return in all thy simple state!
Confirm the tales her sons relate!

MUSIC.

Dryden.

By Music, minds an equal temper know,
Not swell too high, nor sink too low;
If in the brief tumultuous joys arise,
Music her soft, assuasive voice applies;
Or, when the soul is press'd with cares,
Exalts her in enliv'ning airs;
Warriors she fires with animated sounds,
Pours balm into the bleeding lover's wounds;
Melancholy lifts her head,
Morpheus rouses from his bed,
Sloth unfolds her arms and wakes,
List'ning Envy drops her snakes,
Intestine war no more our Passions wage,
And giddy Factions bear away their rage.

Music the fiercest grief can charm,
And fate's severest rage disarm;
Music can soften pain to ease,
And make despair and madness please;
Our joys below it can improve,
And antedate the bliss above.

NATURE MUSICAL.

Andrew James Symington.

There is music in the storm, love,
When the tempest rages high;
It whispers in the summer breeze
A soft, sweet lullaby.
There is music in the night,
When the joyous nightingale,
Clear warbling, filleth with his song
The hillside and the vale.
Then sing, sing, sing,
For music breathes in everything.

There is music by the shore, love,
Where foaming billows dash:
It echoes in the thunder peal,
When vivid lightnings flash.
There is music by the shore,
In the stilly noon of night,
When the murmurs of the ocean fade
In the clear moonlight.

There is music in the soul, love,
When it hears the gushing swell,
Which, like a dream intensely soft,
Peals from the lily-bell.
There is music—music deep
In the soul that looks on high,
When myriad sparkling stars sing out
Their pure sphere harmony.

There is music in the glance, love,
Which speaketh from the heart,
Of a sympathy in souls
That nevermore would part.
There is music in the note
Of the cooing turtle-dove;
There is music in the voice
Of the dear ones whom we love.

There is music everywhere, love,
To the pure of spirit given;
And sweetest music heard on earth
But whispers that of heaven.
Oh, all is music there—
'Tis the language of the sky—
Sweet hallelujahs there resound
Eternal harmony.
Then sing, sing, sing,
For music breathes in everything.

THE PIPES AT LUCKNOW.

Whittier.

PIPES of the misty moorlands,
  Voices of the glens and hills;
The droning of the torrents,
  The treble of the hills!
Not the braes of broom and heather,
  Nor the mountains dark with rain,
Nor maiden bower, nor border tower
  Have heard your sweetest strain!

Dear to the lowland reaper,
  And plaided mountaineer,—
To the cottage and the castle
  The Scottish pipes are dear;—
Sweet sounds the ancient pibroch
  O'er mountain, loch, and glade;
But the sweetest of all music
  The pipes of Lucknow played.

Day by day the Indian tiger
  Louder yelled and nearer crept;
Round and round the jungle serpent
  Near and nearer circles swept.
"Pray for rescue, wives and mothers,—
  Pray to-day!" the soldier said;
"To-morrow, death's between us
  And the wrong and shame we dread."

Oh! they listened, looked, and waited,
  Till their hope became despair;
And the sobs of low bewailing
  Filled the pauses of their prayer.
Then up spake a Scottish maiden,
  With her ear unto the ground:
"Dinna ye hear it?—dinna ye hear it?
  The pipes o' Havelock sound!"

Hushed the wounded man his groaning;
  Hushed the wife her little ones;
Alone they heard the drum-roll
  And the roar of Sepoy guns.
But to sounds of home and childhood
  The Highland ear was true;
As her mother's cradle crooning,
  The mountain pipes she knew.

Like the march of soundless music
  Through the vision of the seer,—
More of feeling than of hearing,
  Of the heart than of the ear,
She knew the droning pibroch
  She knew the Campbell's call.
"Hark! hear ye no' MacGregor's,
  The grandest o' them all!"

Oh! they listened, dumb and breathless,
  And they caught the sound at last;
Faint and far beyond the Goomtee
  Rose and fell the piper's blast!
Then a burst of wild thanksgiving
  Mingled woman's voice and man's:
"God be praised!—the march of Havelock!
  The piping of the clans!"

Louder, nearer, fierce as vengeance,
  Sharp and shrill as swords at strife,
Came the wild MacGregor's clan-call,
  Stinging all the air to life.
But when the far-off dust cloud
  To plaided legions grew,
Full tenderly and blithesomely
  The pipes of rescue blew!

Round the silver domes of Lucknow,
  Moslem mosque and pagan shrine,
Breathed the air to Britons dearest,
  The air of "Auld Lang Syne;"
O'er the cruel roll of war-drums
  Rose that sweet and homelike strain;
And the tartan clove the turban,
  As the Goomtee cleaves the plain.

Dear to the corn-land reaper,
  And plaided mountaineer,—
To the cottage and the castle
  The piper's song is dear;
Sweet sounds the Gaelic pibroch
  O'er mountain, glen, and glade,
But the sweetest of all music
  The pipes at Lucknow played!

Poems about Singing.

TROUBLE IN THE "AMEN CORNER."

T. C. Harbaugh.

'Twas a stylish congregation, that of Theophrastus Brown,
And its organ was the finest and the biggest in the town,
And the chorus—all the papers favourably commented on it,
For 'twas said each female member had a forty-dollar bonnet.

Now in the "amen corner" of the church sat Brother Eyer,
Who persisted every Sabbath-day in singing with the choir;
He was poor, but genteel looking, and his heart as snow was white,
And his old face beamed with sweetness when he sang with all his
might.

His voice was cracked and broken, age had touched his vocal chords,
And nearly every Sunday he would mispronounce the words
Of the hymns, and 'twas no wonder, he was old and nearly blind,
And the choir rattling onward always left him far behind.

The chorus stormed and blustered, Brother Eyer sang too slow,
And then he used the tunes in vogue a hundred years ago;
At last the storm-cloud burst, and the church was told, in fine,
That the brother must stop singing, or the choir would resign.

Then the pastor called together in the lecture room one day
Seven influential members who subscribe more than they pay,
And having asked God's guidance in a printed prayer or two
They put their heads together to determine what to do.

They debated, thought, suggested, till at last "dear Brother York,"
Who last winter made a million on a sudden rise in pork,
Rose and moved that a committee wait at once on Brother Eyer,
And proceed to rake him lively "for disturbin' of the choir."

Said he: "In that 'ere organ I've invested quite a pile,
And we'll sell it if we cannot worship in the latest style;
Our Philadelphy tenor tells me 'tis the hardest thing
For to make God understand him when the brother tries to sing.

"We've got the biggest organ, the best dressed choir in town,
We pay the steepest sal'ry to our pastor, Brother Brown;
But if we must humour ignorance because it's blind and old—
If the choir's to be pestered, I will seek another fold."

Of course the motion carried, and one day a coach and four,
With the latest style of driver, rattled up to Eyer's door;
And the sleek, well-dressed committee, Brothers Sharkey, York, and
Lamb,
As they crossed the humble portal took good care to miss the jamb.

They found the choir's great trouble sitting in his old arm chair,
And the summer's golden sunbeams lay upon his thin white hair,
He was singing "Rock of Ages" in a voice both cracked and low,
But the angels understood him, 'twas all he cared to know.

Said York: "We're here, dear brother, with the vestry's approbation
To discuss a little matter that affects the congregation;"
"And the choir too!" said Sharkey, giving Brother York a nudge,
"And the choir too!" he echoed with the graveness of a judge

"It was the understanding when we bargained for the chorus
That it was to relieve us, that is, do the singing for us;
If we rupture the agreement, it is very plain, dear brother,
It will leave our congregation and be gobbled by another.

"We don't want any singing except what we've bought!
The latest tunes are all the rage—the old ones stand for naught:
And so we have decided—are you listening Brother Eyer?—
That you'll have to stop your singin' for it flurrytates the choir."

The old man slowly raised his head, a sign that he did hear,
And on his cheek the trio caught the glitter of a tear;
His feeble hands pushed back the locks white as the silky snow,
As he answered the committee in a voice both sweet and low;

"I've sung the Psalms of David for nearly eighty years,
They've been my staff and comfort and calmed life's many fears!
I'm sorry I disturb the choir, perhaps I'm doing wrong;
But when my heart is filled with praise, I can't keep back a song.

I wonder if beyond the tide that's breaking at my feet,
In the far-off heavenly temple, where the Master I shall greet—
Yes, I wonder when I try to sing the songs of God up higher
If the angel band will church me for disturbing heaven's choir."

A silence filled the little room; the old man bowed his head:
The carriage rattled on again, but Brother Eyer was dead!
Yes, dead! his hand had raised the veil the future hangs before us,
And the Master dear had called him to the everlasting chorus.

The choir missed him for awhile, but he was soon forgot,
A few church-goers watched the door; the old man entered not.
Far away, his voice no longer cracked, he sings his heart's desires,
Where there are no church committees and no fashionable choirs!

Poems about Praise and Fame.

THE VOICE OF PRAISE.

Mary Russel Mitford.

THERE is a voice of magic power
  To charm the old, delight the young—
In lordly hall, in rustic bower,
  In every clime, in every tongue,
  Howe'er its sweet vibration rung,
In whispers low, in poet's lays,
  There lives not one who has not hung
Enraptured on the voice of praise.

The timid child, at that soft voice,
  Lifts, for a moment's space, the eye:
It bids the fluttering heart rejoice,
  And stays the step prepared to fly;
  'Tis pleasure breathes that short, quick sigh,
And flushes o'er that rosy face;
  While shame and infant modesty,
Shrink back with hesitating grace.

The lovely maiden's dimpled cheek
  At that sweet voice still deeper glows,
Her quivering lips in vain would seek
  To hide the bliss her eyes disclose!
  The charm her sweet confusion shows,
Oft springs from some low broken word;
  Oh! praise to her how sweetly flows,
Their accents from the loved one heard.

The hero, when a people's voice
  Proclaims their darling victor near,
Feels he not then his soul rejoice,
  Their shouts of love, of praise to hear?
  Yes! fame to generous minds is dear;—
It pierces to their inmost core:
  He weeps, who never shed a tear;
He trembles, who never shook before.

The poet, too—ah! well I deem
  Small is the need the tale to tell—
Who knows not that his thoughts, his dream,
  On thee at noon, at midnight dwell?
Who knows not that thy magic spell
Can charm his every care away?
  In memory cheer his gloomy cell;
In hope can lend a deathless ray?

'Tis sweet to watch affection's eye:
  To mark the tear with love replete;
To feel the softly-breathing sigh
  When friendship's lips the tones repeat.
  But, oh! a thousand times more sweet,
The praise of those we love to hear!
  Like balmy showers in summer heat,
It falls upon the greedy ear.

The lover lulls his rankling wound
  By dwelling on his fair one's name;
The mother listens for the sound
  Of her young warrior's growing fame.
  Thy voice can soothe the mourning dame,
Of her soul's wedded partner riven,
  Who cherishes the hallowed flame,
Parted on earth to meet in heaven!

That voice can quiet passion's mood,
  Can humble merit raise on high;
And from the wise and from the good
  It breathes of immortality!
  There is a lip, there is an eye,
Where most I love to see it shine,
  To hear it speak, to feel it sigh—
My mother! need I say, 'tis thine!

PRAISE.

Young.

THE love of praise, howe'er concealed by art,
Reigns, more or less, and glows in every heart:
The proud, to gain it, toils on toils endure;
The modest shun it but to make it sure.
O'er globes, and sceptres, now on thrones it swells;
Now, trims the midnight lamp in college cells.
'Tis tory, whig; it plots, prays, preaches, pleads,
Harangues in senates, squeaks in masquerades.
Here to Steel's humour makes a bold pretence;
There, bolder, aims at Pultney's eloquence.
It aids the dancer's heel, the writer's head,
And heaps the plain with mountains of the dead
Nor ends with life; but nods in sable plumes,
Adorns our hearse, and flatters on our tombs.

FAME.

Johanna Baillie.

OH, who shall lightly say that Fame
Is nothing but an empty name!
Whilst in that sound there is a charm
The nerves to brace, the heart to warm,
As, thinking of the mighty dead,
The young from slothful couch will start,
And vow, with lifted hands outspread,
Like them to act a noble part?

Oh, who shall lightly say that Fame
Is nothing but an empty name!
When, but for those, our mighty dead,
All ages past a blank would be,
Sunk in oblivion's murky bed,
A desert bare, a shipless sea?
They are the distant objects seen,—
The lofty marks of what have been.

Oh, who shall lightly say that Fame
Is nothing but an empty name!
When memory of the mighty dead
To earth-worn pilgrim's wistful eye
The brightest rays of cheering shed,
That point to immortality?

Poems about War.

THE SONG OF THE SWORD.

WEARY and wounded and worn, wounded and ready to die,
A soldier they left, all alone and forlorn, on the field of battle to lie.
The dead and the dying alone could their presence and pity afford,
Whilst, with a sad and terrible tone, he sang . . . . the song of the Sword.

"Fight—fight—fight! though a thousand fathers die;
Fight—fight—fight! though a thousand children cry!
Fight—fight—fight! while mothers and wives lament;
And fight—fight—fight! while millions of money are spent.
Fight—fight—fight! should the cause be foul or fair,
Though all that's gained is an empty name, and a tax too great to bear;
An empty name, and a paltry fame, and thousands lying dead;
Whilst every glorious victory must raise the price of bread.
War—war—war! fire, and famine, and sword;
Desolate fields and desolate towns, and thousands scattered abroad,
With never a home and never a shed, whilst kingdoms perish and fall;
And hundreds of thousands are lying dead, ... and all for nothing at all!
War—war—war! musket, and powder, and ball—
Ah! what do we fight so for? ah! why have we battles at all?
'Tis Justice must be done, they say, the nation's honor to keep!
Alas! that Justice should be so dear, and human life so cheap!
War—war—war! misery, murder, and crime
Are all the blessings I've seen in thee, from my youth to the present time.
Misery, murder and crime—crime, misery, murder and woe;
Ah! would I had known in my younger days half the horrors which now I know!"
Weary and wounded and worn, wounded and ready to die,
A soldier they left, all alone and forlorn, on the field of battle to lie.
The dead and the dying alone could their presence and pity afford,
And the sad and terrible cry was still the horrible Song of the Sword.

THE MISERIES OF WAR.

Scott.

I HATE that drum's discordant sound,
Parading round, and round, and round;
To thoughtless youth it pleasure yields,
And lures from cities and from fields:
To me it talks of ravaged plains,
And burning towns, and ruin'd swains,
And mangled limbs, and dying groans,
And widows' tears, and orphans' moans,
And all that misery's hand bestows,
To fill the catalogue of human woes.

THE SINFULNESS OF WAR.

Lowell.

Ez fer war, I call it murder—
  There you hev it plain an' flat;
I don't want to go no furder
  Than my Testyment fer that;
God hez sed so plump an' fairly,
  It's ez long ez it is broad,
An' you've gut to git up airly
  Ef you want to take in God.

'Taint your eppyletts an' feathers
  Make the thing a grain more right;
'Taint a-follerin' your bell-wethers
  Will excuse ye in His sight.
Ef you take a sword an' dror it,
  An' go stick a feller thru,
Guv'ment aint to answer for it,
  God 'll send the bill to you.

KNOWLEDGE WILL ANNIHILATE WAR.

Longfellow.

WERE half the power that fills the world with terror,
  Were half the wealth bestowed on camps and courts,
Given to redeem the human mind from error,
  There were no need of arsenals nor forts:

The warrior's name would be a name abhorred;
  And every nation that should lift again
Its hand against a brother, on its forehead
  Would wear for evermore the curse of Cain!

Down the dark future, through long generations,
  The echoing sounds grow fainter and then cease;
And like a bell, with solemn, sweet vibrations,
  I hear once more the voice of Christ say, "Peace!"

ELIZA. *Darwin.*

Now stood Eliza on the wood-crowned height,
O'er Minden's plain, spectatress of the fight;
Sought with bold eye, amid the bloody strife,
Her dearer self, the partner of her life;
From hill to hill the rushing host pursued,
And viewed his banner, or believed she viewed.
Pleased with the distant roar, with quicker tread
Fast by his hand one lisping boy she led;
And one fair girl amid the loud alarm
Slept on her kerchief, cradled by her arm;
While round her brow bright beams of honour dart,
And love's warm eddies circle in her heart.
Near and more near the intrepid beauty pressed,
Saw through the driving smoke, his dancing crest;
Heard the exulting shout, "They run! they run!"
"O joy!" she cried, "he's safe! the battle's won!"
A ball now hisses through the airy tides,
Some Fury wings it, and some Demon guides,
Parts the fine locks, her graceful head that deck,
Wounds her fair ear, and sinks into her neck;
The red stream issuing from her azure veins,
Dyes her white veil, her ivory bosom stains.
"Ah me!" she cried, and sinking on the ground,
Kissed her dear babes, regardless of the wound;
"Oh, cease not yet to beat, thou vital urn!
Wait, gushing life, oh, wait my love's return!
Hoarse barks the wolf, the vulture screams from far!
The angel, Pity, shuns the walks of war!
O spare, ye war-hounds, spare their tender age!—
On me, on me," she cried, "exhaust your rage!"
Then with weak arms, her weeping babes caressed,
And, sighing, hid them on her blood-stained vest.
  From tent to tent the impatient Warrior flies,
Fear in his heart and frenzy in his eyes;
"Eliza!" loud along the camp he calls,
"Eliza!" echoes through the canvas walls;
Quick through the murmuring gloom his footsteps tread,
O'er groaning heaps, the dying and the dead;
Vault o'er the plain, and in the tangled wood,
Lo! dead Eliza weltering in her blood!
  Soon hears his listening son the welcome sounds,
With open arms and sparkling eyes he bounds:—
"Speak low," he cries, and gives his little hand,
"Mamma's asleep upon the dew-cold sand.
Alas! we both with cold and hunger quake—
Why do you weep!—Mamma will soon awake."
"She'll wake no more!" the hopeless mourner cried,
Upturned his eyes, and clasped his hands, and sighed:
Stretched on the ground a while entranced he lay,
And pressed warm kisses on the lifeless clay:
And then upsprung with wild convulsive start,
And all the father kindled in his heart.
"O, heaven!" he cried, "my first rash vow forgive!
These bind to earth, for these I pray to live!"
Round his chill babes he wrapped his crimson vest,
And clasped them, sobbing, to his aching breast.

THE BURIAL OF SIR JOHN MOORE.

Rev. Charles Wolfe.

NOT a drum was heard, not a funeral note,
  As his corse to the ramparts we hurried ;
Not a soldier discharged his farewell shot
  O'er the grave where our hero we buried.

We buried him darkly, at dead of night,
  The sod with our bayonets turning,
By the struggling moonbeam's misty light,
  And the lantern dimly burning.

No useless coffin enclosed his breast,
  Nor in sheet nor in shroud we bound him ;
But he lay like a warrior taking his rest,
  With his warrior cloak around him.

Few and short were the prayers we said,
  And we spoke not a word of sorrow ;
But we steadfastly gazed on the face of the dead,
  And we bitterly thought of the morrow.

We thought as we hollow'd his narrow bed,
  And smoothed down his lonely pillow,
That the foe and the stranger would tread o'er his head,
  And we far away on the billow.

Lightly they'll talk of the spirit that's gone,
  And o'er his cold ashes upbraid him ;
But nothing he'll reck if they let him sleep on,
  In the grave where a Briton has laid him.

But half of our heavy task was done,
  When the clock toll'd the hour for retiring,
And we heard by the distant and random gun
  That the foe were sullenly firing.

Slowly and sadly we laid him down,
  From the field of his fame fresh and gory ;
We carved not a line—we raised not a stone,
  But left him alone in his glory.

LIBERTY WITHOUT MURDER.

Mackay.

WE want no flag—no flaunting rag—
In Liberty's cause to fight;
We want no blaze of murderous guns
To struggle for the right;
Our spears and swords are printed words—
The mind's our battle-plain;
We've won our victories thus before,
And so we shall again.

We love no triumphs gained by force—
They stain the brightest cause:
'Tis not in blood that Liberty
Inscribes her sacred laws;
She writes them on the people's hearts,
In language clear and plain:
True thoughts have moved the world before,
And so they shall again.

We yield to none in earnest love
Of Freedom's cause sublime;
We join the cry—"Fraternity!"
We keep the march of Time.
And yet we grasp no spear nor sword
Our victories to obtain;
We've won without such help before,
And so we shall again.

We want no aid of barricade
To show a front to wrong;
We have a fortress in the Truth
More durable and strong.
Calm words, great thoughts, unflinching faith
Have never striven in vain;
They've won our victories many a time,
And so they shall again.

Peace, progress, knowledge, brotherhood,
The ignorant may sneer—
The bad deny; but we rely
To see their triumph near,
No widow's groans shall mar our cause,
No blood of brethren slain:
Kindness and Love have won before,
And so they shall again.

THE WARRIOR'S PRAYER.

THE morning broke—the glorious sun arose
Gilding all nature—even nature's foes,
Up starts the warrior full of health and life,
With heart and arm all ready for the strife.
The muster-roll is called, and every name is there.
But hark! the signal!! 'tis the hour of prayer.
"Of Prayer! for what!! how can they hopes express
What are the deeds they ask their God to bless?"
I almost tremble when I humbly dare
Put in its true sense the Warrior's Prayer—
"Grant us, O Lord, that health and power to-day
That thousands of my creatures we may slay,
To drive our horse hoofs thine image o'er,
And stain our arms and hands in brethren's gore.
And if a glorious victory we gain
We'll shout hurrah! over the thousands slain,
And sing, 'Praise God' upon the battle plain."

BEAUTIFUL WAR.

J. R. Planche.

To her mother's heart she hath press'd him,
Her brave, her only boy!
She hath smil'd, and kiss'd, and bless'd him,
With a mother's pride and joy!

Hark! the lively bugle rings!
To the ranks the soldier springs!
Gaze on the line glittering far!
Beautiful war! Beautiful war!

Again they flock to greet them,
With shout and laurel bough!
But where is she should meet them
With tenfold transport now?

While others clasp a lover,
Father, husband, view
Her hands her pale face cover,
And the bitter drops start through!

Go, and boast of battles won!
Ye, who never lost a son!
Wildly her cry echoes afar,
Terrible war! Terrible war!

Poems about Slaves.

THE SLAVE'S DREAM.

Longfellow.

Beside the ungathered rice he lay,
His sickle in his hand
His breast was bare, his matted hair
Was buried in the sand.
Again, in the mist and shadow of sleep,
He saw his Native Land.

Wide through the landscape of his dreams
The lordly Niger flowed;
Beneath the palm-trees on the plain
Once more a king he strode:
And heard the tinkling caravans
Descend the mountain-road.

He saw once more his dark-eyed queen
Among her children stand:
They clasped his neck, they kissed his cheeks,
They held him by the hand!—
A tear burst from the sleeper's lids
And fell into the sand.

And then at furious speed he rode
Along the Niger's bank;
His bridle-reins were golden chains,
And, with a martial clank,
At each leap he could feel his scabbard of steel
Smiting his stallion's flank.

Before him, like a blood-red flag,
The bright flamingoes flew:
Form morn to night he followed their flight,
O'er plains where the tamarind grew,
Till he saw the roofs of Caffre huts,
And the ocean rose to view.

At night he heard the lion roar,
And the hyæna scream;
And the river-horse as he crushed the reeds
Beside some hidden stream;
And it passed, like a glorious roll of drums,
Through the triumph of his dream.

The forests, with their myriad tongues,
Shouted of liberty;
And the blast of the Desert cried aloud,
With a voice so wild and free,
That he started in his sleep and smiled
At their tempestuous glee.

He did not feel the driver's whip,
Nor the burning heat of day;
For death had illumined the Land of Sleep,
And his lifeless body lay
A worn-out fetter, that the soul
Had broken and thrown away!

THE AFRICAN CHIEF.

William Cullen Bryant.

Chained in the market-place he stood—
A man of giant frame.
Amid the gathering multitude,
That shrunk to hear his name;
All stern of look, and strong of limb,
His dark eye on the ground:—
And silently they gaze on him,
As on a lion bound.

Vainly, but well, that chief had fought—
He was a captive now;
Yet pride, that fortune humbles not,
Was written on his brow.
The scars his dark broad bosom wore,
Showed warrior true and brave;
A prince among his tribe before—
He could not be a slave!

Then to his conqueror he spake—
"My brother is a king:
Undo this necklace from my neck,
And take this bracelet ring,
And send me where my brother reigns,
And I will fill thy hands
With store of ivory from the plains,
And gold-dust from the sands."

"Not for thy ivory nor thy gold,
Will I unbind thy chain;
That fettered hand shall never hold
The battle-spear again.
A price thy nation never gave
Shall yet be paid for thee;
For thou shalt be the Christian's slave,
In lands beyond the sea."

Then wept the warrior-chief, and bade
To shred his locks away
And, one by one, each heavy braid
Before the victor lay.
Thick were the plaited locks, and long;
And deftly hidden there,
Shone many a wedge of gold, among
The dark and crispèd hair.
"Look, feast thy greedy eyes with gold,
Long kept for sorest need;
Take it—thou askest sums untold,—
And say that I am freed.
Take it!—my wife, the long, long day
Weeps by the cocoa-tree,
And my young children leave their play,
And ask in vain for me."
"I take thy gold—but I have made
Thy fetters fast and strong,
And ween that by the cocoa-shade
Thy wife will wait thee long."
Strong was the agony that shook
The captive's frame to hear,
And the proud meaning of his look
Was changed to mortal fear.
His heart was broken—crazed his brain;
At once his eye grew wild;
He struggled fiercely with his chain;
Whispered, and wept, and smiled:
Yet wore not long those fatal bands;
For soon at close of day,
They drew him forth upon the sands,
The foul hyena's prey.

VIRGINIA—A Lay of Ancient Rome.

Macaulay.

[Virginius, a Plebeian of Rome, kills his daughter Virginia to save her from being enslaved and dishonored by Appius Claudius, one of the Patrician tyrants of Rome.]

OVER the Allan mountains, the light of morning broke;
From all the roofs of the Seven Hills curled the thin wreaths of smoke
The city gates were opened; the Forum, all alive
With buyers and with sellers, was humming like a hive:
Blithely on brass and timber the craftsman's stroke was ringing,
And blithely o'er her panniers the market-girl was singing:
And blithely young Virginia came smiling from her home—
Ah! woe for young Virginia, the sweetest maid in Rome,
With her small tablets in her hand, and her satchel on her arm,
Forth she went bounding to the school, nor dreamed of shame or harm.
She crossed the Forum shining with the stalls in alleys gay,
And just had reached the very spot whereon I stand this day,
When up the varlet Marcus came; not such as when, erewhile,
He crouched behind his patron's wheels, with the true client smile:
He came with lowering forehead, swollen features and clenched fist,
And strode across Virginia's path, and caught her by the wrist:
Hard strove the frighted maiden, and screamed with look aghast—
And at her scream from right and left the folk came running fast;
And the strong smith Muræna gave Marcus such a blow,
The caitiff reeled three paces back, and let the maiden go:
Yet glared he fiercely round him, and growled, in harsh, fell tone,
"She's mine, and I will have her: I seek but for mine own.
She is my slave, born in my house, and stolen away and sold,
The year of the sore sickness, ere she was twelve hours old.
I wait on Appius Claudius; I waited on his sire:
Let him who works the client wrong, beware the patron's ire!"
—But ere the varlet Marcus again might seize the maid,
Who clung tight to Muræna's skirt, and sobbed, and shrieked for aid,
Forth through the throng of gazers the young Icilius pressed,
And stamped his foot and rent his gown, and smote upon his breast,
And beckoned to the people, and, in bold voice and clear,
Poured thick and fast the burning words which tyrants quake to hear!
"Now, by your children's cradles, now, by your fathers' graves,
Be men to-day Quirites, or be for ever slaves;
Shall the vile fox-earth awe the race that stormed the lion's den?
Shall we, who could not brook one lord, crouch to the wicked Ten?
Exult, ye proud Patricians! the hard-fought fight is o'er:
We strove for honour—'twas in vain: for freedom—'tis no more.
Our very hearts, that were so high, sink down beneath your will:
Riches and lands, and power and state, ye have them—keep them still!
Heap heavier still the fetters: bar closer still the gate;
Patient as sheep we yield us up unto your cruel hate:—
But, by the shades beneath us, and by the God above,
Add not unto your cruel hate your yet more cruel love!
Have ye not graceful ladies, whose spotless lineage springs
From Consuls, and high Pontiffs, and ancient Alban Kings?
Ladies, who deign not on our paths to set their tender feet—
Who from their cars look down with scorn upon the wondering street—
Who, in Corinthian mirrors, their own proud smiles behold,
And breathe of Capuan odours, and shine with Spanish gold?

Then leave the poor Plebeian his single tie to life—
The sweet, sweet love of daughter, of sister, and of wife!—
Spare us the inexpiable wrong, the unutterable shame,
That turns the coward's heart to steel, the sluggard's blood to flame;
Lest when our latest hope is fled, ye taste of our despair,
And learn, by proof, in some wild hour, how much the wretched dare!"

[Act of the Heart-broken Father—]

Straightway Virginius led the maid a little space aside,
To where the reeking shambles stood, piled up with horn and hide;
Hard by, a flesher on a block had laid his whittle down—
Virginius caught the whittle up, and hid it in his gown;
And then his eyes grew very dim, and his throat began to swell,
And in a hoarse, changed voice he spake, "Farewell, sweet child, farewell!
Oh! how I loved my darling! Though stern I sometimes be,
To thee, thou know'st, I was not so. Who could be so to thee?
And how my darling loved me! How glad she was to hear
My footstep on the threshold when I came back last year!
And how she danced with pleasure to see my civic crown,
And took my sword, and hung it up, and brought me forth my gown!
Now, all those things are over—yes, all thy pretty ways—
Thy needlework, thy prattle, thy snatches of old lays;
And none will grieve when I go forth, or smile when I return,
Or watch beside the old man's bed or weep upon his urn.
—The time is come! See, how he points his eager hand this way!
See, how his eyes gloat on thy grief, like a kite's upon the prey.
With all his wit he little deems, that, spurned, betrayed, bereft,
Thy father hath, in his despair, one fearful refuge left.
He little deems, that, in this hand, I clutch what still can save
Thy gentle youth from taunts and blows, the portion of the slave;
Yea, from nameless evil, that passeth taunt and blow—
Foul outrage, which thou knowest not, which thou shalt never know!
Then clasp me round the neck once more, and give me one more kiss;
And now, my own dear little girl, there is no way—but this!"
—With that he lifted high the steel, and smote her in the side,
And in her blood she sank to earth, and with one sob she died!
When Appius Claudius saw that deed, he shuddered and sank down,
And hid his face, some little space, with the corner of his gown,
Till, with white lips, and blood shot eyes, Virginius tottered nigh,
And stood before the judgment-seat, and held the knife on high:
"Oh! dwellers in the nether gloom, avengers of the slain,
By this dear blood I cry to you, do right between us twain;
And even as Appius Claudius hath dealt by me and mine,
Deal you by Appius Claudius, and all the Claudian line!"
He writhed, and groaned a fearful groan, and then with steadfast feet
Strode right across the Market-place into the Sacred Street.
Then up sprang Appius Claudius: "Stop him; alive or dead!
Ten thousand pounds of copper to the man who brings his head!"
He looked upon his clients—but none would work his will;
He looked upon his lictors—but they trembled and stood still;
And, as Virginius through the press his way in silence cleft,
Ever the mighty multitude fell back to right and left:
And he hath passed in safety unto his woeful home,
And there ta'en horse to tell the Camp what deeds are done in Rome!

Poems of Freedom.

Whittier.

OUR fellow-countrymen in chains!
  Slaves—in a land of light and law!
Slaves—crouching on the very plains
  Where rolled the storm of Freedom's war
A groan from Eutaw's haunted wood,—
  A wail where Camden's martyrs fell,—
By every shrine of patriot blood,
  From Moultrie's wall and Jasper's well!

By storied hill and hallowed grot,
  By mossy wood and marshy glen,
Whence rang of old the rifle shot,
  And hurrying shout of Marion's men
The groan of breaking hearts is there,—
  The falling lash,—the fetter's clank!
Slaves,—SLAVES are breathing in that air,
  Which old De Kalb and Sumter drank!

What, ho!—*our* countrymen in chains!
  The whip on WOMAN'S shrinking flesh!
Our soil yet reddening with the stains
  Caught from her scourging, warm and fresh!
What! mothers from their children riven?
  What! God's own image bought and sold!
AMERICANS to market driven,
  And bartered as the brute for gold!

Speak! shall their agony of prayer
  Come thrilling to our hearts in vain?
To us whose fathers scorned to bear
  The paltry *menace* of a chain:
To us, whose boast is loud and long
  Of holy Liberty and Light,—
Say, shall those writhing slaves of Wrong
  Plead vainly for their plundered Right?

What! shall we send, with lavish breath,
  Our sympathies across the wave,
Where Manhood, on the field of death,
  Strikes for his freedom or a grave?
Shall prayers go up, and hymns be sung
  For Greece, the Moslem fetter spurning,
And millions hail with pen and tongue
  Our light on all her altars burning?

Shall Belgium feel, and gallant France,
  By Vendome's pile and Schoenbrun's wall,
And Poland, gasping on her lance,
  The impulse of our cheering call!
And shall the SLAVE, beneath our eye,
  Clank o'er *our* fields, his hateful chain!
And toss his fettered arms on high,
  And groan for Freedom's gift, in vain?

O, say, shall Prussia's banner be
  A refuge for the stricken slave?
And shall the Russian serf go free
  By Baikal's lake and Neva's wave?
And shall the wintry-bosomed Dane
  Relax the iron hand of pride,
And bid his bondmen cast the chain,
  From fettered soul and limb, aside?

Shall every flap of England's flag
  Proclaim that all around are free,
From "farthest Ind" to each blue crag
  That beetles o'er the Western Sea?
And shall we scoff at Europe's kings,
  When Freedom's fire is dim with us,
And round our country's altar clings
  The damning shade of Slavery's curse?

Go—let us ask of Constantine
  To loose his grasp on Poland's throat;
And beg the lord of Mahmoud's line
  To spare the struggling Suliote,—
Will not the scorching answer come
  From turbaned Turk, and scornful Russ:
"Go, loose your fettered slaves at home,
  Then turn, and ask the like of us!

Just God! and shall we calmly rest,
  The Christian's scorn,—the heathen's mirth,—
Content to live the lingering jest
  And by-word of a mocking Earth?
Shall our own glorious land retain
  That curse which Europe scorns to bear?
Shall our own brethren drag the chain
  Which not even Russia's menials wear?

Up, then, in Freedom's manly part,
  From graybeard old to fiery youth,
And on the nation's naked heart
  Scatter the living coals of Truth!
Up,—while ye slumber, deeper yet
  The shadow of our fame is growing!
Up,—while ye pause our sun may set
  In blood, around our altars flowing!

Oh! rouse ye, ere the storm comes forth,—
  The gathered wrath of God and man,—
Like that which wasted Egypt's earth,
  When hail and fire above it ran.
Hear ye no warnings in the air?
  Feel ye no earthquake underneath?
Up,—up! why will ye slumber where
  The sleeper only wakes in death?

Up *now* for Freedom!—not in strife
  Like that your sterner fathers saw,—
The awful waste of human life,—
  The glory and the guilt of war:
But break the chain,—the yoke remove
  And smite to earth Oppression's rod,
With those mild arms of Truth and Love,
  Made mighty through the living God!

Down let the shrine of Moloch sink,
  And leave no traces where it stood;
No longer let its idol drink
  His daily cup of human blood;
But rear another altar there,
  To Truth and Love and Mercy given,
And Freedom's gift, and Freedom's prayer
  Shall call an answer down from Heaven!

Poems about Steam.

THE SONG OF STEAM.

HARNESS me down with your iron bands;
  Be sure of your curb and rein,
For I scorn the power of your puny hands
  As the tempest scorns a chain.
How I laughed, as I lay concealed from sight
  For many a countless hour,
At the childish boast of human might,
  And the pride of human power

When I saw an army upon the land
  A navy upon the seas,
Creeping along, a snail-like band,
  Or waiting the wayward breeze;
When I mark'd the peasant faintly reel
  With the toil which he daily bore,
As he feebly turn'd at the tardy wheel,
  Or tugged at the weary oar.

When I measured the panting courser's speed,
  The flight of the carrier dove,
As they bore the law a king decreed,
  Or the lines of impatient love;
I could not but think how the world would feel,
  As these were outstripp'd afar,
When I should be bound to the rushing keel,
  Or chained to the flying car.

Ha! ha! ha! they found me at last;
  They invited me forth at length,
And I rush'd to my throne with thunder blast,
  And laugh'd in my iron strength.
Oh! then ye saw a wondrous change
  On the earth and ocean wide,
Where now my fiery armies range,
  Nor wait for wind or tide.

Hurrah! hurrah! the waters o'er
  The mountain's steep decline;
Time—space—have yielded to my power—
  The world! the world is mine!
The rivers the sun hath earliest blest,
  Or those where his beams decline,
The giant streams of the queenly West,
  Or the orient floods divine.

The ocean pales where'er I sweep,
  To hear my strength rejoice,
And the monsters of the briny deep
  Cower, trembling, at my voice.
I carry the wealth and the lord of earth,
  The thoughts of the god-like mind;
The wind lags after my flying forth,
  The lightning is left behind.

In the darksome depths of the fathomless mine
  My tireless arm doth play,
Where the rocks never saw the sun decline,
  Or the dawn of the glorious day.
I bring earth's glittering jewels up
  From the hidden cave below,
And I make the fountain's granite cup
  With a crystal gush overflow.

I blow the bellows, I forge the steel,
  In all the shops of trade;
I hammer the ore, and turn the wheel,
  Where my arms of strength are made;
I manage the furnace, the mill, the mint;
  I carry, I spin, I weave:
And all my doings I put into print
  On every Saturday eve.

I've no muscle to weary, no breast to decay,
  No bones to be "laid on the shelf,"
And soon I intend you may "go and play,"
  While I manage the world by myself.
But harness me down with your iron bands,
  Be sure of your curb and rein,
For I scorn the strength of your puny hands,
  As the tempest scorns a chain.

THE STEAMBOAT.

SEE how yon flaming herald treads
The ridged and rolling waves,
As, crashing o'er their crested heads,
She bows her surly slaves!
With foam before and fire behind,
She rends the clinging sea,
That flies before the roaring wind,
Beneath her hissing lee.

The morning spray, like sea-born flowers,
With heap'd and glistening bells,
Falls round her fast, in ringing showers,
With every wave that swells;
And, burning o'er the midnight deep,
In lurid fringes thrown,
The living gems of ocean sweep
Along her flashing zone.

With clashing wheel, and lifting keel,
And smoking torch on high,
When winds are loud, and billows reel,
She thunders foaming by;
When seas are silent and serene,
With even beam she glides,
The sunshine glimmering through the green
That skirts her gleaming sides.

Now, like a wild nymph, far apart,
She veils her shadowy form,
The beating of her restless heart
Still sounding through the storm;
Now answers, like a courtly dame,
The reddening surges o'er,
With flying scarf of spangled flame,
The Pharos of the shore.

THE RAILROAD.

THROUGH the mould and through the clay,
Through the corn and through the hay,
By the margin of the lake,
O'er the river, through the brake,
On we hie with screech and roar!
Splashing! flashing!
Crashing, dashing!

Over ridges,
Gullies, bridges!
By the bubbling rill,
And mill—
Highways,
Byeways,
Hollow hill—
Jumping—bumping—
Like forty thousand giants snoring!

O'er the aqueduct and bog,
On we fly with ceaseless jog,
Every instant something new;
Every moment lost to view,
Now a tavern—now a steeple—
Now a crowd of gaping people—
Now a hollow—now a ridge—
Now a crossway—now a bridge—

Grumble—stumble—
Rumble—tumble—
Fretting—getting in a stew!
Church and steeple, gaping people,
Quick as thought are lost to view!
Everything that eye can survey
Turns hurly-burly, topsy-turvy!

Glimpse of lonely hut and mansion,
Glimpse of ocean's wide expansion,
Glimpse of foundry and of forge,
Glimpse of plain and mountain gorge,
Dash along!
Slash along!
Flash along!
On! on with a jump,
And a bump,
And a roll!
Hies the fire-fiend to its destined goal!

ASLEEP AT THE SWITCH.

As recited by Harry Bruno in his famous Railroad Speciality.

The first thing that I remember was Carlo tugging away,
With the sleeves of my coat fast in his teeth, pulling as much as to say:
"Come, master, awake, and tend to the switch, lives now depend upon you,
Think of the souls in the coming train and the graves you're sending them to;
Think of the mother and babe at her breast, think of the father and son,
Think of the lover, and loved one, too, think of them doomed every one
To fall, as it were, by your very hand, into yon fathomless ditch,
Murdered by one who should guard them from harm, who now lies asleep at the switch."

I sprang up amazed, scarce knew where I stood, sleep had o'er-mastered me so;
I could hear the wind hollowly howling and the deep river dashing below,
I could hear the forest leaves rustling as the trees by the tempest were fanned,
But what was that noise at a distance? That—I could not understand!
I heard it at first indistinctly, like the rolling of some muffled drum,
Then nearer and nearer it came to me, and made my very ears hum;
What is this light that surrounds me and seems to set fire to my brain?
What whistle's that yelling so shrilly! Oh, God! I know now—it's the train.

We often stand facing some danger, and seem to take root to the place;
So I stood with this demon before me, its heated breath scorching my face,
Its headlight made day of the darkness, and glared like the eyes of some witch;
The train was almost upon me, before I remembered the switch.
I sprang to it, seized it wildly, the train dashing fast down the track,
The switch resisted my efforts, some devil seemed holding it back;
On, on, came the fiery-eyed monster and shot by my face like a flash;
I swooned to the earth the next moment, and knew nothing after the crash.

How long I laid there unconscious 'twere impossible for me to tell,
My stupor was almost a heaven, my waking almost a hell—
For I then heard the piteous moaning and shrieking of husbands and wives,
And I thought of the day we all shrink from, when I must account for their lives;
Mothers rushed like maniacs, their eyes staring madly and wild;
Fathers, losing their courage, gave way to their grief like a child;
Children searching for parents, I noticed as by me they sped,
And lips that could form naught but "Mamma," were calling for one perhaps dead.

My mind was made up in a second, the river should hide me away;
When, under the still burning rafters, I suddenly noticed there lay
A little white hand, she who owned it was doubtless an object of love;
To one whom her loss would drive frantic, tho' she guarded him now from above;
I tenderly lifted the rafters and quietly laid them one side;
How little she thought of her journey, when she left for this last fatal ride;
I lifted the last log from off her, and while searching for some spark of life,
Turned her little face up in the starlight, and recognised—Maggie, my wife!

Oh, Lord! Thy scourge is a hard one, at a blow Thou hast shattered my pride:
My life will be one endless night-time, with Maggie away from my side;
How often we've sat down and pictured the scenes in our long happy life;
How I'd strive through all of my life-time to build up a home for my wife.
How people would envy us always in our cosy and neat little nest.
When I would do all the labor, and Maggie should all the day rest;
How one of God's blessings might cheer us, when some day I p'r'aps should be rich,
But all my dreams have been shattered, while I lay there asleep at the switch.

I fancied I stood on my trial, the jury and judge I could see,
And every eye in the court room was steadfastly fixed upon me,
And fingers were pointing in scorn, till I felt my face blushing red,
And the next thing I heard were the words, "Hung by the neck until dead."
Then I felt myself pulled once again, and my hand caught tight hold of a dress,
And I heard, "What's the matter, dear Jim? You've had a bad nightmare, I guess,"
And there stood Maggie, my wife, with never a scar from the ditch,
I'd been taking a nap in my bed and had not been asleep at the switch.

THE DEATH-BRIDGE OF THE TAY.

Will Carleton.

THE night and the storm fell together upon the old town of Dundee;
And, trembling, the mighty Firth river held out its cold hand towards the sea.
Like the dull-booming bolts of a cannon, the wind swept the streets and the shores;
It wrenched at the roofs and the chimneys, it crashed 'gainst the windows and
doors.

Like a mob that is drunken and frenzied, it surged through the streets up and down
And screamed the sharp, shrill cry of "murder!" o'er river, and hill-top, and town
It leaned its great breast 'gainst the belfries; it perched upon minaret and dome;
Then sprang on the shivering Firth river, and tortured its waves into foam.

Look! the moon has come out, clad in splendour, the turbulent scene to behold;
She smiles at the night's devastation—she dresses the storm-king in gold.
Away to the north, ragged mountains climb high through the shuddering air;
They bend their dark brows o'er the valley, to read what new ruin is there.

Along the shore-line creeps the city, in crouching and sinuous shape,
With fire-sides so soon to be darkened, and doors to be shaded with crape!
To the south, like a spider-web waving, there curves, for a two-mile away,
This world's latest man-devised wonder--the far-famous bridge of the Tay.

It stretches and gleams into distance; it creeps the broad stream o'er and o'er,
Till it rests its strong, delicate fingers in the palm of the opposite shore.
But look! through the mists of the southward, there flash to the eye, clear an
plain—
Like a meteor that's bound to destruction—the lights of a swift-coming train.

'Mid the lights that so gaily are gleaming yon city of Dundee within,
Is one that is waiting a wanderer, who long o'er the ocean has been.
His age-burdened parents are watching from the window that looks on the Firth,
For the train that will come with their darling—their truest-loved treasure on
earth.

"He'll be coming' the nicht," says the father, "for sure the handwritin's his ain;
'The letter says, 'Ha' the lamp lichted—I'll come on the seven o'clock train.
For years in the mines I've been toiling, in this wonderfu' West o'er the sea;
My work has brought back kingly wages—there's plenty for you an' for me.
So sit ye an' wait for my coming (ye will na' watch for me in vain),
An' see me glide over the river, along o' the roar o' the train.'"

So they sit at the southernmost window, the parents with hand clasped in hand,
And gaze o'er the tempest-vexed waters, across to the storm-shaken land.
They see the bold acrobat-monster creep out on the treacherous line;
Its cinder-breath glitters like star-dust—its lamp-eyes they glimmer and shine.

It braces itself 'gainst the tempest; it fights for each inch with the foe;
With torrents of air all around it—with torrents of water below.
But look! look! the monster is stumbling, while trembles the fragile bridge-wall;
They struggle like athletes entwining—then both like a thunder-bolt fall!

Down, down, through the dark the train plunges, with speed unaccustomed and dire;
It glows with its last dying beauty—it gleams like a hailstorm of fire!
No wonder the mother faints dead-like, and clings like a clod to the floor;
No wonder the man flies in frenzy, and dashes his way through the door!

He fights his way out through the tempest; he is beaten, and baffled, and tossed;
He cries, "*The train's gang off the Tay Brig! Lend help here to look for the lost!*"
Oh, little to him do they listen, the crowds to the river that flee;
The news, like the shock of an earthquake, has thrilled through the town of Dundee.

Out, out creep two brave sturdy fellows, o'er danger-strewn buttress and piers;
They can climb 'gainst that blast, for they carry the blood of old Scotch mountaineers;
But they leave it along as they clamber, they mark all their hand-path with red;
Till they come where the torrent leaps bridgeless—a grave dancing over its dead.

A moment they gaze down in horror; then creep from the death-laden tide,
With the news, "There's nae help for our loved ones, save God's mercy for them who have died!"

The morning broke bright with the sunshine, and the Firth threw its gold glances back,
While yet on the heart of the people death's cloud rested heavy and black;

And the couple who waited last evening their man-statured son to accost,
Now laid their heads down on the table, and mourned for the boy that was lost.
"'Twas sae sad," moaned the crushed, aged mother, each word dripping o'er with a tear,
"Sae far he should come for to find us, and then he should perish sae near!

"O Robin, my bairn! ye did wander far from us for mony a day,
And when ye ha' come back sae near us, why could na' ye come a' the way?"
"I hae come all the way!" said a strong voice, and a bearded and sun-beaten face
Smiled on them the first joyous pressure of one long and filial embrace.

"I cam' on last night far as Newport; but Maggie, my bride that's to be,
She ran through the storm to the station, to get the first greetin' o' me.
I leaped from the carriage to kiss her; she held me sae fast and sae ticht,
The train it ran off and did leave me; I could na' get over the nicht.

"I tried for to walk the brig over—my head it was a' in a whirl—
I could na'—ye knew the sad reason—I had to go back to my girl!
I hope ye'll tak' kindly to Maggie—she's promised to soon be my wife;
She's a darling wee bit of a lassie—and her fondness it saved me my life!"

Poems about the Sea.

THE OCEAN. *Byron.*

ROLL on, thou deep and dark blue ocean—roll!
Ten thousand fleets sweep over thee in vain;
Man marks the earth with ruin—his control
Stops with the shore;—upon the watery plain
The wrecks are all thy deed, nor doth remain
A shadow of man's ravage, save his own
When for a moment, like a drop of rain,
He sinks into thy depths with bubbling groan,
Without a grave, unknell'd, uncoffin'd, and unknown.
His steps are not upon thy paths,—thy fields
Are not a spoil for him,—thou dost arise
And shake him from thee; the vile strength he wields
For earth's destruction thou dost all despise,
Spurning him from thy bosom to the skies,
And send'st him, shivering, in thy playful spray,
And howling to the gods, where haply lies
His petty hope in some near port or bay,
And dashes him again to earth:—there let him lay.
The armaments which thunder-strike the walls
Of rock-built cities, bidding nations quake,
And monarchs tremble in their capitals,—
The oak leviathans, whose huge ribs make
Their clay creator the vain title take
Of lord of thee, and arbiter of war;
These are thy toys, and as the snowy flake,
They melt into thy yeast of waves, which mar
Alike the Armada's pride, or spoils of Trafalgar.
Thy shores are empires, changed in all save thee—
Assyria, Greece, Rome, Carthage, what are they?
Thy waters wasted them while they were free,
And many a tyrant since; their shores obey
The stranger, slave, or savage: their decay
Has dried up realms to deserts:—not so thou,
Unchangeable save to thy wild waves' play—
Time writes no wrinkle on thy azure brow—
Such as creation's dawn beheld, thou rollest now.
Thou glorious mirror, where the Almighty's form
Glasses itself in tempest; in all time,
Calm or convuls'd—in breeze, or gale, or storm,
Icing the pole, or in the torrid clime
Dark heaving; boundless, endless, and sublime—
The image of Eternity—the throne
Of the Invisible; even from out the slime
The monsters of the deep are made; each zone
Obeys thee; thou goest forth, dread, fathomless, alone.
And I have loved thee, Ocean; and my joy
Of youthful sport was on thy breast to be
Borne, like thy bubbles, onward: from a boy
I wanton'd with thy breakers—they to me
Were a delight; and if the freshening sea
Made them a terror—'twas a pleasing fear.
For I was as it were a child of thee,
And trusted to thy billows far and near,
And laid my hand upon thy mane—as I do here.

THE SHIPWRECK.

Byron.

THERE were two fathers in this ghastly crew,
  And with them their two sons, of whom the one
Was more robust and hardy to the view
  But he died early: and when he was gone,
His nearest messmate told his sire, who threw
  One glance on him, and said, "Heaven's will be done!
I can do nothing;" and he saw him thrown
Into the deep, without a fear or groan.

The other father had a weaklier child,
  Of a soft cheek, and aspect delicate;
But the boy bore up long, and with a mild
  And patient spirit held aloof his fate:
Little he said, and now and then he smiled,
  As if to win a part from off the weight
He saw increasing on his father's heart,
With the deep, deadly thought, that they must part.

And o'er him bent his sire, and never raised
  His eyes from off his face, but wiped the foam
From his pale lips, and ever on him gazed:
  And when the wished-for shower at length was come,
And the boy's eyes, with the dull film half glazed,
  Brightened, and for a moment seemed to roam,
He squeezed from out a rag some drops of rain
Into his dying child's mouth;—but in vain!

The boy expired. The father held the clay,
  And looked upon it long; and when at last
Death left no doubt, and the dead burden lay
  Stiff on his heart, and pulse and hope were past,
He watched it wistfully until away
  'Twas borne by the rude wave wherein 'twas cast;
Then he himself sank down all dumb and shivering,
And gave no sign of life, save his limbs quivering.

* * * * *

Then rose from sea to sky the wild farewell—
  Then shrieked the timid, and stood still the brave—
Then some leaped overboard with dreadful yell,
  As eager to anticipate their grave;
And the sea yawned around her, like a hell,
  And down she sucked with her the whirling wave,
Like one who grapples with his enemy,
And strives to strangle him before he die.

And first one universal shriek there rushed,
  Louder than the loud ocean—like a crash
Of echoing thunder; and then all was hushed,
  Save the wild wind and the remorseless dash
Of billows; but at intervals there gushed,
  Accompanied by a convulsive splash,
A solitary shriek, the bubbling cry
Of some strong swimmer in his agony.

THE SHIP ON FIRE.

THE storm o'er the ocean flew furious and fast,
And the waves rose in foam at the voice of the blast,
And heavily laboured the gale-beaten ship
Like a stout-hearted swimmer, the spray at his lip.
And dark was the sky o'er the mariner's path,
Except where the lightning illum'd it in wrath.

A young mother knelt in the cabin below,
And pressing her babe to her bosom of snow.
She pray'd to her God, 'mid the hurricane wild,
"Oh, Father, have mercy; look down on my child!"

It passed; the fierce whirlwind careered on its way
And the ship like an arrow divided the spray;
The sails glimmered white in the beams of the moon;
And the breeze up aloft seemed to whistle a tune.
There was joy in the ship as she furrowed the foam,
For fond hearts within her were dreaming of home.
The fond mother pressed the fond babe to her breast,
And sang a sweet song as she rocked it to rest;
And the husband sat cheerily down by his side,
And look'd with delight on the face of his bride.

"Oh, happy," said she, "when our roaming is o'er,
We'll dwell in our cottage that stands by the shore;
Already, in fancy, its roof I descry,
And the smoke of its hearth curling up to the sky;
It's garden so green, and its vine-cover'd wall,
And kind friends awaiting to welcome us all;
And the children that sport by the old oaken tree."
Ah! gently the ship glided over the sea.

Hark! What was that? Hark, hark to the shout—
"Fire, fire!" Then a tramp, then a rout,
And an uproar of voices arose in the air;
And the mother knelt down, and the half-utter'd prayer
That she offer'd to God in her agony wild
Was, "Father, have mercy, look down on my child!"
She flew to her husband, she clung to his side,
Oh, there was her refuge, whate'er might betide.

Fire, fire! It was raging above and below,
'Midst shrieks intermittent of wailing and woe;
And the cheeks of the sailors grew pale at the sight,
And their eyes glistened wild in the glare of the light;
'Twas vain o'er the ravage the waters to drip,
The pitiless flame was lord of the ship,
And the smoke in thick wreaths mounted higher and higher;
Oh, God! it is fearful to perish by fire!
Alone with destruction, alone on the sea,
Great Father of Mercy! our hope is in thee!

Sad at heart, and resign'd, yet undaunted and brave,
They lower'd the boat, a mere speck on the wave;
First entered the mother, enfolding her child,
It knew she caress'd it, look'd upwards and smil'd.

Cold, cold was the night as they drifted away,
And mistily dawned o'er the pathway the day:
And they prayed for the light, and at noontide about,
The sun o'er the waters shone joyously out.
"Ho, a sail—ho, a sail!" cried the man on the lee,
"Ho, a sail!" and they turned their glad eyes on the sea
"They see us, they see us! the signal is wav'd,
They bear down upon us! thank God we're all sav'd!"

A LEAP FOR LIFE.

Walter Colton.

OLD Ironsides at anchor lay,
In the harbour of Mahon;
A dead calm rested on the bay—
The waves to sleep had gone;
When little Hal, the captain's son,
A lad both brave and good,
In sport, up shroud and rigging ran,
And on the main truck stood!

A shudder shot through every vein;
All eyes were turned on high!
There stood the boy, with dizzy brain,
Between the sea and sky.
No hold had he above, below;
Alone he stood in air;
To that far height none dared to go—
No aid could reach him there.

We gazed, but not a man could speak!
With horror all aghast—
In groups, with pallid brow and cheek,
We watched the quivering mast.
The atmosphere grew thick and hot,
And of a lurid hue;
As riveted unto the spot,
Stood officers and crew.

The father came on deck. He gasped,
"O God! Thy will be done!"
Then suddenly a rifle grasped,
And aimed it at his son.
"Jump, far out, boy, into the wave!
Jump, or I fire," he said.
"That only chance your life can save;
Jump, jump, boy!" He obeyed.

He sunk—he rose—he lived—he moved,
And for the ship struck out.
On board we hailed the lad beloved
With many a manly shout.
The father drew, in silent joy,
Those wet arms round his neck,
And folded to his heart his boy—
Then fainted on the deck.

DRIFTED OUT TO SEA.

Two little ones, grown tired of play,
Roamed by the sea one Summer day,
Watching the great waves come and go,
Prattling, as children will, you know,
Of dolls and marbles, kites and strings—
Sometimes hinting at graver things.

At last they spied within their reach
An old boat cast upon the beach:
Helter skelter, with merry din,
Over its sides they clambered in—
Ben, with his tangled nut-brown hair,
Bess, with her sweet face flushed and fair

Rolling in from the briny deep,
Nearer, nearer, the great waves creep,
Higher, higher, upon the sands,
Reaching out with their giant hands,
Grasping the boat with a boisterous glee,
Tossing it up and out to sea.

The sun went down 'mid clouds of gold;
Night came, with footsteps damp and cold,
Day dawned; the hours crept slowly by.
And now across the sunny sky
A black cloud stretches far away.

A storm comes on with flash and roar,
While all the sky is clouded o'er;
The great waves rolling from the rest,
Bring night and darkness on their breast;
Still floats the boat through driving storm
Protected by God's powerful arm.

The home-bound vessel, *Seabird*, lies
In ready trim 'twixt sea and skies;
Her captain paces reckless now,
A troubled look upon his brow,
While all his nerves with terror thrill
At shadow of some coming ill.

The mate comes up to where he stands,
And grasps his arm with eager hands;
"A boat has just swept by," says he,
"Bearing two children out to sea,
'Tis dangerous now to put about,
Yet they cannot be saved without."

"Naught but their safety will suffice,
They must be saved," the captain cries,
"By every thought that's just and right,
By lips I hoped to kiss to-night,
I'll peril vessel, life and men,
And God will not forsake me then."

With anxious faces, one and all,
Each man responded to his call;
And when at last through driving storm,
They lifted up each little form,
The captain started with a groan;
"My God!" he cried, "they are my own!"

Poems about Water,

THE BROOK.

Wordsworth.

BROOK! whose society the poet seeks
Intent his wasted spirits to renew;
And whom the curious painter doth pursue
Through rocky passes, among flowery creeks,
And tracks thee dancing down thy waterbreaks;
If I some type of thee did wish to view,
Thee,—and not thyself, I would not do
Like Grecian artists, give thee human cheeks
Channels for tears; no Naiad shouldst thou be,
Have neither limbs, feet, feathers, joints, nor hairs;
seems the eternal soul is clothed in thee
With purer robes than those of flesh and blood,
And hath bestowed on thee a better good—
Unwearied joy, and life without its cares.

THE STREAM.

Clough.

O STREAM descending to the sea,
Thy mossy banks between,
The flow'rets blow, the grasses grow,
Thy leafy trees are green.

In garden plots the children play,
The fields the labourers till,
And houses stand, on either hand,
And thou descendest still.

O life descending into death,
Our waking eyes behold,
Parent and friend, thy lapse attend,
Companions young and old.

Strong purposes our minds possess,
Our hearts' affections fill,
We toil and earn, we seek and learn,
And thou descendest still.

O end to which our currents tend
Inevitable sea,
To which we flow, what do we know,
What shall we guess of thee?

A roar we hear upon thy shore,
As we our course fulfil!
Scarce we divine a sun will shine
And be above us still.

THE STREAMLET.

Mary Anne Stod[illegible]

I saw a little streamlet flow
Along a peaceful vale,
A thread of silver, soft and slow,
It wandered down the dale;
Just to do good it seemed to move,
Directed by the hand of love.

The valley smiled in living green;
A tree which near it gave
From noontide heat a friendly screen,
Drank from its limpid wave.
The swallow brush'd it with her wing,
And followed its meandering.

But not alone to plant and bird
That little stream was known,
Its gentle murmur far was heard—
A friend's familiar tone!
It glided by the cottage door,
It blessed the labour of the poor.

And would that I could thus be found,
While travelling life's brief way,
An humble friend to all around.
Where'er my footsteps stray,
Like that pure stream, with tranquil breast,
Like it, still blessing, and still blest.

THE FOUNTAIN.

Lowell.

INTO the sunshine,
Full of light,
Leaping and flashing
From morn till night!

Into the moonlight
Whiter than snow,
Waving so flower like,
When the winds blow!

Into the starlight,
Rushing in spray,
Happy at midnight,
Happy by day!

Ever in motion,
Blithsome and cheery,
Still climbing heavenward,
Never weary;

Glad of all weathers,
Still seeming best,
Upward or downward,
Motion thy rest;

Full of a nature
Nothing can tame,
Changed every moment—
Ever the same;

Ceaseless aspiring,
Ceaseless content,
Darkness or sunshine
Thy element.

Glorious fountain,
Let my heart be
Fresh, changeful, constant,
Upward like thee!

Poems about Clouds.

THE CLOUD.

Percy Bysshe Shelley.

I bring fresh showers for the thirsting flowers,
From the seas and the streams;
I bear the light shades for the leaves when laid
In their noon-day dreams;
From my wings are shaken the dews that waken
The sweet birds every one,
When rocked to rest on their mother's breast.
As she dances about the sun.
I wield the flail of the lashing hail,
And whiten the green plains under:
And then again I dissolve it in rain,
And laugh as I pass in thunder.

I sift the snow on the mountains below,
And their great pipes groan aghast!
And all the night 'tis my pillow white.
While I sleep in the arms of the blast.
Sublime on the towers of my skyey bowers,
Lightning, my pilot, sits;
In a cavern under is fettered the thunder—
It struggles and howls by fits.
Over earth and ocean, with gentle motion,
This pilot is guiding me,
Lured by the love of the genii that move
In the depths of the purple sea;
Over the rills, and the crags, and the hills,
Over the lakes and the plains,
Wherever he dream, under mountain or stream,
The spirit he loves remains;
And I, all the while, bask in heaven's blue smile
Whilst he is dissolving in rains.

The sanguine sunrise, with his meteor eyes,
And his burning plumes outspread,
Leaps on the back of my sailing rack,
When the morning-star shines dead;
As on the jag of a mountain crag,
Which an earthquake rocks and swings,
An eagle alit, one moment may sit,
In the light of its golden wings.
And when sunset may breathe, from the lit sea beneath,
Its ardours of rest and love,
And the crimson pall of eve may fall
From the depth of heaven above,
With wings folded I rest on mine airy nest,
As still as a brooding dove.

That orbèd maiden, with white fire laden,
Whom mortals call the moon,
Glides glimmering o'er my fleece like floor,
By the midnight breezes strewn;
And wherever the beat of her unseen feet,
Which only the angels hear,
May have broken the woof of my tent's thin roof
The stars peep behind her and peer!
And I laugh to see them whirl and flee,
Like a swarm of golden bees,
When I widen the rent in my wind-built tent,
Till the calm rivers, lakes, and seas,
Like strips of the sky fallen through me on high,
Are each paved with the moon and these.

I bind the sun's throne with a burning zone,
And the moon's with a girdle of pearl;
The volcanoes are dim, and the stars reel and swim,
When the whirlwinds my banners unfurl.
From cape to cape, with a bridge-like shape
Over a torrent sea,
Sunbeam proof, I hang like a roof,
The mountains its columns be.
The triumphal arch through which I march
With hurricane, fire, and snow,
When the powers of the air are chained in my chair,
Is the million-coloured bow;
The sphere-fire above its soft colours wove,
While the moist air was laughing below.

I am the daughter of earth and water,
And the nursling of the sky;
I pass through the pores of the ocean and shores;
I change, but I cannot die:
For, after the rain, when, with never a stain,
The pavilion of heaven is bare,
And the winds and sunbeams, with their convex gleams,
Build up the blue dome of air,
I silently laugh at my own cenotaph,
And out of the caverns of rain,
Like a child from the womb, like a ghost from the tomb,
I arise and upbuild it again."

Poems about the Wind.

THE WIND.

Mrs. Hawkshawe.

THE wind it is a mystic thing,
  Wand'ring o'er ocean wide,
And fanning all the thousand sails
  That o'er its billows glide.

It curls the blue waves into foam
  It snaps tho strongest mast,
Then like a sorrowing thing it sighs,
  When the wild storm is past.

And yet how gently does it come
  At ev'ning through the bow'rs,
As if it said a kind "good night"
  To all the closing flowers.

It bears the perfume of the rose
  It fans the insect's wing:
'Tis round me, with me everywhere,
  Yet 'tis an unseen thing.

How many sounds it bears along,
  As o'er the earth it goes;
The song of many joyous hearts,
  The sounds of many woes.

It enters into palace halls,
  And carries thence the sound
Of mirth and music;—but it creeps
  The narrow prison round,

And bears away the captive's sigh
  Who sits in sorrow there;
Or from the martyr's lonely cell
  Conveys his evening prayer.

It fans the reaper's heated brow;
  It through the window creeps,
And lifts the fair child's golden curls,
  As on her couch she sleeps.

'Tis like the light, a gift to all,
  To prince, to peasant given;
Awake, asleep, around us still,
  There is this gift of Heaven.

This strange, mysterious thing we call
  The breeze, the air, the wind;
We call it so, but know no more,—
  'Tis mystery, like our mind.

Think not the things most wonderful
  Are those beyond our ken,—
For wonders are around the paths,
  The daily paths of men.

SONG OF THE NORTH WIND.

I AM here from the north, the frozen north,
  'Tis a thousand leagues away;
And I left, as I came from my cavern forth,
  The streaming lights at play.

From the deep sea's verge to the zenith high,
  At one last leap they flew,
And kindled a blaze in the midnight sky,
  O'er the glittering icebergs blue.

The frolicsome waves they shouted to me,
  As I swept their thousands past,
"Where are the chains that can fetter the sea?"
  But I bound the boasters fast.

In their pride of strength, the pine trees tall
  Of my coming took no heed;
But I bowed the proudest of them all,
  As if it had been a reed.

I found the tops of the mountains bare,
  And gave them a crown of snow;
And roused the hungry wolf from his lair,
  To hunt the Esquimaux.

I saw where lay in the forest spent,
  The fire of the embers white;
And I breathed on the lordly element,
  And nursed it into might.

It floateth amain, my banner red,
  With a proud and lurid glare;
And the fir-clad hills, as torches dread,
  Flame in the wintry air.

O'er valley and hill, and mere I range,
  And, as I sweep along,
Gather all sounds that are wild and strange
  And mingle them in my song.

My voice hath been uttered everywhere,
  And the sign of my presence seen;
But the eye of man the form I wear
  Hath never beheld, I ween!

Poems about Sunshine.

COMMON THINGS.

Mrs. Hawkshawe.

The sun is a glorious thing,
That comes alike to all,
Lighting the peasant's lonely cot,
The noble's painted hall.

The moonlight is a gentle thing,
It through the window gleams
Upon the snowy pillow where
The happy infant dreams.

It shines upon the fisher's boat,
Out on the lonely sea;
Or where the little lambkins lie,
Beneath the old oak tree.

The dewdrops on the summer morn,
Sparkle upon the grass;
The village children brush them off,
That through the meadows pass.

There are no gems in monarch's crowns
More beautiful than they;
A d yet we scarcely notice them,
But tread them off in play.

Poor Robin on the pear-tree sings
Beside the cottage door;
The heath-flower fills the air with sweets
Upon the pathless moor.

There are as many lovely things,
As many pleasant tones,
For those who sit by cottage hearths
As those who sit on thrones.

THE SUNSHINE.

Mary Howitt.

I love the sunshine everywhere—
In wood, and field, and glen;
I love it in the busy haunts
Of town-imprisoned men.

I love it, when it streameth in
The humble cottage door,
And casts the chequered casement shade
Upon the red-brick floor.

I love it, where the children lie
Deep in the clovery grass,
To watch among the twining roots
The gold-green beetle pass.

I love it, on the breezy sea,
To glance on sail and oar,
While the great waves, like molten glass,
Come leaping to the shore.

I love it, on the mountain-tops,
Where lies the thawless snow;
And half a kingdom, bathed in light,
Lies stretching out below.

O! yes, I love the sunshine!
Like kindness, or like mirth,
Upon a human countenance,
Is sunshine on the earth.

Upon the earth—upon the sea—
And through the crystal air—
Or piled-up clouds—the gracious sun
Is gracious everywhere.

Poems about Spring.

THE VOICE OF SPRING.

Mrs. Hemans.

I COME, I come! ye have call'd me long—
I come o'er the mountains with light and song!
Ye may trace my step o'er the waking earth
By the winds which tell of the violet's birth,
By the primrose stars in the shadowy grass,
By the green leaves opening as I pass.

I have breathed on the South, and the chestnut flowers,
By thousands, have burst from the forest-bowers,
And the ancient graves, and the fallen fanes
Are veil'd with wreaths on Italian plains:—
But it is not for me, in my hour of bloom,
To speak of the ruin or the tomb!

I have looked on the hills of the stormy North,
And the larch has hung all his tassels forth,
The fisher is out on the sunny sea,
And the reindeer bounds through the pasture free,
And the pine has a fringe of a softer green,
And the moss looks bright where my foot hath been.

I have sent through the wood-paths a glowing sigh,
And call'd out each voice of the deep-blue sky;
From the night-bird's lay through the starry time,
In the groves of the soft Hesperian clime,
To the swan's wild note by the Iceland lakes,
When the dark fir-branch into verdure breaks.

From the streams and founts I have loosed the chain,
They are sweeping on to the silvery main,
They are flashing down from the mountain brows,
They are flinging spray o'er the forest boughs,
They are bursting fresh from their sparry caves,
And the earth resounds with the joy of waves!

THE VOICE OF SPRING.

I AM coming! I am coming!—hark! the little bee is humming;
See, the lark is soaring high in the blue and sunny sky;
And the gnats are on the wing, wheeling round in airy ring.

See the yellow catkins cover all the slender willows over;
And on banks of mossy green star-like primroses are seen;
And, their clustering leaves below, white and purple violets grow.

Hark! the new-born lambs are bleating, and the cawing rooks are meeting,
In the elms—a noisy crowd! all the birds are singing loud;
And the first white butterfly in the sunshine dances by.

Look around thee—look around! flowers in all the fields abound;
Every running stream is bright; all the orchard trees are white,
And each small and waving shoot promises sweet flower and fruit.

Poems about Summer.

SUMMER.

I'M coming along with a bounding pace,
To finish the work that spring begun;
I've left them all with a brighter face,
The flowers in the vale through which I've run.

I have hung festoons from laburnum trees,
And clothed the lilac, the birch, and broom;
I've wakened the sound of humming bees,
And decked all nature in brighter bloom.

I've roused the laugh of the playful child,
And tired it out in the sunny noon;
All nature at my approach hath smiled,
And I've made fond lovers seek the moon.

For this is my life, my glorious reign,
And I'll queen it well in my leafy bower;
All shall be bright in my rich domain;
I'm queen of the leaf, the bud, and the flower.

And I'll reign in triumph till autumn time
Shall conquer my green and verdant pride;
Then I'll hie me to another clime,
Till I'm called again as a sunny bride.

THE BEAUTIES OF SUMMER. *John Houseman.*

THE Summer! the Summer! the exquisite time
Of the red rose's blush, and the nightingale's chime;
The chant of the lark, and the boom of the bee—
The season of brightness, and beauty, and glee!
It is here—it is here! it is lighting again,
With sun-braided smiles, the deep heart of the glen;
It is touching the mountain and tinging the hill,
And dimpling the face of the low laughing rill;
It is flooding the forest-trees richly with bloom;
And flinging gold showers in the lap of the broom.
I have heard the lark warble his hymn in the sky;
I have seen the dew-tear in the meek daisy's eye;
I have scented the breath of the fresh open'd flowers;
I have plucked a rich garland from bright hawthorn bowers
My footsteps have been where the violet sleeps,
And where arches of eglantine hang from the steeps;
I have startled the linnet from thickets of shade;
And roused the fleet stag as he basked in the glade;
And my spirit is blithe—as a rivulet clear,
For the Summer, the golden-crown'd Summer, is here!

Poems about Horses.

THE ARAB'S FAREWELL TO HIS STEED.

Mrs. Norton.

MY beautiful, my beautiful! that standest meekly by,
With thy proudly-arched and glossy neck, and dark and fiery eye!
Fret not to roam the desert now with all thy wing'd speed:
I may not mount on thee again!—thou'rt sold, my Arab steed!

Fret not with that impatient hoof, snuff not the breezy wind;
The farther that thou fliest now, so far am I behind!
The stranger hath thy bridle-rein, thy master hath his gold;—
Fleet-limbed and beautiful, farewell; thou'rt sold, my steed, thou'rt sold.

Farewell!—Those free, untired limbs full many a mile must roam,
To reach the chill and wintry clime that clouds the stranger's home;
Some other hand, less kind, must now thy corn and bed prepare;
That silky mane I braided once must be another's care.

The morning sun shall dawn again—but never more with thee
Shall I gallop o'er the desert paths where we were wont to be—
Evening shall darken on the earth: and, o'er the sandy plain,
Some other steed, with slower pace, shall bear me home again.

Only in sleep shall I behold that dark eye glancing bright—
Only in sleep shall hear again that step so firm and light;
And when I raise my dreamy arms to check or cheer thy speed,
Then must I startling wake, to feel thou'rt sold! my Arab steed.

Ah, rudely then, unseen by me, some cruel hand may chide,
Till foam-wreaths lie, like crested waves, along thy panting side,
And the rich blood that in thee swells, in thy indignant pain,
Till careless eyes that on thee gaze may count each starting vein!

Will they ill-use thee;—If I thought—but no,—it cannot be;
Thou art too swift, yet easy curbed, so gentle, yet so free;—
And yet, if haply when thou'rt gone, this lonely heart should yearn,
Can the hand that casts thee from it now, command thee to return?

"Return!"—alas! my Arab steed! what will thy master do,
When thou that wast his all of joy, hast vanished from his view?
When the dim distance greets mine eyes, and through the gathering tears
Thy bright form for a moment, like the false mirage, appears?

Slow and unmounted will I roam, with wearied foot, alone,
Where, with fleet step, and joyous bound, thou oft hast borne me on;
And sitting down by the green well, I'll pause and sadly think—
"'Twas here he bowed his glossy neck when last I saw him drink."

When *last* I saw thee drink!—Away! the fevered dream is o'er!
I could not live a day, and know that we should meet no more;
They tempted me, my beautiful! for hunger's power is strong—
They tempted me, my beautiful! but I have loved too long.

Who said, that I had given thee up? Who said that thou wert sold?
'Tis false! 'tis false, my Arab steed! I fling them back their gold!
Thus—thus, I leap upon thy back, and scour the distant plains!
Away! who overtakes us now shall claim thee for his pains.

SHERIDAN'S RIDE.

Thomas Buchanan Read

Up from the south at break of day,
Bringing to Winchester fresh dismay,
The affrighted air with a shudder bore,
Like a herald in haste, to the chieftain's door,
The terrible grumble and rumble and roar,
Telling the battle was on once more—
And Sheridan twenty miles away!
And wilder still those billows of war
Thundered along the horizon's bar;
And louder yet into Winchester rolled
The roar of that red sea uncontrolled,
Making the blood of the listener cold—
As he thought of the stake in that fiery fray,
With Sheridan *twenty* miles away!

But there is a road from Winchester town,
A good, broad highway leading down;
And there, through the flash of the morning light,
A steed as black as the steeds of night,
Was seen to pass as with eagle flight;—
As if he knew the terrible need,
He stretched away with the utmost speed;
Hills rose and fell—but his heart was gay
With Sheridan *fifteen* miles away!
Still sprung from these swift hoofs, thundering South
The dust, like the smoke from the cannon's mouth,
Or the trail of a comet sweeping faster and faster;
Foreboding to traitors the doom of disaster:
The heart of the steed and the heart of the master
Were beating like prisoners assaulting their walls,
Impatient to be where the battle-field calls;
Every nerve of the charger was strained to full play,
With Sheridan only *ten* miles away!
Under his spurning feet, the road
Like an arrowy Alpine river flowed;
And the landscape sped away behind
Like an ocean flying before the wind;
And the steed, like a bark fed with furnace ire,
Swept on with his wild eyes full of fire:
But, lo! he is nearing his heart's desire—
He is snuffing the smoke of the roaring fray,
With Sheridan only *five* miles away!
The first that the General saw, were the groups
Of stragglers, and then the retreating troops!—
What was done—what to do—a glance told him both
And striking his spurs, with a terrible oath,
He dashed down the line 'mid a storm of huzzahs,
And the wave of retreat checked its course there because
The sight of the master compelled it to pause.
With foam and with dust the black charger was grey;
By the flash of his eye, and his red nostril's play,
He seemed to the whole great army to say,
"I have brought you Sheridan, all the way
From Winchester down to save the day!"

Hurrah, hurrah, for Sheridan!
Hurrah, hurrah for horse and man!
And when their statues are placed on high,
Under the dome of the Union sky,—
The American soldier's Temple of Fame,—
There with the glorious general's name,
Be it said in letters both gold and bright:
"Here is the steed that saved the day
By carrying Sheridan into the fight,
From Winchester—twenty miles away!"

Poems about Dogs.

BETH GELERT.

Hon. Wm. Robert Spencer.

THE spearman heard the bugle sound,
And cheerily smiled the morn;
And many a brach, and many a hound,
Attend Llewellyn's horn:

And still he blew a louder blast,
And gave a louder cheer:
"Come, Gelert! why art thou the last
Llewellyn's horn to hear!

"Oh! where does faithful Gelert roam?
The flower of all his race!
So true, so brave: a lamb at home,
A lion in the chase!"

In sooth he was a peerless hound,
The gift of royal John;
But now no Gelert could be found,
And all the chase rode on.

And now, as over rocks and dells
The gallant chidings rise,
All Snowdon's craggy chaos yells
With many mingled cries.

That day Llewellyn little loved
The chase of hart or hare!
And small and scant the booty proved,
For Gelert was not there.

Unpleased, Llewellyn homeward hied,
When near the portal-seat,
His truant Gelert he espied,
Bounding his lord to greet.

But when he gained the castle door,
Aghast the chieftain stood;
The hound was smeared with gouts of gore,
His lips and fangs ran blood!

Llewellyn gazed with wild surprise,
Unused such looks to meet:
His favourite checked his joyful guise,
And crouch'd and lick'd his feet.

Onward in haste Llewellyn pass'd—
And on went Gelert too—
And still, where'er his eyes were cast,
Fresh blood-gouts shocked his view.

O'erturn'd his infant's bed, he found
The blood-stained covert rent;
And all around, the walls and ground
With recent blood besprent.

He call'd the child—no voice replied;
He search'd—with terror wild;
Blood! blood! he found on every side,
But nowhere found his child!

"Hell-hound! by thee my child's devoured!"
The frantic father cried;
And, to the hilt, his vengeful sword
He plunged in Gelert's side!

His suppliant, as to earth he fell,
No pity could impart:
But still his Gelert's dying yell
Pass'd heavy o'er his heart.

Arous'd by Gelert's dying yell
Some slumberer waken'd nigh:
What words the parent's joy can tell,
To hear his infant cry!

Conceal'd beneath a mangled heap,
His hurried search had miss'd,
All glowing from his rosy sleep,
His cherub-boy he kissed!

Nor scratch had he, nor harm, nor dread—
But, the same couch beneath,
Lay a great wolf, all torn and dead—
Tremendous still in death!

Ah! what was then Llewellyn's pain!
For now the truth was clear:
The gallant hound the wolf had slain,
To save Llewellyn's heir.

Vain, vain was all Llewellyn's woe:
"Best of thy kind, adieu!
The frantic deed which laid thee low
This heart shall ever rue!"

And now a gallant tomb they raise,
With costly sculpture deck'd;
And marbles, storied with his praise,
Poor Gelert's bones protect.

Here never could the spearman pass
Or forester unmoved!
Here oft the tear-besprinkled grass
Llewellyn's sorrow proved.

And here he hung his horn and spear,
And oft, as evening fell,
In fancy's piercing sounds would hear
Poor Gelert's dying yell.

Poems about Animals.

THE RING OF DEATH.

Thomas Gregory.

PEACEFULLY nipping the grass at his feet,
With glance thrown furtively round his retreat,
The monarch of prairies looks on his own,
Far, far from his herd stands in grandeur alone—
Heedless of danger though watchful his eye,
The buffalo is grazing in stern majesty.
Who can behold the huge monster's repose,
And not give a thought to the terrible throes
That shake him when roused and furiously bent
To conquer a foe or menace resent.
'Mid stillness like death he now treads the ground,
When a rustling bush breaks the silence profound,
Up goes his head with a sniff in the air,
While in a moment he gazes with ominous stare,
But, snorting with scorn, returns to his feed,
Proof against danger—a hero, indeed.
From the cov'ring bush has just sprang to sight
A hungry jowl, with fangs pearly white—
A bloodthirsty wolf, with ill-omened glance,
Glares on to the monarch, and woos an advance.
A second bush trembles, another wolf glides—
And the two gaze upon him from opposite sides.
Supreme in his strength the mammoth pursues
His meal of soft herbage, and presently views,
With look of disdain, those flashing eyes bent,
In ravenous greed, on his body intent.
Yet stay; still another grim spectre is seen,
Who seems to come up from the long, waving green.
And followed by one, two, three, aye, a score,
Who form a dread circle as onward they pour.
Thus hemmed in on all his sides, he coolly surveys
The gathering ring, nor an instant betrays
By gesture or sound the peril that greets
From each hungry look which nobly he meets.
But now, with a bellow of triumph that wakes
The echoing hills, he plunges and breaks
The circle of death, with terrific sound,
And wolf upon wolf lies dead on the ground,
Like thunder he roars, like lightning he darts,
Again and again the deadly ring parts,
Nor pause for an instant his death-dealing blows,
But foe after foe swiftly upward he throws,
Till gory his horns, his brows steeped in blood—
He hungers for more of the ravenous brood—
His steaming red nostrils expand with each gust,
And the fire in his eyes ignites at each thrust.
Now he paws the green earth, grand in his might,
And lowers his horns to renew the fierce fight:
Again with a rush the buffalo swings,
While hither and thither the enemy flings.
Gaunt, quiv'ring wolves in agony fly
From his bloody embrace to fall there and die.
Though scored by a hundred wounds, he maintains
The battle undaunted—still the earth stains
With trophies of death, in pools at his feet,
Each time the grim pack their onslaught repeat.
Nearer they draw, more compact in their ranks
And oftener now their teeth gall his flanks,
Tufts of long hair are tossed to and fro—
And fierce as the vulture's their wolfish eyes glow.
Still he fights gamely, the earth still he paws,
Although the boundary of death closer draws:
Strong in his fury, and awful to sight,
Backward he drives them to left and to right,
Then follows them up, and scatters them wide.
Once more they close in, once more they divide—
Again he pursues, each thrust a cruel death,
Till weakened and torn he pauses for breath.
Now from his fiery red lips falls a sound,
A low, plaintive note, in which terror is found—
One wounded foot scarcely touches the grass;
And languid, his eye is now fixed on the mass:
His bright blazing orb, relaxed in its fire,
No longer is gleaming with furious ire,
And now, with a rush, the gluttonous pack
Cling to his neck, to his loins, to his back.
He wheels on his centre, his blood ebbing fast—
Though proudly the battle contests to the last;
But weaker the blows, uncertain the aim,
He staggers and limps for he is quite lame.
Over each other the wolves lightly vault,
Spurred by their hunger to urge the assault,
Howling and snarling as onward they press;
With courage that grows with the buffalo's stress,
They mount on each other and fix on his hide,
Scoring the skin which a bullet defied.
The noble beast wavers—ah! look he is down,
And victory now the wolves' efforts crown—
Swirling they leap, prepared for the feast,
And tear the hot flesh from the prostrate beast.
'Tis all over now—the mighty has fell;
They gather round with triumphant yell,
Till death puts an end to the harrowing sight,
Leaving the brutes o'er his carcass to fight,
True nerve and true grit—a hero lay there,
His bones left to bleach in the sun's scorching glare.
But who will gainsay, if those relics he finds,
That they should be buried by statelier minds.

BIRDS.

William H. Thompson.

BIRDS—birds! ye are beautiful things,
With your earth-treading feet and your cloud-cleaving wings;
Where shall man wander, and where shall he dwell,
Beautiful birds, that ye come not as well?
Ye have nests on the mountain all rugged and stark,
Ye have nests in the forest all tangled and dark:
Ye build and ye brood 'neath the cottagers' eaves,
And ye sleep on the sod 'mid the bonnie green leaves;

Ye hide in the heather, ye lurk in the brake,
Ye dive in the sweet flags that shadow the lake:
Ye skim where the stream parts the orchard-decked land,
Ye dance where the foam sweeps the desolate strand.
Beautiful birds! ye come thickly around,
When the bud's on the branch, and the snow's on the ground;
Ye come when the richest of roses flush out,
And ye come when the yellow leaf eddies about.

Beautiful birds! how the schoolboy remembers
The warblers that chorussed his holiday tune;
The robin that chirped in the frosty Decembers,
The blackbird that whistled through flower-crowned June.
That schoolboy remembers his holiday ramble,
When he pulled every blossom of palm he could see,
When his finger was raised as he stopped in the bramble,
With "Hark! there's the cuckoo; how close he must be."

THE SKYLARK.

James Hogg.

BIRD of the wilderness,
Blithesome and cumberless,
Sweet be thy matin o'er moorland and lea!
Emblem of happiness,
Blest is thy dwelling-place—
O to abide in the desert with thee!
Wild is thy lay and loud,
Far in the downy cloud,
Love gives it energy, love gave it birth;
Where, on thy dewy wing,
Where art thou journeying?
Thy lay is in heaven, thy love is on earth.

O'er fell and fountain sheen,
O'er moor and mountain green,
O'er the red streamer that heralds the day,
Over the cloudlet dim,
Over the rainbow's rim,
Musical cherub, soar, singing, away;
Then, when the gloaming comes,
Low in the heather blooms,
Sweet will thy welcome and bed of love be.
Emblem of happiness,
Blest is thy dwelling-place—
O to abide in the desert with thee!

THE CUCKOO.

John Logan.

HAIL, beauteous stranger of the grove,
Thou messenger of spring,
Now heaven repairs thy rural seat,
And woods thy welcome sing.

What time the daisy decks the green,
Thy certain voice we hear;
Hast thou a star to guide thy path,
Or mark the rolling year?

Delightful visitant! with thee
I hail the time of flowers,
And hear the sound of music sweet
From birds among the bowers.

The schoolboy wandering through the wood,
To pluck the primrose gay,
Starts, thy curious voice to hear,
And imitates thy lay.

What time the pea puts on the bloom,
Thou fliest the vocal vale,
An annual guest, in other lands
Another spring to hail.

Sweet bird! thy bower is ever green,
Thy sky is ever clear;
Thou hast no sorrow in thy song,
No winter in thy year.

Oh! could I fly, I'd fly with thee;
We'd make, with joyful wing,
Our annual visit o'er the globe,
Companions of the spring.

THE RAVEN.

Edgar Allan Poe.

Once upon a midnight dreary, while I ponder'd weak and weary,
Over many a quaint and curious volume of forgotten lore—
While I nodded, nearly napping, suddenly there came a tapping,
As of someone gently rapping, rapping at my chamber-door.
"'Tis some visitor," I muttered, "tapping at my chamber-door—
Only this, and nothing more."

Ah! distinctly I remember it was in the bleak December,
And each separate dying ember wrought its ghost upon the floor.
Eagerly I wish'd the morrow;—vainly I had sought to borrow
From my books surcease of sorrow—sorrow for the lost Lenore—
For the rare and radiant maiden whom the angels name Lenore—
Nameless here for evermore.

And the silken sad uncertain rustling of each purple curtain
Thrill'd me—fill'd me with fantastic terrors never felt before;
So that now, to still the beating of my heart, I stood repeating,
"'Tis some visitor entreating entrance at my chamber-door—
Some late visitor entreating entrance at my chamber-door;
That it is, and nothing more."

Presently my soul grew stronger, hesitating then no longer,
"Sir," said I, "or madam, truly your forgiveness I implore;
But the fact is I was napping, and so gently you came rapping,
And so faintly you came tapping, tapping at my chamber-door,
That I scarce was sure I heard you:"—here I open'd wide the door;—
Darkness there, and nothing more.

Deep into that darkness peering, long I stood there wondering, fearing,
Doubting, dreaming dreams no mortal ever dared to dream before
But the silence was unbroken, and the stillness gave no token,
And the only word there spoken was the whispered word, "Lenore?"
This I whisper'd, and an echo murmured back the word, "Lenore!"—
Merely this, and nothing more.

Back into my chamber turning, all my soul within me burning,
Soon again I heard a tapping, something louder than before.
"Surely," said I, "surely that is something at my window lattice;
Let me see, then, what thereat is, and this mystery explore—
Let my heart be still a moment, and this mystery explore:—
'Tis the wind, and nothing more."

Open here I flung the shutter, when, with many a flirt and flutter,
In there stepp'd a stately raven of the saintly days of yore.
Not the least obeisance made he; not a minute stopp'd or stay'd he;
But, with mien of lord or lady, perch'd above my chamber-door—
Perch'd upon a bust of Pallas, just above my chamber-door—
Perch'd, and sat, and nothing more.

Then this ebony bird beguiling my sad fancy into smiling,
By the grave and stern decorum of the countenance it wore:
"Though thy crest be shorn and shaven, thou," I said, "art sure no craven;
Ghastly, grim, and ancient raven, wandering from the nightly shore,
Tell me what thy lordly name is on the night's Plutonian shore?"
Quoth the raven, "Never more."

Much I marvelled this ungainly fowl to hear discourse so plainly,
Though its answer little meaning, little relevancy bore:
For we cannot help agreeing that no living human being
Ever yet was blessed with seeing bird above his chamber-door—
Bird or beast upon the sculptured bust above his chamber-door
With such name as "Never more."

But the Raven, sitting lonely on that placid bust, spoke only
That one word, as if his soul in that one word he did outpour;
Nothing further then he uttered, not a feather then he fluttered,
Till I scarcely more than muttered—"Other friends have flown before,
On the morrow *he* will leave me, as my hopes have flown before."
Then the bird said, "Never more."

Startled by the stillness broken by reply so aptly spoken,
"Doubtless," said I, "what it utters is its only stock and store,
Caught from some unhappy master, whom unmerciful disaster
Followed fast and followed faster, till his songs one burden bore—
Till the dirges of his hope this melancholy burden bore—
Of 'Never, never more.'"

But the Raven still beguiling all my sad soul into smiling,
Straight I wheeled a cushioned seat in front of bird, and bust, and door;
Then upon the velvet sinking, I betook myself to linking
Fancy into fancy, thinking what this ominous bird of yore—
What this grim, ungainly, ghastly, gaunt, and ominous bird of yore
Meant in croaking, "Never more."

Thus I sat engaged in guessing, but no syllable expressing
To the fowl whose fiery eyes now burned into my bosom's core;
This and more I sat divining, with my head at ease reclining,
On the cushion's velvet lining, that the lamp-light gloated o'er,
But whose violet velvet lining, with the lamp-light gloating o'e
She shall press, ah, never more

Then methought the air grew denser, perfumed from an unseen censer
Swung by seraphim, whose footfalls tinkled on the tufted floor.
"Wretch," I cried, "thy God hath lent thee—by these angels he hath sent thee
Respite—respite and nepenthe from my memories of Lenore!
Quaff, oh quaff this kind nepenthe, and forget this lost Lenore!"
Quoth the Raven, "Never more."

"Prophet," said I, "thing of evil!—prophet still, if bird or devil!
Whether tempter sent, or whether tempest tossed thee here ashore
Desolate, yet all undaunted, on this desert land enchanted,
On this home by horror haunted—tell me truly, I implore,
Is there—*is* there balm in Gilead?—tell me truly, I implore!"
Quoth the Raven, "Never more."

"Prophet!" said I "thing of evil!—prophet still, if bird or devil!—
By that Heaven that bends above us—by that God we both adore—
Tell this soul with sorrow laden if within the distant Aidenn,
It shall clasp a sainted maiden whom the angels name Lenore—
Clasp a rare and radiant maiden whom the angels name Lenore?"
Quoth the Raven, "Never more."

"Be that word our sign of parting, bird or fiend!" I shriek'd, upstarting,
"Get thee back into the tempest and the Night's Plutonian shore!
Leave no black plume as a token of that lie thy soul hath spoken!
Leave my loneliness unbroken!—quit the bust above my door!
Take thy beak from out my heart, and take thy form from off my door!"
Quoth the Raven, "Never more."

And the Raven, never flitting, still is sitting, still is sitting,
On the pallid bust of Pallas, just above my chamber-door;
And his eyes have all the seeming of a demon's that is dreaming,
And the lamp-light o'er him streaming throws his shadow on the floor,
And my soul from out that shadow that lies floating on the floor,
Shall be lifted—never more.

Poems about Plants.

THE SENSITIVE PLANT.

A SENSITIVE plant in a garden grew,
And the young winds fed it with silver dew,
And it open'd its fan-like leaves to the light,
And closed them beneath the kisses of night.

And the Spring arose on the garden fair,
Like the Spirit of Love, felt everywhere ;
And each flower and herb on Earth's dark breast
Rose from the dreams of its wintry rest.

But none ever trembled and panted with bliss
In the garden, the field, or the wilderness,
Like a doe in the noontide with love's sweet want,
As the companionless Sensitive Plant.

The snowdrop, and then the violet,
Arose from the ground with warm rain wet,
And their breath was mix'd with fresh odour, sent
From the turf, like the voice and the instrument.

Then the pied wind-flowers and the tulip tall,
And narcissi, the fairest among them all,
Who gaze on their eyes in the stream's recess,
Till they die of their own dear loveliness ;

And the Naiad-like lily of the vale,
Whom youth makes so fair, and passion so pale,
That the light of its tremulous bells is seen
Through their pavilions of tender green ;

And the hyacinth purple, and white, and blue,
Which flung from its bells a sweet peal anew
Of music, so delicate, soft, and intense,
It was felt like an odour within the sense

And the rose like a nymph to the bath addrest,
Which unveil'd the depth of her glowing breast,
Till, fold after fold, to the fainting air
The soul of her beauty and love lay bare ;

And the wand-like lily, which lifted up,
As a Mænad, its moonlight-coloured cup,
Till the fiery star, which is its eye,
Gazed through clear dew on the tender sky ;

And the jessamine faint, and the sweet tuberose,
The sweetest flower for scent that blows ;
And all rare blossoms from every clime
Grew in that garden in perfect prime.

THE VOICE OF THE GRASS.

Mary Howitt.

HERE I come creeping, creeping everywhere;
By the dusty roadside,
On the sunny hillside,
Close by the noisy brook,
In every shady nook
I come creeping, creeping everywhere.

Here I come creeping, creeping everywhere ;
All round the open door,
Where sit the aged poor,
Here where children play
In the bright and merry May
I come creeping, creeping everywhere.

Here I come creeping, creeping everywhere;
In the noisy city street,
My pleasant face you'll meet,
Cheering the sick at heart,
Toiling his busy part,
Silently creeping, creeping everywhere.

Here I come creeping, creeping everywhere;
You cannot see me coming,
Nor hear my low sweet humming ;
For in the starry night,
And the glad morning light,
I come creeping, creeping everywhere.

Here I come creeping, creeping everywhere
More welcome than the flowers
In summer's pleasant hours
The gentle cow is glad,
And the merry bird not sad,
To see me creeping, creeping everywhere.

Here I come creeping, creeping everywhere;
When you're number'd with the dead
In your still and narrow bed,
In the happy spring I'll come
And deck your silent home,
Creeping, silently creeping everywhere.

Here I come creeping, creeping everywhere ;
My humble song of praise
Most gratefully I raise
To Him, at whose command
I beautify the land,
Creeping, silently creeping everywhere.

Poems Miscellaneous.

TRIUMPHS OF THE ENGLISH LANGUAGE.

J. G. Lyons.

Now gather all our Saxon bards,
Let harps and hearts be strung,
To celebrate the triumphs of
Our own good Saxon tongue;
For stronger far than hosts that march
With battle-flags unfurled,
It goes with *freedom, thought,* and *truth*
To rouse and rule the world.

Stout Albion learns its household lays
On every surf-worn shore,
And Scotland hears its echoing far
As Orkney's breakers roar—
From Jura's crags and Mona's hills
It floats on every gale,
And warms with eloquence and song
The homes of Innisfail.

* * * *

It spreads where winter piles deep snows
On bleak Canadian plains,
And where, on Essequibo's banks,
Eternal summer reigns:

It glads Arcadia's misty coasts,
Jamaica's glowing isle:
And bides where, gay with early flowers,
Green Texan prairies smile.
It tracks the loud swift Oregon
Through sunset valleys rolled,
And soars where Californian brooks
Wash down their sands of gold.

It sounds in Borneo's camphor groves;
On seas of fierce Malay,
In fields that curb old Ganges' flood,
And towers of proud Bombay:

It wakes up Aden's flashing eyes,
Dusk brows and swarthy limbs—
The dark Liberian soothes her child
With English cradle hymns.

Tasmania's maids are wooed and won
In gentle Saxon speech;
Australian boys read Crusoe's life
By Sydney's sheltered beach:
It dwells where Afric's southmost capes
Meet oceans broad and blue,
And Nieuveld's rugged mountains gird
The wide and waste Karroo.

It kindles realms so far apart,
That while its praise you sing,
These may be clad with autumn's fruits,
And *those* with flowers of spring:
It quickens lands whose meteor-lights
Flame in an Arctic sky,
And lands for which the Southern Cross
Hangs its orbed fires on high.

Mark, as it spreads, how deserts bloom,
And error flies away,
As vanishes the mist of night
Before the star of day!
But grand as are the victories
Whose monuments we see,
These are but as the dawn which speaks
Of noontide yet to be.

Go forth, and jointly speed the time,
By good men prayed for long,
When Christian states, grown just and wise,
Will scorn revenge and wrong:
When earth's oppressed and savage tribes
Shall cease to pine or roam,
All taught to prize these English words—
Faith, freedom, heaven, and *home.*

THE BLIND MEN AND THE ELEPHANT.

[A HINDOO FABLE.]

J. G. Saxe.

It was six men of Indostan
  To learning much inclined,
Who went to see the elephant
  (Though all of them were blind),
That each by observation
  Might satisfy his mind.

The *First* approached the Elephant,
  And happening to fall
Against his broad and sturdy side,
  At once began to bawl:
"God bless me!—but the Elephant
  Is very like a wall!"

The *Second* feeling of the tusk,
  Cried: "Ho!—what have we here
So very round and smooth and sharp?
  To me 'tis mighty clear
This wonder of an Elephant
  Is very like a spear!"

The *Third* approached the animal,
  And happening to take
The squirming trunk within his hands,
  Thus boldly up and spake:
"I see," quoth he, "the Elephant
  Is very like a snake!"

The *Fourth* reached out his eager hand,
  And felt about the knee,
"What most this wondrous beast is like
  Is mighty plain," quoth he;
"'Tis clear enough the Elephant
  Is very like a tree!"

The *Fifth*, who chanced to touch the ear,
  Said: "E'en the blindest man
Can tell what this resembles most;
  Deny the fact who can,
This marvel of an Elephant
  Is very like a fan."

The *Sixth* no sooner had begun
  About the beast to grope,
Than, seizing on the swinging tail
  That fell within his scope,
"I see," quoth he, "the Elephant
  Is very like a rope!"

And so these men of Indostan
  Disputed loud and long,
Each in his own opinion
  Exceeding stiff and strong,
Though each was partly in the right,
  And all were in the wrong!

MORAL.

So, oft in theologic wars
  The disputants, I ween,
Rail on in utter ignorance
  Of what each other mean
And prate about an Elephant
  Not one of them has seen!

ALEXANDER SELKIRK.

Cowper.

I am monarch of all I survey,
  My right there is none to dispute;
From the centre all round to the sea
  I am lord of the fowl and the brute.
O Solitude, where are the charms
  That sages have seen in thy face?
Better dwell in the midst of alarms
  Than reign in this horrible place.

I am out of humanity's reach;
  I must finish my journey alone;
Never hear the sweet music of speech—
  I start at the sound of my own.
The beasts that roam over the plain
  My form with indifference see;
They are so unacquainted with men,
  Their tameness is shocking to me.

Society, friendship, and love,
  Divinely bestowed upon man,
O had I the wings of a dove,
  How soon would I taste you again!
My sorrows I then might assuage
  In the ways of religion and truth;
Might learn from the wisdom of age,
  And be cheer'd by the sallies of youth.

Religion! what treasure untold
  Resides in that heavenly word!
More precious than silver and gold,
  Or all that this earth can afford.
But the sound of the church-going bell
  These valleys and rocks never heard—
Never sigh'd at the sound of a knell,
  Or smiled when a Sabbath appear'd.

Ye winds that have made me your sport,
  Convey to this desolate shore
Some cordial endearing report
  Of a land I shall visit no more.
My friends, do they now and then send
  A wish or a thought after me?
O tell me I yet have a friend,
  Though a friend I am never to see.

How fleet is a glance of the mind!
  Compared with the speed of its flight,
The tempest itself lags behind,
  And the swift winged arrows of light.
When I think of my own native land,
  In a moment I seem to be there;
But, alas! recollection at hand
  Soon hurries me back to despair.

But the sea-fowl is gone to her nest;
  The beast is laid down in his lair;
Even here is a season of rest,
  And I to my cabin repair,
There's mercy in every place;
  And mercy, encouraging thought!
Gives even affliction a grace,
  And reconciles man to his lot.

THE GLOVE AND THE LIONS.

Leigh Hunt.

KING FRANCIS was a hearty king, and loved a royal sport;
And one day as his lions fought, sat looking on the Court;
The nobles filled the benches round, the ladies by their side,
And 'mongst them Count de Lorge, with one he hoped to make his bride;
And truly 'twas a gallant thing to see that crowning show—
Valour and love, and a king above, and the royal beasts below.

Ramped and roared the lions, with horrid laughing jaws;
They bit, they glared, gave blows like beams—a wind went with their paws;
With wallowing might and stifled roar, they rolled on one another,
Till all the pit, with sand and mane, was in a thunderous smother;
The bloody foam above the bars came whizzing through the air;
Said Francis then, "Faith! gentlemen, we're better here than there!"

De Lorge's love o'erheard the king,—a beauteous lively dame,
With smiling lips and sharp bright eyes, which always seemed the same.
She thought, "The Count my lover is brave as brave can be—
He surely would do wondrous things to show his love for me:
King, ladies, lovers, all look on; the occasion is divine!
I'll drop my glove, to prove his love: great glory will be mine!"

She dropped her glove to prove his love, then looked at him and smiled;
He bowed, and in a moment leaped among the lions wild.
The leap was quick, return was quick—he has regained his place—
Then threw the glove—but not with love—right in the lady's face!
"In truth," cried Francis, "rightly done!" and he rose from where he sat.
"No love," quoth he, "but vanity, sets love a task like that."

HARMOSAN.

Dr. Trench

Now the third and fatal conflict for the Persian throne was done,
And the Moslem's fiery valour had the crowning victory won:
Harmosan, the last of the foemen, and the boldest to defy,
Captive, overborne by numbers, they were bringing forth to die.

Then exclaimed that noble Satrap, "Lo, I perish in my thirst;
Give me but one drink of water, and let then arrive the worst."
In his hand he took the goblet, but awhile the draught forbore,
Seeming doubtfully the purpose of the victors to explore.

"But what fear'st thou?" cried the Caliph: "dost thou dread a secret blow?
Fear it not; our gallant Moslems no such treacherous dealings know,
Thou may'st quench thy thirst securely; for thou shalt not die before
Thou hast drunk that cup of water:—this reprieve is thine—no more."

Quick the Satrap dashed the goblet down to earth with ready hand,
And the liquid sunk,—for ever lost, amid the burning sand:
"Thou hast said that mine my life is, till the water of that cup
I have drained:—then bid thy servants that spilled water gather up."

For a moment stood the Caliph, as by doubtful passions stirred;
Then exclaimed, "For ever sacred must remain a monarch's word:
Bring forth another cup, and straightway to the noble Persian give:—
Drink, I said before, and perish;—now, I bid thee drink and live!"

DEATH-DOOMED.

Will Carleton.

THEY'RE taking me to the gallows, mother—they mean to hang me high;
They're going to gather round me there, and watch me till I die;
All earthly joy has vanished now, and gone each mortal hope—
They'll draw a cap across my eyes, and round my neck a rope;
The crazy mob will shout and groan—the priest will read a prayer,
The drop will fall beneath my feet and leave me in the air.
They think I murdered Allen Bayne; for so the judge has said,
And they'll hang me to the gallows, mother—hang me till I'm dead!

The grass that grows in yonder meadow, the lambs that skip and play,
The pebbled brook behind the orchard, that laughs upon its way,
The flowers that bloom in the dear old garden, the birds that sing and fly,
Are clear and pure of human blood—and, mother, so am I!
By father's grave on yonder hill—his name without a stain—
I ne'er had malice in my heart, or murdered Allen Bayne!
But twelve good men have found me guilty, for so the judge has said,
And they'll hang me to the gallows, mother—hang me till I'm dead!

The air is fresh and bracing, mother; the sun shines bright and high;
It is a pleasant day to live—a gloomy one to die!
It is a bright and glorious day the joys of earth to grasp—
It is a sad and wretched one to strangle, choke, and gasp!
But let them damp my lofty spirit, or cow me if they can,
They send me like a rogue to death—I'll meet it like a man;
For I never murdered Allen Bayne! but so the judge has said,
And they'll hang me to the gallows, mother—hang me till I'm dead!

Poor little sister 'Bell will weep, and kiss me as I lie!
But kiss her twice and thrice for me, and tell her not to cry;
Tell her to weave a bright, gay garland, and crown me as of yore,
Then plant a lily upon my grave, and think of me no more,
And tell that maiden whose love I sought, that I was faithful yet;
But I must lie in a felon's grave, and she had best forget.
My memory is stained for ever; for so the judge has said.
And they'll hang me to the gallows, mother—hang me till I'm dead!

Lay me not down by my father's side; for once, I mind, he said
No child that stained his spotless name should share his mortal bed.
Old friends would look beyond his grave, to my dishonoured one,
And hide the virtues of the sire behind the recreant son.
And I can fancy, if there my corse its fettered limbs should lay,
His frowning skull and crumbling bones would shrink from me away;
But I swear to God I'm innocent, and never blood have shed!
And they'll hang me to the gallows, mother—hang me till I'm dead!

Lay me in my coffin, mother, as you've sometimes seen me rest;
One of my arms beneath my head, the other on my breast.
Place my Bible upon my heart—nay, mother, do not weep—
And kiss me as in happier days you kissed me when asleep.
And for the rest—for form or rite—but little do I reck;
But cover up that cursèd stain—*the black mark on my neck!*
And pray to God for His great mercy on my devoted head;
For they'll hang me to the gallows, mother—hang me till I'm dead

But hark! I hear a mighty murmur among the jostling crowd!
A cry!—a shout!—a roar of voices!—it echoes long and loud!
There dashes a horseman with foaming steed and tightly-gathered rein;
He sits erect!—he waves his hand!—good heaven! 'tis Allen Bayne!
The lost is found, the dead alive, my safety is achieved!
For he waves his hand again, and shouts, "The prisoner is reprieved!"
Now, mother, praise the God you love, and raise your drooping head;
For the murderous gallows, black and grim, is cheated of its dead!

OH, WHY SHOULD THE SPIRIT OF MORTAL BE PROUD?

William Knox.

(President Lincoln's Favourite Poem.)

OH, why should the spirit of mortal be proud?
Like a swift, fleeing meteor, a fast flying cloud,
A flash of the lightning, a break of the wave,
Man passes from life to his rest in the grave.

The leaves of the oak and the willows shall fade;
Be scatter'd around and together be laid;
And the young and the old, and the low and the high,
Shall moulder to dust, and together shall lie.

The infant a mother attended and loved;
The mother that infant's affection who proved;
The husband that mother and infant who blessed,
Each, all, are away to their dwelling of rest.

The maid on whose cheek, on whose brow, in whose eye,
Shone beauty and pleasure—her triumphs are by;
And the memory of those who loved her and praised,
Are alike from the minds of the living erased.

The hand of the king that the sceptre hath borne;
The brow of the priest that the mitre hath worn;
The eye of the sage and the heart of the brave,
Are hidden and lost in the depth of the grave.

The peasant, whose lot was to sow and to reap;
The herdsman, who climbed with his goats up the steep
The beggar, who wandered in search of his bread,
Have faded away like the grass that we tread.

The saint who enjoyed the communion of heaven,
The sinner who dared to remain unforgiven,
The wise and the foolish, the guilty and just,
Have quietly mingled their bones in the dust.

So the multitude goes like the flowers or the weed
That withers away to let others succeed;
So the multitude comes, even those we behold,
To repeat every tale that has often been told.

For we are the same our fathers have been;
We see the same sights our fathers have seen—
We drink the same stream and view the same sun,
And run the same course our fathers have run.

The thoughts we are thinking our fathers would think;
From the death we are shrinking our fathers would shrink,
To the life we are clinging they also would cling;
But it speeds for us all, like a bird on the wing.

They loved, but the story we cannot unfold;
They scorned, but the heart of the haughty is cold;
They grieved, but no wail from their slumbers will come
They joyed, but the tongue of their gladness is dumb.

They died, ay! they died! and we things that are now,
Who walk on the turf that lies over their brow,
And make in their dwelling a transient abode,
Meet the things that they met on their pilgrimage road.

Yea! hope and despondency, pleasure and pain,
Are mingled together in sunshine and rain;
And the smile and the tear, the song and the dirge,
Still follow each other, like surge upon surge.

'Tis the wink of an eye, 'tis the draught of a breath,
From the blossom of health to the paleness of death,
From the gilded saloon to the bier and the shroud—
Oh, why should the spirit of mortal be proud?

WAITING FOR MOTHER.

Mary D. Brine.

THE old man sits in his easy chair,
Slumbering the moments away,
Dreaming a dream that is all his own,
On this gladsome peaceful day.
His children have gathered from far and near,
His children's children beside,
And merry voices are echoing through
The "Homestead's" halls so wide.

But far away in the years long flown
Grandfather lives again;
And his heart forgets that it ever knew
A shadow of grief and pain.
For he sees his wife as he saw her then—
A matron comely and fair,
With her children gathered around his board,
And never a vacant chair.

Oh! happy this dream of the "Auld Lang Syne,"
Of the years long slipped away!
And the old man's lips have gathered a smile,
And his heart grows young and gay.
But a kiss falls gently upon his brow,
From his daughter's lips so true:
"Dinner is ready; and, Father dear,
We are *only waiting for you!*"

The old man wakes at his daughter's call,
And he looks at the table near.
"There's *one* of us missing, my child," he says.
"We will wait till *Mother* is here."
There are tears in the eyes of the children then,
As they gaze on an empty chair;
For many a lonely year has passed
Since "*Mother*" sat with them there.

But the old man pleads still wistfully:
"We must *wait for Mother*, you know!"
And they let him rest in his old arm-chair
Till the sun at last sinks low.
Then, leaving a smile for the children here,
He turns from the earth away,
And has gone to "Mother," beyond the skies,
With the close of the quiet day.

POOR HUMANITY.

[Beside a skeleton in the Royal College of Surgeons, more than fifty years ago, the following lines were found. Every effort made to discover the author proved fruitless. Even the offer of a reward of 50 guineas did not induce the writer to make himself known. The lines were afterwards published in the London *Morning Chronicle.*]

BEHOLD this ruin! 'Twas a skull
Once of ethereal spirit full.
This narrow cell was life's retreat;
This space was thought's mysterious seat.
What beauteous visions filled this spot
With dreams of pleasure long forgot!
Nor hope, nor joy, nor love, nor fear,
Have left one trace of record here.

Beneath this mouldering canopy
Once shone the bright and busy eye;
But start not at the dismal void!
If social love that eye employed,
If with no lawless fire it gleamed,
But through the dews of kindness beamed,
That eye shall be for ever bright
When sun and stars are sunk in night.

Within this hollow cavern hung
The ready, swift, and tuneful tongue;
If falsehood's honey it disdained,
And, when it could not praise, was chained;
If bold in virtue's cause it spoke,
Yet gentle concord never broke,
The silent tongue shall plead for thee
When time unveils eternity.

Say, did these fingers delve the mine,
Or with the envied ruby shine?
To hew the rock or wear the gem
Can little now avail to them.
But if the page of truth they sought,
Or comfort to the mourner brought,
These hands a richer meed shall claim
Than all that wait on wealth or fame.

Avails it whether bare or shod
These feet the path of duty trod?
If from the bowers of ease they fled,
To seek affliction's humble shed;
If grandeur's guilty bribe they spurned,
And home to virtue's cot returned,
These feet with angel's wings shall rise,
And tread the palace of the skies.

PRE-EXISTENCE OR TRANSMIGRATION.

Wordsworth.

OUR birth is but a sleep and a forgetting:
The Soul that rises with us, our life's Star,
Hath had elsewhere its setting,
And cometh from afar:
Not in entire forgetfulness,
And not in utter nakedness,
But trailing clouds of glory do we come
From God, who is our home:
Heaven lies about us in our infancy!
Shades of the prison-house begin to close
Upon the growing Boy,
But he beholds the light, and whence it flows
He sees it in his joy:
The Youth, who daily farther from the east
Must travel, still is Nature's Priest,
And by the vision splendid
Is on his way attended;
At length the man perceives it die away,
And fade into the light of common day.

A GEM OF GEMS;

OR,

THE BEST VERSES OF THE BEST POETS.

Unappreciated Genius.

Full many a gem, of purest ray serene,
The dark, unfathom'd caves of ocean bear;
Full many a flower is born to blush unseen,
And waste its sweetness on the desert air.
Gray.

Universal Gravitation.

That very law which moulds a tear,
And bids it trickle from its source,
That law preserves the earth a sphere;
And guides the planets in their course.—*Rogers.*

Intellectual Expansion.

For I doubt not through the ages,
One increasing purpose runs,
And the thoughts of men are widened
By the process of the suns.—*Tennyson.*

Harmony of Nature.

All Nature is but art, unknown to thee;
All chance, direction which thou canst not see;
All discord, harmony not understood;
All partial evil, universal good.—*Pope.*

Words.

But words are things, and a small drop of ink,
Falling like dew, upon a thought, produces
That which makes thousands, perhaps millions, think.—*Byron.*

The Pen.

Use the pen! there's magic in it,
Never let it lag behind;
Write thy thought, the pen can win it
From the chaos of the mind.—*Carpenter.*

Writing and Printing.

Blest be that gracious power, who taught mankind
To stamp a lasting image of the mind;
Beasts may convey, and tuneful birds may sing,
Their mutual feelings in the opening spring;
But man alone has skill and power to send
The heart's warm dictates to the distant friend;
'Tis his also to please, instruct, advise,
Ages remote, and nations yet to rise.—*Crabbe.*

The Press.

But mightiest of the mighty means,
On which the arm of progress leans,
Man's noblest mission to advance,
His woes assuage, his weal enhance,
His rights enforce, his wrongs redress—
Mightiest of mighty is the Press.—*Bowring.*

Books.

This, books can do;—nor this alone; they give
New views to life, and teach us how to live;
They soothe the grieved, the stubborn they chastise,
Fools they admonish, and confirm the wise:
Their aid they yield to all; they never shun
The man of sorrow, nor the wretch undone:
Unlike the hard, the selfish and the proud,
They fly not sullen from the supplicant crowd!
Nor tell to various people various things,
But show to subjects what they show to kings.
Crabbe.

Books.

Books show the joys, griefs, hopes, and fears
Of every race and clan;
Books show, by unity of thought,
The brotherhood of man.
'Tis books will cause the flag of peace
Through earth to be unfurled—
Produce "the parliament of man,"
And federate the world.—*Cole.*

Education.

Delightful task! to rear the tender thought,
To teach the young idea how to shoot,
To pour the fresh instruction o'er the mind,
To breathe the enliv'ning spirit, and to fix
The generous purpose in the glowing breast.
Thomson.

Learning.

A little learning is a dangerous thing.
Drink deep, or taste not the Pierian spring.
For shallow draughts intoxicate the brain,
But drinking largely sobers us again.—*Pope.*

Philosophy.

How charming is divine philosophy!
Not harsh and crabbed, as dull fools suppose,
But musical as is Apollo's lute,
And a perpetual feast of nectar'd sweets,
Where no crude surfeit reigns.—*Milton.*

Mind.

My mind to me a kingdom is;
Such perfect joy therein I find,
As far exceeds all earthly bliss
That God or nature hath assign'd.—*Byrd.*

Mind.

Were I so tall to reach the pole,
Or grasp the ocean with my span,
I must be measured by my soul:
The mind's the standard of the man.—*Watts.*

Mental Freedom.

Stone walls do not a prison make,
Nor iron bars a cage;
Minds innocent and quiet, take
That for an hermitage.—*Lovelace.*

Music.

Music!—oh! how faint, how weak,
Language fades before thy spell!
Why should feeling ever speak,
When thou canst breathe her soul so well?
Moore.

Music.

Oh, surely melody from heaven was sent
To cheer the soul, when tired with human strife,
To soothe the wayward heart by sorrow rent,
And soften down the rugged road of life.
Kirke White.

Music.

Music the fiercest grief can charm,
And fate's severest rage disarm,
Music can soften pain to ease,
And make despair and madness please,
Our joys below it can improve,
And antedate the bliss above.—*Pope.*

Music Everywhere.

There's music in the sighing of a reed;
There's music in the gushing of a rill;
There's music in all things, if men had ears;
There, earth is but an echo of the spheres.—*Byron.*

Love.

In peace, Love tunes the shepherd's reed;
In war, he mounts the warrior's steed:
In halls, in gay attire is seen:
In hamlets, dances on the green.
Love rules the court, the camp, the grove,
And men below, and saints above—
For Love is heaven, and heaven is Love.—*Scott.*

Disappointed Love.

Had we never loved so kindly,
Had we never loved so blindly,
Never met or never parted,
We had ne'er been broken-hearted.—*Burns.*

Disappointed Love.

I hold it true, whate'er befall,
I feel it when I sorrow most;
'Tis better to have loved and lost,
Than never to have loved at all.—*Tennyson.*

A Mother's Love.

A mother's love—how sweet the name!
What is a mother's love?
A noble, pure, and tender flame,
Enkindled from above.
To bless a heart of earthly mould,
The warmest love that can't grow cold—
This is a mother's love.—*Montgomery.*

A Mother's Love.

Hast thou sounded the depth of yonder sea,
And counted the sands that under it be?
Hast thou measured the height of heaven above,
Then mayest thou mete out a mother's love.
There is not a grand, inspiring thought,
There is not a truth by wisdom taught,
There is not a feeling pure and high,
That may not be read in a mother's eye.
Emily Taylor.

A Father's Love.

Fathers alone a father's heart can know:
What secret tides of sweet enjoyment flow
When brothers love! But if then hate succeeds,
They wage the war, but 'tis the *father* bleeds.
Young.

Woman.

Oh! woman in our hours of ease,
Uncertain, coy, and hard to please,
And variable as the shade
By the light, quivering aspen made;
When pain and anguish wring the brow,
A ministering angel thou!—*Scott.*

Woman.

And say, without our hopes, without our fears,
Without the home that plighted love endears,
Without the smile from partial beauty won,
Oh! what were man?—a world without a sun.
Campbell.

Woman.

O woman! lovely woman! Nature made thee
To temper man; we had been brutes without you.
Angels are painted fair to look like you:
There's in you all that we believe of heaven
Amazing brightness, purity and truth,
Eternal joy, and everlasting love.—*Otway.*

Woman.

Oh, woman! whose form and whose soul
Are the spell and the light of each path we pursue;
Whether sunned in the tropics, or chilled at the pole,
If woman be there, there is happiness too.
Moore.

Woman's Love.

Alas! the love of woman! it is known
To be a lovely and a fearful thing;
For of all theirs upon that die is thrown,
And if 'tis lost, life hath no more to bring.
Byron.

A Woman's Answer.

Do you know you have asked for the costliest thing
E'er made by the hand above?
A woman's heart and a woman's life,
And a woman's wonderful love?

Woman's Mission.

'Tis thine to curb the passions' madd'ning sway,
And wipe the mourner's bitter tear away;
'Tis thine to soothe, when hope itself has fled,
And cheer with angel smile the sufferer's bed;
To give to earth its charm, to life its zest,
One only task—to bless, and to be blest.—*Graham.*

Marriage.

Though fools spurn Hymen's gentle powers,
We who improve his golden hours,
By sweet experience know
That marriage, rightly understood,
Gives to the tender and the good
A paradise below.—*Cotton.*

Marriage.

Oh! who the exquisite delights can tell,
The joy which mutual confidence imparts?
Or who can paint the charm unspeakable,
Which links in tender bands two faithful hearts.
Mrs. Tighe.

Marriage.

The kindest and the happiest pair
Will find occasion to forbear;
And something, every day they live,
To pity, and perhaps forgive.—*Cowper.*

Wife.

His house she enters, there to be a light,
Shining within, when all without is night;
A guardian-angel o'er his life presiding,
Doubling his pleasure, and his cares dividing.
Rogers.

Wife.

'Tis sweet to hear the watchdog's honest bark
Bay deep-mouth'd welcome as we draw near home;
'Tis sweet to know there is an eye will mark
Our coming, and look brigher when we come.
Byron.

Children.

Yes! there are angels of the earth,
Pure, innocent, and mild,
The angels of our hearts and homes,
Each loved and loving child.—*Carpenter.*

Let the Child Play.

He who checks a child with terror
Stops its play and stills its song,
Not alone commits an error,
But a great and moral wrong.
Give it play, and never fear it;
Active life is no defect.
Never, never break its spirit;
Curb it only to direct.
Would you stop the flowing river,
Thinking it would cease to flow?
Onward it must flow for ever;
Better teach it where to go.

Baby Gone Before.

Ere sin could blight or sorrow fade,
DEATH came with friendly care;
The opening bud to Heaven conveyed,
And bade it blossom there.—*Coleridge.*

The Lost Little One.

We miss her footfall on the floor,
Amidst the nursery din,
Her tip-tap at our bedroom door,
Her bright face peeping in.

The Golden Stair.

Put away the little dresses,
That the darling used to wear,
She will need them on earth never,
She has climb'd the golden stair:
She is with the happy angels,
And I long for her sweet kiss,
Where her little feet are waiting,
In the realm of perfect bliss.

Graves of Children.

There's many an empty cradle,
There's many an empty bed,
There's many a lonesome bosom,
Whose joy and light have fled;
For thick in every graveyard
The little hillocks lie—
And every hillock represents
An angel in the sky.

Bear with Baby.

If we knew the baby fingers
Press'd against the window pane,
Would be cold and stiff to morrow—
Never trouble us again—
Would the bright eyes of our darling
Catch the frown upon our brow?
Would the prints of rosy fingers
Vex us then as they do now?—*K.A.S.*

Meeting Again.

Oh! when a mother meets on high
The BABE she lost in infancy.
Hath she not then, for pains and fears,
The day of woe, the watchful night,
For all her sorrow, all her tears,
An over-payment of delight?—*Southey*.

Home.

Breathes there a man with soul so dead,
Who never to himself hath said,
This is my own, my native land!
Whose heart hath ne'er within him burn'd,
As home his footsteps he hath turn'd,
From wandering on a foreign strand.—*Scott.*

Home.

Man, through all ages of revolving time,
Unchanging man, in every varying clime,
Deems his own land of every land the pride,
Belov'd of heaven o'er all the world beside;
His home, the spot of earth supremely blest,
A dearer, sweeter spot than all the rest.
Montgomery.

Home.

And when from wholesome labour he doth come,
With wishes to be there, and wish'd-for home,
He meets at door the softest human blisses,
His chaste wife's welcome and dear children's kisses.—*Cowley.*

Home, Sweet Home.

Mid pleasures and palaces, though we may roam,
Be it ever so humble, there's no place like home;
A charm from the skies seems to hallow us there,
Which, seek through the world, is ne'er met with elsewhere.
Home, home, sweet home,
There's no place like home.—*Payne.*

God.

Father of ALL; in every age,
In every clime adored.
By saint, by savage, and by sage,
Jehovah, Jove, or Lord!—*Pope.*

God.

O thou Eternal One! whose presence bright
All space doth occupy—all motion guide:
Unchanged through time's all devastating flight;
Thou only God; there is no God beside;
Being above all beings! Holy One!
Whom none can comprehend and none explore,
Who fill'st existence with THYSELF alone,
Embracing all—supporting—ruling o'er—
Being whom we call God—and know no more!
Derzhavin.

God.

I know not what the future hath
Of marvel or surprise,
Assured alone that life and death
His mercy underlies.

I know not where His islands lift
Their fronded palms in air;
I only know I cannot drift
Beyond his love and care.—*Whittier*

God.

The spacious firmament on high,
With all the blue ethereal sky,
And spangled heavens, a shining frame,
Their great original proclaim.—*Addison.*

Heaven.

Beyond these chilling winds and gloomy skies,
Beyond death's cloudy portal,
There is a land where beauty never dies,
And love becomes immortal.

Heaven.

Eye hath not seen it, my gentle boy!
Ear hath not heard its deep song of joy;
Dreams cannot picture a world so fair,
Sorrow and death may not enter there.—*Hemans.*

Heaven.

Go, wing thy flight from star to star,
From world to luminous world, as far
As the universe spreads its flaming wall;
Take all the pleasures of all the spheres,
And multiply each through endless years,
One minute of heaven is worth them all!
Moore.

Death.

There is no death! What seems so is transition;
This life of mortal breath
Is but a suburb of the life Elysian,
Whose portal we call death.—*Longfellow.*

A Spirit Leaving the Body.

I hear a VOICE you cannot hear,
Which says I must not stay;
I see a hand you cannot see,
Which beckons me away.—*Tickell.*

Immortality.

Life is real! Life is earnest!
And the grave is not its goal;
Dust thou art, to dust returnest,
Was not spoken of the soul.

Immortality.

It must be so—Plato, thou reasonest well—
Else whence this pleasing hope, this fond desire,
This longing after IMMORTALITY?
Or whence this secret dread and inward horror
Of falling into naught? Why shrinks the soul
Back on herself, and startles at destruction?
'Tis the Divinity that stirs within us;
'Tis Heaven itself that points out an hereafter,
And intimates eternity to man.—*Addison.*

Immortality.

The soul, secured in her existence, smiles
At the drawn dagger, and defies its point.—
The stars shall fade away, the sun himself
Grow dim with age, and nature sink in years;
But thou shalt flourish in immortal youth,
Unhurt amidst the war of elements,
The wreck of matter, and the crash of worlds.
Addison.

Hope.

Hope leads the child to plant the flower, the man to sow the seed,
Nor leaves fulfilment to her hour, but prompts again to deed,
And ere upon the old man's dust the grass is seen to wave,
We look through falling tears to trust hope's sunshine on the grave.—*Sarah F. Adams.*

Hope of Immortality.

Unfading Hope! when life's last embers burn,
When soul to soul, and dust to dust return!
Heaven to thy charge resigns the awful hour!
Oh! then, thy kingdom comes! Immortal Power!
Cease, every joy, to glimmer on my mind,
But leave—oh! leave the light of HOPE behind!
What thou my winged hours of bliss have been,
Like angel-visits, few and far between.—*Campbell.*

Eternal Hope.

Eternal Hope! when yonder spheres sublime
Pealed their first notes to sound the march of Time,
Thy joyous youth began—but not to fade—
When all the sister planets have decayed;
When wrapt in fire the realms of ether glow,
And Heaven's last thunder shakes the world below.
Thou, undismayed, shalt o'er the ruins smile,
And light thy torch at Nature's funeral pile.
Campbell.

Religion.

My religion is Love—'tis the noblest and purest;
And my temple the Universe—widest and surest.
I worship my God, through His works, which are fair,
And the joy of my heart is perpetual prayer.
John Critchely Prince.

Prayer.

Prayer is the soul's sincere desire,
Uttered or unexpressed,
The motion of a hidden fire
That trembles in the breast.
Montgomery.

Prayer.

He prayeth best who loveth best
All things both great and small;
For the dear God who loveth us,
He made and loveth all.—*Coleridge*

Conscience.

Yet still there whispers the small voice within,
Heard through Gain's silence, and o'er Glory's din.
Whatever creed be taught or land be trod,
Man's conscience is the oracle of God!—*Byron.*

Creed.

Shall I ask the brave soldier who fights by my side
In the cause of mankind, if our creeds agree?
Shall I give up the friend I have valued and tried,
If he kneel not before the same altar with me?
Moore.

Deeds not Creeds.

Perplex'd in FAITH, but pure in deeds,
At last he beat his music out,
There lives more faith in honest doubt,
Believe me, than in half the creeds.—*Tennyson.*

Sorrowing Remembrance.

Still o'er these scenes my memory wakes
And fondly broods with miser care.
Time but th' impression deeper makes,
As streams their channels deeper wear!—*Burns.*

The Common Lot.

Once in the flight of ages past,
There liv'd a man:—and who was he?
Mortal! howe'er thy lot be cast,
That man resembled thee.—*Montgomery.*

Suffering the Common Lot.

To each his sufferings: all are men
Condemn'd alike to groan;
The tender for another's pain,
The unfeeling for his own.—*Gray.*

Death, the Common Lot.

There is no flock, however watched and tended,
But one dead lamb is there!
There is no fireside, howso'er defended,
But has one vacant chair!—*Longfellow.*

The Village Preacher.

At church, with meek and unaffected grace,
His looks adorned the venerable place;
Truth from his lips prevail'd with double sway,
And fools, who came to scoff, remained to pray.
Goldsmith.

The Village Schoolmaster.

His words of learned length and thundering sound
Amaz'd the gazing rustics rang'd around!
And still they gaz'd and still the wonder grew,
How one small head could carry all he knew.
Goldsmith.

A Loving Wish.

Bright be the future which lieth before thee,
Loving and loved may'st thou go on thy way;
God in his mercy watch tenderly o'er thee,
Guarding thee ever by night and by day.

A Wish for Both Worlds.

May every joy be yours on earth,
Your every day be free from care;
Where all desires are satisfied,
May you become immortal there.

In Loving Remembrance.

Bright be the place of thy soul!
No lovelier spirit than thine
E'er burst from its mortal control,
In the orbs of the blessed to shine.
On earth thou wert all but divine,
As thy soul shall immortally be;
And our sorrow may cease to repine,
When we know that thy God is with thee.
Byron on Kirke White.

Bacon and Cromwell.

If parts allure thee, think how BACON shin'd,
The wisest, brightest, meanest of mankind!
Or, ravish'd with the whistling of a name,
See Cromwell, damn'd to everlasting fame!—*Pope.*

Burke.

Here lies our good Edmund, whose genius was such,
We scarcely can praise it, or blame it, too much;
Who, born for the Universe, narrow'd his mind,
And to party gave up what was meant for mankind.
Goldsmith.

Charles the Second.

Here lies our sovereign lord the KING,
Whose word no man relies on;
He never says a foolish thing,
Nor ever does a wise one.—*Earl of Rochester.*

The Ruling Passion.

Search then the ruling passion; there alone
The wild are constant, and the cunning known,
The fool consistent, and the false sincere!
Priests, princes, women—no dissemblers here.

Bashfulness.

I pity bashful men, who feel the pain
Of fancied scorn, and undeserv'd disdain,
And bear the marks upon a blushing face,
Of needless shame, and self-impos'd disgrace.
Cowper.

Industry.

Ho, all who labour, all who strive!
Ye wield a lofty power!
Do with your might, do with your strength,
Fill every golden hour!
The glorious privilege to do
Is man's most noble dower,
Oh, to your birthright and yourselves,
To your own souls be true!
A weary, wretched life is theirs
Who have no work to do.—*Orne.*

Industry.

In works of labour, or of skill,
I would be busy too,
For Satan finds some mischief still
For idle hands to do.—*Watts.*

Industry.

Each morning sees some task begun,
Each evening sees its close;
Something attempted, something done,
Has earned a night's repose.—*Longfellow.*

Labour is Rest.

Labour is rest—from the sorrows that greet us,
Rest from all petty vexations that meet us,
Rest from the sin promptings that ever entreat us;
Rest from world-sirens that lure us to ill.
Work—and pure slumbers shall wait on the pillow,
Work—thou shalt ride over Care's coming billow;
Lie not down wearied 'neath Woe's weeping willow!
Work with a stout heart and resolute will!
Work for some good—be it ever so slowly;
Cherish some flower, be it ever so lowly;
Labour!—all labour is noble and holy!
Let thy great deeds be thy prayer to God.
Frances Osgood.

Perseverance.

Lives of great men all remind us
We can make our lives sublime;
And departing, leave behind us
Footprints on the sands of time.
Longfellow.

Perseverance.

Not enjoyment, and not sorrow,
Is our destined end or way;
But to act, that each to-morrow
Finds us farther than to-day.

Let us, then, be up and doing,
With a heart for any fate;
Still achieving, still pursuing,
Learn to labour and to wait.
Longfellow.

Perseverance.

Never give up! it is wiser and better
Always to hope, than once to despair:
Fling off the load of doubt's cankering fetter,
And break the dark spell of tyrannical care.

Never give up! If adversity presses,
Providence wisely has mingled the cup;
And the best counsel, in all your distresses,
Is the stout watchword of, "Never give up."
Tupper.

Persevere.

Drive the nail aright, boys—
Hit it on the head;
Strike with all your might, boys,
While the iron's red.

Duty.

One by one thy duties wait thee,
Let thy whole strength go to each;
Let not future dreams elate thee,
Learn thou first what those can teach.
Miss Procter.

Duty.

Onward, onward, let us press,
Through the path of duty;
Virtue is true happiness,
Excellence true beauty.
Minds are of celestial birth;
Let us make a heaven of earth.
Montgomery.

Duty.

What might be done if men were wise—
What glorious deeds, my suffering brother,
Would they unite
In love and right,
And cease their scorn for one another?—*Mackay.*

Duty.

This world is full of beauty
As other worlds above;
And, if we did our duty,
It might be full of love.—*Massey.*

Little Things.

There is many a gem in the path of life,
Which we pass in our idle pleasure,
That is richer far than a jewelled crown,
Or the miser's hoarded treasure;
It may be the love of a little child,
Or a mother's prayer to heaven,
Or only a beggar's grateful thanks,
For a cup of water given.

Little Things.

Since trifles make the sum of human things
And half our misery from foibles springs—
Since life's best joys consist in peace and ease,
And few can save or serve, but all can please—
Oh! let the ungentle spirit learn from hence
A small unkindness is a great offence:
Large bounties to bestow we wish in vain,
But all may shun the guilt of giving pain.
Dr. Johnson.

Little Things.

We cannot all be heroes,
And thrill a hemisphere
With some great daring venture,
Some deed that mocks at fear;
But we can fill a lifetime
With kindly acts and true,
There's always noble service
For noble souls to do.—*C. A. Mason.*

Good Temper.

There's not a cheaper thing on earth,
Nor yet one half so dear;
'Tis worth more than distinguish'd birth,
Or thousands gain a year;
Good temper!—'tis the choicest gift
That woman homeward brings,
And can the poorest peasant lift
To bliss unknown to kings.
Charles Swain.

The Happy Mind.

Out upon the calf, I say,
Who turns his grumbling head away,
And quarrels with his feed of hay,
Because it is not clover,
Give to me the happy mind,
That will ever seek and find
Something fair and something kind,
All the wide world over.—*Eliza Cook.*

Contentment.

Look always on the sunny side,
'Twill make us happier far,
Why should we try to find the cloud,
When brightly shines the star!
Some people only see the world,
As through a smoky glass,
They go half way to meet the woe,
And let the sunshine pass.

Peace of Mind.

And the night shall be filled with music,
And the CARES that infest the day
Shall fold their tents like the Arabs,
And as silently steal away.—*Longfellow.*

Mercy.

The quality of mercy is not strain'd,
It droppeth as the gentle dew from heaven
Upon the place beneath; it is twice blessed—
It blesseth him that gives, and him that takes.
Shakespere.

Mercy.

Teach me to feel another's woe,
To hide the fault I see;
That mercy I to others show,
That mercy show to me.—*Pope.*

Pity.

No flocks that range the valley free
To slaughter I condemn;
Taught by that Power that pities me,
I learn to pity them.—*Goldsmith.*

Charity.

Then gently scan your brother man,
Still gentler sister woman;
Though they may gang a kennin' wrang,
To step aside is human.—*Burns.*

Charity.

If we knew the cares and crosses,
Crowded round our neighbour's way,
If we knew the little losses,
Sorely grievous day by day,
Would we then so often chide him
For the lack of thrift and gain,
Leaving on his heart a shadow,
Leaving on our lives a stain.—*Mrs. Charles.*

Charity.

Thy neighbour?—it is him whom thou
Hast power to aid and bless,
Whose aching heart and burning brow
Thy soothing hand may press.

Kindness.

There's no dearth of kindness
In this world of ours;
Only in our blindness
We gather thorns for flowers!
Oh, cherish God's best giving,
Falling from above;
Life were not worth living,
Were it not for love.—*Massey.*

Speak Gently.

Speak gently! it is better far
To rule by love than fear;
Speak gently! let not harsh words mar
The good we might do here.—*Bates.*

Kindness.

Ah! be kind—life hath no secret
For our happiness like this;
Kindly hearts are seldom sad ones,
Blessing ever bringeth bliss.—*Hobbins.*

Humanity.

Then let us learn to help each other,
Hoping unto the end;
Who sees in every man a brother,
Shall find in each a friend.

Humanity.

I would not have a slave to till my ground,
To carry me, to fan me while I sleep,
And tremble when I wake, for all the wealth
That sinews bought and sold have ever earn'd.
Cowper

Humanity.

I would not enter on my list of friends,
Though grac'd with polish'd manners and fine sense
(Yet wanting sensibility), the man,
Who needlessly sets foot upon a worm.—*Cowper.*

Human Sympathy.

No radiant pearl which crested fortune wears,
No gem that twinkling hangs from beauty's ears,
Not the bright stars which night's blue arch adorn,
Nor rising sun that gilds the vernal morn,
Shine with such lustre as the tear that flows
Down Virtue's manly cheek for other's woes.
Darwin.

The True Fatherland.

Where'er a single slave doth pine,
Where'er one man may help another—
Thank God for such a birthright, brother—
That spot of earth is thine and mine!
There is the true man's birthplace grand,
His is a worldwide fatherland!—*Lowell.*

War.

One to destroy is MURDER, by the law,
And gibbets keep the lifted hand in awe;
To murder thousands takes a specious name—
War's glorious art—and gives immortal fame.
Young.

The Miseries of War.

I hate that drum's discordant sound,
Parading round, and round, and round;
To thoughtless youth it pleasure yields,
And lures from cities and from fields;
To me, it talks of ravaged plains,
And burning towns, and ruin'd swains,
And mangled limbs, and dying groans,
And widow's tears, and orphan's moans,
And all that misery's hand bestows,
To fill the catalogue of human woes.—*John Scott*

The Sinfulness of War.

Ez fer war, I call it murder—
There you hev it plain an' flat;
I don't want to go no furder
Than my Testyment fer that;
Ef you take a sword an' dror it,
An' go stick a feller thru,
Guv'ment ain't to answer for it,
God 'll send the bill to you.—*Lowell.*

War.

Were half the power that fills the world with terror,
Were half the wealth bestow'd on camps and courts,
Given to redeem the human mind from error,
There were no need of arsenals nor forts.
Longfellow

Freedom Without War.

We want no flag—no flaunting rag—
In Liberty's cause to fight;
We want no blaze of murderous guns
To struggle for the right:
Our spears and swords are printed words—
The mind's our battle plain.
We've won our victories thus before,
And so we shall again.—*Mackay.*

Duelling.

Am I to set my life upon a throw
Because a bear is rude and surly?—No;
A moral, sensible, and well-bred man
Will not affront me, and no other can.—*Cowper.*

Equality.

All men are equal in their birth,
Heirs of the earth and skies;
All men are equal when that earth
Fades from their dying eyes.

All Men Equal.

Why do the proud insult the poor,
And boast the large estates they have?
How vain are riches to secure
Their haughty owners from the grave!
Why doth he treat the poor with scorn,
Made of the self-same clay;
And boast as though his flesh was born
Of better dust than they?

Mental Slaves.

They are slaves who will not choose
Hatred, scoffing and abuse,
Rather than in silence shrink
From the truth they needs must think;
They are slaves who dare not be
In the right with two or three.

Moral Courage.

He who seeks the truth and trembles
At the dangers he must brave
Is not fit to be a freeman;
He at best is but a slave.

Speak! no matter what betide thee,
Let them strike but make them hear;
Be thou like the noble Jesus,
Scorn the threat that bids thee fear.

Face thine enemies, accusers;
Scorn the prison, rack, or rod!
And if thou hast truth to utter,
Speak, and leave the rest to God!—*Gallagher*

The Reformer.

I look'd: aside the dust cloud roll'd—
The waster seem'd the builder too
Up-springing from the ruin'd Old
I saw the New.
'Twas but the ruin of the bad—
The wasting of the wrong and ill;
Whate'er of good the old time had
Was living still.—*Whittier.*

Truth and Error.

Truth crushed to earth shall rise again:
The eternal years of God are hers;
But Error, wounded, writhes with pain,
And dies amongst his worshippers.—*Bryant.*

Goodness only is Nobility.

Howe'er it be, it seems to me
'Tis only noble to be good;
Kind hearts are more than coronets,
And simple faith than Norman blood.
Tennyson.

Goodness only is Nobility.

Ye proud, ye selfish, ye severe,
How vain your mask of state;
The good alone have joy sincere,
The good alone are great.

The Noblest Works of God.

Honour and shame from no condition rise,
Act well your part, there all the honour lies.
Worth makes the man, the want of it the fellow;
The rest is all but leather or prunella!
A wit's a feather, and a chief a rod!
An honest man's the noblest work of God!—*Pope.*

True Nobility.

I ask not for his lineage,
I ask not for his name;
If manliness be in his heart,
He noble birth may claim.

The palace or the hovel
Where first his life began,
I seek not of; but answer this—
"Is he an honest man?
Robert Nicoll.

True Nobility.

What is noble? 'Tis the finer
Portion of our mind and heart
Linked to something still diviner
Than mere language can impart!

E'en though scorn's malignant glances
Prove him poorest of his clan,
He's the Noble who advances
Freedom and the Cause of Man.—*Swain.*

True Nobility.

In that all glorious land beyond
The grave's dark wilderness,
Where titles, riches, sounding names,
Sink into nothingness,
The wretched beggar's tatter'd garb,
By honest virtue worn,
Shall laugh the crime-stain'd diadems
Of guilty kings to scorn.

True Heroism.

Let others tell of battles fought
On bloody, ghastly fields,
Where honour greets the man who wins,
And death the man who yields;
But I will speak of him who fights
And vanquishes his sins,
Who struggles on through weary years
Against himself, and wins.
He may not wear a hero's crown,
Or fill a hero's grave;
But truth will place his name among
The bravest of the brave.

How to Live.

We live in *deeds*, not years; in *thoughts*, not breaths;
In feelings, not in figures on a dial.
We should count time by *heart-throbs*. He most lives
Who thinks most—feels the noblest—acts the best.
Bailey.

Live to some Purpose.

Seize, then, the minutes as they pass;
The woof of life is thought!
Warm up the colours! let them glow
With fire of fancy fraught.
Live to some purpose; make thy life
A gift of use to thee:
A joy, a good, a golden hope,
A heavenly argosy.

Good Advice to All.

Think truly, and thy thoughts
Shall the world's famine feed;
Speak truly, and each word of thine
Shall be a fruitful seed;
Live truly, and thy life shall be
A great and noble creed.—*Bonar.*

ADDITIONAL POEMS

TO BE

CLASSIFIED IN A LATER EDITION.

BABY.

George Macdonald.

WHERE did you come from, baby dear?
Out of the everywhere into here.

Where did you get those eyes so blue?
Out of the sky as I came through.

What makes the light in them sparkle and
spin?
Some of the starry spikes left in.

Where did you get that little tear?
I found it waiting when I got here.

What makes your forehead so smooth and
high?
A soft hand stroked it as I went by.

What makes your cheek like a warm white
rose?
I saw something better than any one
knows.

Whence that three-cornered smile of bliss?
Three angels gave me at once a kiss.

Where did you get this pearly ear?
God spoke, and it came out to hear.

Where did you get those arms and hands?
Love made itself into bonds and bands.

Feet, whence did you come, you darling
things?
From the same box as the cherubs' wings.

How did they all just come to be you?
God thought about me, and so I grew.

But how did you come to us, you dear?
God thought about you, and so I am here.

THE COMING MAN.

A PAIR of very chubby legs,
Encased in scarlet hose;
A pair of stubby little boots
With rather doubtful toes
A little kilt, a little coat,
Cut as a mother can—
And lo! before us strides, in state,
The future "coming man."

His eyes perchance will read the stars,
And search their unknown ways;
Perchance the human heart and soul
Will open to their gaze;
Perchance their keen and flashing glance
May be a nation's light—
Those eyes that now are wistful bent
On some "big fellow's" kite.

That brow, where mighty thoughts will
dwell
In solemn secret state,
Where fierce Ambition's restless strength
Shall war with future fate;
Where Science from now hidden caves
New treasures will outpour—
'Tis knit now with a troubled doubt:
Are two, or three, pence more?

Those lips—that, in the coming years,
Will plead, or pray or teach,
Whose whispered words, on lightning
flash,
From world to world may reach;
That, sternly grave, may speak command,
Or, smiling, win control—
Are coaxing now for gingerbread
With all a baby's soul!

Those hands—those little busy hands—
So sticky, small, and brown;
Those hands, whose only mission seems
To tear all order down;
Who knows what hidden strength may lie
Within their chubby grasp,
Though now 'tis but a toffy-stick
In sturdy hold they clasp.

Ah, blessings on those little hands,
Whose work is not yet done!
And blessings on those little feet,
Whose race is yet unrun!
And blessings on the little brain
That has not learned to plan!
Whate'er the future holds in store,
God bless "the coming man!"

THE PATTER OF LITTLE FEET.

Watson.

Over my head, in the morning early,
I heard the patter of little feet,
Rising above the hurly-burly
Out in the fast-awakening street.
I like my nap in the morning early—
That drowsy, sleeping waking time—
And am apt to give way to a touch of the surly
With one who breaks on its soothing rhyme.

And so this morn when I heard the clatter,
I turned uneasily in my bed,
And bothered my brain to guess the matter
With the little ones pattering over my head.
My nap was gone, and in humour sulky
I stretched a loud and imperious yawn,
And then, with a word both big and bulky,
I blessed the hour those babes were born.

With a knitted brow and a hasty toilet,
I made up my mind as I mounted the stairs
Whatever the fun, I would quickly spoil it
By coming upon them unawares.
I never had seen my top-floor neighbours;
This only I knew that the tidy house,
Save and except for those infantile labours,
Was silent and still as a baby mouse.

I knocked at the door, and a moment waited;
The noise was hushed to a whispered word;
The patter of little feet abated,
And a tiny hand on the knob I heard.
The door, with a laboured opening, started,
And full in its light a vision appeared,
That carried my heart to the days departed,
And the one to whom it was ever endeared.

Oh, vision of life in the darkened palace
Where I have enshrined the one of my love!
What vestige remained of the wrath and the malice
I threatened to wreak on the noise above?
What memoried thought is the one I am meeting?
What hands are they stretched as I entered the door?
"Are you my papa?" was the baby-like greeting;
"Are you my papa, come home from the war?"

"No, darling," I said, with a choking emotion,
"I am not your papa, come home from the war;
I am only a waif on the fathomless ocean,
With no one to love me the weary world o'er."
"With no one to love you?" the baby replies;
"I will love you myself—you shall be my papa."
And I caught the sweet child with the wondering eyes
Up close to my breast where the memories are.

Oh, where was my heart as I lay in bed dozing,
And the noise overhead could not quicken its beat?
The chambers of memory surely were closing
When no entrance was found for those dear little feet;
For had I the riches we read of in story,
I would give up the whole to sweep away years—
To bring back the pleasure, the wealth, and the glory,
The patter of dear little feet to my ears.

THE TENEMENT HOUSE.

Sarah T. Bolton.

I WENDED my way through frost and snow
One winter's night to a tenement row;
The place seemed under the ban and blight
Of a ghastly spell that winter's night;
Unearthly footsteps seemed to fall
In the dismal darkness down the hall,
Unearthly voices deep and low
Seemed to whisper a tale of woe,
From reeking angle and rotten stair,
As through the foul and fettered air
I groped my way to a certain room, or rather a den,
Such as some wealthy or prosperous men
Build and rent to the homeless poor.

The door was ajar, within all dark,
Never an ember, never a spark
Glowed or glimmered athwart the gloom
That hung like a pall in that wretched room.
But I heard the patter of children's feet,
And the sound of voices sad and sweet,
And one—he was only three years old—
Said, "Sissy, 'at makes mamma so told?
P'ease 'et me 'ak 'er," the sweet voice pled;
"I'es so 'undery, I 'ants some b'ed—
Only ze littless pease 'll do—
And Donny 'ill give a bit to zoo."
"Hush, Johnny, hush," the sister said,
"There is not a single crust of bread—
Don't wake poor mamma; she's sick, you know,
So sick and weak that she cannot sew.
Don't you remember how she cried,
When she bade me put the work aside,
And how she blessed us when she said:
'The Father in heaven will give us bread'?
All day long through the snow and sleet,
I wander up and down the street,
And Johnny, I held my freezing hand
To crowds of ladies rich and grand,
But they didn't hear me when I said:
'Please give me a penny to buy some bread.'

One beautiful lady turned and smiled,
But she only said, 'Don't touch me, child.'
In their beautiful clothes they all passed by,
And I was so cold, but I did not cry.
Oh, Johnny, I never begged before,
But I went to-day from door to door,
Till my very heart was faint and weak,
And I shivered so I could hardly speak,
But when I remembered what mamma said,
That the Father in heaven would give us bread,
I quite forgot the shame and pain,
And went on asking, but asking in vain.
But I scarce could move my frozen feet;
And when they lighted the lamps in the street,
I came away through the fog and mire,
With nothing to eat or make a fire,
But as I was passing Dennie's shop,
Some one called out—'Stop, Kattie, stop!'
And out came little Sammy Dole,
And filled my basket with wood and coal.
So now we shall have a fire, you see,
And oh, how nice and warm it shall be;
And, Johnny, if you'll be still and good,
I'll tell you 'Little Red Riding Hood.'"
"No, no, I'es hundry," the wee one said;
"Tan't you dive me a tum of bread?
P'ease dive me sum, I sink yoo tood,
And Donny 'll do to seep and be good."
"There isn't a crumb of bread; hush, don't cry,
Soon in the morning, Sissy will try
To get poor mamma a bit of meat
And some nice white bread for Johnny to eat."
By this time, her little cold blue hands
Had gathered some half-charred brands
And lighted a fire. Surely the light
Never revealed a sadder sight
Than greeted my eyes that winter night:
Walls broken and damp, a window bare,
A rickety table, a bottomless chair,
A floor discoloured with soil and stain,
Snow driving through a missing pane;
Wee, womanly Kattie, scarce nine years old,
Pinched and shrunken with hunger and cold,
Sweet baby Johnny, with dimpled feet,
Sobbing, crying for something to eat;
A tattered bed, where the eye could trace
A human form with a thin white face—
A thin white face that had once been fair,
Framed in tangles of bright brown hair;
The sad eyes closed, the lips apart,
Pale hands crossed on a silent heart.
Softly Kattie approached it now
And pressed a kiss on the marble brow;
Then with a sudden cry, she said—
"Johnny, oh, Johnny, mamma is dead!
Speak to me, mamma—one word——" she cried,
"Oh, speak to Kattie!"—no voice replied,
But Johnny crept to the pulseless breast,
Where his golden head was wont to rest,
And nestling close to the icy form,
Said, "I tan teep sweet mamma 'arm."
But the mother, out-worn with trouble and strife,
With the sad hard toil in the battle of life,
Had silently gone to the beautiful shore,
Where the rich man has need of his gold never more.

THE CHILDREN.

(Ascribed to Charles Dickens.)

When the lessons and tasks are all ended,
And the school for the day is dismissed,
And the little ones gather around me
To bid me "good-night," and be kissed,
Oh, the little white arms that encircle
My neck in a tender embrace;
Oh, the smiles that are halos of heaven,
Shedding sunshine and joy on my face.

And when they are gone I sit dreaming
Of my childhood too lovely to last;
Of love that my heart will remember,
While it wakes to the pulse of the past,
Ere the world and its wickedness made me
A partner of sorrow and sin;
When the glory of God was about me,
And the glory of gladness within.

Oh, my heart grows as weak as a woman's,
And the fountains of feeling will flow,
When I think of the paths steep and stony
Where the feet of the dear ones must go;
Of the mountains of sin hanging o'er them,
Of the tempests of fate blowing wild;
Oh, there's nothing on earth half so holy
As the innocent heart of a child.

They are idols of hearts and of households;
They are angels of God in disguise;
His sunlight still sleeps in their tresses;
His glory still gleams in their eyes.
Oh, those truants from home and from heaven,
They have made me more manly and mild;
And I know now how Jesus could liken
The Kingdom of God to a child.

I ask not a life for the dear ones
All radiant as others have done;
But that life may have just enough shadow
To temper the glare of the sun.
I would pray God to guard them from evil,
But my prayer would bound back to myself;
Oh, a seraph may pray for a sinner,
But a sinner must pray for himself.

The twig is so easily bended,
I have banished the rule and the rod;
I have taught them the goodness of knowledge,
They have taught me the goodness of God.
My heart is a dungeon of darkness
When I shut them from breaking a rule;
My frown is sufficient correction;
My love is the law of the school.

I shall leave the old house in the autumn,
To traverse its threshold no more;
Ah! how I shall sigh for the dear ones
That mustered each morn at the door!
I shall miss the "good-nights" and the kisses,
And the gush of their innocent glee,
The group on the green, and the flowers
That are brought every morning to me.

I shall miss them at morn and at evening,
Their songs in the school and the street;
I shall miss the low hum of their voices,
And the tramp of their delicate feet.
When the lessons and tasks are all ended,
And Death says: "The school is dismissed,"
May the little ones gather around me,
To bid me "good-night," and be kissed

LET THEM LAUGH AND PLAY.

E. T.

Parents, when you hear your children
Laugh and shout in childish glee,
Do not let the noise annoy you,
Even though you harassed be;
There are hours in every life-time
When we feel confused I know,
By the hurry and the worry
Of Life's tangling ways below!

Such times, hearts are vainly longing
For a calm and quiet hour,
Then disturbances from children
Come with strangely vexing power.
Oh! subdue that angry feeling,
Let no word their joys dispel,
But be glad you hear their voices
And are sure that they are well.

I have seen the eyes of parents
Wild with tears they could not shed,
Bending in distracting sorrow
O'er a darling's suffering bed;
Oh! could they but hear such laughter
From the lips so pale with pain,
They had thanked God for the token
That their child was well again!

I have heard the broken heart-sighs
Bursting from a mother's breast,
As she neared the green enclosure
Where her little children rest!
Silent was her lofty mansion,
Boyish shouts no more were there,
Not a laugh or kiss awakened
Her lone heart from deep despair!

Once, she told me, that their noises
Almost crazed her aching head,
While she shadowed every frolic
By the hushing words she said;
"Now," she cried, "could I but hear them
Bounding round in merry glee,
Could their voices break this stillness,
What a mercy it would be!"

Mothers, let your children frolic;
Let them run and jump and play;
Bear their noises, do not check them,
In a stern and angry way:
Oh! thank God, that in the hurry
Of Life's work, from wood and dell,
Cot and palace, come sweet noises,
Telling that each child is well.

DORKINS' NIGHT.

Bobby Newcomb.

The theatre was full, it was Dorkins' night,
That is Dorkins was going to appear
At night in a favourite comedy part,
For he was comedian here.
Funny? why, he'd make you laugh
Till the tears ran down your cheeks like rain,
And as long as Dorkins was on the stage
You'd try to stop laughing in vain.
A family? yes, he'd a family,
And he loved them as dear as life,
And you'd scarcely find a happier lot
Than Dorkins' children and wife,
And you'd scarcely find a happier lot
Than Dorkins' children and wife.

There came one night, and I was in front,
And Dorkins was going to play
A character new to himself and the stage
That he'd trod for so many a day.
By eight the theatre was perfectly crammed,
All awaiting a pleasant surprise,
For they knew they would laugh
Till their sides would ache,
And they longed for the curtain to rise.
The play soon began;
Each neck was stretched forth,
And eagerly watched each eye
For Dorkins to make his "first entrance,'
And then to give him a cheerful "Hi, hi!"

He soon appeared amid loud applause,
But something was wrong you could see,
"Dorkins is playing quite badly to night,"
The people said sitting round me.
A hiss? yes, it was. I saw Dorkins start
As though stung by a serpent's fang;
Then he'd cast a beseeching glance all around,
And his head on his breast would hang.
He's drunk, and really I thought so myself.
For to me it was awful at times
To see how he'd struggle along with his part,
And continually stick in his lines.

The footlights at last he approached very slow
And "Ladies and Gentlemen," said,
"If I cannot please you to-night,
The fault's not the heart, but the head.

There's many a night I've made you all laugh
When I could scarcely well stand,
And every effort was pain to me then,
Yes, if even I raised but my hand.
You hiss me to-night,
And think that I'm drunk
(From his heart came a sob and a moan);
I'll tell you the reason—
I know you won't laugh—
I've a little one dying at home."

THE SKATERS.

Watson.

I STOOD on the frozen river,
Watching the skaters go by;
They were laughing and shouting merrily,
Under the cold grey sky;
Joyfully greeting the calls of a friend,
Heartily meeting the jibes they may send,
Kissing the lips of the loved ones that stay,
Missing the lips of the loved ones away.

There was one in the midst of the skaters,
A beautiful boy of ten,
With a dreamy, dark-eyed beauty,
Who flitted among the men;
Laughingly winning his way along,
Scarcely beginning to feel himself strong,
Stumbling and catching his step from a fall,
Tumbling and rolling about like a ball.

There was one in the crowd of watchers
Who watched the boy in his play,
Whose eye was ever upon him
Whenever he wandered away;
Smilingly gazing at each new start,
Silently praising the child in her heart,
Willing to follow the steps of her boy,
Filling her soul with his frolicsome joy.

I stood in the midst of the skaters,
And looked at it all as a dream;
But my heart was suddenly wakened
With a single death-like scream;
Fearfully filling the chill winter air,
Instantly stilling the song that was there,
Crushing the light from a thousand of eyes,
Hushing in terror a thousand of sighs.

Where is the dark-eyed boy?
And the ever-watching mother?
A shrieking woman clings to her waist,
And her hands are held by another;
Terribly standing, in accents wild,
Idly demanding her beautiful child,
Staring with eyes in a fire-like glow,
Tearing the lace from her bosom of snow.

There is running to and fro,
And the talking of many men;
But an hour goes by before they find
The beautiful boy of ten;
Quietly raising him under their breath,
Earnestly praising his beauty in death,
Putting his limbs in a natural way,
Shutting his eyes from the light of the day.

But the mother has broken her guard
And lies on the breast of her child;
She is kissing the pallid, oozing lips
That the waters have defiled;
Gloomily pressing the baby-like corse,
Fondly caressing, and mourning her loss,
Trying to waken the voice of the dead,
Crying to God for the soul that is fled.

She has raised the babe in her arms,
Rejecting all offer of aid;
His arm falls over her shoulder,
And his head on her bosom is laid;
Wearily bearing her burden of death,
Tenderly caring as though he had breath,
Creeping along with a staggering pace,
Weeping, and kissing the little pale face.

I stand on the frozen river,
But the skaters no longer go by;
They are gathered in groups at the landings,
Under the cold grey sky;
Woefully talking of what they had seen,
Steadily walking where late they had been,
Running with terror at every sound,
Shunning the spot where the boy was drowned.

THE REAPER AND THE FLOWERS.

Longfellow.

There is a Reaper, whose name is Death,
And, with his sickle keen,
He reaps the bearded grain at a breath,
And the flowers that grow between.

"Shall I have nought that is fair?" saith he;
"Have nought but the bearded grain?
Though the breath of these flowers is sweet to me,
I will give them all back again."

He gazed at the flowers with tearful eyes,
He kissed their drooping leaves;
It was for the Lord of Paradise
He bound them in his sheaves.

"My Lord has need of these flowerets gay,"
The Reaper said, and smiled;
"Dear tokens of the earth are they,
Where he was once a child.

"They shall all bloom in fields of light,
Transplanted by my care,
And saints, upon their garments white,
These sacred blossoms wear."

And the mother gave, in tears and pain,
The flowers she most did love;
She knew she should find them all again
In the fields of light above.

O, not in cruelty, not in wrath,
The Reaper came that day;
'Twas an angel visited the green earth,
And took the flowers away.

TRUE LOVELINESS.

She who thinks a noble heart
Better than a noble mein,
Honours virtue more than art,
Though 'tis less in fashion seen;
Whatsoe'er her fortune be,
She's the bride, the wife for me.

She who deems that inward grace
Far surpasses outward show,
She who values less the face
Than that charm the soul can throw;
Whatsoe'er her fortune be,
She's the bride, the wife for me.

She who knows the heart requires
Something more than lips of dew,
That when Love's brief repose expires,
Love itself dies with it too;
Whatsoe'er her fortune be,
She's the bride, the wife for me.

TRUE UNION.

Byron.

There is a mystic thread of life
So dearly wreath'd with mine alone,
That destiny's relentless knife
At once must sever both or none.

There is a form on which these eyes
Have often gazed with fond delight;
By day that form their joys supplies,
And dreams restore it through the night.

There is a voice whose tones inspire
Such thrills of rapture through my breast;
I would not hear a seraph choir,
Unless that voice could join the rest.

There is a face whose blushes tell
Affection's tale upon the cheek;
But, pallid at one fond farewell,
Proclaims more love than words can speak.

There is a lip which mine hath prest,
And none have ever prest before,
It vow'd to make me sweetly blest,
And mine—mine only, prest it more.

There is a bosom—all my own—
Hath pillow'd oft this aching head;
A mouth which smiles on me alone,
An eye whose tears with mine are shed.

There are two hearts whose movements thrill
In unison so closely sweet!
That, pulse to pulse responsive still,
They both must heave—or cease to beat.

There are two souls whose equal flow
In gentle streams so calmly run.
That when they part—they part!—ah, no!
They cannot part—those souls are one.

THE TWO BRIDES.

We two will stand in the shadow here,
To see the bride as she passes by;
Ring soft and low, ring loud and clear,
Ye chiming bells that swing on high!
Look! look! she comes! The air grows sweet
With the fragrant breath of the orange blooms,
And the flowers she treads beneath her feet
Die in a flood of rare perfumes.

She comes! she comes! the happy bells
With their joyous clamour fill the air,
While the great organ dies and swells,
Soaring to trembling heights of prayer!
Oh! rare are her robes of silken sheen,
And the pearls that gleam on her bosom's snow:
But rare the grace of her royal mein,
Her hair's fine gold, and her cheeks' young glow.

Dainty and fair as a folded rose,
Fresh as a violet dewy sweet,
Chaste as a lily she hardly knows
That there are rough paths for other feet;
For love hath shielded her; honour kept
Watch beside her by night and by day,
And evil out from her sight hath crept,
Trailing with slow length far away.

Now in her perfect womanhood,
In all the wealth of her matchless charms,
Lovely and beautiful, pure and good,
She yields herself to her lover's arms,
Hark! how the jubilant voices ring,
Lo! as we stand in the shadow here,
While far above us the gay bells swing
I catch the gleam of a happy tear.

The pageant is over. Come with me
To the other side of the town, I pray,
Ere the sun goes down in the darkening sea,
And the night falls around us chill and gray.

In the dim church porch an hour ago
We waited the bride's fair face to see;
Now life has a sadder sight to show,—
A darker picture for you and me.

No need to seek for the shadow here;
There are shadows lurking everywhere,
These streets in the brightest day are drear,
And black as the blackness of despair.
But this is the house. Take heed, my friend,
The stairs are rotten, the way is dim,
And up the flights as we still ascend,
Creep stealthy phantoms dark and grim.

Enter this chamber. Day by day,
Alone in this chill and ghostly room
A child—a woman—which is it, pray?
Despairingly waits for the hour of doom;
Alas! she wrings her hands so pale,
No gleam of a wedding-ring you see;
There is nothing to tell. You know the tale,
God help her now in her misery!

I dare not judge her. I only know
That love was to her a sin and a snare!
While to the bride of an hour ago
It brought all blessings its hands could bear.
I only know that to one it came
Laden with honour and joy and peace;
Its gifts to the other were woe and shame,
And a burning pain that shall never cease.

I only know that the soul of one
Had been a pearl in a golden case!
That of the other a pebble thrown
Idly down in a wayside place,
Where all day long strange footsteps trod,
And the bold bright sun drank up the dew!
Yet both were women. Oh, righteous God!
Thou only can judge between the two!

NOT OURS THE VOWS.

Barton.

NOT ours the vows of such as plight
  Their troth in sunny weather,
While leaves are green, and skies are bright,
  To walk on flowers together.

But we have loved as those who trend
  The thorny path of sorrow,
With clouds above, and cause to dread
  Yet deeper gloom to-morrow.

That thorny path, those stormy skies,
  Have drawn our spirits nearer;
And render'd us, by sorrow's ties,
  Each to the other dearer.

Love, born in hours of joy and mirth,
  With mirth and joy may perish;
That to which darker hours gave birth
  Still more and more we cherish.

It looks beyond the clouds of time,
  And through death's shadowy portal;
Made by adversity sublime,
  By faith and hope immortal.

THE TIRED WIFE.

ALL day had the wife been toiling,
  From an early hour in the morn,
And her hands and feet were weary
  With the burdens that they had borne.
But she said to herself, "The trouble
  That weighs on my heart is this—
That Tom never thinks to give me
  A comforting hug or a kiss.

"I'm willing to do my duty,
  To use all my strength and skill,
In making the home attractive,
  In striving my place to fill.
But though the approval of conscience
  Is sweet, I am free to say,
That if Tom would give me a hug or a kiss,
  'Twould take all the tire away."

And she counted over and over
  The years she had been Tom's wife,
And thought of the joys and sorrows
  She had known in her married life.
To be sure, there was money plenty,
  And never a lack of food;
But a kiss now and then, and a word of praise
  Would have done a world of good.

Ah! many a one is longing
  For the words that are never said,
And many a heart goes hungry
  For something better than bread.
But Tom had an inspiration,
  And when he went home that day,
He petted his wife, and kissed her
  In the old-time, lover-like way.

And she—such enigmas are women,
  Who had held herself up with pride,
At her husband's display of fondness,
  Just hung on his neck and cried.
And he by her grief reminded
  Of troubles he might have shared,
Said—"Bless my heart! What a fool I've been,
  Ann, I didn't suppose you cared!"

WOMAN OUR ANGEL.

(Not our Legislator.)

E. W. Cole.

This serio-comic trifle of my own is somewhat out of place in this collection, and is only added at the request of my wife, who, although a spirited woman, yet fully agrees with the sentiment of it.

OH! woman, loving, patient woman,
  Best blessing in our house,
So brave to bear the greatest pain,
  Yet frightened by a mouse!

Oh! woman, gentle soothing woman,
  To us in wisdom sent,
You rear the greatest, noblest men,
  Yet nothing you invent.

Oh! woman, sympathetic woman,
  You reason less than feel;
But reason only safe can guide
  Aright the public weal.

Oh! woman, careful, tasteful woman,
  This truth you must confess,
That politics are not your forte,
  But love, and home, and dress.

Oh! woman, tender, tearful woman,
  You are not formed for strife,
But happy homes to make on earth,
  That is your sphere of life.

Oh! woman, fairest flower of earth,
  Since first our race began,
Oh! be our love, our angel still,
  Don't try to be a man!

WOMAN'S RIGHTS.

Temple Bar.

A WOMAN'S rights. What do these words convey?
What depths of old-world wisdom do they reach?
What is their real intent? O sisters say;
And strive in daily life their truth to teach.

The right to minister to those that need;
With quiet song the weary to beguile;
With words of peace the hungry hearts to feed,
And cheer the sad and lonely with a smile.

The right in others' joys a joy to find;
The right divine to weep when others weep;
The right to be all unceasing kind:
The right to wake and pray while others sleep.

Right to be noble, right to be true,
Right to think rightly—and rightly to do;
Right to be tender, right to be just,
Right to be worthy of infinite trust.

To be little children's truest friend,
To know them in their ever-changing mood;
Forgetting self to labour to the end
To be a gracious influence for good.

To be the ladies of creation's lords,
As mothers, daughters, sisters, or as wives;
To be the best that earth to them affords;
To be to them the music of their lives.

The right is strength and honour to be free;
In daily work accomplished finding rest!
The right in "trivial round" a sphere to see;
The right, in blessing, to be fully blest.

Right to be perfect, right to be pure,
Right to be patient, and strong to endure;
Right to be loving, right to be good—
Those are the rights of true womanhood.

THE COMPLAINTS OF THE POOR

Southey.

AND wherefore do the poor complain?
The rich man ask'd of me; . . .
Come walk abroad with me, I said,
And I will answer thee.

'Twas evening, and the frozen streets
Were cheerless to behold,
And we were wrapt and coated well,
And yet we were a-cold.

We met an old bare-headed man,
His locks were thin and white:
I ask'd him what he did abroad
In that cold winter's night:

The cold was keen, indeed, he said,
But at home no fire had he,
And therefore he had come abroad
To ask for charity.

We met a young bare-footed child,
And she begg'd loud and bold:
I ask'd her what she did abroad
When the wind it blew so cold:

She said her father was at home,
And he lay sick a-bed,
And therefore was it she was sent
Abroad to beg for bread.

We saw a woman sitting down
Upon a stone to rest,
She had a baby at her back.
And another at her breast:

I ask'd her why she loiter'd there
When the night-wind was so chill:
She turn'd her head and bade the child
That scream'd behind, be still;

Then told us that her husband served,
A soldier, far away,
And therefore to her parish she
Was begging back her way.

We met a girl, her dress was loose,
And sunken was her eye,
Who with a wanton's hollow voice
Address'd the passers-by;

I ask'd her what there was in guilt
That could her heart allure
To shame, disease, and late remorse:
She answer'd she was poor.

I turn'd me to the rich man then,
For silently stood he, . . .
You ask'd me why the poor complain,
And these have answer'd thee!

GIRLS THAT ARE IN DEMAND.

THE girls that are wanted are good girls—
Good from the heart to the lips;
Pure as the lily is white and pure,
From its heart to its sweet leaf tips.
The girls that are wanted are home girls—
Girls that are mother's right hand,
That fathers and brothers can trust to,
And the little ones understand.

Girls that are fair on the hearthstone,
And pleasant when nobody sees;
Kind and sweet to their own folks,
Ready and anxious to please.
The girls that are wanted are wise girls,
That know what to do and to say:
That drive with a smile and a soft word
The wrath of the household away.

The girls that are wanted are girls of sense,
Whom fashion can never deceive;
Who can follow whatever is pretty,
And dare what is silly to leave.
The girls that are wanted are careful girls,
Who count what a thing will cost,
Who use with a prudent generous hand,
But see that nothing is lost.

The girls that are wanted are girls with hearts;
They are wanted for mothers and wives,
Wanted to cradle in loving arms
The strongest and frailest lives.
The clever, the witty, the brilliant girl,
There are few who can understand;
But, oh! for the wise, loving home girls
There's a constant steady demand.

GO, FEEL WHAT I HAVE FELT.

HATRED TO ALCOHOLIC DRINKS.

[A poor woman recently conversing in New York with a lady on the subject of total abstinence, which had been discussed at a large meeting of the reclaimed drunkards from Baltimore, when the lady said, "Why, you are almost a monomaniac in your hatred to alcoholic drinks." The following verses, containing an excuse for her warmth, were afterwards written.]

Go, feel what I have felt,
Go, bear what I have borne;
Sink 'neath a blow a father dealt,
And the cold, proud world's scorn.
Thus struggle on from year to year,
Thy sole relief the scalding tear.

Go, weep as I have wept
O'er a loved father's fall;
See every cherished promise swept,
Youth's sweetness turned to gall;
Hope's faded flowers strewed all the way,
That led me up to woman's day.

Go, hear what I have heard,—
The sobs of sad despair,
As memory's feeling fount hath stirred,
And its revealings there
Have told him what he might have been,
Had he the drunkard's fate foreseen.

Go to my mother's side,
And her crushed spirit cheer;
Thine own deep anguish hide,
Wipe from her cheek the tear;
Mark her dimmed eye, her furrowed brow,
The grey that streaks her dark hair now,
The toil-worn frame, the trembling limb,
And trace the ruin back to him
Whose plighted faith in early youth
Promised eternal love and truth,
But who, forsworn, hath yielded up
This promise to the deadly cup.

Go, kneel as I have knelt:
Implore, beseech, and pray,
Strive the besotted heart to melt,
The downward course to stay;
Be cast with bitter curse aside,—
Thy prayers burlesqued, thy tears defied.

Go, stand where I have stood,
And see the strong man bow;
With gnashing teeth, lips bathed in blood,
And cold and livid brow;
Go, catch his wandering glance, and see
There mirrored his soul's misery.

And led her down from love and light,
From all that made her pathway bright,
And chained her there mid want and strife,
That lowly thing,—a drunkard's wife!
And stamped on childhood's brow, so mild,
That withering blight—a drunkard's child!

Go, hear, and see, and feel, and know
All that my soul hath felt and known,
Then look within the wine-cup's glow,
See if its brightness can atone;
Think of its flavour would you try,
If all proclaimed, '*Tis drink and die.*

Tell me I hate the bowl,—
Hate is a feeble word;
I loathe, abhor, my very soul
By strong disgust is stirred
Whene'er I see, or hear, or tell
Of the DARK BEVERAGE OF HELL!

THE LADY'S DREAM.

Hood.

The lady lay in her bed,
  Her couch so warm and soft,
But her sleep was restless and broken still,
  For turning often and oft
From side to side, she mutter'd and moan'd,
  And toss'd her arms aloft.

At last she startled up,
  And gazed on the vacant air,
With a look of awe, as if she saw
  Some dreadful phantom there—
And then in the pillow she buried her face
  From visions ill to bear.

The very curtain shook,
  Her terror was so extreme;
And the light that fell on the broider'd quilt
  Kept a tremulous gleam;
And her voice was hollow, and shook as she cried:—
  "Oh me! that awful dream!

"That weary, weary walk,
  In the churchyard's dismal ground!
And those horrible things, with shady wings,
  That came and flitted round,—
Death, death, and nothing but death,
  In every sight and sound!

"And oh! those maidens young,
  Who wrought in that dreary room,
With figures drooping and spectres thin,
  And cheeks without a bloom;
And the Voice that cried, 'For the pomp of pride,
  We haste to an early tomb!

"'For the pomp and pleasure of Pride,
  We toil like Afric slaves,
And only to earn a home at last,
  Where yonder cypress waves;'—
And then they pointed—I never saw
  A ground so full of graves!

"And still the coffins came,
  With their sorrowful trains and slow;
Coffin after coffin still,
  A sad and sickening show;
From grief exempt, I never had dreamt
  Of such a World of Woe!

"Of the hearts that daily break,
  Of the tears that hourly fall,
Of the many, many troubles of life
  That grieve this earthly ball—
Disease and Hunger, and Pain, and Want,
  But now I dreamt of them all!

"For the blind and the cripple were there,
  And the babe that pined for bread,
And the houseless man and the widow poor
  Who begged—to bury the dead;
The naked, alas, that I might have clad,
  The famish'd I might have fed!

"The sorrow I might have sooth'd,
  And the unregarded tears;
For many a thronging shape was there,
  From long forgotten years,
Ay, even the poor rejected Moor,
  Who rais'd my childish fears!

"Each pleading look, that long ago
  I scann'd with a heedless eye,
Each face was gazing as plainly there,
  As when I passed it by;
Woe, woe for me if the past should be
  Thus present when I die!

"No need of sulphurous lake,
  No need of fiery coal,
But only that crowd of human kind
  Who wanted pity and dole—
In everlasting retrospect—
  Will wring my sinful soul!

"Alas! I have walked through life
  Too heedless where I trod;
Nay, helping to trample my fellow worm,
  And fill the burial sod—
Forgetting that even the sparrow falls
  Not unmark'd of God!

"I drank the richest draughts;
  And ate whatever is good—
Fish, and flesh, and fowl, and fruit,
  Supplied my hungry mood;
But I never remember'd the wretched ones
  That starve for want of food!

"I dress'd as the noble dress,
  In cloth of silver and gold,
With silk, and satin, and costly furs
  In many an ample fold;
But I never remember'd the naked limb
  That froze with winter's cold.

"The wounds I might have heal'd!
  The human sorrow and smart!
And yet it never was in my soul
  To play so ill a part:
But evil is wrought by want of Thought,
  As well as want of Heart!"

She clasp'd her fervent hands,
  And tears began to stream;
Large, and bitter, and fast they fell,
  Remorse was so extreme:
And yet, oh yet, that many a Dame
  Would dream the Lady's Dream!

THE CHANGE.

Morgan.

I SAW him when a beauteous babe
Untouched by care or guile;
So fair and smooth his dimpled cheek,
So innocent his smile;
Unfolding to admiring eyes
Fresh beauties as he grew,
With many sounds the sense of which
No living creature knew;
From hour to hour the mother sat
Beside his cradle bed,
And built fine dreams of future fame
O'er his unconscious head.

I saw him when a comely child,
No fairer could be seen;
The first in feats of skill and speed
Upon the village green;
So gentle, and beloved by all
His mates in task and play;
So good and noble in his ways
And honest as the day;
So full of thoughtful love at home,
His parents' pride and joy;
And oft the village folks would say,
"There goes the model boy."

I saw him in the spring of youth,
His purpose strong and high!
He walked with well-directed step,
He looked with single eye.
He bowed to nought but truth and right,
He dreaded nought but sin;
Of nobler form, yet nobler still
The soul that dwelt within;
As means of good he valued gold,
But hated sordid love;
His aims and plans, his light and strength
Were drawn from things above.

I saw him in his ripened strength,
Life in its glorious prime;
The seal of goodness pressed upon
His talents and his time.
But see, alas! some subtle foe
Draws nigh and twines around
Our hero's limbs a massive chain,
Then smites him to the ground;
Enslaved and crushed by tyrant force
He lies on ruin's brink;
Of peace and all but hope despoiled—
That subtle foe was drink!

I saw him in declining age,
O'ershadowed by the tomb;
The present felt a weary weight,
The future full of gloom.
In sultry heat and biting cold
He strayed from door to door;
His mind so rent with keen regret,
His limbs so weak and sore;
No gentle love his age to cheer,
No power himself to save,
His body borne by stranger's hands
To a dishonoured grave.

TWO PICTURES.

Evan E. Rexford.

I SAT in the gathering shadows,
And look'd t'ward the west away,
Where the hand of an unseen artist,
Was painting at close of day.
A strange and a beautiful picture,
That fill'd my soul with awe,
And made me think of the city
No mortal ever saw.

"Paint me, O wonderful artist,"
I cried when the shadows came,
And hid the marvellous glory
Of the western hills aflame,
"Paint me the face of an angel."
And lo! before mine eyes,
Was the face of my sainted mother,
Who dwells in Paradise.

"Paint me the face of a sinner,"
A darker shadow swept
Down the hills, and I thought in the twilight
The unseen artist wept.
And lo! from his magical pencil,
A face in a moment had grown,
The sad, white face of a sinner,
And I knew it for my own.
The sad, white face of a sinner,
And I knew it for my own,
I knew it for my own.

THE CONVICT SHIP.

Hervey.

Morn on the waters! and, purple and bright
Bursts on the billows the flashing of light;
O'er the glad waves, like a child of the sun,
See the tall vessel goes gallantly on;
Full to the breeze she unbosoms her sail,
And her pennon streams onward, like hope, in the gale;
The winds come around her, and murmur and song,
And the surges rejoice as they bear her along.
See! she looks up to the golden-edged clouds,
And the sailor sings gaily aloft in her shrouds.
Onward she glides, amid ripple and spray,
Over the waters, away and away!
Bright as the visions of youth ere they part,
Passing away, like a dream of the heart!
Who, as the beautiful pageant sweeps by,
Music around her, and sunshine on high,
Pauses to think, amid glitter and glow,
Oh! there be hearts that are breaking below.
Night on the waves! and the moon is on high,
Hung like a gem on the brow of the sky,
Treading its depths in the power of her might,
And turning the clouds, as they pass her, to light;
Look to the waters! asleep on their breast,
Seems not the ship like an island of rest?
Bright and alone on the shadowy main,
Like a heart-cherish'd home on some desolate plain!
Who, as she smiles in the silvery light,
Spreading her wings on the bosom of night,
Alone on the deep, as the moon in the sky,
A phantom of beauty,—could deem, with a sigh,
That so lovely a thing is the mansion of sin,
And souls that are smitten lie bursting within!
Who, as he watches her silently gliding,
Remembers that wave after wave is dividing
Bosoms that sorrow and guilt could not sever,
Hearts that are parted and broken for ever?
Or dreams that he watches afloat on the wave
The death-bed of hope, or the young spirit's grave?

THE FELON.

M. G. Lewis.

Oh! mark his wan and hollow cheeks,
And mark his eye-balls glare,
And mark his teeth in anguish clenched—
The anguish of despair!

Know, three days since his penance o'er,
Yon culprit left a jail;
And since three days no food has passed
His lips, so parched and pale.

"Where shall I turn?" the wretch exclaims,
"Where hide my shameful head?
How fly from scorn, or how contrive
To earn my honest bread?

"This branded hand would gladly toil;
But where for work I pray,
Who views this mark, 'A felon!' cries,
And loathing turns away.

"My heart has greatly erred,—but now
Would fain return to good!
My hand has deeply sinned,—but yet
Has ne'er been stained with blood!

"For alms, or work, in vain I sue—
The scorners both deny;
I starve! I starve! Then what remains?
This choice—to sin or die!

"Here Virtue spurns me with disdain,—
There pleasure spreads her snare;
Strong habit drives me back to vice;
And, urged by fierce despair,

"I strive, while hunger gnaws my heart,
To fly from shame, in vain!
World! 'tis thy cruel will! I yield,
And plunge in guilt again!

"There's mercy in each ray of light
That mortal eyes e'er saw;
There's mercy in each breath of air
That mortal lips e'er draw;

"There's mercy both for bird and beast
In heaven's indulgent plan;
There's mercy in each creeping thing,
But man has none for man!

"Ye proudly honest, when you heard
My wounded conscience groan,
Had generous hand or feeling heart
One glimpse of mercy shown,

"That act had made from burning eyes
Sweet tears of virtue roll,
Had fixed my heart, assured my faith,—
And Heaven had gained a soul!"

HER COMING HOME.

Up and down the streets of the city
She wanders, this desolate night,
While the elves of the snow are busy
Robing the world in white.
For the morrow is Christmas morning,
And the jubilant bells will ring,
And the world must be pure in raiment
On the birthday of its King.

She pauses by shining windows
Of homes where the hearts within
Are warm with love for each other,
While she is alone with her sin.
She sees them drinking and feasting,
And her heart makes sorrowful moan,
If she asks for the bread they are breaking
They will answer with a stone.

The light on the hearthstones mock her,
Astray in the stormy night,
And she hides her face in the darkness,
To shut them out from sight.
To the outcast from love and friendship,
The poor wayfarers of earth,
Like a glimpse of forbidden Heaven
Is the home-light on the hearth.

On, on! in the storm and darkness!
Where shall the wanderer go?
If she only could hide for ever
From the thoughts which hurt her so!
She moans as again she remembers
The years when her soul was white,
A heart that is human is breaking,
Alone in the pitiless night.

She stops by another window,
And sees in the fire's red glow
A girl with pure eyes stand smiling
As she used to, long ago.
Then her mother comes from the shadow,
And kisses the face so fair,
And her hand lays like a blessing
On her daughter's shining hair.

The sight stabs home like a dagger,
She turns with a cry of pain,
And a face as white as the dead are,
And is lost in the dark again.
The winds laugh out like demons,
And smite her shivering form,
And the heart is growing colder,
That the home-fires cannot warm.

On, in the storm's fierce tumult,
And her brain is growing wild,
She thinks she is going homeward,
An erring, repentant child.
"I wonder if mother is watching,
And praying to-night for me?"
And her eyes are strained in the darkness,
The light on home's hearth to see.

"Will she kiss me again, I wonder,
As she used to, long ago?
My soul is black as the night is,
And hers is as pure as snow.
Oh, my soul! if she could see it
When I kneel at her feet to-night,
She would shrink from the child she prays for,
And cry out at the sight.

"And yet I think she would take me
In her loving arms at last,
In her love for the child come homeward
Forgetting the shameful past.
Ah, me! but the night is chilly
And it's wearisome work to roam,
But her kiss will be rest and comfort
To the wanderer, safe at home.

"Ah! there is the light outshining
Along the homeward track,
I knew she would keep it burning
To guide my footsteps back.
At last I am coming, coming,
Weary and sick with sin.
Oh! love me a little, mother,
And let the wanderer in!"

She fancies she reaches the threshold
Of the home where mother is,
And her loving arms enfold her,
And she feels the mother-kiss.
Then her heart cries out in sorrow,
For the touch of lips so pure
Makes the burden of sin upon her
Seem more than she can endure.

"I am not the child you loved so
In the summers long ago,"
She moans at the feet of her mother,
"For she was as pure as the snow.
She has lost in the world's grim darkness,
And your innocent child is dead.
And I, with my shame all covered,
Kneel here at your feet in her stead."

Then her mother kneels down beside her
  And lifts her head on her breast,
And the wanderer feels on her bosom
  A thrill of infinite rest.
And the mother whispers to her,
  As she kisses her tenderly,
"Though your sins be red like scarlet
  You are always my child to me!"

Then the world seems flooded with brightness
  Through all the stormy night;
She forgets in the wayward fancies
  That her soul is no longer white.
And she cries, in a wild, strange gladness,
  As the wild flakes swifter come,
"Oh! mother has welcome to give me,
  And her child has at last come home!"

Then morning breaks in splendour
  And the bells for gladness ring,
And the world is clad in white raiment
  On the birthday of its King.
In a shining drift by the roadside,
  No more in the dark to roam,
A dead face smiles in the sunshine:
  God, lead all the wanderers home!

THE TWO FACES.

Montagu Vere.

An artist wished to paint a face,
  The symbol of innocence and joy;
He sought a child for his ideal,
  And drew the likeness of a boy.

Long years past on. The artist now
  A grey old man, one picture more
Designed to make, and call it Guilt—
  A contrast to the child of yore.

He went into a dungeon dark,
  Its cold wall damp with slime,
And painted a wretched man chained there.
  Condemned to death for crime.

Beside the other he placed the last:
  And when he heard the prisoner's name,
He found the innocent, laughing child
  And hardened man were both the same.

THE OLD MAN'S DREAM.

Holmes.

"Oh for one hour of youthful joy!
  Give back my twentieth spring!
I'd rather laugh a bright-hair'd boy
  Than reign a grey-beard king!

"Off with the wrinkled spoils of age!
  Away with learning's crown!
Tear out life's wisdom-written page,
  And dash its trophies down!

"One moment let my life-blood stream
  From boyhood's fount of flame!
Give me one giddy, reeling dream
  Of life all love and fame!"

—My listening angel heard the prayer,
  And calmly smiling, said,
"If I but touch thy silver'd hair,
  Thy hasty wish hath sped.

"But is there nothing in thy track
  To bid thee fondly stay,
While the swift seasons hurry back
  To find the wish'd-for day?"

"—Ah, truest soul of womankind!
  Without thee, what were life?
One bliss I cannot leave behind:
  I'll take—my—precious—wife!"

—The angel took a sapphire pen,
  And wrote in rainbow dew,
"The man would be a boy again,
  And be a husband, too!

"—And there is nothing yet unsaid
  Before the change appears?
Remember, all their gifts have fled
  With these dissolving years!"

"Why, yes; for memory would recall
  My fond paternal joys;
I could not bear to leave them all;
  I'll take—my—girl—and—boys!"

The smiling angel dropp'd his pen,—
  "Why this will never do;
The man would be a boy again,
  And be a father, too!"

And so I laugh'd,—my laughter woke
  The household with its noise,—
And wrote my dream, when morning broke,
  To please the grey-hair'd boys.

A DEAD MARCH.

Cosmo Monkhouse.

Play me a march low-toned and slow, a march for a silent tread,
Fit for the wandering feet of one who dreams of the silent dead,
Lonely—between the bones below and the souls that are overhead.

Here for a while they smiled and sang, alive in the interspace;
Here with the grass beneath the feet, and the stars above the face.
Now are the feet beneath the grass, and whither has flown their grace?

Who shall assure us whence they come, or tell us the way they go?
Verily life with them was joy, and now they have left us woe;
Once they were, and now they are not; and this is the sum we know.

Orderly range the seasons dew, and orderly roll the stars.
How shall we deem the soldier brave who frets of his wounds and scars?
Are we as senseless brutes that we should dash at the well-seen bars?

No, we are here with feet unfixed, but ever as if with lead
Drawn from the orbs which shine ove to the orb on which we tread,
Down to the dust from which we came and with which we shall mingle, dead.

No, we are here to wait, and work, and strain our banished eyes
Weary and sick of soil and toil, and hungry, and fair for skies
Far from the reach of wingless men, and not to be scaled with cries.

No, we are here to bend our necks to the yoke of Tyrant Time,
Welcoming all the gifts he gives us—glories of youth and prime;
Patiently watching them all depart as our heads grow white as rime.

Why do we mourn the days that go?—for the same sun shines each day;
For every Spring her primrose hath and ever a May her may;
Sweet as the rose that died last year is the rose that is born to-day.

Do we not too return, we men, as ever the round earth whirls?
Never a head is dimmed with grey but another is sunned with curls.
She was a girl and he was a boy, but yet there are boys and girls.

Ah, but alas for the smile of smiles that never but one face wore!
Ah, for the voice that has flown away like a bird to an unseen shore!
Ah, for the face, the flower of flowers, that blossoms on earth no more!

THE UNSEEN WORLD.

It lies around us like a cloud,
A world we do not see;
Yet the sweet closing of an eye
May bring us there to be.
Its gentle breezes fan our cheek
Amid our worldly cares;
Its gentle voices whisper love,
And mingle with our prayers.

Sweet hearts around us throb and beat,
Sweet helping hands are stirred,
And palpitate the veil between
With breathings almost heard.
So thin, so soft, so sweet they glide,
So near to press they seem;
They lull us gently to our rest,
They melt into our dream.

And in the hush of rest they bring,
'Tis easy now to see
How lovely and how sweet a pass
The hour of death may be;
Scarce knowing if we wake or sleep,
Scarce asking where we are,
To feel all evil sink away,
All sorrow and all care.

Sweet friends around us watch us still
Press nearer to our side,
Into our thoughts, into our prayers,
With gentle helpings glide.
Let death between us be as nought,
A dried and vanished stream
Your joy be the reality,
Our suffering like the dream.

THE NEW BIRTH.

Death is the fading of a cloud—
  The breaking of a chain:
The rending of a mortal shroud
  We ne'er shall need again.

Death is the conqueror's welcome home—
  The heavenly city's door:
The entrance of the world to come;
  'Tis life for evermore.

Death is the mightier, second birth—
  Th' unveiling of the soul:
'Tis freedom from the chains of Earth,
  The pilgrim's heavenly goal.

Death is the close of life's alarms—
  The watchlight on the shore;
The clasping in immortal arms
  Of loved ones gone before.

Death is a song from seraph lips—
  The day-spring from on high:
The ending of the soul's eclipse,
  Its transit to the sky.

CONTENTMENT.

Dyer.

My mind to me a kingdom is;
  Such perfect joy therein I find,
As far exceeds all earthly bliss
  That world affords, or grows by kind:
Though much I want what most men have,
Yet doth my mind forbid me crave.

Content I live—this is my stay:
  I seek no more than may suffice:
I press to bear no haughty sway;
  Look—what I lack, my mind supplies!
Lo! thus I triumph like a king,
Content with that my mind doth bring.

I see how plenty surfeits oft,
  And hasty climbers soonest fall;
I see how those that sit aloft
  Mishap doth threaten most of all;
These get with toil, and keep with fear:
Such cares my mind could never bear.

I laugh not at another's loss;
  I grudge not at another's gain;
No worldly wave my mind can toss;
  I brook that is another's pain.
I fear no foe: I scorn no friend:
I dread not death: I fear no end.

Some have too much, yet still they crave;
  I little have, yet seek no more:
They are but poor, though much they have,
  And I am rich, with little store.
They poor, I rich: they beg, I give:
They lack, I lend: they pine, I live.

I wish but what I have at will:
  I wander not to seek for more:
I like the plain, I climb no hill:
  In greatest storm I sit on shore,
And laugh at those that toil in vain,
To get what must be lost again.
—This is my choice; for why?—I find
No wealth is like a quiet mind.

WE CAN MAKE HOME HAPPY.

Though we may not change the cottage
  For a mansion tall and grand,
Or exchange the little grass plot
  For a boundless stretch of land—
Yet there's something brighter, dearer,
  Than the wealth we'd thus command.

Though we have not means to purchase
  Costly pictures, rich and rare—
Though we have not silken hangings
  For the walls, so cold and bare,
We can hang them o'er with garlands,
  For flowers bloom everywhere.

We can always make home cheerful,
  If the right course we begin,
We can make its inmates happy,
  And their truest blessings win.
It will make the small room brighter
  If we let the sunshine in.

We can gather round the fireside
  When the evening hours are long—
We can blend our hearts and voices
  In a happy social song;
We can guide some erring brother—
  Lead him from the path of wrong.

We may fill our home with music,
  And with sunshine brimming o'er,
If against all dark intruders
  We will firmly close the door—
Yet, should evil shadows enter,
  We must love each other more.

There are treasures for the lowly
  Which the greatest fail to find,
There's a chain of sweet affection
  Binding friends of kindred mind—
We may reap the choicest blessings,
  From the poorest lot assigned.

ORANGE AND GREEN.

Gerald Griffin.

THE night was falling dreary,
In merry Bandon town,
When in his cottage weary,
An Orangeman lay down.
The summer sun in splendour
Had set upon the vale,
And shouts of "No surrender!"
Arose upon the gale.

Beside the waters, laving
The feet of aged trees,
The Orange banners, waving,
Flew boldly in the breeze—
In mighty chorus meeting,
A hundred voices join,
And fife and drum were beating
The *Battle of the Boyne.*

Ha! tow'rd his cottage hieing,
What form is speeding now,
From yonder thicket flying,
With blood upon his brow?
"Hide—hide me, worthy stranger,
Though green my colour be,
And in the day of danger,
May heaven remember thee!

"In yonder vale contending
Alone against that crew,
My life and limbs defending,
An Orangeman I slew.
Hark! hear that fearful warning,
There's death in every tone—
Oh, save my life till morning,
And heaven prolong your own!"

The Orange heart was melted
In pity to the Green;
He heard the tale and felt it,
His very soul within.
"Dread not that angry warning,
Though death be in its tone—
I'll save your life till morning,
Or I will loose my own."

Now, round his lowly dwelling,
The angry torrent press'd,
A hundred voices swelling,
The Orangeman addressed—
"Arise, arise, and follow
The chase along the plain!
In yonder stony hollow
Your only son is slain!"

With rising shouts they gather
Upon the tracks amain,
And leave the childless father
Aghast with sudden pain.
He seeks the righted stranger,
In covert where he lay—
"Arise!" he said, "all danger
Is gone and passed away."

"I had a son—one only,
One lovèd as my life,
Thy hand has left me lonely,
In that accursed strife.
I pledged my word to save thee
Until the storm should cease,
I keep the pledge I gave thee—
Arise, and go in peace!"

The stranger soon departed,
From that unhappy vale;
The father, broken-hearted,
Lay brooding o'er the tale.
Full twenty summers after
To silver turned his beard;
And yet the sound of laughter
From him was never heard.

The night was falling dreary,
In merry Wexford town,
When in his cabin weary,
A peasant laid him down.
And many a voice was singing
Along the summer vale,
And Wexford town was ringing
With shouts of "Granua Uile."

Beside the waters laving
The feet of aged trees,
The green flag, gaily waving
Was spread against the breeze—
In mighty chorus meeting,
Loud voices filled the town,
And fife and drum were beating,
"*Down, Orangemen, lie down!*"

Hark! 'mid the stirring clangor
That woke the echoes there,
Loud voices, high in anger,
Rise on the evening air.
Like billows of the ocean,
He sees them hurry on—
And 'mid the wild commotion,
An Orangeman alone.

"My hair," he said, "is hoary,
And feeble is my hand,
And I could tell a story
Would shame your cruel band.
Full twenty years and over
Have changed my heart and brow,
And I am grown a lover
Of peace and concord now.

"It was not thus I greeted
Your brother of the Green;
When, fainting and defeated
I freely took him in.
I pledged my word to save him,
From vengeance rushing on,
I kept the pledge I gave him,
Though he had killed my son."

That aged peasant heard him,
And knew him as he stood,
Remembrance kindly stirr'd him,
And tender gratitude.
With gushing tears of pleasure,
He pierced the listening train.
"I'm here to pay the measure,
Of kindness back again!"

Upon his bosom falling,
That old man's tears came down,
Deep memory recalling
That cot and fatal town.
"The hand that would offend thee,
My being first shall end;
I'm living to defend thee,
My saviour and my friend!"

He said, and slowly turning,
Address'd the wondering crowd,
With fervent spirit burning,
He told the tale aloud.
Now pressed the warm beholders,
Their aged foe to greet;
They raised him on their shoulders
And chaired him through the street.

As he had saved that stranger,
From peril scowling dim,
So in his day of danger
Did Heav'n remember him.
By joyous crowds attended,
The worthy pair were seen,
And their flags that day were blended
Of Orange and of Green.

BETTER THAN GOLD.

Mrs. J. M. Winton.

Better than grandeur, better than gold,
Than rank and title a thousand fold,
Is a healthy body, a mind at ease,
And simple pleasures that always please;
A heart that can feel for a neighbour's woe
And share his joys with a genial glow.—
With sympathies large enough to enfold.
All men as brothers,—is better than gold.

Better than gold is a conscience clear,
Though toiling for bread in an humble sphere:
Doubly blest with content and health,
Untried by the lust of cares or wealth.
Lowly living and lofty thought
Adorn and ennoble a poor man's cot;
For manners and morals on nature's plan
Are the genuine test of a gentleman.

Better than gold is the sweet repose
Of the sons of toil when their labours close;
Better than gold is the poor man's sleep,
And the balm that drops on his slumbers deep.
Bring sleeping draughts to the downy bed,
Where luxury pillows his aching head;
His simpler opiate labour deems
A shorter road to the land of dreams.

Better than gold is a thinking mind
That in the realm of books can find
A treasure surpassing Australian ore,
And live with the great and good of yore.
The sage's lore and the poet's lay,
The glories of empires pass'd away.
The world's great drama will thus unfold
And yield a pleasure better than gold.

Better than gold is a peaceful home
Where all the fireside charities come;—
The shrine of love and the heaven of life,
Hallowed by mother, or sister, or wife.
However humble the home may be,
Or tried by sorrow with Heaven's decree,
The blessings that never were bought or sold,
And centre there, are better than gold.

A DINNER AND A KISS.

"I've brought your dinner, father,"
The blacksmith's daughter said,
As she took from her arm the kettle
And lifted its shining lid.
"There is no pie or pudding,
So I will give you this."
And upon his toil-worn forehead
She left the childish kiss.

The blacksmith took off his apron,
And dined in happy mood,
Wondering much at the savour
Hid in his humble food;
While all about him were visions
Full of prophetic bliss;
But he never thought of magic
In his little daughter's kiss.

While she, with her kettle swinging,
Merrily trudged away,
Stopping at sight of a squirrel,
Catching some wild bird's lay.
And I thought how many a shadow
Of life and fate we should miss,
If always our frugal dinners
Were seasoned with a kiss.

A POET'S EPITAPH.

Ebenezer Elliott.

Stop, Mortal! Here thy brother lies—
The Poet of the Poor.
His books were rivers, woods, and skies,
The meadow and the moor;
His teachers were the torn heart's wail,
The tyrant and the slave,
The street, the factory, the gaol,
The palace—and the grave!
Sin met thy brother everywhere!
And is thy brother blamed?
From passion, danger, doubt, and care,
He no exemption claim'd.
The meanest thing, earth's feeblest worm,
He fear'd to scorn or hate;
But, honouring in a peasant's form
The equal of the great,
He bless'd the steward, whose wealth makes
The poor man's little, more;
Yet loathed the haughty wretch that takes
From plunder'd Labour's store.
A hand to do, a head to plan,
A heart to feel and dare—
Tell man's worst foes, here lies the man
Who drew them as they are.

REAL LIFE.

W. H. Wood.

The world's great soul is weary
With "eloquence" misplaced;
And modern days made sadly dreary
By lifeless forms strait-laced.

Let's break the spell of Folly's rule,
That freely we may steer
Our course to health and logs of yule
Whose blaze burns bright and clear.

We'll quit the race for selfish end,
Where bubbles swell and break,
And dwell where peace and virtue blend
And thus life's music wake.

We'll cheat no more, nor cheated be,
By blare or glare or cry;
But wash the feet, the face, and see
Real life with open eye.

If God be God, we'll worship Him
As Father of mankind;
If man's His child, we'll nourish him
As brother true and kind.

If mind be mind, we'll mindful be,
Let matter be the husk:
If souls were soulful none would see
A man with swinish tusk.

If heart be heart, we'll hearty be,
As hearth-fire's ruddy glow;
Or lamp whose light is pure and free
To flame with golden flow.

If life be life, we'll be alive
With living energy:
In all the stress of life we'll strive
For true ability—

God's blessed boon of human grace
To crown each useful act;
And on the soul his likeness trace,
And seal the sacred pact.

We'll seek the Centre of all good;
The Sun of love and truth;
Whose healthful rays refine the blood,
And give immortal youth.

O Life of life, and Love of love!
Thou Truth of all that's true!
Heart of all the heavens above,
Our souls with life imbue!

THE STORY OF A DOLL.

Watson.

I STOOD in the semi-darkness and watched a child at her play;
Her cares were of multiform nature, and the daylight was speeding away.
Her dolly demanded attention, to be petted and kissed and be fed;
To have on its little nightgown, and then to be put in its bed.
All this with a motherly yearning she had learned by the instinct of love;
And the dolly but faintly presented a gift from the heaven above.
The dear little creature had finished and was just about turning to go,
When the scene was all changed in a moment and turned into weeping and woe.
A boy, almost reaching to manhood, dashed wildly from outside the room,
And seizing the doll from the cradle rushed out again into the gloom.
There was one wild scream from the maiden, a clasp of the hands and a chase;
But the boy thought the thing was funny and was in for a brotherly race.
But soon, when the screaming grew louder and he saw all the pain he had caused,
He threw down the doll on the flooring, and sneering, he suddenly paused.
"I wouldn't be such a cry-baby," he said with a half-mocking drawl;
"I can buy plenty more that's just like it. It is only a plaster doll.
Why don't you get one made of china, instead of that plaster thing?
And then I would try and respect it," and he took himself off with a fling.
"Oh! my dolly, my dolly is broken," and quick in her bosom she hid
The maimed little bit of her sunshine. "I loved it, I loved it, I did.
I don't care if it was only plaster; 'twas my dolly, my dolly, my own."
And she knelt by the mangled plaything. "And now I am left all alone."

* * * * * * * * * *

Ten years from that very evening, I stood by the couch of a child,
While a man knelt and wept beside it, with a face both haggard and wild.
'Twas the old scene of dolly repeated, the boy had to manhood grown:
A hand crushed his plaster idol and left him to mourn all alone.
Ah me! how the world is repeating the work of each day o'er and o'er.
We all have our broken dollies away on the golden shore.
Did he think, I wonder, of that one he threw on the carpetless floor?

POOR TIRED MOTHER.

Margaret Eytinge.

THEY were talking of the glory of the land beyond the skies,—
Of the light and of the gladness to be found in paradise,—
Of the flowers ever blooming, of the never-ceasing songs,—
Of the wand'rings through the golden streets of happy white-robed throngs;
And, said father, leaning cosily back in his easy-chair
(Father always was a master-hand for comfort everywhere):
"What a joyful thing 'twould be to know that when this life is o'er,
One would straightway hear a welcome from the blessed shining shore!"
And Isabel our eldest girl, glanced upward from the reed
She was painting on a water-jug, and murmured, "Yes, indeed."
And Marian, the next in age, a moment dropped her book,
And "Yes, indeed," repeated with a most ecstatic look.
But mother, gray-haired mother, who had come to sweep the room,
With a patient smile on her thin face, leaned lightly on her broom—
Poor mother; no one ever thought how much she had to do—
And said, "I hope it is not wrong not to agree with you;
But seems to me that when I die, before I join the blest,
I'd like just for a little while to lie in my grave and rest."

THE KISS IN THE STREET.

Watson.

THE world is a world of glorious themes,
The world is a world of wonder—
A web and a tissue of beautiful dreams,
To be torn by the world asunder.
The world is an image of beauty,
The world is a type of bliss;
If the world would but do its duty,
There would be no world like this.

I walked on the street on a sunshiny day,
I walked, and I watched the crowd—
The crowd that were looking so happy and gay
That they almost shouted aloud.
I held by my hand my darling girl,
She skipped and she danced along,
And, childlike, laughed at the hum and the whirl
Of the countless moving throng.

I walked, and I watched the myriad mass
That was sweeping idly by,
And it made me glad to see them pass
With a smiling lip and a laughing eye.
And so I sang to myself a song—
A song on the happiest theme—
To the crowd that was slowly passing along
Like the mythical forms in a dream.

And so I sang as I walked along,
Led by my baby guide,
And a man came out of the midst of the throng
Who walked by my darling's side.
He was pale, and haggard, and marked with woe,
But his clothes they were rich and fine,
And a diamond gleamed on his shirt of snow
Which I wished at the moment were mine.

He walked for a while with a downcast eye,
Then stooped with a sudden bow,
And I heard the moan of an inward sigh
As he kissed my darling's brow.
In the crowded street we quietly stand,
While neither offered to stir,
And he softly said, as he pressed my hand,
"I have lost a child like her."

Then silently passed that haggard man
To the midst of the crowd again,
And the song I had in my heart began
Was hushed in a throb of pain.

NOTHING TO WEAR.

SERIO-COMIC. ABRIDGED. CONTAINS A MORAL.

An Episode of Fashionable Life.

WELL, having thus woo'd Miss M'Flimsy and gained her,
With the silks, crinolines, and hoops that contained her,-
I had, as I thought, a contingent remainder
At least in the property, and the best right
To appear as its escort by day and by night:
And it being the week of the Stuckups' grand ball—
  Their cards had been out a fortnight or so,
  And set all the Avenue on the tiptoe—
I consider'd it only my duty to call,
  And see if Miss Flora intended to go.
I found her—as ladies are apt to be found,
When the time intervening between the first sound
Of the bell and the visitor's entry is shorter
Than usual—I found, I won't say I caught her—
Intent on the pier-glass, undoubtedly meaning
To see if perhaps it didn't need cleaning.
She turned as I entered—"Why, Harry, you sinner,
I thought that you went to the Flashers' to dinner!"
"So I did," I replied, "but the dinner is swallowed,
  And digested, I trust, for 'tis now nine and more;
So being relieved from that duty, I followed
  Inclination, which led me, you see, to your door.
And now will your ladyship so condescend
As just to inform me if you intend
Your duty and grace and presence to lend
(All which, when I own, I hope no one will borrow)
To the Stuckups', whose party you know is to-morrow?"
The fair Flora looked up with a pitiful air,
And answer'd quite promptly, "Why, Harry, *mon cher*,
I should like above all things to go with you there;
But really and truly—I've nothing to wear!"
"Nothing to wear! Go just as you are;
Wear the dress you have on, and you'll be by far,
I engage, the most bright and particular star
  On the Stuckup horizon." I stopp'd, for her eye,
Notwithstanding this delicate onset of flattery,
Open'd on me at once a most terrible battery
  Of scorn and amazement. She made no reply,
But gave a slight turn to the end of her nose
  (That pure Grecian feature), as much as to say,
"How absurd that any sane man should suppose
That a lady would go to a ball in the clothes,
  No matter how fine, that she wears every day!"
So I ventured again—"Wear your crimson brocade"
(Second turn up of nose)—"That's too dark by a shade."
"Your blue silk."—"That's too heavy."
"Your pink."—"That's too light."
"Wear tulle over satin."—
"I can't endure white."
"Your rose-coloured, then, the best of the batch."—
"I haven't a thread of point lace to match."

"Your brown moiré antique."—"Yes, and look like a Quaker."
"The pearl-coloured."—"I would, but that plaguy dressmaker
Has had it a week."—"Then that exquisite lilac,
In which you would melt the heart of a Shylock."
(Here the nose took again the same elevation.)—
"I wouldn't wear that for the whole of creation."
"Why not? It's my fancy there's nothing could strike it
As more *comme il faut*——" "Yes, but, dear me! that lean
Sophronia Stuckup has got one just like it,
And I won't appear dress'd like a chit of sixteen."
"Then that splendid purple, that sweet Mazarine;
That superb point d'aiguille, that imperial green,
That zephyr-like tarlatan, that rich grenadine."—
"Not one of all which is fit to be seen,"
Said the lady, becoming excited and flushed.
"Then wear," I exclaimed, in a tone which quite crush'd
Opposition, "that gorgeous toilette which you sported
In Paris last Spring, at the grand presentation,
When you quite turn'd the head of the head of the nation;
And by all the grand court were so very much courted."
The end of the nose was portentously tipped up,
And both the bright eyes shot forth indignation,
As she burst upon me with the fierce exclamation,
"I have worn it three times at the least calculation,
And that and the most of my dresses are ripped up!"
Here I ripp'd out something, perhaps rather rash,
Quite innocent, though; but to use an expression
More striking than classic, it "settled my hash,"
And proved very soon the last act of our session.
"Fiddlesticks, is it, sir? I wonder the ceiling
Doesn't fall down and crush you. Oh, you men have no feeling!
You selfish, unnatural, illiberal creatures!
Who set yourselves up as patterns and preachers.
Your silly pretence—why, what a mere guess it is!
Pray, what do you know of a woman's necessities?
I have told you and shown you I've nothing to wear,
And 'tis perfectly plain you not only don't care,
But you do not believe me." (Here the nose went still higher.)
"I suppose if you dared you would call me a liar.
Our engagement is ended, sir—yes, on the spot!
You're a brute and a monster, and—I don't know what!"
I mildly suggested the words Hottentot,
Pickpocket and cannibal, Tartar and thief,
As gentle expletives which might give relief.
But this only proved a spark to the powder,
And the storm I had raised came faster and louder;
It blew and it rain'd, thunder'd, lighten'd, and hail'd,
Interjections, verbs, pronouns, till language quite fail'd
To express the abusive; and then its arrears
Were brought up all at once by a torrent of tears
And my last faint, despairing attempt at an obs-
Ervation was lost in a tempest of sobs.
Well, I felt for the lady, and felt for my hat too;
Improvised on the crown of the latter a tattoo,
In lieu of expressing the feelings which lay
Quite too deep for words, as Wordsworth would say.

Then, without going through the form of a bow,
Found myself in the entry—I hardly knew how—
On doorstep and sidewalk, past lamp-post and square,
At home and upstairs, in my own easy chair;
  Poked my feet into slippers, my fire into blaze,
And said to myself, as I lit my cigar,
Supposing a man had the wealth of the Czar
  Of the Russias to boot, for the rest of his days,
On the whole, do you think he would have much to spare
If he married a woman with nothing to wear?

Since that night, taking pains that it should not be bruited
Abroad in society, I've instituted
A course of inquiry, extensive and thorough,
On this vital subject; and find, to my horror,
That the fair Flora's case is by no means surprising,
  But that there exists the greatest distress
In our female community, solely arising
  From this unsupplied destitution of dress,
Whose unfortunate victims are filling the air
With the pitiful wail of "Nothing to wear!"

* * * * * *

Oh, ladies, dear ladies! the next sunny day
Please trundle your hoops just out of Broadway,
From its whirl and its bustle, its fashion and pride,
And the temples of Trade which tower on each side
To the alleys and lanes, where Misfortune and Guilt
Their children have gather'd, their city have built;
Where Hunger and Vice, like twin beasts of prey,
  Have hunted their victims to gloom and despair;
Raise the rich, dainty dress, and the fine broider'd skirt,
Pick your delicate way through the dampness and dirt,
  Grope through the dark dens, climb the rickety stair
To the garret, where wretches, the young and the old,
Half-starved and half-naked, lie crouch'd from the cold.
See those skeleton limbs, those frost-bitten feet,
All bleeding and bruised by the stones of the street;
Hear the sharp cry of childhood, the deep groans that swell
  From the poor dying creature who writhes on the floor;
Hear the curses that sound like the echoes of hell,
  As you sicken and shudder, and fly from the door!
Then home to your wardrobes, and say,—if you dare,—
Spoil'd children of Fashion, you've nothing to wear!
And oh, if perchance there should be a sphere
Where all is made right which so puzzles us here,
Where the glare and the glitter, and the tinsel of Time,
Fade and die in the light of that region sublime,
Where the soul, disenchanted of flesh and of sense,
Unscreen'd by its trappings, and shows, and pretence,
Must be clothed for the life and the service above,
With purity, truth, faith, meekness, and love—
O, daughters of Earth! foolish virgins! beware,
Lest in that upper realm you have nothing to wear!

THE ARSENAL AT SPRINGFIELD.

Longfellow.

THIS is the Arsenal. From floor to ceiling,
Like a huge organ, rise the burnished arms;
But from their silent pipes no anthem pealing
Startles the villagers with strange alarms.

Ah! what a sound will rise, how wild and dreary,
When the death-angel touches those swift keys!
What loud lament and dismal Miserere
Will mingle with their awful symphonies!

I hear even now the infinite fierce chorus—
The cries of agony, the endless groan,
Which through the ages that have gone before us,
In long reverberations reach our own.

On helm and harness ring the Saxon hammer;
Through Cimbric forest roars the Norseman's song;
And loud amid the universal clamour,
O'er distant deserts sounds the Tartar gong.

I hear the Florentine, who from his palace
Wheels out his battle-bell with dreadful din;
And Aztec priests upon their teocallis
Beat the wild war-drums made with serpents' skins;

The tumult of each sacked and burning village;
The shout that every prayer for mercy drowns;
The soldiers' revels in the midst of pillage;
The wail of famine in beleaguered towns;

The bursting shell, the gateway wrenched asunder,
The rattling musketry, the clashing blade—
And ever and anon, in tone of thunder,
The diapason of the cannonade.

Is it, O man, with such discordant noises,
With such accursed instruments as these,
Thou drownest Nature's sweet and kindly voices,
And jarrest the celestial harmonies?

Were half the power that fills the world with terror,
Were half the wealth bestowed on camps and courts,
Given to redeem the human mind from error,
There were no need of arsenals nor forts

The warrior's name would be a name abhorred:
And every nation that should lift again
Its hand against a brother, on its forehead
Would wear for evermore the curse of Cain!

Down the dark future, through long generations,
The echoing sounds grow fainter and then cease;
And like a bell, with solemn, sweet vibrations,
I hear once more the voice of Christ say, "Peace!"

Peace! and no longer from its brazen portals,
The blast of war's great organ shakes the skies!
But, beautiful as songs of the immortals,
The holy melodies of love arise.

MURDERED BY DRINK.

Carleton, Jun

SHE was scarcely more than a girl, it is true,
  If you measured her life by its years;
Yet still she was old by the sorrows she knew,
  For her life was a winter of tears:
And yet she was fair, and her tresses of gold,
  Which often *his* hand had caressed,
Were wavy and light; but uncared for they rolled
  Down her shoulders and lay on her breast.

She sat by the hearth that was sparkless and bare,
  And she heard the night-tempest's shriek wild,
And she pressed to her bosom, cold home of despair,
  The form of her slumbering child.
"God help us," said she, as her tears trickled fast,
  And streamed on the sleeping one's head;
"Our lives are as wintry and bleak as the blast,
  And I often could wish I were dead."

Then she pressed her cold lips to the sleeper's pale brow,
  As she drew the loved one to her heart;
"Yes, yes," she spoke on, "I could wish it were now:
  Yet how could I wish we should part?"
Then she bent down her ear and she listened awhile
  For the words that the little one said;
For she spoke in her sleep with a sorrowful smile,
  "When father comes home we'll get bread.

"And he'll give up the drink and he'll beat us no more,"
  Then the sleeper grew silent again;
But, after a space, she spoke on as before,
  "'Tis the drinking that maddens his brain."
Then again she grew silent, and sighed in her sleep,
  And she shook at her fond mother's touch,
As she muttered once more, "'Tis no wonder we weep,
  For, father, you beat us too much."

She started and opened her bonny blue eyes,
  And she clung to her mother in fear,
And she said, "Was it you, mother, gave the loud cries
  That I heard in my sleep, and still hear?
I thought *he* came in with a log from the yard,
  And that you were just there at the door
Then I thought he was beating you ever so hard,
  And kicking you, too, on the floor.

"Was it only a dream," said the child, "mother dear?
Well, it made me grow sick with the fright;
And I'm cold, and my hands are shaking with fear
Pray God he won't beat us to-night.
Oh! I wish there was nothing in all the whole land,
Oh! nothing but water to drink,
And then, mother dear, we could all live so grand,
And we'd all be so happy, I think."

The mother bent down, and she kissed the child's lips,
While sad were the tears that she shed;
But little she dreamed of the deadly eclipse
That was gathering over each head;
And though the wild tempest was loud in its shout
They heard not its shrieking and roar,
For mother and child had detected without
A footstep approaching the door.

Then they clung to each other in fear and dismay,
And their faces grew pallid and shrunk·
"Oh, 'tis he," said the child, "and I know by the way
That he's cursing you, mother, he's drunk.
Steal out to the back, and keep quiet outside,
And hide yourself down in the shed.
O dear! mother, please, do steal outside and hide,
And I'll strive and get father to bed."

"Too late," said the mother; "my darling, he's here,"
And the father reeled in through the door;
And he said, "By the Lord, if you haven't got beer,
I will strangle you there on the floor."
The child clasped her hands in a heartrending way,
And she looked in his face with affright,
And she said, "We've had nothing to eat all the day,
Then, father, don't beat her to-night."

"Are you deaf," said the drunkard, "and do you not hear?"
As he grasped the long hair of his wife:
"Do you hear me? I say, if you haven't got beer
You may take your farewell of this life."
She gasped for a space like a person who dies,
And her lips for a moment were dumb,
Then she said, "Charley, don't!" as she looked in his eyes.
"For the sake of the child that's to come."

Then she strove to embrace him, yes, strove to embrace,
For her love for him still was profound:
But his cruel hands smote on and crimsoned her face,
And she tottered and fell to the ground.
Then a pitiful moaning arose on the air,
Arose for a moment and fled:
And the dream of the child, it was acted out there,
And the *hero* then staggered to bed.

Then the little child went and lay down by the side
Of the mother and silently wept,
But through the long waste of that dismal night-tide
The mother, unheeding her, slept.
"Oh! mother, dear mother!" the little one said,
And she spoke very low in her ear,
"Won't you speak to me now *he* is gone to his bed,
And there's no one at all but me here?

"Oh! mother, what is it that makes you grow cold,
As cold as a mortal can be?
You often have said that I never was bold;
Speak now and say something to me."
But silent and coldly the mother still lay,
While the child nestled close to her breast,
And wept on that pillow; but ere it was day
She slept, with her sorrow oppressed.

And the being round whom their affections had twined
Awoke and arose with the sun;
And with his red hand he uplifted the blind,
And he looked on the deed he had done.
"Jess, Jessie," said he; and the sleeping child woke
With a start at the words he had said;
And she gazed on her mother, and shrinking back spoke,
"Look! father, my mother is dead."

He went from the room, and his visage was white
As the face of the victim he'd slain,
And he gave a wild groan as he passed out of sight,
And his child never saw him again.
The Yarra flows silent, and softly, and deep,
For ever and aye o'er its bed;
And still it flowed onward, unheeding his leap,
And rolled o'er the murderer's head.

And years have ran on since that pitiful day,
And what is the little child *now?*
A down-trodden thing on the earth's crowded way,
With the brand of disgrace on her brow.
A palpable curse, an exponent of sin,
From which, in our horror, we shrink:
And where did the plague-spot that kills her begin?
She will answer and tell you, "In Drink."

THE TWO GLASSES.

Ella Wheeler

There stood two glasses, filled to the brim,
On a rich man's table, rim to rim:
One was ruddy, and red as blood,
And one was clear as the crystal flood.
Said the glass of wine to his paler brother,
"Let us tell tales of the past to each other;
I can tell of banquet, and revel, and mirth,
Where I was king, for I ruled in might,
And the proudest and grandest souls on earth
Fell under my touch, as though struck with blight

"From the heads of kings I have torn the crown,
From the heights of fame I have hurled men down
I have blasted many an honoured name,
I have taken virtue and given shame;
I have tempted the youth with a sip, a taste,
That has made his fortune a barren waste.
Far greater than any king am I,
Or than any army beneath the sky.

"I have made the arm of driver fail,
And sent the train from its iron rail.
I have made good ships go down at sea,
And the shrieks of the lost were sweet to me;
For they said, 'Behold how great you be!
Fame, strength, wealth, genius, before you fall,
And your might and power are over all.'
Ho! oh! pale brother," laughed the wine,
"Can you boast of deeds so great as mine?"

Said the water-glass, "I cannot boast
Of a king dethroned or a murdered host;
But I can tell of hearts that were sad
By my crystal drops made light and glad,
Of thirst I have quenched, and brows I've laved,
Of hands I have cooled, and lives I've saved.
I have leaped thro' the valley, dashed down the mountain;
Slept in the sunshine, and dripped from the fountain;
I have burst my cloud fetters, and dropped from the sky,
And everywhere gladdened the landscape and eye."

Y

ADDRESS TO THE MUMMY IN BELZONI'S EXHIBITION.

Horace Smith.

And thou hast walked about (how strange a story!)
  In Thebe's streets three thousand years ago.
When the Memnonium was in all its glory,
  And time had not begun to overthrow
Those temples, palaces, and piles stupendous,
Of which the very ruins are tremendous.

Speak! for thou long enough hast acted dummy;
  Thou hast a tongue—come let us hear its tune;
Thou'rt standing on thy legs, above ground, mummy;
  Revisiting the glimpses of the moon,
Not like thin ghosts or disembodied creatures,
But with thy bones, and flesh, and limbs, and features.

Tell us—for thou canst recollect—
  To whom shall we assign the Sphynx's fame;
Was Cheops or Cephrenes architect
  Of either pyramid that bears his name?
Is Pompey's pillar really a misnomer?
Had Thebes a hundred gates, as sung by Homer?

Perchance that very hand, now pinioned flat,
  Has hob-a-nobbed with Pharaoh, glass to glass;
Or dropped a halfpenny in Homer's hat,
  Or doffed thine own to let Queen Dido pass:
Or held, by Solomon's own invitation,
A torch at the great Temple's dedication.

I need not ask thee if that hand, when armed,
  Has any Roman soldier mauled and knuckled;
For thou wert dead, and buried, and embalmed,
  Ere Romulus and Remus had been suckled:
Antiquity appears to have begun
Long after thy primeval race was run!

Thou couldst develop, if that withered tongue
  Might tell us what those sightless orbs have seen,
How the World looked when it was fresh and young,
  And the great Deluge still had left it green—
Or was it then so old, that History's pages
Contained no record of its early ages?

Still silent? Incommunicative elf,
  Art sworn to secrecy? then keep thy vow
But pr'ythee tell us something of thyself—
  Reveal "the secrets of thy prison-house;"
Since in the world of spirits thou hast slumbered,
What hast thou seen? what strange adventures numbered?

Since first thy form was in this box extended,
  We have, above-ground, seen some strange mutations.
The Roman empire has begun—and ended,—
  New worlds have risen—we have lost old nations;
And countless kings have into dust been humbled,
While not a fragment of thy flesh has crumbled.

Didst thou not hear the pother o'er thy head,
When the great Persian conqueror, Cambyses,
Marched armies o'er thy tomb with thundering tread,
O'erthrew Osiris, Orus, Apis, Isis,
And shook the Pyramids with fear and wonder,
When the gigantic Memnon fell asunder?

If the tomb's secrets may not be confessed,
The nature of thy private life unfold:
A heart has throbbed beneath that leathern breast,
And tears adown that dusty cheek have rolled:—
Have children climbed those knees, and kissed that face?
What was thy name and station, age and race?

Statue of flesh—Immortal of the dead!
Imperishable type of evanescence!
Posthumous man, who quitt'st thy narrow bed,
And standest undecayed within our presence,—
Thou wilt hear nothing—till the Judgment morning,
When the great Trump shall thrill thee with its warning!

Why should this worthless tegument endure
If its undying guest be lost for ever?
Oh! let us keep the Soul embalmed and pure
In living virtue; that when both must sever,
Although Corruption may our frame consume,
The immortal Spirit in the skies may bloom!

REVELATIONS OF THE DIVINE.

Harris.

Though nature is a veil, of lightnings woven,
Most beautiful and glorious to see,
And registers, in each progressive motion,
The beatings of the heart of Deity;
Yet, through its folds, His loftiest revelations
Of law and essence have been never made;
His voice, that awes and thrills the adoring nations,
Comes not with sensual imagery arrayed,
It ripples, bathed in everlasting splendour,
Through veins where Deity hath ever ran;
And speaks, in tones with Love's rich breathings tender,
From the child-lips and heaven-bright soul of man.

God speaketh in their lives of truth and beauty;
God speaketh in their words of prophet fire;
God speaketh in their acts of loving duty,
And noiseless charities that never tire.
And, haloed round with everlasting lustre,
They shine transfigured in the might of soul;
And thronging generations round them cluster
To hear the music from their spirits roll.
For them earth shines more joyfully and fairer;
Each word and deed of right lives on for aye;
Each heart-beat of their lives to man brings nearer
The golden sunrise of the Eden day

THE LAND WHERE OUR DREAMS COME TRUE.

Far over some mist-hidden river,
And under a wonderful sky,
Where the rain never blots out the sunshine,
And our loves never weary or die;
Where the flowers never fade, but, in changing,
Their magical sweetness renew,
Lies a glorified realm of enchantment—
The land where our dreams come true!

By mystical symbols and tokens
We know of that mystical land;
But alas! on the threshold of manhood,
The frail clue slips out of our hand!
And the wild river wanders between us,
The white gates are hidden from view,
And only in sleep we remember
The land where our dreams come true!

We shall find the lost treasures we seek for
Revealed in that wonderful sphere;
All the aims and the dreams of the bygone,
All the good that eluded us here.
The innocent faiths of our childhood,
The one flawless friendship we knew,
Arrayed in our vanished illusions
In the land where our dreams come true!

We know in divinest fulfilment
Our vain hopes are gathered at home;
The jewels we mourn here are hoarded
Where the moth and the rust cannot come,
And oft when the sunset is fairest,
We catch, through a rift in the blue,
A far-away glimpse of the glories
Of the land where our dreams come true!

There are garnered the prayers of our mothers,
And the soft cradle songs that they sung;
There they move, in the midst, with white garments
And faces immortally young!
And out of the mist of that river
Their sweet hands shall lead us the clue
That leads through the Valley of Shadow
To the land where our dreams come true!

So, weeping we lay down our idols,
And bury our bones out of sight,
Tho' we know, in our hearts, we shall find them
By-and-by in the Mansions of Light.
And the salt tears that fall on their ashes,
And blossom in pansy and rue,
Over there shall be lilies immortal,
In the land where our dreams come true!

RING THE BELL SOFTLY.

SOME one has gone from this strange world of ours,
No more to gather its thorns and its flowers,
No more to linger where sunbeams must fade,
Where, on all beauty, death's fingers are laid;
Weary with mingling life's bitter and sweet,
Weary with parting though soon we shall meet,
Some one has gone to the bright golden shore;
Ring the bell softly, there's one gone before!

Some one is resting from sorrow and sin,
Happy where earth's conflicts enter not in;
Joyous as birds, when the morning is bright,
When the sweet sunbeams have brought us their light;
Weary with sowing, in sorrow to reap,
Weary with labour, and welcoming sleep,
Some one's departed for heaven's bright shore;
Ring the bell softly, there's one gone before!

Angels were anxiously longing to meet
One who walks with them in heaven's bright street;
Loved ones have whispered that some one is blest;
Free from earth's trials and taking sweet rest;
Yes! there is one more in angelic bliss,
One more to cherish, and one more to kiss;
One more departed to heaven's bright shore;
Ring the bell softly, there's one gone before!

ALWAYS A FUTURE.

I BEHELD a golden portal in the visions of my slumber,
  And through it streamed the radiance of a never-setting day;
While angels tall and beautiful, and countless without number,
  Were giving gladsome greeting to all who came that way.
And the gate, for ever swinging, made no grating, no harsh ringing,
  Melodious as the singing of one that we adore;
And I heard a chorus swelling, grand beyond a mortal's telling;
  And the burden of that chorus was Hope's glad word, "Evermore."

And, as I gazed and listened, came a mortal wildly weeping:
  "I have lost my hopes for ever; one by one they went away;
The idols of my patient love the cold grave hath in keeping.
  Life is one long lamentation; I know no night nor day!"
Then the angel, softly speaking, "Stay, mourner, stay thy shrieking,
  Thou shalt find those thou art seeking, beyond that golden door.
Then I heard the chorus swelling, grand beyond a mortal's telling,
  "They whom thy sad soul loveth shall be with thee evermore."

I saw a toiler enter, to rest for aye from labour;
  The weary-hearted exile there found his native land;
The beggar there could greet the king as equal and a neighbour;
  The crown had left the kingly brow, the staff the beggar's hand;
And the gate, for ever swinging, made no grating, no harsh ringing,
  Melodious as the singing of one that we adore;
And the chorus still was swelling, grand beyond a mortal's telling,
While the vision faded from me, with the glad word, "Evermore!"

PEOPLE WILL TALK.

You may go through the world, but 'twill be very slow,
If you listen to all that is said as you go.
You'll be worried and fretted and kept in a stew,
For meddlesome tongues must have something to do,
And people will talk.

If quiet, and modest, 'twill then be presumed,
That your humble position is only assumed.
You're a wolf in sheep's clothing, or else you're a fool,
But don't get excited—keep perfectly cool,
For people will talk.

If generous and noble, they'll vent out their spleen,
You'll hear some loud hints that you're selfish and mean.
If upright and honest, and fair as the day,
They'll call you a rogue in a sly sneaking way,
For people will talk.

Then if you should show the least boldness of heart,
Or a slight inclination to take your own part,
They'll call you an upstart conceited and vain,
But keep straight ahead, and don't stop to explain,
For people will talk.

If threadbare your coat, or old fashioned your dress,
Someone of course will take notice of this,
And hint rather close that you can't pay your way,
But don't get excited whatever they say,
For people will talk.

They'll talk fine before you, but then at your back,
Of venom and spite there is never a lack;
How kind and polite, in all that they say,
But bitter as gall, when you're out of the way,
For people will talk.

Good friend, take advice, and just do as you please,
For your mind (if you have one) will then be at ease.
Through life you'll meet with all sorts of abuse,
But don't think to stop them, 'twill be of no use,
For people will talk.

WAS LOST AND IS FOUND.

Rt. Rev. W. W. How, Bishop of Bedford

"COME in! Come in!" the lady said—the door stood open wide—
The church was bright, and young and old were ranging side by side;
The lady's look was soft and grave, her voice was low and sweet;
The girl half stopped and turned—and then went faster down the street.
One moment, and a gentle hand upon her arm was pressed:
"Oh, won't you stay?" the kind voice said; "Come in, come in and rest;
The missioner will preach to-night, and all the church is free:
You won't refuse me now, my child; come in, and sit by me."
"No, no," she said, yet stopped and looked (it was not hard to trace
The conflict passing like a cloud across that fair young face),—
Then hastily, as though she feared her heart at last might fail,
Passed in and sat beside the door, so weary, sad, and pale.
The preacher spoke of God's great love, and how the Saviour blest
Called weary souls to come to Him, that He might give them rest.
He spoke no grand or learned words, he used no studied art,
He simply spoke as one who tried to reach his brother's heart.
It was the old, old story, that can never pall or tire
When the lips with grace are fervent, and the heart with love on fire
And the lady marked how, one by one, the tear-drops grew and fell,
While eagerly those wistful eyes were fixed as by a spell.
And then a hymn rose all around—no cultured choir's display,
For every voice and every heart seemed moved to sing that day;
And faster, faster, rained the tears, for with the well-known air
Came back her childhood's happy days, her childhood's home so fair.
She sees her father's thin white locks, her mother's loving eyes—
This night she cannot put aside the memory, if she tries:
She sees—she cannot help but see—the little sister sweet;
She hears upon the broad old stairs the little pattering feet;
They laid her in the old churchyard beneath the sombre yew:—
And "Oh! my God!" the poor girl sobs, "that I were laid there too!"
And now the preacher stands and waits, and bids who will to stay,
For he is yearning for their souls, and he has more to say.

The lady still is kneeling there, but kneeling all alone:
She lifts her head—alas! the girl has left the church and gone.
She had so yearned to take her hand and help her, and she sighs
To think of that poor suffering face, those eager tearful eyes.

The pleading voice has ceased, yet still a scattered few are there,
As one by one the missioner kneels by their side in prayer;
And one by one they pass away, with hearts that throb to feel
They have been very near to One whose touch hath power to heal.
Oh! had that poor child only stayed and told her tale of grief,
The lady thinks, perchance, she too had found the blest relief!
And now from out the silent church she with a friend departs;
Their words are few, but fewest words speak best from fullest hearts.
They part at last; and there, behold! half eager and half shy,
The girl with those poor tear-stained cheeks, that sad beseeching eye.
"Oh! it was long to wait," she said, "I thought it ne'er would end;
And then I could not speak to you, for you were with your friend;
Oh, help me, help me, if you can!" The lady gently smiled—
"I will," she said; "but God is love, and He will help His child."
"Oh, no! oh, no!" the poor girl cried, despair in every tone,
"You cannot know how far away from his true fold I've gone.
I'm not as one who never knew, time was I used to pray,
I tried to do the right, but oh, I've sinned his love away!
Five years have passed since I wrote home, and now I cannot tell
Whether my parents are alive! they don't know where I dwell.
And all that time I never once have crossed the church's door.
Until this night; and now, O God! there's hope for me no more!"
"Nay, nay, that can't be true, my child" (and oh! like gentle rain
The words fell on that withered heart, and softened it again);
"Why did God let me come to you? Why did He let you stay,
Unless He had some word of hope to speak to you to-day?
Oh, offer Him this very night that worthiest sacrifice—
The broken and the contrite heart, which He will not despise:
We both have need of pardoning grace: yes, sister, we will lay
Our sin-stained souls before His feet, and for His mercy pray:
And promise me one thing—this night, before aught else you do,
That you will to your mother write, and ask her pardon too."
"I will," she sobbed; and then her hand the lady kindly took,
And bade her read the blessed words of peace in God's own Book.

"I have no Bible now," she said: the lady sadly smiled;
"That must not be," she said, "take mine; and now, good-night, my child."

Next morning at a hospital the lady needs must call.
Ah! little dreamt she of the tale that on her ears would fall
Why runs the nurse to meet her there ere she can speak a word?
"Oh, is it not most strange and sad! Nay, surely you have heard?
A girl has been brought in to-day, but only just to die;
By some rough driver in the street struck down and left to lie.
We know her not, but you may know; for strange as it may sound,
A Bible with your name in it was all the clue we found."
"Oh, let me see," the lady said, "I think I know too well—
Yes, it is she—but tell me, nurse, whate'er there is to tell."
"Not much," she said, "but once she spoke, before she passed away;
We thought she gasped, 'Thank God, thank God, this was not yesterday!'"
Next day there stood before the gate, with hearts too full too speak,
A father with his thin white locks, a mother grave and meek.
The kind folk at the lodging-house had guessed their errand well,
And sent them on, but had not heart the thing they knew to tell.
The lady sees them standing there; she knows who it must be;
No need to ask them who they are, or whom they come to see.
She runs to meet them—"Yes," she cries, "I know what you would say;
Your child is here; my poor, poor friends, it happened yesterday.
Come in, come in: God comfort you, and make you firm and brave,
For oh! your child has gone to Him, and found Him strong to save."
And then she took them by the hand, like little children weak;
They went with her, scarce knowing aught, too stunned to think or speak.
And then she told them all the tale, in loving words and slow:—
Ah me! they came to find their child—and they have found her so!

She lay there white and beautiful, no trace of conflict now,
No lines that told of sin and shame upon that marble brow:
The aged pair they knelt beside the bed where she was laid,
And "Not our will but Thine be done!" amid their sobs they prayed.
What though the flower of childhood's grace no more be blooming there,
His snow-white lily Death has laid upon that form so fair.
"Blest are the pure in heart"—so once the Friend of sinners cried:—
Yet not unblest, methinks, are those whom he has purified!

THE OLD OAKEN BUCKET.

Wordsworth.

How dear to this heart are the scenes of my childhood,
When fond recollection presents them to view!
The orchard, the meadow, the deep-tangled wildwood,
And every loved spot which my infancy knew;
The wide-spreading pond, and the mill that stood by it,
The bridge and the rock where the cataract fell,
The cot of my father, the dairy-house nigh it,
And e'en the rude bucket that hung in the well—
The old oaken bucket, the iron-bound bucket,
The moss-covered bucket, that hung in the well

The moss-covered vessel I hailed as a treasure,
For often at noon, when returned from the field,
I found it the source of an exquisite pleasure,
The purest and sweetest that nature can yield.
How ardent I seized it, with hands that were glowing,
And quick to the white-pebbled bottom it fell;
Then soon with the emblem of truth overflowing,
And dripping with coolness, it rose from the well—
The old oakeu bucket, the iron-bound bucket,
The moss-covered bucket, arose from the well.

How sweet from the green mossy brim to receive it,
As poised on the curb it inclined to my lips!
Not a full-blushing goblet could tempt me to leave it,
The brightest that beauty or revelry sips.
And, now, far removed from the loved habitation,
The tear of regret will intrusively swell,
As fancy reverts to my father's plantation,
And sighs for the bucket that hangs in the well—
The old oaken bucket, the iron-bound bucket,
The moss-covered bucket, that hangs in the well.

FLOWERS.

A very pretty poem which appeared in *Chambers's Journal* with the signature of John Palmer.

Wildings of nature, or cultured with care,
Ye are beautiful, beautiful everywhere!
Gemming the woodland, the glen, and the glade,
Drinking the sunbeams, or courting the shade;
Gilding the moorland and mountain afar,
Shining in glory in garden parterre.

Ye bloom in the palace, ye bloom in the hall,
Ye bloom on the top of the mouldering wall;
Ye bloom in the cottage, the cottager's pride—
The window looks cold with no flowers by its side;
Ye twine up the trellis, ye bloom in our bowers,
Ye carpet creation, ye beautiful flowers.

Did angels descend from their home in the skies,
To pencil those petals with exquisite dyes?
To store in your cells the rich odours of heaven,
Was employment so meet unto seraphim given?
Ye answer me: No; 'twas an Almighty hand
That clothed ye in beauty, and bade ye expand.
Rich gems of creation, that ravish the sight,
And pour on the senses supernal delight;
Wildings of nature, or cultured with care,
Ye are beautiful, beautiful everywhere!

When morn's early beams gild the glorious east,
Your incense ascends unto nature's high priest;
When sunset foreshadows the day's dewy close,
Ye fold up your petals for welcome repose;
Your odours impregnate with odours the breeze,
Ye furnish a feast for the banqueting bees;
Ye promise in eloquent language, though mute,
Boughs bending with offerings of delicate fruit;
Ye tell, when your glory and fragrance is o'er,
That autumn shall come with his rich gushing store.

Sweetness of life, ye are infancy's play;
To boyhood's bright dream, O what charms ye display!
In years more mature we but love ye the more,
As tracing veil'd beauties undreamt of before.
To childhood, to manhood, to age ye are dear;
Ye are strewn at the bridal and strewn on the bier;
Fair flowers even there soothe the lone mourner's woes,
And hallow the turf where loved ashes repose.
Wildings of nature, or cultured with care,
Ye are beautiful, beautiful everywhere!

DOING GOOD, TRUE NOBILITY.

Carlos Wilcox.

Wouldst thou from sorrow find a sweet relief?
Or is thy heart oppressed with woes untold?
Balm wouldst thou gather for corroding grief?
Pour blessings round thee like a shower of gold.
'Tis when the rose is wrapped in many a fold,
Close to its heart, the worm is wasting there
Its life and beauty; not when, all unrolled,
Leaf after leaf, its bosom, rich and fair,
Breathes freely its perfumes throughout the ambient air

Some high or humble enterprise of good
Contemplate, till it shall possess thy mind,
Become thy study, pastime, rest, and food,
And kindle in thy heart a flame refined.
Pray Heaven for firmness thy whole soul to bind
To this thy purpose—to begin, pursue,
With thoughts all fixed and feelings purely kind;
Strength to complete and with delight review,
And grace to give the praise where all is due.

SIMILES.

One taper lights a thousand,—yet doth beam
No dimmer, giving all, but losing naught.
By one faint glimmering taper light is brought
To altar candles, many branched, that gleam
Against high vaulted chancel roofs, and stream
Through painted panes with vivid splendours fraught
And shine on effigies of saints, fair wrought,
Whose folded hands for ever praying seem.
These two things have I known; and this beside,—
Fire kindled by a failing flame, which died
That self-same moment. Lord, my flame burns low—
Great fires are kindled by a feeble spark—
Let my poor taper lighten some, whose glow
Shall bless the world when I am cold and dark!

Page to write or paste any Gems of Poetry in that you may come across.

Page to write or paste any Gems of Poetry in that you may come across.

Page to write or paste any Gems of Poetry in that you may come across.

Page to write or paste any Gems of Poetry in that you may come across.

Page to write or paste any Gems of Poetry in that you may come across.

Page to write or paste any Gems of Poetry in that you may come across.

Page to write or paste any Gems of Poetry in that you may come across.

Page to write or paste any Gems of Poetry in that you may come across.

Printed in the USA
CPSIA information can be obtained
at www.ICGtesting.com
LVHW080411080823
754482LV00015B/1482